TIMING AND TEMPORALITY
IN ISLAMIC PHILOSOPHY AND PHENOMENOLOGY OF LIFE

Islamic Philosophy and Occidental Phenomenology in Dialogue

VOLUME 3

Timing and Temporality in Islamic Philosophy and Phenomenology of Life

Edited by

Anna-Teresa Tymieniecka

The World Institute for Advanced Phenomenological Research and Learning

 Springer

Library of Congress Cataloging-in-Publication Data is available

ISBN 978-90-481-7553-6
ISBN 978-1-4020-6160-8 (e-book)

Published by Springer,
P.O. Box 17, 3300 AA Dordrecht, The Netherlands.

www.springer.com

TABLE OF CONTENTS

ACKNOWLEDGEMENTS

It is with a considerable joy and pride that I am bringing the present collection of studies to the public. In the main it comprises studies read at, or intended for, our fifth symposium held by the World Institute for Advanced Phenomenological Research and Learning at our Annual convention of American Philosophical Association, Eastern Division, in New York, December 27–30, 2005, in the Institute's program of "Islamic Philosophy and Phenomenology of Life in Dialogue".

My appreciation and thanks go first of all to the authors, whose enthusiasm and dedication to the cause of the dialogue keeps this research project going. I thank in particular Professor William Chittick for his precious advice and to Dr. Nader El-Bizri for his editorial help.

My secretary Jeff Hurlburt deserves warm thanks for his expert work at the logistics of this enterprise, and Springer Publishers for the moral support and technical help in copy-editing.

I believe that in these three volumes of the series we have set down cornerstones for the desired dialogue between two great traditions of thought as they stay at the present moment, dialogue, which will not fail to unfold toward the enrichment of our philosophical culture.

A-T.T.

PREFACE

1. Timing and temporality has become the great issue of our times. Our civilization must meet their puzzling requirements in order to survive. The striking scientific discoveries of modernity, whose far-reaching implications we are slowly deciphering, along with technological inventions unforeseeable in the past are not only transforming the modalities of human existence on earth but are also reaching into the cosmos. Most of all, these developments enter into the systems of our gregarious and societal sharing-in-life and communication and into the singular individual and personal realm. It is the timing of life and life's essential temporality that are at stake.

Timing is so primordial to our existence that we are as if permeated by it. Indeed, all the factors and lines of vital development as well as all undertakings and projects, whether human, animal, or vegetative, turn on some or other modality of "timing," or to put it better, "time themselves" in order to evolve.

Temporality pervades our human horizon of life, feeling, reflection, hope. Whatever our mind encounters and conceives of is timed in its own turn. The timing of events, encounters, plans, etc. is the reference point not only for human communication but also of the symphony of nature's life. Every functional operation times itself in an irrevocable way.

From time immemorial our temporality has suffused us to the bone. Seemingly it governs existence. Indeed, awareness of timing and temporality has so grown in our minds as to assume an autonomous sovereign position and to loom over us like the monstrous Chronos of Greek mythology, who devours his own offspring.

In sum our inmost human concern with the timing of life and with life's temporal nature is an axis upon which turns our vision of existence, our worldview, into an embrace of the universe, reality, nature-life, and transcendent realms, and that in life's practice, in personal experience, and so in human destiny. *This combination of theoretical and practical concerns, of ultimate and immediate, of knowing and doing, makes the right apprehension of temporality's and timing's meaning an extremely urgent charge for philosophers.*

2. With the great progress made in deciphering the results of scientific inquiry, we have been made more and more aware of the role of temporality, seeing timing variously, the part it plays in such diverse fields as genetics, embryology, biology, psychology, sociology and even in so rigorous and abstract a field as mathematics (as has been demonstrated by René Thom). But human beings have always been interested in the history of their ancestors, nations, the world itself. Sagas, myths have been handed down from generation to generation. We have always seen in the past dependencies and influences on the present, not only the effects of cataclysmic events that in their drama insure their memory (earthquakes, hurricanes, famines, wars) but imponderable effects also that can only be guessed at (of language, literature, law, religion, representative figures). Modern discoveries have only sharpened the questions of evolution and historical development, of generation and interaction, and of prospects. All of the sciences, physics, chemistry, biology, ecology, medicine, psychology, sociology are brought to bear on the discovery of the inner workings of individualizing life in its symbiotic exchange with circumambient conditions and within life's networks. The inquiry into the ecological conditions of life stretches far into geological spheres, into elementary organic processes and how they are affected by ground conditions and changing climatic and atmospheric conditions. The emphasis on change and evolution has also radically transformed our view of the "heavens," with the stars no longer being seen as permanently affixed but as participating and carrying on the transformative course of the universe. This is modern astronomy/astrophysics. Origin, genesis, extinction – these hidden yet crucial questions have brought emphasis on change and development to the fore. Emphasis is on questions of change, transformation, continuity, succession, articulation, of existential dependencies and conditions subject to change. The sphere of life/existence, whether of nature or of human society, sharing-in-life, is beset with concerns of temporality, with how to negotiate change, with latching on to available opportunities and with losing them.

Given the depth of awareness now had of human subjective, inner psychological temporality, of how the experienced duration of existence is expressed in the stream of consciousness, of the foundational role this plays in life, there can hardly be any illusion left among philosophers that Time constitutes a unique and autonomous force or that duration is a mysterious and absolute infinity. Change has become now the measure of things.

One most significant upshot of this is that consciousness can no longer be given priority over the unfolding of life and the cosmos. We see that consciousness calls for explanation of its origin, development, inner symbiotic genetic conditions. In short, it calls for the justification of its own temporality, its own "time" of origins and ends. Consciousness may overwhelmingly govern our lives and our experience of it, but it is itself subject to life's timing.

To use Husserlian phenomenological parlance, finding the unconditioned status of our knowledge does not involve its "reduction" to consciousness. Already Husserl found that to be so. Though Husserl ultimately came to believe that our knowledge can be reduced to the lifeworld, that also cannot be so, for as I have suggested above, the lifeworld is conditioned by a net of factors in cosmos and bios, from which net the world and life are suspended. This is life at its fulcrum, the cosmic network and conditions to which life refers.

3. In our times it seems as if the temporality of the moves of the lifeworld is undergoing further intrinsic variation. Time together with space is "shrinking" and acquiring new modes of significance according to a new inventive \ interpretation of life. It is a general phenomenon of our life today that owing to the already spoken of unprecedented technological developments we cannot rely on a temporal routine; in our everyday life we now feel as if we compete with "time." We feel as if all current world affairs, societal life, and personal existence have lost their "usual" pace, that is, the pace to which we had become accustomed, and have so "accelerated" that we as human beings now have to be "reeducated" to meet the requirements of the life struggle. We wonder how far this acceleration of human affairs can and may go. We calculate the probabilities in order to counter the unforeseeable and so avoid insoluble difficulties and so work to arrange "sustainable" circumstances for our societal and individual existence.

And so timing has become a critical theoretical and practical concern for us. What accounts for the acceleration of our lives in spite of our protest against it? In spite of ourselves we are left breathless by life's pace. What is the nature of temporality? This question takes on an urgency as we seek to orient our lives in today's world and estimate our prospects for the future. Is indomitable Kronos itself undergoing transformation along with the changes in our way of life? Or are changes in how we live affecting our overall experience of temporality? Is it not that life practices are shaping time differently?

4. As philosophical thinkers we find here a striking situation in that the practical and the theoretical now meet so intimately in our concern with the temporality of existence that they seem almost to convert into each other. The necessities of practical life are here as stringent as the driven theoretical interrogation seeking understanding of the metaphysical quest.

These two seemingly quite divergent concerns in fact inform each other and have done so in the depths of the human struggle for life from time immemorial. In the present day the generation of knowledge for the betterment of human life proceeds along with human consciousness' asking ultimate questions. They both take part in the basic human attention to ways and means of objectifying, measuring, comparing the occurrences of life so that an intersubjective coordination indispensable to human vital existence may be established. In this interaction we clarify our speculative understanding of the world also.

This unique convergence of theory and practice is particularly obvious in the history of how Islamic and Occidental cultures took wisdom from the inheritance of the great Greek thinkers, from Plato and Aristotle in particular, and so share innumerable insights.

The succinct historical account given by Nader El-Bizri (pp. XXX) shows how Aristotle refers to motion and number to specify time's nature – a measure pertinent to physics and practicality equally, and pertinent to psychology also given the soul's observing and measuring. This perspective has resonated through history. El-Bizri details how it entered medieval Islamic philosophy after Ishaq Ibn Hunayn's translation of Aristotle's *Physics* into Arabic (and covers as well other views, in particular views inspired by atomism). And he covers reflections of classical thought in Occidental philosophy too, in Augustine, Maimonides, and the Scholastics. He tells as well of the divide in modern Occidental philosophy between analytic and a priori approaches to time, an era that most sharply went in two directions, making either the timing of nature or the timing of the soul prime. Turning to phenomenology, El-Bizri again visits the subject of time in its theoretical and practical aspects – in in-depth reviews of time in the ontic thought of Heidegger and the ethical thought of Levinas.

With all the speculative efforts of philosophy and science, temporality and the timing of all life horizons remain still a puzzling mystery that, as argued above, has become in our times a pressing urgency to be resolved. The temporality of life, of everything in our horizon, demands fresh attention.

I present here to the reader a gamut of approaches to the questions on our theme. They share the insight that a renewed inquiry must take into account the dramatic transformation of life now essential to our vision of life. The world and our destiny depend on our treating this theme in a spirit that harmonizes perennial wisdom and the contemporary climate.

Anna-Teresa Tymieniecka

SECTION I

WILLIAM C. CHITTICK

THE VIEW FROM NOWHERE: IBN AL-'ARABĪ ON
THE SOUL'S TEMPORAL UNFOLDING

Discussion of the soul was foundational to Islamic philosophy.[1] Seekers of
wisdom wanted to become wise, and that demanded the soul's transformation.
To achieve transformation, they had to know the nature of both the soul and
the world, for the soul is the subjective counterpart of the outside realm—
one of many meanings that Muslim thinkers saw in the Koranic verse, "God
taught Adam the names, all of them" (2:31).

In the view of Avicenna, the philosopher's goal is to transform the soul
into "an intellective world within which is represented the form of everything,
the arrangement intelligible in everything, and the good that is effused upon
everything," beginning with the Origin of all things and comprising knowledge
of "all of existence." The soul must turn into an intelligible world, parallel
with the whole existent world, and it must witness "absolute comeliness,
absolute good, and real, absolute beauty while being united with it."[2]

A full grasp of what Avicenna is saying here would demand explication
of his world view as detailed in his metaphysics, cosmology, psychology,
and ethics, which is not at all my task here. I simply want to stress that
transformation of the soul was a basic concern even for the relatively staid
Peripatetic philosophers, not just the more "mystically-minded" thinkers such
as Ibn al-'Arabī (d. 1240).[3] Although not classified as a *faylasūf* by historians
of Islamic philosophy, he was certainly a philosopher in the sense of the
term *ḥakīm*, "sage," or in the broad sense in which the word "philosopher"
is used nowadays. The specific issue I want to address here is how he
understands temporality; and, given the tradition's stress on transformation
and self-realization, I want to look specifically at how temporality is involved
with the soul's becoming.

In order to keep the discussion focused—which is not easy when dealing
with Ibn al-'Arabī—I will talk about temporality mainly in terms of
ḥudūth, though several other words could easily be used for the same
ends. *Ḥudūth* means to arrive newly, to come to be, to happen, to occur. It
is contrasted with *qidam*, which means to precede, to be old, to be ancient.

3

A-T. Tymieniecka (ed.),
Timing and Temporality in Islamic Philosophy and Phenomenology of Life, 3–10.
© 2007 *Springer*.

In technical language, *ḥudūth* means to have an origin and to enter into time; *qidam* means to have no origin, to be outside of time, to be eternal.

The Unique Reality that gives rise to the universe—Avicenna's Necessary Being and Ibn al-'Arabī's Real Being (*al-wujūd al-ḥaqq*)—has the attribute of *qidam*, and everything else partakes of *ḥudūth*. In other words, the cosmos, which Ibn al-'Arabī typically defines as "everything other than God" (*mā siwa'llāh*), is an occurrence, a new arrival, and so also is everything within it. This does not mean, however, that the world came into being at some moment in the past and has continued to be, but rather that new arrival is a real and permanent attribute of everything other than God at every moment always and forever.

In discussing the Real Being, Ibn al-'Arabī often develops the implications of the broad range of meanings found in the word *wujūd*. For him it can never mean the dry fact of simply being there. Although the word may have been used this way by some of the philosophers, it also means finding, grasping, perceiving, knowing, experiencing, enjoying. When Ibn al-'Arabī speaks of the Real Being, he is talking about that which fully and actually possesses all these attributes and effuses them on creation. Simply to speak of the Real as *wujūd* is to say that the Source of all is alive, conscious, and loving, and that its manifestations are governed by the same attributes. Indeed, Ibn al-'Arabī tells us that the divine name Alive (*al-ḥayy*) is a Koranic synonym for *wujūd*, and the cosmos is nothing but the ebullient manifestation of life and all of its concomitants.

In Ibn al-'Arabī's perspective, the cosmos itself is alive, because it partakes of the Living One from whom it appears. Like any living thing, it is constantly changing and transforming, but always in keeping with the principles demanded by the divine life, that is, consciousness, desire, power, generosity, wisdom, justice. To say that the cosmos is constantly changing is to say that new arrival is on-going and never-ending. One of the better known ways in which Ibn al-'Arabī expresses this notion is his doctrine of "the renewal of creation at each instant" (*tajdīd al-khalq ma' al-ānāt*).

The term creation (*khalq*) is typically contrasted with Real (*ḥaqq*), in which case it designates the cosmos, everything other than God. The Real alone is *wujūd* by definition. Everything other than God is not *wujūd*, which is to say that in itself and for itself, it is not truly there, nor is it truly alive, conscious, and active. In itself it is nonexistent (*ma'dūm*).

Given that we observe the essentially nonexistent things that are collectively known as "creation" living and flourishing in some way, this can only be by virtue of reception of *wujūd*'s attributes and qualities from that which is truly alive. In the standard philosophical language that Ibn al-'Arabī often employs, this is to say that possibility or contingency (*imkān*) is intrinsic to all things, and that nothing can give them *wujūd* except that which is *wujūd* by definition, that is, the Necessary *Wujūd*.

The Necessary or Real *Wujūd* is one. Its status is perfectly clear, in the sense that it alone is truly real, permanent, and eternal, truly alive and aware; it alone is the point of reference from which unreal, impermanent, and newly arrived things can be understood. Hence, the basic philosophical problem is to discern the status of "unreal" or "nonexistent" things. How is it that they manifest attributes of Real *Wujūd*, such as life and awareness, and even wisdom and compassion?

Ibn al-'Arabī maintains that *wujūd* in the case of both the Real and creation, the Eternal and the newly arriving, is the self-same reality. As he puts it, "In its own essence *wujūd* may be divided into that which has a first, that is, the newly arriving, and that which has no first, that is, the eternal."[4] The fact that *wujūd* remains a single reality in whatever form it appears is what is typically meant when it is said, famously but not quite accurately, that Ibn al-'Arabī believed in *waḥdat al-wujūd*, "the Oneness of Being."[5] In his terms, the Necessary Being is *wujūd* in its unknowable "essence" (*dhāt*) or selfhood, and the possible thing is *wujūd*'s "self-disclosure" (*tajallī*). In other words, newly arrived things are the manifestation of the infinite possibilities latent in the Real Being.

For Ibn 'Arabī, the axiom of *wujūd*'s self-disclosure is that it never repeats itself (*lā takrār fi'l-tajallī*). Each being in the universe is a unique appearance of the Unique Being, and each moment of each being is a unique moment of new arrival. This means that the cosmos and all things within it undergo constant change always and forever.

The self-disclosure of the Real Being is essentially ambiguous, since the constantly transforming vistas that appear as the universe are neither Real *Wujūd* per se, nor completely other than it. As Ibn al-'Arabī remarks, everything is a changing image of the Real. Inasmuch as *Wujūd* appears in its own images, the images are real, but inasmuch as *Wujūd* stays hidden, they are unreal. Looking at the Koranic verse, "Wherever you turn, there is the face of God" (2:115), he tells us that everything is simultaneously God's face (*wajh*) and his veil (*ḥijāb*).[6] He sometimes expresses the ambiguity of things by saying that the cosmos is God's dream, or, much more commonly, that it is imagination or image (*khayāl*).

Everything other than the Essence of the Real is in the station of transmutation, speedy and slow. Everything other than the Essence of the Real is intervening imagination and vanishing shadow.[7]

Ibn al-'Arabī describes the imaginal status of things in many contexts and with diverse analogies. For example:

> No one knows what the newly arrived things are except he who knows what a rainbow is. The diversity of its colors is like the diversity of the forms of the newly arrived things. You know that no colored thing is there, nor any color, even though you witness it like that. So also is your witnessing of the forms of the newly arrived things in the *wujūd* of the Real, which is *wujūd* per se. Thus you say, "What is there is not there."[8]

* * *

In terms of new arrival, the human soul is no different from anything else: What is there is not there. Renewed at every moment by the divine self-disclosure, the soul manifests and conceals the face of the Real. Nonetheless, it has a unique status among all newly arrived things, a status announced by the prophetic saying, "God created Adam in His own form."[9] In other words, the human soul is a divine self-disclosure in respect of the fullness of the Real's ontological implications. "The fact that you are in the Form is the fact that you are a locus of manifestation for the divine names."[10]

This understanding of the cosmos and the soul in terms of the attributes of Real *Wujūd* is of course standard fare in the philosophical tradition, though Ibn al-'Arabī stresses it much more strongly than most. Avicenna, for instance, ascribes seven essential attributes to the Necessary Being—unity, eternity, knowledge, desire, power, wisdom, and generosity—and then explains that the implications of contingency can be understood only in terms of these attributes.

Although the soul was created in the divine form and is thereby a single locus in which the full range of the divine attributes may become manifest, the extent to which these attributes do in fact become manifest depends upon many factors, not least the free activity of the soul in its day-to-day experience of newly arriving *wujūd*. The purpose of striving for wisdom, in Ibn al-'Arabī's terms, is to actualize the diverse attributes latent in the divine form in perfect balance. He and many others call this actualization *al-takhalluq bi'l-akhlāq al-ilāhiyya*, "assuming as one's own the divine character traits." The philosophical tradition is thoroughly familiar with this discussion, though it is more likely to use expressions like *al-tashabbuh bi'l-ilāh*, "similarity to God," or *al-ta'alluh*, "theomorphism" or "deiformity."

Wujūd, as noted, is of two sorts, eternal and newly arriving, or *wujūd* in itself and *wujūd* in its self-disclosure. To speak of deiformity is to have in mind the integrated disclosure of the multiple attributes of *wujūd* in a single locus, namely the human soul. But in itself *wujūd* is one, with no multiplicity whatsoever, and the soul must also strive to actualize the full implications of its oneness.

The oneness of the Real *Wujūd* transcends all number, limits, and forms. None knows the One *Wujūd* in its essence but the One *Wujūd* itself; things that partake of new arrival can only know the One through its multiple self-disclosures. The divine self-disclosures are realized globally and comprehensively in two loci: the differentiated form that is the cosmos and the undifferentiated form that is the soul (that is, in macrocosm and microcosm). Individual cosmic things are parts of the whole; their differentiation, specification, and partiality do not allow them to actualize the full range of the divine self-disclosure. In other words, everything in the universe manifests this or that face of God, and thereby it acts as a veil for all other faces. The soul, however, though a part of the cosmos in its bodily manifestations, partakes of the undifferentiated form of Real *Wujūd* in its invisible dimensions.

The form of the undisclosed divine Essence—of *wujūd* per se, not of *wujūd* in this face or that face—can be called "the form of formlessness," and only the soul has access to it. To say that it may achieve this formless form is to say that in itself it has no essential form defining it as this or that. Its only essential form is not to have an essential form, in contrast to everything else in the universe. It has the potential to manifest all the divine attributes, all the divine faces, but in itself it has no defining attribute or face. It is essentially indefinable, so its development and unfolding over the course of a newly arriving human lifetime can never be known beforehand.

Ibn al-'Arabī sometimes talks about the indefinability of the soul in terms of the Koranic verse put into the mouth of the angels, "None of us there is but has a known station" (37:164). Everything other than human beings, he says, was created in a station (*maqām*) that does not change. There can be no surprises in nonhuman creatures. But human beings dwell in unknown stations until death.[11] In the case of our own selves, we do not and cannot know what we are dealing with. The more we try to limit and define ourselves, the more we miss our essential nature.

The Peripatetics talk about the soul as a "hylic intellect" (*'aql hayūlānī*), meaning that it is the prime matter in which the intellect can take form and be fully actualized. The extent to which the intellect does in fact become actualized determines the soul's ultimate destiny. In Ibn al-'Arabī's terms, the soul's hylic nature is established by the divine form, which is formless and hence capable of assuming every form.

The renewal of creation at each instant means that all things are constantly dressed in new forms, not just human beings. What distinguishes the human form is its ability to assume an infinity of forms, in contrast to other things, which are limited and confined to "known stations." To the objection that people are limited by their physical and psychological natures, Ibn al-'Arabī replies that the soul in itself has no such limitations. Simply to begin with, its realm opens up into the *mundus imaginalis*, the World of Imagination, which is the most inclusive realm of cosmic existence, since it embraces all the possibilities of heaven and earth, the spiritual and corporeal realms. Imagination is precisely the realm of *taṣawwur*, "assuming forms" (though this term is typically translated as "concept" in keeping with its meaning in logic); there is no form that cannot appear in the imaginal world. As Ibn al-'Arabī writes,

Through its reality [imagination] exercises its properties over every thing and non–thing. It gives form to absolute nonexistence, the impossible, the Necessary, and possibility. It makes existence nonexistent and nonexistence existent.[12]

Given that new forms arrive constantly, the soul at any given point of its unfolding manifests a specific divine face and stands in a determinate station— like the angels or other creatures. But, because of its essential formlessness, it has the possibility to assume any form and the freedom to shape the modalities in which it assumes them, and these are the "stations" through which it passes.

In Avicenna's terms, the goal of the philosopher is to achieve the virtues and perfections of the soul and to actualize the intellect. In Ibn al-'Arabī's terms, the goal is to pass through all the stations while achieving the perfections of each, and then to return to the indefinability of the original divine form. He calls this original indefinability "the station of no station" (*maqām lā maqām*).

In brief, then, new arrival is an attribute of everything other than God, including the human soul. Whatever our definition of "time," new arrival is a name for the cosmic situation that makes it manifest. To cite the words of two philosophical observers of a parallel tradition, "It is the pervasive and collective capacity of the events [read "new arrivals," *ḥawādith*] of the world to transform continuously that is the actual meaning of time."[13] The soul, however, has no essential limits tying it to one form or another, even though its very essence demands that it arrive newly forever.[14]

The perfect soul—the soul that has realized the fullness of its own possibilities as divine form—has achieved a situation in which every perfection of Real *Wujūd* has been actualized in a manner appropriate to its constant new arrival. These perfections include the nondelimitation and nonspecificity of *wujūd* per se, the fact that it stands outside of every station, every limitation, every essence, every quiddity. As Ibn al-'Arabī puts it,

The most all-inclusive specification is that a person not be delimited by a station whereby he is distinguished.... His station is that of no station.[15]

The people of perfection have realized all stations and states and passed beyond these to the station above both majesty and beauty, so they have no attribute and no description.[16]
The highest of all human beings are those who have no station. The reason for this is that the stations determine the properties of those who stand within them, but without doubt, the highest of all groups themselves determine the properties. They are not determined by properties.[17]

* * *

What I have just said touches briefly on two or three of Ibn al-'Arabī's themes relevant to the temporal situation of the soul. Let me simply make one more point: Despite the fact that he is one of the most voluminous and non-repetitive authors in Islamic history, in a very real sense his only topic is the exposition of the never-ending new arrival of the soul. What he is doing in diverse ways is to map out the possible modalities of the soul's understanding of its own unfolding, placing emphasis on those that lead to the perfect realization of the form of formlessness. This is especially obvious in the way he situates most if not all of the 560 chapters of his magnum opus, *al-Futūḥāt al-makkiyya*, in the context of specific sorts of knowledge that are granted to specific sorts of self-realization, as embodied in various prophets and sages. Each understanding of scripture, God, the cosmos, and the human soul pertains to a specific station of knowledge, a specific standpoint in reality. Only the Station of No Station provides the view from nowhere.[18]

NOTES

[1] The word I have in mind is *nafs* (cognate with Hebrew *nephesh*), the main reflexive pronoun in Arabic, which is to say that in many contexts it needs to be translated as "self." If I prefer "soul," it is for reasons of English usage. In the unvocalized Arabic script, *nafs* is written exactly the same way as *nafas*, "breath," and this congruence of breath and self has correlations with terms from other traditions, not least Sanskrit *atman*.
[2] For the Arabic text and a different translation, see Michael E. Marmura, *Avicenna. The Metaphysics of the Healing* (Provo: Brigham Young University Press, 2005), p. 350.
[3] For an introduction to Ibn al-'Arabī's philosophical teachings, see Chittick, *Ibn 'Arabī: Heir to the Prophets* (Oxford: Oneworld, 2005). For detailed expositions of the issues discussed here, see idem, *The Sufi Path of Knowledge: Ibn al-'Arabī's Metaphysics of Imagination* (Albany: State University of New York Press, 1989).
[4] *al-Futūḥāt al-makkiyya* (Cairo, 1911), vol. IV, p. 226, line 5; quoted also in Chittick, *The Self-Disclosure of God* (Albany: State University of New York Press, 1998), p. 238.
[5] For a history of the inaccurate ascription of this term to Ibn al-'Arabī and its use by his detractors and followers, see Chittick, "Rūmī and *Waḥdat al-wujūd*," *Poetry and Mysticism in Islam: The Heritage of Rūmī*, edited by A. Banani, R. Hovannisian, and G. Sabagh (Cambridge: Cambridge University Press, 1994), pp. 70–111.
[6] On the interplay of face and veil, see Chittick, *Sufism* (Oxford: Oneworld, 2000), chapter 10; for details, see *Self-Disclosure*, chapters 3 and 4.

[7] *Futūhāt* II 313.17; quoted in *Sufi Path* 118.

[8] *Futūhāt* IV 167.12; quoted in *Self-Disclosure* 71.

[9] One could follow the Biblical example and translate the word *sūra* as "image," but *sūra* is the same term that is used by philosophers in their discussions of hylomorphism (and "image" should be saved for translating the technical terms *khayāl* and *mithāl*). In the Koran, God is the "Form-giver" (*musawwir*), and, we are told, "He formed you, and made your forms beautiful" (40:64). In Ibn al-'Arabī's usage, "form" rarely designates the intelligible reality or quiddity of a thing (for which he uses *sūra*'s correlative, *ma'nā*, "meaning"), but rather the appearance of things, or the distinctive attributes that make them what they are, or their bodily guise. Like everything else, form undergoes constant change.

[10] *Futūhāt* II 102.31. On the divine form, see *Self-Disclosure* 27–29.

[11] See *Sufi Path* 295.

[12] *Futūhāt* I 306.6. See *Sufi Path* 122–23.

[13] Roger T. Ames and David L. Hall, *Daodejing, "Making This Life Significant": A Philosophical Translation* (New York: Ballantine Books, 2003), p. 15.

[14] On never-ending divine self-disclosure as the secret of the soul's endless life, see Chittick, *Sufi Path* 156.

[15] *Futūhāt* IV 76.31; *Sufi Path* 377.

[16] *Futūhāt* II 133.19; *Sufi Path* 376.

[17] *Futūhāt* III 506.30; *Sufi Path* 376.

[18] Contra Ames and Hall, who maintain that "There is no view from nowhere," given that "The field of experience is always construed from one perspective or another" (*Daodejing* 18).

ANNA-TERESA TYMIENIECKA

THE GREAT METAMORPHOSIS OF THE LOGOS
OF LIFE IN ONTOPOIETIC TIMING

11

A-T. Tymieniecka (ed.),
Timing and Temporality in Islamic Philosophy and Phenomenology of Life, 11–71.
© 2007 *Springer*.

PREFACE: The present study draws upon an extensive and lifelong inquiry of the author, an inquiry that has branched in numerous directions. This study may seem then to be a synopsis of my hitherto established system of thought. While in many respects it is, I here approach the great philosophical issues, which have hitherto been treated each in its own right, within the overall perspective of timing and the temporality of beingness, which perspective brings to them all a common denominator since whatever we human beings may have mental access to manifests itself in its essential timing. Temporality pervades existence, both the known and the knower through and through. It emerges in its particular modalities from the bowels, from the womb of life—where the first seminal elements acquire their logoic shape and life is molded forthwith through the unfolding of living beingness out of and within its circumambient conditions.

Thus timing and the temporality of life assume such a preponderant role in the life of each living beingness that we human beings feel ourselves to be its captives. It seems to pervade our life and yet is always escaping our grasp. There is no wondering why the ancient Greeks in the myth of Kronos spoke of Time devouring his own children. In philosophical schemata, time has been given the standing of an absolute—one that distinguishes and brings together the modalities of everything in the purview of human knowledge.

Most significantly, we have in our inquiry identified the first and last ontopoietic fact of beingness at large, namely, the logos of life, life's prompting force and the shaper of its course—in its innermost workings, in its constructive/destructive progress, in the genesis, growth, decay, and extinction of living beingness. Since timing is crucial in all those steps, our phenomenology/ontopoiesis of life puts the classic substantial conception of time on its head. Our being is becoming.

In contrast to the traditional view, the ontopoiesis of life unravels the "absolute" of the logos, which as a prompting force carries becoming onward. As we will see, it is in their temporality that beings, things, events manifest themselves as modalities of the logos of life.

This is a perspective that deprives time of its traditional absolute status. Still timing and temporality remain emblematic of becoming at its innermost.

I propose to follow succinctly time's unfolding modalities within the entire compass of the logos of life, and that at the crucial level of the inner workings of beingness, of the logos of life's timing itself in its unfolding. Going step by step, from brink to brink of the cadences of its continuity/discontinuity, we will follow the long series of constructive transformations, transmutations, conversions of sense by which the logos of life has procured ever new devices and brought forth ever new modalities of intergenerative, symbiotic, interactive, communicative linkage. In pondering the reversals in which over time one modality grows while another declines and how one function serves as a spring-board for another in its surging forth, we must ask, "Where does this ever renewing current come from and where does it lead?" Amidst the transformations of sense, what sense does the current itself bear?

The meandering transformative, transmutative, sublimating, converting operations of the logos of life in the temporal ontopoietic spread of life's self-individualizing networks intimate for us an answer to that ultimate metaphysical question—THE GREAT METAMOR-PHOSIS.

INTRODUCTION

1. BEFORE ENTERING INTO THE HEART OF THE MATTER (LEGITIMATING THE ACCESS TO TRUTH)

1.1. The Question of Life as the Radical Beginning

It is all about the philosophical quest. Our urge to understand all around us—the world, other beings, the soil under our feet and the firmament above—springs forth from our innermost as an imperative desire to find the enigmatic sense of it all. Considering the philosophical quest as a journey through the dense jungle of intuitions, ideas, and flashes of insight, through the desert of dead ends, through the "stormy sea without a compass" as Kant saw it, it is of utmost significance to recognize our point of departure. It is from within our being in itself as a whole that we will delineate life's path, and not through the promptings of our cognitive urge in isolation. And there is an even greater question than that of from where we shall commence our quest, namely, that of with what shall we equip ourselves for our quest. Shall we heed an intuitive grasp of the essences of beingness around us? Taking that as our starting point will give us only an ossified view of things, beings. This starting point usually leads us to so-called "ontology." Shall we, in contrast, instead scrutinize our cognitive apparatus, differentiating the variety of cognitive modalities and their contrasting claims to certainty, probability—the path usually called "epistemology"? Or shall we venture into the highly elevated sphere of spiritual speculation, privileging the direct swing of our deepest subterranean yearning for ultimate truth toward its absolute destination free from all contingent certitude?

All three of these lines of thought have been pursued by great truth seekers. Each of them seems indispensable for the situating of our quest. None alone, however, bears complete witness to the truth we seek. Thus I ask—Can there be a more fundamental grounding, a firmer and more indicative point of departure than life itself? *I submit that the living being recognizes itself as "himself" or "herself," not by a cognitive act but by "being alive"*— by experiencing oneself within one's milieu of beingness, directing one's instincts and appetites, recognizing the elements of the circumambient world in their vital relatedness to oneself, and lastly, but foremostly, by recognizing oneself as *the acting center of the universe of existence,* as a self-sustaining agent who directs within this universe of existence through experience, observation, reflection, and deliberation his or her own course and who, finally, endows that course with moral and aesthetic values, and upon the wings of the spirit seeks to understand the reasons of it all and soars to the metaphysical and spiritual realm above, carrying within a thoroughly felt self-aware conviction that to be is to be alive.

The starting point of our quest has to be situated from its incipient instance in the very midst of all three of the perspectives mentioned and all their subsidiary considerations. It has, then, to be *life.*

1.2. The Point of Departure

There is indeed an undeniable primal state of living beingness: *to be means to be alive.* This state cannot be identified with any one experience and yet it underlies all experiences. The "spark of life," which I have isolated as the event of its manifestation in reality, radiates from the coalescence of the propitious factors of life that favor dynamic consolidation in self-individualization. The force of the logos shaping life drives the subsequent escalation of more and more complex individualizing steps and finds its apogee in the human individual. Here lies the point of vital confidence, that of existential certainty that the identification of one's very beingness lies in this, that to be is to be alive! This is to feel oneself in a primogenital mode as being expanded and integrated into the world by one's own body in performance, to be dimly aware of one's vital bodily/psychic participation in the world's performances, to be from the inside out oriented toward close integration with the world's/life's progress. Therein, *in the actio/passio context of being alive my certitude lies.*

Yet this first awareness—self-awareness—of beingness, which carries all the virtualities of its entire unfolding—comes last to the reflective awareness of the mind. When I propose it as the "starting point" of the metaphysical journey, I have to point to the preparatory phases of the phenomeno-logical/philosophical investigation that have to be traversed in order to reach it.

Let us then indicate succinctly the steps and stations on the way preliminary to our mounting the primogenital ontopoietic platform upon which we will discover the primordial state of life. It is the logos of life that we will pursue which will be our conducting thread, our *filum Ariadnae.* The classical ways proposed by philosophy—ontology, epistemology, metaphysics, aesthetics, anthropology, etc.—all have their source in this logos and yet escape from it into the labyrinths of their singular intellective approaches, getting more and more remote from the sources and from each other, getting lost in endless intel-lective speculation. In contrast, phenomenology/ontopoiesis of life takes from life poignant evidence of the self as the firm ground from which to delineate life's course, retracing in the work of the mind the dynamic vital/existential lineaments of the logos of life. Proceeding in this way retrieves all the above-mentioned perspectives and situates them in their proper place.

1.3. Survey of the Initial Itinerary Legitimating Access to Truth

It is customary in contemporary philosophy and especially in the Husserlian tradition to legitimate not only the point of departure but also the procedure of philosophizing. I submit that our thread of inquiry will directly focus on the intuition of the logos of life. In various writings I have trekked a tortuous path toward the oasis of the primogenital logos of life, and before we enter I will briefly indicate the main phases of the journey.

1.3.1. The Human Creative Act   First and foremost the discovery of human creative experience allowed us access to the logos of life,[1] for it is reflected in human creative experience in its manifold radiation.

1.3.2. The Human Creative Condition Within the Unity-of-Everything-There-Is-Alive   We found a definitive station (platform) and our compass not in cognition but in the human creative act, which enters the sphere of becoming-individualizing life. We thus interpret in its original nature the becoming that reveals the logos of life within pristine nature. With only one step further (but what an intuitive step!), the entire field of the becoming of life, of the *ontopoiesis of life,* lies open.

1.3.3. The Ontopoietic Plane of Life   With the uncovering of the ontopoietic plane of life's becoming, the forces and the arteries of the logos of life are revealed for metaphysical inspection. This is a plane of inquiry that combines *the dynamic ontology of beingness in becoming* with metaphysical insight and conjectural reaching beyond toward the great enigmas of the Universal Logos.

Only a quest that does not shrink before the peaks of the All may satisfy the dynamic interrogating thrust of human genius.

Within this field we will dwell forthwith in order to show how the timing of life and temporality as such belong to the essential ways in which the vital spheres of life emerge and unfold, and the specifically human moral and intellective spheres also; we are led on as well toward the spheres of the sacred that lay beyond and toward the Fullness of the All. We will find, indeed, within the sacral sphere of the logos of life links to the logoic phase that lies beyond. Briefly, led by the logos of life's supreme timing, its constructive/destructive ways, we will be led from the unconditioned generation of modes of interdependence in existence toward the Fullness of all. But All is logos, and with the logos we have to start our journey on the ontopoietic platform, which the three preparatory phases of philosophy just covered tend toward.

1.4. The Revelation of the Logos in Reality

The revelation of the logos of life in reality—and its conjectured reaching Beyond—is a unique state of individualizing/becoming in which the evolving logos of life acquires its existential plenitude within the full-fledged development of the human individual. Not being a product of the intellective function of the human mind, nor of any single one of the mind's powers or dependencies, the revelation of the logos of life engages the entire sentient human person in its logoic expansion. It ties the ever-renewing living synthesis of the person into a final knot. Not only does it surge into awareness according to the level of completeness in the individual's development, but it acquires the clarity of an experiential vision only through unveiling itself in the gradual ascent of the steps of the metaphysical itinerary of the full mind.

This calls for a gradual unveiling because it is the first and the last fruit yielded in the ontopoietic course of a human person. This is not simply the fruit of the human mind's intellective cognition but is a revelation to the entire mind, one awarded to it through its climbing the itinerary of life's becoming.

We do not need to seek any "certitude" of this revelation's validity other than its very own unveiling. Human experience and human cognitive powers are part and parcel of this revelation. This revelation carries absolute certitude within itself. That is to say, it cannot be "reduced" to anything that would stand for it; it reposes in itself. It is truth to be unveiled fully at the end of the mind's journey. Beyond the networks of relative "truth" of the concrete lifeworld of earthly existence, we find in the revelation of the logos of life the absolute truth of Beingness in its sense, in the sense of the logos of life itself.

However, this last phase of the journey does not mean its absolute termination. To the contrary, the wondrous transformability of the progress of the logos of life in establishing reality intimates from the beginning its expansion into Imaginatio Creatrix, which accounts first of all for the great transformation of sense in the Human Condition as well as, secondly, for its refinement into the Sacral Imagination, which through its works of conjectural inference inspires and informs the Great Passage leading onward to and beyond the Great Sacral Metamorphosis.

PART ONE

2. THE LOGOS OF LIFE IN THE CONSTRUCTIVE VIRTUALITIES FOR LIFE'S UNFOLDING

On entering the ontopoietic field upon which we will pursue our investigation of timing and temporality, we have been instructed by our journey to that point about numerous features of the logos of life and about the logos itself as the originator and promoter of life. We have now to review our findings in order to prepare ourselves to continue our quest.

2.1. Logos as Force

The force of the Logos manifests itself in the logos' effusion of life. It acquires "shape" in its performance and is then intuited through that performance, from the inside, as it were. First of all, logos, the reason of reasons and the sense of everything, is not simply a set of principles articulating "matter." It is above all a force, a *driving force* that through its modalities is accountable not only for the incipient instance of originating life in its self-individualizing process but also for the pre-origination, pre-ontopoietic ground and for the subsequent striving toward the abyss of the spirit. Life, as the ontopoietic progress of the logos' drive in the self-individualization of beingness, emerges then as a manifestation of the ontopoietic process.[2] It appears *sua sponte* but not from "nowhere." It surges in an effusion from itself, it has no beginning and no end. "Beginning" and "end" are in time. But it is from the unfolding of the logos of life that "time" emerges. The logos is a primogenital force striving without end, surging in its impetus and seeking equipoise.

But what is force? Leaving aside speculative query, let us stress that force means, in the first place, the constructive prompting of the logos of life as it manifests itself in the progress of life. Further, this force for its own advance prepares its own means/organs. Thirdly, its advance means the fulfillment of constructive steps toward transformations, steps by step unfolding projects of progressive conversion of constructive forces into new knots of sense (in the terms of classical philosophy, "substances" undergo a "transubstantial" change). Fourthly, in this progress of the transformation of sense, the inner modality of the logoic force undergoes an essential transmutation. Having seemingly brought the crucial factum of life out of "nowhere," it reveals its purpose in preparing scrupulously in a long progression the constructive route of individualizing life so that Imaginatio Creatrix emerges as an autonomous modality of force with its own motor, the human will. To crown this development, the force of the logos, with will as a novel modality of force, advances from the vital/ontopoietic round of significance into two novel dominions of sense: the creative/spiritual and the sacral. But this is to anticipate our further discourse.

2.2. *The Interrogative Mode of the Logos of Life*

The force of the logos does not explode blindly. It proceeds by throwing itself from the already achieved to the presumed that it partly indicates and partly leaves to a further determination by the circumambient situation. Each step posited throws up a "question" for the next, that is, establishes an order for the dynamic.[3] Through this interrogative relay the logos of life, operating within the network of the ontopoietic constructive designs that it brings with itself, transforms the stream of its forces from a chaos into an organized becoming, the becoming of life and life-coordinated elements. *Life is, then, a dynamic flux, but is far from a wild Heraclitean flux, for it articulates itself. First of all, it "times" itself.* The moves of life in their constructive ontopoietic patterns time life. Life throughout its advancing interrogative steps of constructive/destructive becoming times itself.

Its prompting force is, indeed, dispersed in this constructive élan, which as élan is interrogating its possibilities: moving one step ahead, it carries within this very step's virtualities for constructive continuation, seeking an opportune situation in which to crystalize them. Life is ever ahead of itself in the actual implementation of its potentialities. This intrinsic feature of the logos of life—of logos as such?—is what carries the progress, and regress, of life. Does this stop with the timing of life? Does it not drive also those inner yearnings to go beyond temporality?

2.3. The Logos of Life as Sentience

Impressed by the intellective capacities of our mind, we are tempted to contrast reason and feeling, seen as an agent of the passions. But in our own inquiry down the main avenues of life, we have discovered that reason, the logos of life precisely, is capable of articulating life's elements owing to its innermost passional orientation: its sentience.

It is most curious that the logos of life brings the thread of its primogenital nature clearly to light only after investigation has uncovered its numerous constructive streaks in various differentiated expressions. Only after gaining an overview of its vital, societal, creative realms of realization do we discover that in its essence the logos of life is quite far away from being just a universal ordering and communicative entity that we may characterize as being intellective. On the contrary, and here lies the radical distinction between life and nonlife: the logos of life is essentially primarily sentient.

Most perceptively, medicine from Paracelsus to John Brown, has defined life as "reactivity", a view affirmed by Schelling. This tradition, however, saw this reactivity as reactivity "to" some exterior factor. Contemporary thinkers (e.g., Michel Henry for one) seem to identify life with the "affectivity" of innermost human consciousness. This view has some merits, but it also lies far from the root of the matter. Only in apprehending the logos of life itself as the motor and carrier of the entire ontopoietic enterprise are we in a position to penetrate into the deepest level of life's becoming, a level at which beingness itself originates in virtue of the logos of life itself.

Now, as I have been pointing out from the very outset of these preliminary remarks, the nature of the logos of life is revealed through life itself. We recognize something as being alive through the mobility that proceeds from within it and is directed by its interior "self," that is, through the force of its movement and its directedness. But foremostly, we recognized life through its sentience. Indeed, *the logos of life is not an uncommitted stream of neutral force; on the contrary, it is a shaping force that it exhibits.* This latter sustains a double line of reason: the reason of constructive ontopoietic unfolding with its innumerable ramifications and varying modalities for inserting the self-individualizing beingness within circumambient forces and vital conditions, and the reason of sharing-in-life that at innumerable opportunities allows life's virtual cognitive and moral modalities to unfold. But both of these lines of "reasoning" are as it were secondary to the primal essence of the logos of life, which is sentience.

In fact, the logos of life IS sentience. Having once burst into the open, the logos unfolds itself in life's becoming. It is not through anticipating its furthest constructive results, such as human consciousness, and not by assuming an outside realm beyond it, but by laying out intuitively the logos' own life involvement and its realization in concrete life development that we may get to its ultimate constructive roots. They lie with the nature of the logos which crystalizes it virtualities in projecting life.

2.4. The Intentionality of Life Is Sentient

Life's essence is, as stated above, SENTIENCE. The incipient individualizing step of life—a step passing over into virtual beingness—involves not the throwing forth of a constructive moment only. No, it does not mean standing as a singular and accidental moment without association with steps to come, without a follow-up of intrinsic reason. Life in its emergence is simultaneously a self-registration within a projected net, a net within which all the moments are linked together by a most intrinsic to the unfolding reciprocal affectivity, the affectivity of life—the sentient nature of the logos which carries it. There is no need for or possibility of an "outside" element's entering or being reacted to. There is no "outside" to the logos of life. This logos itself lays out spacing. This logos brings with itself the very distinction between "outside" and "inside" as the modality of its proceeding. The process of the ontopoietic unfolding of the living being (that is, of its self-individualization-in-existence) proceeds at its incipient moment with a doubly directed move—one inwardly and outwardly directed. The logos of life in action in this seemingly fleeting moment introduces "sentience": the sentience of the logos of life itself, which means sentience is the primal feature of the intentional correlatedness of the constructive processes of life's unfolding. In brief, the logos of life manifests itself not simply as a neutral ordering factor of life but as its essentially sentient artery bringing about and receiving an infinite array of signals informing the constructive continuity/discontinuity of life's progress.[4]

2.5. Logoic Sentience and the Dianoiac Thread of Life

From that it is but one step to recognition that to be means essentially to be sentient, that is, to emit and evoke sense-imbued responses. Sentience leads us to recognize that in this guise the logos of life establishes the means of intergenerative and social communication. Sentience is key to life's communal sharing at all levels of complexity. In the final analysis it is geared to the *intellective sense* that surges in higher living beings and attains its full measure in the creative mind of the human being, through which it acquires full-fledged *cognitive measure*. I have called this sentient-cognitive streak of logoic sentience a *dianoiac thread* that runs through the entire spread of life's differentiated functions and which at the cognitive level of sentience makes us aware of and feel deeply a basic existential solidarity with all creation. The recognition of the sentient essence of the logos of life is, as we will see, the key not only to societal life-connectedness as sharing in life but also to the seemingly discontinuous coherence of the individual life-progress of the human soul on its path to transcending the vicissitudes of existence.

2.6. The Measuring Stick: the Ontopoietic Sequence of Self-Individualizing Life

This driving force of life which brings with itself its germinal endowment for constructive endeavor, is by no means a vital élan, a wild stream of force without direction other than the paths hazard opens. On the contrary, the logos as force not only carries within itself its virtual endowment toward constructive employment—its seminal arsenal—and its vertiginous networks of constructive virtualities, varying with circumambient conditions, but also leads them in their constructive articulations from within, applying its own measure. It carries within itself a prototype of singular beingness to be infinitely molded and yet remain enduringly the same: *the ontopoietic sequence.*[5] It is the ontopoietic sequence of the logos which serves as its ontic, infinitely variable and yet at its core essentially perduring model/measure of constructive becoming as well as the ontopoietic yardstick for life's articulations. Through its dynamic, variable, and yet relatively perduring ontopoietic model, the logos of life is not only force and shaping but also the ordering principle of life. With this insight into the very nature of the logos force, it is but one big step to discovering its dynamics.

2.7. The Interrogative Prompting

Exploring the ontopoietic field of the primogenital logos of life further, we learn also its specifically own ways of proceeding constructively from within. The force/élan of the logos proceeds by simultaneously bringing forth the elemental chaos and harnessing it constructively into a streaming flux of becoming. We discover immediately its "interrogative nature" in its stepwise projection of a line of constructive moves while only halfway *fulfilling* those projected constructive moves.

The logos' prompting force is, indeed, dispensed in this constructive élan, which as élan interrogates its possibilities; moving one step ahead it carries within this very step virtualities for a constructive continuation and seeks an opportune situation in which to crystalize it. It is ever ahead of itself in the actual implementation of its potentialities. This intrinsic feature of the logos of life (of logos as such?) is what carries the progress, and the regress, of life. Does it stop with the timing of life? Does it not drive its innermost strivings beyond?

We will conclude our very brief statement of the inward nature of the logos of life, merely outlined here but gathered from our preceding work and in need of further elaboration, by emphasizing the crucial telic sense of its construc-tivity, what amounts to a transmutation of sense that drives the entire logoic route toward transformation. First and foremost logos involves taking some step, whether it be a fusion, coalescence, redirection in living beings of least complexity, or the unfolding of the vital sense of life, or using sharing-in-life networks, or advancing on the path of the sacral logos within the human soul, it means a transformation of the status quo. Each step is, further, a more near or more remote provision for significant moments of transformation. All of them in a web of transformation lead stepwise toward an overall metamorphosis to be fulfilled. We will follow this path, distinctive in every tiniest step of the constructive advance that the line of the logos of life pursues. These steps may be tentatively and provisorily distinguished as having hyletic, morphic, convertible, instrumental, manifesting, kairic creative, or sacral transformative modalities according to the milestone that it is meant to be reached along the transformative route of life significance. We may say that the enterprise of the logos of life is escalating a differentiated metamorphic flow that finds its fulfillment in a Great Metamorphosis of life that has been projected in germ from the very incipient instance and in which we will find our destiny.

PART TWO

3. THE ONTOPOIETIC TIMING OF LIFE—THE DIFFUSION
OF THE LOGOS-FORCE IN THE ONTOPOIETIC
SHAPING OF LIFE

3.1. The Corporeal Vortex of Timing and the Temporality of Life

Setting out from the absolute evidence of our primogenital selfhood's being alive we will map ontopoietically its expansion on two trajectories: that which concerns its individual evolving and that which concerns its symbiotic processes/transactions within its sustaining and limiting world. There is, however, no real distinction here, for it is one reality that is being measured in the different processes or constructive divisions of labor. There is a constructive application of vital/intellective forces in one great and continuous thrust. The distinctive significances that these forces bring to their confluence express only different constructive lines. These are indeed to be ontopoietically distinguished but only as being mutually completing of each other, indispensable to each other, for together they fulfill one and the same constructive design.

Ultimately these constructive lines express and crystalize in their confluence, in their coherence, that they are the devices of the logos in its dynamic effusion. Along these trajectories of individual evolution and symbiosis the logos of life is timing and spacing life. Or, to put it inversely, life in evolving is bringing about timed and spaced reality.

3.2. Embodiment: Vortex and Blueprint of Life—the Creation of the Real World

To live means to be embodied, but since life is essentially sentient, life also means to be besouled. Living beingness surges into life with an ontopoietic project to be embodied. The logos of life that prompts it unfolds its primary steps in the self-individualization of beingness, which means its progressive embodiment. The body is the vehicle of its project, the knots of its articulations, the source and processor of its energies in ontopoietic unfolding and metamorphosis.

3.3. The Creation of Our World Means In-carnation in a Body

Life means embodiment. The creation of our world means in-carnation in a body. Embodiment calls for two basic dimensions, spacing and timing, to carry out its basic blueprint in generation and becoming, for the reception of the effusion of the logos and its launching as the logos of life. Thus embodiment does not mean inert matter's taking various shapes. Embodiment does not mean the occupation of space. From its simplest forms (such as a cell), *corporeality means sentient motility,* which proceeds from its core, wherefrom it is directed. In short, *to be a living body means to be "besouled".* In the besouled body the ontopoietic individualizing process is focused, and here is centered the interactive origin of the world of life, as well as of the sharing-in-life spheres of simple as well as most complex societal existence.

All the prelife physical and organic operations of the ontopoietic origination of life are primed for the vitally significant purpose of establishing, first of all, bodily operations and sentient and physically aware fleshly beingness. Living beingness consists existentially in this essential foundational complex. Most significantly in the other direction, it is in virtue of embodiment and in strict fulfillment of its postulates that the setup of life—its nest and womb—the world is established now within life's network: the cosmos, the earth (and the presumed beyond). In their purposeful springing forth the constructive processes of the world in a continuous stream of transformation foster self-sustaining types of living beingness, self-sustaining within the generic and interactive networks of life. The prodigious inventiveness of the logos of life develops along the way numerous instruments of metamorphic advance; it is enough to mention the building of vital organs.

The greater station of transmutation within the progress/regress of life is the Human Condition, prepared for by the purposive unfolding of the organic system as its interrogative steps of constructive/destructive becoming timed itself.

3.4. The Ontopoietic Intentionality of Life

Thus the dynamic constructive flux is in its ordering not a self-contained—window-and-doorless—train. On the contrary, there are generative articulations that are operative in this flux's overall substantial shaping and fit. But this very operativeness, the smooth adjustment that we witness along the entire spread of the genesis and the deterioration of life's progress or regress in myriads of intergenerative and interactive moves also occurs, first of all, in virtue of the crucial sensitivity—sentience—of the logos of life itself. The logos of life projects itself onwards by sending out sentient links in myriad registers according to the modalities of the entities that it links with or generates, with all being communicated to the innermost sentient modalities. Thus all living beings are symbiotic beings, that is, they all partake essentially in the sentience that they share. This is not a neutral intellectually grasped causal chain but the congenital communality of the living, which delimits their common conditions of existence as well as their interdependence upon each other and the All. If we denominate the schema of interdependence in generation, sharing-in-life, psychic communication, etc. as intentionality, then the intentionality of life is primordially sentient, for communicable signs, language, is essentially accessible through sentience. Only with the human mind at the peak of its abstract performance is intentionality intellective.

Intentionality as the thread of the interconnectedness of life is essentially sentient and only as such does it bind together all its various modes. It not only conducts the elementary symbiotic communication of life's program but also plays an essential role in the specifically human sphere. In fact, the force of the logos of life manifests in its exercise that it is suspended on an overarching network of human sharing-in-life within which human vital interests, personal relations with others, etc. are intertwined and within which it is molded in innumerable and protean ways that are informed by specifically human sentience.

3.5. The Ontopoietic Sequence: Endowment, Impulse, Force, Direction, Adjustment, Coordination

Having enumerated the various functional features and factors of the logos of life in its promoting life's deployment, let us now focus on its essential organizing-constructive-directional device, with reference to which their constructive orchestration occurs, that is, on *the ontopoietic sequence.*

In the self-individualization of beingness, that is, in its differentiation of beings from each other as they assume each their own selfhoods, the device of the logos lies in the dynamic adaptiveness of its "essence" to the circumambient conditions. This is a persistently perduring project—blueprint—of the course that self-individualizing may and "should" take. The "project" in limbo contains all its virtualities. It is in virtue of this project that all the operational unfoldings of individualizing beingness take place. It is in virtue of its indications' prescriptive formation of the living beingness-in-course that all the distinctive as well as coalescing operations occur, insofar as the circumambient situation allows. The constructive sequence is an intrinsic endowment of the emerging beingness. It is the "gift" of the logos that prompts its surging amid already favorable conditions. How does the logos of life come by it? How does it fit beforehand into the set of conditions found virtually ready to unfold? These are among the last cosmologico-metaphysical questions to which we will come. For our present purpose let us emphasize the sequence in its *entelechial aspect*—an entelechy that in its dynamic unfolding brings together all the moves of life, that is, of life's timing. This sequence's intrinsic ontopoietic intentionalities in correspondence with those of the living network within which it unfolds, synchronize the existential mix of living occurrences into vitally significant concurrent networks, in vitally significant successive phases whose vital telos is virtually foretraced by the ontopoietic sequence containing its various "possibilities." These phases are right-there-in-wait, ready to emerge full force if the proper symbiotic response be encountered.

The ontopoietic sequence is not only an intrinsic model of a project but most significantly it is also its engine. The timing of life's orchestrated individualizing steps follows with vital *necessity* its intrinsic prescriptions—even if allowing for considerable variation in adaptation to existential circumstances. We may speak of life's "vital timing," which advances in myriad synchronizing streams of events. I call this timing kronos.

In a dramatic contrast to the kronos temporality of the vital significance of life, however, there is to be distinguished an altogether different timing brought about with the emergence and unfolding of the Human Condition, namely, that of kairos, the timing of human creative existence.

It is the ontopoietic sequence that 1) controls and prompts the consistency of individualizing-in-beingness; 2) controls its integrative immersion in the turmoil of life's onward rush and retreats; 3) is the principle of ordering at life's platform of individual becoming as well as of symbiotic coexistence; and 4) maintains the identity of types through perpetual transforming adjustments.

However, and this is of crucial significance for the progress of life's timing, amid the ontopoietic sequence's inner transformations in adjustment to surrounding conditions and its maintainence of its concrete constructive core (its *ipseitas*) and its simultaneous maintenence of a set of "essential existentials" (a corresponding *haeccitas*), it undergoes inner transformations that lead to transmutations of type, accounting for the evolution of the "types" of beingness.

3.6. Ontopoietic Timing Conjectured: The Cosmic Relevancies of Bios

With this basic clarification we enter directly into the puzzling issue of "cosmic time" as well as that of "mechanical" temporality. As I have pointed out before, not only is life the point of a specific convergence of forces, one that may emerge only within a conundrum of specific cosmic conditions, but life in all its forms also "implements" the specific laws, of the cosmos itself. Although these laws (e.g., gravitation) are not directly "present" within the structuring of the forms of life, they are re-presented within its specific forms and processes through what I have called the system of "cosmic relevancies." Thus when we ask about the nature of cosmic movements and their temporality, we are already raising and formulating these questions "from within" those very cosmic relevancies in accord with which we are constituted as living beings, even as we participate through our very endowments in that system. In short, we approach the cosmos with our life-established notions of and devices for measuring motion and time. Our estimation of cosmic developments over billions of years is made by transposing onto a sphere unknown in itself our own very specific, uniquely specific, life factors. We do not discover in the cosmos, at least we have not so far, other forms of life. Should they exist, how would we be able to recognize them from within our own form of life and specify their means and relevancies? We can identify the motions of the stars, the falling of meteors, the streaming of cosmic forces, etc., but can only partially ken the constructive moves, processes, and operations that we distinguish in the sphere of bios as they orient and surge from "within" and work a constructive achievement.

Thus, having no evidence of "movement timing itself" in the cosmos, we approach these moves and processes as stripped down versions of the timing of life and so posit for it an abstract line of succession, of causation, seeing only lifeless mechanical motion without sentience. In this fashion, we arrive at both "cosmic time" and the "time of mechanical motion" as well as the uniform abstraction of all of time's qualitative life-coordinates in the measurement of time by clepsydra, clock, metronome. We empty the prototype of living time of all its genetic content, leaving a mere skeleton.

3.7. The Penultimate Question

The penultimate question that occurs here is this: "How are these dynamic constructive adjustments of each singular individualizing beingness spontaneously coordinated in a mesh of generating and unfolding types and their conditions; How is this organization and evolving brought about?; Where does this penultimate coordination come from?" There is certainly a spontaneously unfolding plan, one malleable and protean yet holding on to the crucial principle of the bodily vortex. To this we will still come.

This is the ultimate question of the logos of life—its "secret" to be pursued.

When we advance to the specifically human realm, here we are bedazzled by the powers bestowed upon us—by which we have an essential say in directing our life course. While on the scale of universal values we favor yet further deployments of the psychic realm with its freedom and of the spiritual realm with its self-awareness of sense, and ultimately we yearn for expansion into the sacral realm seeking the redemption of the finiteness of earthly life, nevertheless it is from and upon the arena offered by the body-flesh-empirical psyche that the great drama of humanness is being played.

The reach of the logos of life in which concrete life on earth is enmeshed seems to be enigmatic. We will come to this further on in our investigations. For the time being, let us state that life's timing of itself through the ontopoietic schema of the logos extends directly only through the concrete reality of life; and yet this timing seems to reverberate much further.

PART THREE

4. THE KAIRIC TIMING OF THE LOGOS OF LIFE THE SECOND BIRTH OF THE HUMAN BEING IN THE MORAL SENSE

4.1. Toward the Kairic Transmutation of Sense

4.1.1. The Advent of the Human Creative Condition   We have glanced at the unfolding of life through the basic moments of its self-individualizing beingness timing itself in its progress and indicating the most intricate devices by which the logos of life projects that individualization onwards by functional "moves" that punctuate in unison life's vital timing. We have indicated the directing reference system of this gigantic dynamically coordinated web and pointed to the ontopoietic sequence as not only coordinating and prompting the appropriate moves at a given phase of an individual's unfolding as it concretizes itself in existence, but as also simultaneously participating in the given palpitating web within which this concretization takes place. And so we have outlined the major arteries of life's vitally significant timing.

Here we encounter a crucial metaphysical issue. Intertwined with it are several questions. What is the metaphysical standing of the logos of life? We begin tracing it from the origin of beingness in an already established form—or a to be established form, that of self-individualization. But what is the relation of the logos of life to the prelife situation? A second intertwined issue lies with the transmutation of types that is prepared in the intergenerative variability of individualizing procreation. Is the scalar-gradual advance of types of living beingness of growing complexity that which is central? Thirdly, what is the standing of the logos of life vis-à-vis the advent of Imaginatio Creatrix, the dramatic advent of the specifically Human Creative Condition?

To answer these questions we have above particularly noted the significance of the ontopoietic sequence and its multiple temporalizing role. While this sequence maintains each given type, all are nevertheless subject to their own inner transformations. This inner transformability of the ontopoietic sequence accounts for the so-called mutation of types and the surging of forms of beingness different from preceding ones. This gives a novel foundation for that we scientifically call "evolution." The notion of evolution is thus not only a fact of scientific inquiry, now universally accepted (despite controversy over details), but foremostly a dynamically ontic trend of life having at its roots ontopoietic unfolding.

Although owing to varying conditions the advancing course of the evolution of types takes various routes, nevertheless we may state from our human point of view that there is a steady advance in complexity of functions, forms, life-manifestations, etc. Along this route there is reached a unique phase of evolutive transmutation that merits to be called *the Human Condition within the unity-of-everything-there-is-alive.* In its "mature" phase this platform of life manifests an extraordinary character. Paradoxically the human being appears to be integrally part and parcel of nature yet to reaches levels "beyond nature," levels of life that endow the human being with special unique significance that is no longer simply vital but is also spiritual.

There are, indeed, three perspectives in which we have now for our present purpose to go back to the Human Condition to which I have long devoted great attention.

First of all, let me propose that the emergence of the Human Condition "out from" and "out of" life seems to mean a second "birth" of the human being, who was born before "out of" Nature. This is an audacious statement, but there are perspectives in which it is substantiated.

The essential differentiation of the Human Condition amid the unity of life is a watershed event, essentially a transformation of the significance of life. In. its root condition the human being draws its vitally significant endowment from Nature-life. There he stands firmly in life's entire functional network of operations; with that network, it stands or falls.

Secondly, we see that concurrently the intricate unfolding of complex bodily organs has formed a most complex vital platform ready to receive—one step further—a unique impulse springing seemingly from within and yet strangely autonomous and defying the drawing of any line of direct continuity with the vitally significant orchestration of organs that has, it seems, prepared it. This new factor of life's significance surges with the entry of Imaginatio Creatrix into the game of life.

Thirdly, we have to return to our description of the sentient nature of the logos of life. It is through the sentience of the logos which permeates all the functional moves of unfolding life, and in which all the constructive designs are processed, that a continuity is maintained throughout. The complexity of the advance in the unfolding of organs has brought about in man configurations of sentience of ampler significance than those serving vital interest alone, and with the conscious apparatus being developed, the gamut of what we call "experience" (from sensory pulsations to presentiment and emotions) comes about.

As the logos of life unfolds stepwise, with living beingness leaving behind each completed step and moving to the next, an essential logoic interconnectedness is maintained as each consecutive move, be it centrifugal or fusing, is inscribed into the common script of the originary unfolding that is self-individualization as well as in the so-called generative code for the transformation of types.

It is to "elementary," that is, vital sensing along with the intermediary elementary conscious apparatus that are addressed the three initiatives of Imaginatio Creatrix that expand animal-vital significance into the specifically human significance of life.

4.1.2. The Vortex of the Great Conversion of Sense   Here we reach the most surprising—if not enigmatic—turn of the logos of life. It appears to us "enigmatic," this surging of Imaginatio Creatrix in the middle of the ontopoietic sequence, surging freely as it floats above the inner workings of nature. It seemingly explodes the tight concatenations of nature's constructive links, clearing the way for seemingly unbound spiritual potentialities. Imaginatio Creatrix, in fact, proceeds from Nature-Life given its appositeness to life situations; still it manifests a striking autonomy in its functioning as well as in its offering a wealth of possibilities unprecedented in the ontopoietic unfolding. It brings into this otherwise self-enclosed orbit a radiating wealth of possibilities allowing for transformative projects for life's advance and the impulse to employ them.

This will seem an amazing intrusion of a special force "out of nowhere" so long as we do not recognize in it just the "next" step, the next phase of the logos of life in its decisive advance; the crucial phase of life's innermost metamorphosis.

With its advent—having seen clearly in it a continuation of the course of the unfolding of the logos through life, we may see and appreciate that Imaginatio Creatrix, while unforeseen, has been prepared for slowly through the entire progress of individualizing life, with each step bringing in further ranges of functioning and preparing organs for the advance to more complex functioning. What is the purpose, aim, telos of this? Of its directive principle? Is there, in fact, a "reason" for this *paradoxical reversal* in the course of the logos of life, which while centering its forces, first on a tight and ever tighter escalation of its constructive thrust was also preparing to loosen its grip on the selective process? This countervailing move comes from its very bowels, yet brings about a complete conversion of its hold on life's individualizing course and opens the entire horizon of freedom. Again, was this outcome a telos inherent in all the incidents leading to it?

And indeed, the crucial point of this reversal consists in the fact that it does not come out of "nowhere" but emerges from a logoic endowment or reservoir of virtual forces. Further, as we come to discern, this great shift was being prepared by the logos' constructive steps, starting obviously at the very beginning of self-individualizing life. Did the outcome lie already within its own ontopoietic project? We will get to that later. But the unfolding was obviously "controlled" by the nature of the logos. This phase of "freedom" synthesizes the evolution of individuality and of types; it manifests a line of the logos within the plan of the creation of the universe. For our present argument let us consider this, that the shift is operated by the metamorphosis of the temporality of beingness that subtends it.

Where is this great transformation leading us? What reason does the logos of life bear in itself? Or is it moved simply by its own creative power?

4.1.3. Imaginatio Creatrix   Imaginatio Creatrix—rooted within the functioning of Nature-life and yet an autonomous sense giver—introduces three new sense giving factors:[6] the intellective sense, the aesthetic sense, and the moral sense, which together inspire the emerging human mind. The *intellective sense* accounts for the human order of the world of life and communication. The *aesthetic sense* accounts for the expansion of experience beyond the strictly pragmatic apprehension of what serves the vital interests of self-individualizing beingness, for the opening of the specifically human realm to beauty, ugliness, and the sublime. It is, however, the *moral sense* that lies at the core of the metamorphosis of the life situation from vital existence into the Human Condition. It is the moral sense that accounts for the world as a human community. It is the engine of the human project and carries within itself the germinal propulsions of the sacral quest.

With these three new factors endowing life with meaning beyond what is geared to and strictly limited to survival, there comes about an inner transformation of the vitally oriented and single-minded functional system of reference into the novum of specifically human creativity. Within the creative modus of human functioning in its specifically creative orchestration there occurs a metamorphosis of the vital system of ontopoiesis and consequently the timing of ontopoiesis is transformed too. But to reach the point of addressing the question of temporality, we have first to cover the ground of the transition from the vital to the human significance of life on the way to the Great Metamorphosis.

4.1.4. The Creative Human Mind's Interpreting the Vital Significance of the Life Course in the Human Condition   With the introduction of the intellective sense, Imaginatio Creatrix accounts for the objectification of the sphere of existence around-and-in us in representation, thus setting up the "world" of beings, spheres, things. Simultaneously—and in order to work this objectification—it introduces sense of proportion, measure, comparison, discrimination, etc. Concurrently, this assessing of matters is referred to *the moral sense, which introduces valuation reflecting the principles of "good" and "evil," "true" and "false"* as these bear on in different respects and to varying degrees different physical and vital elements. Differentiation and valuation serve the free exercise of selection among the options presented for individual implementation in life.

We are reaching here an absolutely new platform of the ontopoiesis of life: *the human platform of freedom* in selection of nutrients etc. Where the direction of the choice had been foretraced by the vital needs to be satisfied and by the fitness of the available material, here the selection is made with deliberation that respects taste and desire but also refers to aims to be accomplished.

These aims are enhanced by the expansion of human experience beyond animal awareness to experience whose points of reference and modulations are the essential work of the aesthetic sense. This latter together with the two other meaning giving senses lift specifically human experience from the vitally regulated plane to the spheres of human appreciation for beauty, gracefulness, harmony....

In brief, through the orchestrated dynamic work of these sense-giving factors, the human mind transforms radically the way in which life's functions time its progress. Instead of carrying out step by step the logoic directions of the ontopoietic sequence fulfilling its individualized course and varying only in changed conditions, we are here dealing with modes of operation newly instaurated by imagination, the creative apparatus of the full-fledged human mind with its main prompting logoic forces: will and imagination. To find proper implementation of these powers we explore, project, aim.

In short, this station of life which is the Human Condition allows not merely foretraced constructive performances but the accomplishment of projected aims, teloi. With this we reach two points: a) specifically human temporality, b) the path to launching and fulfilling the course of the sacral logos.

4.1.5. The Centrality of the Besouled Body-Flesh-Psyche Complex for the Human Drama   The essential feature of life, its "nervous system," is the temporality within which its intricate shaping moves are performed. As a matter of fact, there are to be distinguished two shaping, constructive, perduring devices of life: first there is vitally significant performance, which follows directly the selective adaptational interactive prompts of the ontopoietic sequence; then with growth in the complexity of selectivity the human creative condition introduces will, deliberation, mind-directed selection, which does not stop at seeking immediate satisfaction but calls for planning and the entire creative operational system of the human being in order to frame and accomplish aims.

4.1.6. The Human Creative Condition as the "Second Birth" of the Human Being in the Moral Sense   The emergence of the moral sense and valuation introduces an order of "insight" that radically alters the significance of life hitherto valid for living beings as all the significant strings leading the experiences of the logos of life come together in a specific net for a new vision of existence, the Human Condition.

Recall that the fall from the Adamic state—from a paradisal existence to one haunted by pain, suffering, disenchantment, loss, etc., to an existence maintained by hard labor and maintained for but a short span till unavoidable death—followed on the discovery of good and evil, of the true and false, in short of the moral sense of life. It is this discovery which is said to have made our first parents fully aware of feelings in relation to the self and the other in the moral sense (e.g., feeling shame in their bodies). With the introduction of the moral perspective on oneself, our merely symbiotic community with the rest of creation was transformed into a communal sharing of my other self with myself. The recognition of good and evil brought to the awareness of the human being a new and different appreciation of life's course, which I will discuss forthwith.

4.1.7. The Experience of Life in the Human Condition: the Human Predicament   The novum of the Human Condition means the transformation of life's significance owing to the human mind's entry into the moral world.

The advent of the Human Condition within the unity-of-everything-there-is-alive is the true birth of the human being out of nature, is the birth of a living being with the capacity of spirit. Should we not consider this development as *the entrance into the game of life of a specific type of logos or rather of a specific thread of the logos of life* (after all, the human spirit is carried by the natural life complex)? Human communion and also the sacral quest are both virtually bound up with this thread.

The expansion of the evaluative perspective of the created living to the point of transformation is worked by the creative mind with its essential sense giving factors, the factor of the moral sense, in particular, which makes the human being distinctively and essentially different from the rest of known animals. Awareness of good and evil is at the root of specifically human consciousness, which is ultimately moral valuation, concurrently and confluent with the subterranean springing forth of the higher yearnings and aspirations of the soul to "understand," to understand what life is all about. This higher awareness is a "second birth" of the human being—second after the "first" Adamic creation, a completion of the Human Condition, which was begun by the entrance into the game of life of the human drama. It is most significant that in Genesis the awakening of this consciousness was seen as involving awareness of the human body.

Moral awareness, and in a way the grounding of the primordial sensibility of human communion, is brought in by the moral sense. It is within the sentient core of the logos of life that the moral sense surges from the numerous lines of sentience of commonality in animality to the re-cognition of another human as being equal to oneself. In this re-cognition resides a novel morality of the logos: a spirit of human communion. A human being cannot become fully aware of himself/herself as a conscientious being other than in relation to another human being.

As a factor of human intersubjectivity, empathy is grounded within the sentient nature of human intentional subjectivity; more will be said about this later. And so the logos of life is prompting, shaping, and carrying the dynamic, never stopping stream of life from its incipient moment of the self-individualization of beingness through its unfolding and growth till it decreases in energies and vital capacities and the extinction of the spark of life which has carried it occurs, timing itself all the while through its ontopoietic moves. But does the logos of life then complete its course with the dissolution of its existential vital articulations?

Does logos of life retire at the nadir of human creative effort along with the system of life's arteries, just suspending its force and vanishing? These questions will come into focus later on. For now we consider the evaluative nature of the entire course of life, which as the overarching shaping schema indicates, is evolving in complexity and shape ad infinitum. As the generative references of the simplest forms of life indicate, there seems to be a deeper and further reach of the original conditions through which the logos of life enters into its full-fledged reign, which also evolves.

We must see how all our senses are bound up with the exercise of the moral sense. But we are inclined/tempted to attribute all our selective freedom as well as the deliberative choice to be exercised by our own will to the specifically human dimension of existence, to assign that a preponderant role and value. We are prone to overlook or forget that this specifically human creative condition emerged upon the back of a giant, the body-flesh-psyche complex, and is in its exercise carried by it. In the final existential-ontopoietic account of the logos of life, it is in virtue of this bodily complex that the living beingness originates and evolves in its varying types; it is ultimately in virtue of the functioning of this bodily complex that the living being's subsistence stands and falls. This otherwise autonomous run of human "higher" intentional functioning and of the unfolding human spirit depends in its forces, energies, proportions, and measures, etc. on those of bodily-fleshly-psychic functioning. The most significant point for our present argument, however, is that the great human drama of good and evil, of charity and cruelty toward others within the evolving human destiny, is participating in, drawing upon, played within the framework of the dynamic conundrum of functional body sustenance. Our innermost spiritual tragedies find responding reverberations within the significance of our vital functioning in the unavoidable course of life.

An interpretation was given to this state of affairs by Confucius, "Fan Chi demanda ce qu'était la connaissance. Le Maître répondit: connaître autrui." It is indeed in relation to another man that "connnaissance" of oneself means con-naissance, that is to say, to become fully aware of oneself as a human being calls for inserting one's novel self into the web of others; the human being as such is born with others.

4.1.8. The Significance of Life Brought by the Human Condition. Pain, Birth, and Death Interpreted as Predicament, and Life as a "Drama"
Sentience, the life carrying thread, carried with itself, or through itself, its own penalty: pain and suffering. At the vegetal plane the failure to encounter the appropriate circumstances for growth results in plants' not being able to benefit from the action of the sun or moisture, with their growth being stunted and their moving toward extinction, mutely bearing their doom. With animals endowed with complex organs of sensitivity, frustration of their natural bent entails physical pain and psychic suffering, given the chain reactions in its functioning from the physical to the psychic. The pain common to all living beings finds, however, its climax in the complex psycho-organic suffering of the human being, where it extends through all the functions of the psyche, informed by imagination and the functions of the mind. While imagination and cogitation play an important role in the qualification, extent, and intensity of suffering, it is their sensory, bodily functional ground that holds the roots of pain. The excruciating suffering of the body challenges endurance, endurance that is maintained through the bastion of our psyche/mind, which interprets situations and calls for heroism of spirit to prevail. Then there are the torments of the mind—facing profound disapproval, a friend's betrayal, the loss of one beloved, despair, keen disappointment, followed by the weakening of our resistance, by the weakening of our poor spirit. Even our successes and accomplishments lose their meaning

when facing inexorable disintegration with the advance of life's timing and its unavoidable extinction.

The human being seeks to remedy, to redress this bent of existence by "continuation in posterity," by accumulating power and exercising it in society, by accumulating wealth and endowing foundations, leaving monuments marking one's glorious deeds or creative genius. This is the predicament of the human condition: having been brought to a peak of growth, power, and vision, we without appeal plunge into an abyss.

All in the end is vain. Is there really no remedy for suffering and for the inexorable, deterioration and extinction of life? Measuring death by the yardstick of life itself, what is its sense? Is there no means available by which to salvage life's seemingly spurious value, by which to find in life an innermost sense that would give lasting meaning to our otherwise seemingly vain effort, endurance, courage, hope? What could be the means for such a salvaging, considering life to be what it appears—an incomprehensible passing venture? Lastly but foremostly we ask: In what preconditions is life, especially human life, situated, conditions that could clarify its situation and endow it with sense, an absolute and a personal "sense"? Can we gather the answers to our queries from the nature of life itself?

We have in fact, approached life in its logos. It is then the sense of the logos of life that is key to answering these questions.

PART FOUR

5. KAIRIC TIMING

5.1. The Specifically Human Kairic Timing of Life; Freedom and Accomplishment—Kairos between Fancy and Arbitrariness

With the full-fledged human creative mind that emerges in the ascent of life to the human condition, there emerges also an altogether different timing of life. We call this "kairic timing" in contradistinction to the "kronos timing" of survival-oriented sharing-in-life, which follows the directives of the ontopoietic design's purposeful unfolding of the living individual. Kronos timing corresponds to the realm of Bios as it times itself, poised as it is between the two extremes of necessity (the constructive entelechial principle) and hazard (the external conditions for the principle's deployment). Kronos and Kairos, which are life's arteries, take shape in this oscillation.[7]

As a matter of fact there occurred a gradual change as the animal species emerged in evolutive progress, growing in the complexity of their forms and the flexibility with which they match inner demand and external supply as they counteract adverse conditions and avail themselves of opportunities. This flexibility reaches its culmination in the surging of a new category of life, namely, that of human freedom. Indeed, it is between freedom and arbitrariness that specifically human self-individualization oscillates. In indicating these bounds, we point to the creative endeavor as the vector moving within them, using them. In the context of the phenomenology of life, I have singled out the Human Condition within the evolutive progress of constructive types of living beings as the Archimedean point of the ontopoietic unfolding, that is, as the point at which Imaginatio Creatrix brings the three main factors of sense into the metaphysical matrix of life.

Let us now focus on the way in which the vital genesis of bios proceeds. Its progressive steps crystalize in a multiple *motio*. Hence, it crystalizes in "time," which lends it a "moment" of fulfillment, the measure of the step onward in the process of growth or decline. Each constructive advance of individualizing life (e.g., the opening of the petals of a flower, the rise of the sap of a tree in early spring, the cross-pollination of flowering plum trees effected by insects,...) is a result of a bundle of results—of numerous operations and processes, each of them crystalizing segments of time that flow together to work a change, a transformation, a moment of constructive progress. Advance is not the effect of a single cause, nor does it singlehandedly contribute or effectuate another change. On the contrary, each occurrence in the course of bios' unfolding is significant in various inward/outward radiating directions (*inwardly,* the opening of a flower is a phase preparatory to fruition; *outwardly,* it is the opening of a source of nectar that nourishes bees, wasps, hummingbirds, etc.).

Thus, whether human cognitive intelligence registers it or not, life—bios— is timing itself. It measures itself, and thus its temporal spread, by its natural constructive advance in the cyclic cosmic order.

It is not time that brings in this order; it is not that time is infused into the constructive operations from the "outside" as if it "existed" or is "just there." The moves of the vital operations beginning with the lurking organic forces that emerge from seemingly non-organic ones, or the moves of a virus entering a cell in order to replicate itself, all these time themselves from "within," and their advance marks and measures temporal progression in itself. Thus, it is from the inward moves of the sentient and living soul of the living being that stems the measure of motion—organic/sentient/psychic motion and the time that crystalizes itself in it.

There is no need for intelligence, nor for any other observer, to register the lapse of time. Life proceeds and temporalizes itself without it.

We must consider that in addition to the universally constructive crystal-ization of time and its contrary, destructive tendencies as seen in the whole cycle of individual life going from generation to extinction, there is that which departs from the pattern, a particularly vital tendency of bios, its self-constructivism.

As I have been pointing out throughout in my treatises, what makes life is its particular, constructive tendency, which is decisive for its unfolding and its spread, nay, for its very taking place. And this constructive tendency is embodied in a *self-individualizing progress.* It is only by consistently deploying forces and directing them from within that a living beingness may establish itself and maintain a course of progress within adverse, neutral, or merely propitious outward conditions. This constructive tendency is then appropriately "embodied" in a life-principle intrinsic to the emerging life process, to the emerging living beingness, in what I call the "entelechial principle of life." According to its direction ontopoietic constructivism unfolds, unfolds while it constructs with each move. There is an intrinsic ontopoietic "agency" of life directives. This amounts to the unfolding of an "entelechial schema" presiding as it were already in its germinal form over life's constructive advance to a self-fulfillment in accord with a "model."

Now is the moment to move on to the ontopoietic crowning point of complexity reached in the Human Condition.

The timing of life's self-unfolding, its self-interpretative course, here undergoes several transformations, with time as kairos coming into its own. Kairos here assumes original, uniquely significant roles with respect to the specifically human significance of life, its projecting of new avenues, history, and the personal quest for transcendence.

Indeed, it is in the crystalization of the creative Human Condition, in which the hitherto relatively strict entelechial decoding of life's enactment, as seen in the progressive unfolding of species in evolution, attains the flexible, inventive, endlessly transformable progress of "free will" or even whim, of human beingness. Kronos, and more particularly kairos, now take on novel modalities and roles.

Cutting through innumerable questions concerning freedom, constraint, arbitrariness, as well as the universal human round of life—order and turmoil, monotony and revolt, peace and crisis in personal and societal life—is timing itself. On the one hand, there are our everyday regular activities, gestures, and, on the other, there is the ceaseless flow of our personal conscious psychic life of stirrings, sensing, emotions, motivations, and conscious acts variously concatenated. From this ever vibrating conundrum, in its variety ungraspable, I will single out the main artery of specifically human self-interpretation in existence, of human self-individualizing, namely, the intrinsic timing of the modalities of kronos and kairos as they work in tandem in the implementation of the unique prerogative of the human being, the creative endeavor.

To cut a long story short, human self-individualizing progress defines itself by striving for accomplishment. The accomplishment of tasks, aims, ideals stands in contrast to the vital organic sentient movements of life's constructive progress heretofore. These are now projected inventively by the human-being, the creator. The tasks themselves emerge as fruits of a human creative reorientation within the circumambient world. The creator's innermost tendencies and desires as transmuted by imagination are tied not into the knot of the appropriate natural response, as with animal life, but by a free deliberated decision and impetus to seek an accomplishment, to undertake the projects that ensue. Natural promptings are transformed into those of the surging will, igniting an initiative to undertake an accomplishment. Due credit must be given to the progress of the evolution of species from entelechial flexibility to the exercise of freedom, to the point where the creative orchestration of emergent specifically human functioning comes into its reign. But I see the crystalization of the creative function in the Human Condition as the instance of the emergence of the unique timing that is kairos. Human will seems to soar on the wings of imaginatio creatrix through open and unlimited skies, "free" from all constraints, and seeming to enjoy all "possibilities" in a play of fancy and the "free" whimsical selection of them, that is, non-directed, altogether arbitrary choice. The human will to undertake, initiate, and institute—which means to move freely in the self-individualizing progress of life—is caught in between fancy and the arbitrary. It is within the new functional creative orchestration that the virtualities of the Human Condition bring in, first, the primordial moves of the human spirit; second, the thrust toward the other; third, the will to undertake; and lastly, the deliberative inventive quest. These functions are not performed alone, however. On the contrary, they may be activated only within the valuative schemata that install the human creative condition, that is, only within the aesthetic, moral, and intellectual perspectives that introduce the specifically human valuation of life.

Furthermore, these factors of human dynamics informing human action operate within the bounds that the world of life projects in structures and rules. Ultimately the human being, although aiming beyond through a creative swing, keeps its inventive creative spread within the human world of life that he or she unfolds, steering a course basically within the bounds of the system of life itself. Hence, as much as the human creative prerogative makes surge and guarantees the exercise of freedom, the same creative spirit does not let freedom be carried away into a wild chase after phantasmagoric possibilities of fancy or to fall into the accidentalness of arbitrariness. It remains within the open and yet not absolutely unrestrained boundaries of the human.

5.2. *Kairos as the Propitious Moment; Accomplishment, and Measure in Human Creative Self-Interpretation in Existence*

The specifically human life operations draw upon the energies, forces, strivings of our animal circuits in the self-individualizing process that extends their orbits, maintaining a balance of freedom between fancy and arbitrariness. Excesses in either direction lead to crises and upheavals in personal and social life. Both directions, however, belong to the "nervous skeleton" of self-individualization, the self-interpretative progress of human beings, and weave the fabric of the creative orchestration of the system of human functioning.

These specifically human operations, then, are "informed," imbued, molded by the significances with which the human being as creator endows life. Thus their timing is their partaking of shades of significance that vary in the infinite modalities and qualitative nuances of the aesthetic, moral, and intellectual sense-giving factors brought into the progress of life by the Human Condition.

The timing of these fulgurating and constant moves, operations, processes is fully imbued by their modalities, tendencies, aims, successes, and failures in striving for accomplishment.

Given that the confluences, fusions, and resultant steps of successive progress occur within the creative milieu of human interactions, individual personal encounter or avoidance of personal encounter are essential elements of human transaction. While kronos diversifies into innumerable streamlets of occurrences, there emerge conundrums of propitious conditions that allow the tying of the knot of accomplishment. It is by the tying of these knots of accomplishment that the human personal—and social—self-interpretive course of existence not only proceeds but is also measured. Indeed, along the path of human creative self-individualizing, kairos is concurrently the timing of the propitious circumstances and forces leading toward the realization of constructive projects, their accomplishment, and concurrently and finally is their measure.

The specifically human existential itinerary advances essentially through two intimately, inextricably interwoven and intermotivating realities: the workings of the inner realm and the workings of the external world. The entire web of inner experience, with its feelings, thoughts, deliberations, judgments, is woven partly by the universal requirements of life and partly— and ultimately—by the innermost striving for accomplishment, for advancing, for self-realization in the attainment of ever "higher" aims in the domain of outward life (from there to be transposed into the inner self). It is through action directed toward others, through activity with others that our intimately personal life within advances. Hence, the accomplishment of an undertaking, the culminating kairos, is in its outward realization prepared in the interior life. And, indeed, with the advent of the human condition we witness an extraordinary expansion of the inward/outward, self-individualizing and self-interpretative agency of living being.

The inner life—considered to be the life of experience or of consciousness—manifests a timing of its own; kronos and kairos become more sharply defined in the advance of life's story.

5.3. Kairic Timing and the Human Mind

But what about the timing of conscious acts themselves? What of their emergence and perdurance or disappearance, their ephemeral existence and its timing? What is the timing of conscious life? Beyond doubt, already at even the lowest complexity of living beingness, living beings time their operations. It is not only that their directives time themselves in relation to functional performance and "objective" accumulation, but also that these living agencies "record" the performances in their succession, simultaneity, and expectation. There is, indeed, a prototype of "inward" timing in action and resistance; a dog "expects" his food at certain intervals, records having received it from the hands of a certain person, is satisfied and content on having filled his stomach .... With the emergence of the human creative mind this inward sphere of psychic and experiential registering of the thus far vitally subservient and vitally significant inwardness expands crucially. It converts into a full-fledged creatively radiating zone in which kairic timing plays a preponderant role. In fact, human consciousness on setting out to work times itself while building up an intermediary zone between the vitally significant registering common to living agents and the creatively radiating inwardness of consciousness. With human consciousness, that is, freedom of choice and will, being set upon accomplishment, the timing of human consciousness is essentially kairic.

Into the rudimentary purposive unfolding of life's moves, the creative human mind introduces deliberation over opportunities, planning, and the envisioning of an innumerable variety of options as one proposes to oneself goals aiming above elemental vitally oriented needs subservient to direct survival. Prompted by creative striving, human beings invent for themselves special systems of deliberative, means preparing moves toward accomplishing aims. The timing of these moves is quite different from the vitally oriented ones.

Steps are taken sweeping toward all horizons, advancing toward projects. "The ground" is "palpated" in all directions to test the most appropriate moves to take. These steps acquire a special nuance of significance in relation to their role in the pursuit of aims. Once an aim is accomplished, the steps that timed our life for its accomplishment recede in their singular significance; whether that accomplishment be a work of art, the enactment of a new law, the consecration of a building to a charitable use, a battle won in war, it dominates in its significance its respective life arena, standing out from the usual course of things. It acquires there its own relative stability, effecting a kind of halt in the incessant timing of life. Its vital registering develops into what we call "memory," a depository of our registered experiences lying-in-wait to be recalled to our attention. They are registered in a creative/kairic fashion and are recalled to assume a kairically significant role in present consciousness.

Human consciousness times itself in its functioning with respect to its basic orientation towards accomplishment. From this proceeds a person's internal organizing of life: the constant objectifying of choices, presenting of courses, recording, synchronizing of moves, coordinating with others' efforts and nature's rhythms, and making decisions.

In contrast to the classic phenomenological vision in which time appears as an absolute factor, an enigmatic "abysmal" realm in which everything has its roots and which we cannot sound out, in our ontopoietic vision, time is the creative work of consciousness, which, stirred and sustained by Imaginatio Creatrix, times its logos itself in a kairic key. The dizzying turmoil within our consciousness as we react to life presses us to make innumerable associative links and interactive modulations, vibrating to a seemingly "infinite" range of choices, adjusting by making innumerable variations and tying and untying myriads of knots, trying to find a "propitious" answer to our queries. In glimpses that come to our minds, the creative kairic timing at work opens up an unsoundable trust that in the turmoil there is that answer.

Only some junctures and stretches of this creative work and the so complex logos at the heart of it come to the surface and are available to our mind. In the complete engagement of our beingness in the kairic ventures of life, most does not come into the open, most occurs and remains within the profound well of the mind, which times itself until its demise.

Before passing to the essential point of our inquiry let us gather our reflections briefly in their most intimate harmony and diversity. The logos of life arranges the advance of human existence. The besouled body is the engine, the stage, and the driver of the course of unique human existence, unique given the specifically human predicament. In awareness of life and death and in the desire to preserve life and insure memory, therein lies the heart of the human predicament and the deep logos of human understanding. Underlying the drama of our existence is this awareness of the narrow space between a person's birth and death, of the narrowness of the space in which the logos of life in its timing conducts its marvelous transformation.

What specific sense does this drama carry? Does not this logos here reveal heretofore secret threads which if followed provide the answer to that question?

PART FIVE

6. THE KAIRIC TIMING OF THE SACRAL LOGOS: THE SACRAL QUEST AS THE IN-BETWEEN

6.1. The Sacral Logos of Life Running through Life's Vital, Creative, and Life-Transcending Course

Let us immediately strike the chord of the leading melody. Advancing through its various constructive phases the logos of life finally opens its sacral font as the innermost sense of its inquiring progress. With the advent of the creative condition there enters into play a novel modality of the logos' questioning. It slowly progresses through kairic fulfillments specific to human life by putting in question the meaningfulness of all human creative accomplishments of all aims, criteria, expectations.

The sacral logos thus unfolding drives a wedge between the logos of life's ownmost life-constituting sense, on the one side, and its ownmost drive to transcend self, on the other. Paradoxically the self and the totally other appear to draw us in two directions in a single process. These are the poles of the human drama. We stand "in-between."

6.2. The Genesis of the Sacral Logos of Life

From times beyond counting, as the saga of Gilgamesh indicates, the human being has been aware of the congenital paradox that is life as it stands within the mind of the human being. Life engages us in a battle with suffering. We have always been facing the finiteness of our existence on earth. This awareness stands in contrast with our unquenchable thirst for perdurance and fills us with dread. To witness the triumphant ascent of our powers in the struggle for survival, to know pain and joy, cruelty, terror, greed, hate, as well as devotion, benevolence, self-sacrifice for others' well being, and pure charity, all this rends the human heart, rending all the way down to the psyche-flesh-body groundwork and motor of individual and societal existence. But in their life performance body and psyche may not be separated or divided. Given our spiritual awareness of the finiteness of life, the quest after its redemption is played out upon their common territory, that of the human soul.

The sacral front is opened, the transnatural quest of the soul is launched in the midst of this communal arena of the struggle for life in all its dimensions. By the "sacral" I mean that virtuality of the logos of life ordered to life's sublimation, to its transcendence of the framework of reality, a consummation not yet accomplished, one beckoning our spirits to mystical heights.

I noted above the first paradox of the human predicament that the advent of the Human Creative Condition introduced. Now let us pinpoint a second paradox of the Human Condition, one that makes this predicament even more acute: the paradox of freedom. We exalt the freedom that the human being enjoys owing to the creative orchestration of the logoic faculties in which the human logos projects and processes its very own creative fruits, making him or her capable of rising above self and the common vital plane. We may lifts ourselves above the plane of the survival-oriented and selected indications of animality to develop our very own personal system of valuation of existential elements and may harness our own creative forces and valuating-judgmental-decision-making faculties into a selecting, judging, and acts-controlling agent. Now not merely a "living agent" but "a *personal* agent" is abroad, one whose very sense is lifted above simply seeking what fits life's needs and the requirements of the individualizing sequence inherent to our kind; ours is deliberation and valuation informed by novel tastes, principles, and aims self-projected on our own existential plane. In the new orchestration of these new evaluative principles the elementary instinctive drives, appetites, inclinations are not culturally given but are molded for a consistent significant schema for which our imaginations guide selection. In this progress, those drives bloom into a new uniquely personal transformation of the vital agent—the self—into a human person. This center of the self does not radiate a new significance of life but does marshall the elementary drives into a performing logoic force, the human will to undertake personal initiatives.

Within the ontopoietic self-individualizing of beingness in its elementary bio-psychic dimensions, the living agent as the centralizing and self-directing focal point of life is now invigorated by creative force and makes its way by the differentiation, and thus distinguishing if not separating, of the individual-in-process from its symbiotic and interactive circumstances, making it responsive of itself. The freedom of personal will (though it raises to an unprecedented degree the interconnectedness of the circumambient world in communal sharing-in-life and also unfolds the specific logoic linkage of intersubjectivity) strengthens this self-centering and consciously motivated autonomy of the self, even propelling it into an existential state of solipsism.

But the second great "gift" of the creative logos is its establishing human existence in a symbiotic ingrownness, in networks on different levels up to and including intersubjectivity, building up a personal-communal world of life, and so working a paradoxical reversal of its heightening of selfhood. This self-conscious intersubjective network actually buttresses the freedom of will that makes human beingness even more extensively and tightly self-centered than was the circuit of vital/animal selfhood. But concurrently it brings about—in accord with the self's expanding significant spheres—a much deeper, more overwhelming yearning for sharing in life, a yearning to share in the logos of personal understanding of the very significance of personal deliberations, hesitations, decision making.... of "all." The human person, however, is so wrapped up in his of her cocoon of never completed interaction that it cannot enter into a clear commerce of understanding with fellow human beings. All the while each of us is desperately struggling to overcome the barrier of selfhood, i.e., of self-enclosure, and to experience deep personal communication with the Other.[8] The search after this interpersonal communication is indeed the basic thread of the struggle of human existence.

However, as I have said in discussion a few times before, in this paradoxical reversal, there is also the engine of the sacral quest, which we here ponder.

With the adamant desire of the human personal self for human communion in the logos itself, we approach a rising witness.

6.3. The Sacral Quest between the Self and the Other: the Witness

Life is a stream of impervious ontopoietic becoming, a flux that does not stop from birth till life's extinction of the individual, and from the beginning of the world that harbors life till its eventual ending. All the passages from day to night, from season to season are punctuated by the timing of life's vitally significant functions and by its sharing-in-life moves, which insure the basic survival of the body-flesh-psyche schema. The animal joys and pains entailed in life's vital-psychic course are endured. But rising up amid all joys and pains and eclipsing them is the isolation, the internal isolation that is to be endured no matter how extensive be the symbiotic empathy of sharing-in-life. That empathy does alleviate the essential self-centeredness separating living beings from each other. We empathize with the suffering dog, which "feels" in turn our sympathizing moves of the heart and shows in its way that it is "grateful," yet the pain remains strictly its own to deal with. An analogous but far more complex situation is to be found with the infinitely more extensive, complex, and existentially intertwined human experience of life, for human "experience" evolves within the creative aspirations and strivings for accomplishment that employ the kairic timing of life.[9]

6.4. The Suffering of the Other

Yes, the gist of our human drama and of our plight is suffering. It goes back to our own suffering but culminates in our enduring the suffering of the other. In our excruciating pain for the other we adjure a witness to share it with us.

All goes back to the sentience that informs the logos of life at its incipient instance and from which the timing of self-individualization starts. Sentience spurs life's diversification through the generative phases in which vital intentionalities articulate the constructive moves of evolving beingness and reach the summit that is the entry of imagination into the human mind, which in turn informs the soul that now reaches deeply into the spheres of organic and vital life and spreads through the entire psychic, intellectual, and spiritual network of human functioning.

Symbiotic groupings of living beings extend from groupings of bacteria, cells, plants, corals, animal herds and packs to the most sophisticated psychic ties of human sharing-in-life. Our primitive human feeling of life-community with every type of living being—whether it be our feeling pain at the sight of a withering plant, a suffering dog, etc. or feeling kinship with another human being—is inspired by the moral sense proceeding from Imaginatio Creatrix and having logoic sentience as its conductor. Not only do we human beings experience pain and suffering in all the registers of our functioning but we also are able to experience more than a "phantasma" of the suffering of others. The witnessed suffering of others is experienced by us in a unique way. We have not simply a symbiotic picture of the other's pain and torment but feel his or her feelings transposed into our system and hitting us full in the heart. This "blow" does not cause bleeding, broken bones, etc. but has nonetheless an altogether overwhelming effect on our soul/psyche, and so we become stricken. All our own personal pursuits are then put on hold. We experience excruciating pain in our innermost being with and for the other whom we love, feeling for him or her as closely as if he or she were ourselves. We are as if paralyzed inside. With our own suffering, we are open in a sense, given that it varies with our endurance and experience of it; it may be objectified, eased by interpretation or by comfort coming from friends or by the prospect of improvement. We may ponder our sufferings and thereby change or at least alleviate them; in this way we may influence our entire experiental schema. But when it comes to our identification with the suffering of a loved one, then in contrast the schema in which his or her pains are embedded and the threads it partakes of are foreign to us; while we may imagine the pain, the vital threads of the pain are outside our own system, and the suffering escapes us. Thus the blow that we feel and through which we participate in our loved one's suffering, while striking some chords of our own virtualities, remains ultimately closed to us, out of reach. Hence when struck by the blow of realizing the suffering of a loved one, of one who is our other self, we feel as though we are paralyzed. Immersed in the suffering of the other in our innermost depths, we "almost" reach the depths of the suffering of our beloved, but we still fail to enter into it completely. This suffering, which we share to such an extent that it reaches through to our innermost being, seemingly down to elemental sentience, does not reach the very core of our beingness. It traverses our entire soul, engulfing all the sentient networks of our bodily sensibility, yet stops at the pain of the flesh as its existential frontier.

As ancient mythologies and cults brought out, there lies in the flesh not only the measure of human endurance but our ultimate cosmic link, through which we seek to partake in universal forces through human sacrifice. Lastly but foremostly, it is through the transformation of the body/flesh/psyche that birth, growth, and descent towards death times life, alternating between the delight and the suffering of living ambitions. Impelled by moral considerations, we often live in inward turmoil, and we struggle as contrasting forces pull us in opposite directions. We often feel torn apart, seeing no remedies to our plight. This interior drama of the human condition is reserved for human beingness alone. It is an elevation of the logos of life, this moral perspective for the interpretation of life situations. Interpretations corroborated become criteria, values, virtues, which deepens feeling. Linked deliberative issues emerge in which the differentiation between the self and the other takes on innumerable threads of significance corresponding to experiences.

When we attempt to present these issues on the stage, we have what we call drama. The drama of human existence, constitutes, in fact, the gist of human life. The human drama essentially concerns our human ontopoietic coexistence, human self-awareness within the circumambient communal fabric of life, and our feelings about ourselves. Lastly, but foremostly, this drama is shaped by our awareness of the irreversible finitude of life and our concern about its ultimate significance. It is not that we live within ourselves in a sort of isolation such that we are left to ourselves. On the contrary, there is nothing in life in which we would be concerned about ourselves alone. In whatever

we turn toward there is also concern for the other, but everything comes
back to us alone to decide on and to act upon. Even as we are torn between
contrary inclinations and appetites ourselves, alternate solutions to problems
propose themselves, reflecting vital, communal, and personal strivings and
at the highest level human moral consciousness, for which, conversely, the
highest price is to be paid: moral struggle involving interior forces that tear
one's life apart in anguish and suffering. But, then in a paradoxical contrary
move, this inner turmoil in the course of life is also the unique device, means,
way to redeem the predicament of human existence, for it challenges the
finiteness (contingency) of life and reaches the sense of the All. At the heart
of the human drama lies the key that opens the closed door to the realms
holding life's ultimate sense.

In fact, as I have emphasized often enough, each human being is intimately
bound up with fellow human beings, for sharing is the essential factor of
human life. Sharing extends from the vital through the moral and spiritual
spheres of the human life in numerous modalities, but what I have principally
in mind here is the sharing in the logos of self-understanding that the human
being seeks continuously. I have spoken already of our sharing in feeling with
animals. With expanded human consciousness and communicative means, in
question here is the sharing in understanding in *full spiritual communion* that
is sought by the human being as the quintessential factor of life. But is it ever
achieved?

At all the problematic turns of life we seek to explain our situation to
another human being. Probing into the intricacies of our feelings about life,
we try, as we unfold it to another, to make him or her privy to our concerns,
our pains, our dilemmas and seek solicitude in his or her assuming our
own position—standing in our own place—to justify the attitude that we
contemplate and would adopt, to be our "witness."

The deeper the validity of life's pursuits erodes before our eyes, the less
important our own egotistic accomplishments appear. Our own happiness or
misery, suffering or joy, triumphs or defeats are blunted. They all evaporate
into futility, and there emerges more clearly consciousness of the common
lot of existence that we share with all others. And so the more clearly does
the other then appear in our concern! Slowly a simultaneous two-way traffic
gradually builds between two inner logoic streaks most intimately interfused:
the advance of our disillusionment with worldly affairs and ambitions and
the opening of an "inner ear" to the Other who stands before us in the same
network of life, sharing with us its ebbs and flows, and whose life course is
interwoven with ours. As we progressively "let go" of our earthly attachments,
the other and his or her plight stands more clearly in our sight.

6.5. *The Transnatural Conversion/Transmutation of the Psychic Soul*

The kairic timing of life takes here another form which will be the object of our attention now. To begin with we have to emphasize that the kairic timing of life in accomplishments—indeed, the entire schema of the creative mind—equips us with the essential apparatus for the real humanness reached with the human condition, namely, human moral consciousness.

Accompanying the surging up of the moral sense of life within the human condition, of the recognition of other living beings, in particular of human beings like ourselves, is the yearning, the pressing need spoken of above to find the meaning of life as such and beyond its orbit the ultimate human communion flowing from knowing the meaning of All. Unsatisfied with all possible accomplishment that creative endeavor may bring forth, we, reflexively ask "And what then?" and let go of our drive to dominate. We become more and more aware of the needs, rights, wishes of others. In our interpersonal acting we begin to give priority to the other, yielding to the other time/life previously spent pursuing our own interests. In yielding space in one's existential dominion to expanding moral sentiment, the human being undergoes an inner transformation.

6.6. *The Inward Sacred or the Sacral Course In-Progress*

As the human soul releases from her innermost its stream of spontaneities there surges a novel type of becoming and a novel kind of phenomena. These spontaneities bring with themselves specific virtualities as well as imaginative powers effecting a crystalization-in-process that will unfold within the entire frame of the human being, one having its center within the soul. Evolving progressively from step to step along its very own route and escaping the thematizing (ciphering) of the mind, as well as the mind's creative/intentional system of conceptualization, it is the soul itself that works from out its hidden resources a line of transformation of the psychic, creative schema of life of the person.

I have written at length about the three "movements of the soul" in this advance, in the unfolding of the sacral logos. Through this inward sacral process, the person's entire human beingness is slowly transformed. Following inwardly surging ciphering pointers, there emerges within a novel type of perception, one that captures an entirely new universe of experience; the evidences of new phenomena, new values of life, values at odds with the current values of the creative logos of life. These values are shaped not by the ideals of life accomplishment but by a contrasting unquenchable thirst to transcend the goals of this life and take hold of the ultimate sense of life itself, the sense of all. This process occurring within the soul simultaneously reveals its hidden resources in the inward manifestation of this universe, the Universe of sacral life.

Outwardly this process shows itself only in that seemingly puzzling sense (puzzling because ungraspable by the creative intellective molds of the mind), but as this sense is implemented in a person's interworldly manifestation it comes to permeate his or her being.

Thus the inner manifestation of the sacral phenomenon is simultaneously its unveiling. The sacral phenomenon does not call for any further legitimation. Its evidences carry within themselves their absolute necessity. In unraveling progressively its stages of unfolding within the human soul, we are only deepening and expanding its circumference within and consequently expanding our entire human beingness. The advancing stages of our metamorphosis lead us toward the Fullness.

Thus does human beingness as a microcosm gain purchase, given its creative fulcrum, on the world of life—the world of life stretching outwardly through the earth to the cosmos. From the person's inmost being, and as prompted by the growth within fostered by the logos of life there emerge spontaneities that surpass the last horizon of this life, escaping any phenomenal grasp.

The timing of creative/inventive accomplishment is oriented toward planning, and its steps navigate, seeking the virtualities available and serviceable for fulfilling plans. And the projects planned—even those undertaken for the most elevated ideals animating a person are geared toward the enhancement of the significance of "real" life. With that horizon opened, our accomplishments remain.

In contrast, engaging in the quest after the ultimate sense of life, the soul finds itself deprived of any interworldly orientation. The steps of this pilgrim's progress actually dismantle precisely the well-established nets of worldly sense. Attention is fixed precisely on the questioning of all that had been considered valid. But this questioning-in-the-dark does not go altogether without answers. As I have pointed out earlier, it belongs to the nature of the logos of life that each and every one of its pressing steps of inquiry contains/indicates the virtualities of the next step. Each of *the three movements of the soul* on her quest indicates the virtuality specific to the next. And so it is in her third movement that the radical conversion of the soul occurs. It is indeed in the soul's third movement, prepared by her two preceding advances, that the "negative" dismantling of the prevailing sense of life accomplishment brings in a positive state through transformative moves of the logos, which loses thereby its force in the concrete constructive thread of life but is strengthened in life's sacral thread, which was already released with the initial impetus of the quest. These moves transform the inmost being of the questioning person.

Here the question of the timing of life takes on a quite different guise. The transformative moves of the sacral thread of the logos of life do not follow any preestablished or projected plan. They keep within the soul. They reach kairic accomplishment in bringing about a new state in the soul's experience. These moves sublimate and convert our primitive egotistic sense of givenness into a bundle of inklings, propulsions, inclinations primed to introduce to the soul a new functioning, even its sense. Such an accomplishment can be prepared only by subterranean realities at work in the soul. Their events manifest in their timing of themselves the psychic flux of natural life, of experience, on the one hand, and constructive steps that follow indicating a progressive hidden transnatural work of the soul, on the other, work that progressively ties the kairic knot. Because they are discontinuous accomplishments, these transnatural moments manifest themselves as interruptions of the "regular" timing of life. They seem to be so, but that is only seeming, for they mark the kairic "right time" when they interrupt the regular course of events, they express the "right measure," and they contribute to true accomplishments. We may thus say that the unique transnatural nature of the "instants" of sacral experience is best grasped in terms of the kairic timing of its subterranean genesis. This kairic prompting of sacral moments that have a continuity of their own occurs within the regular continuity of interworldly processes. Human history as such also proceeds through the kairic tying of new knots of meaning when the old lines of intentional significance are disrupted, but that kairic timing has no relation to the genesis of the sacred, which occurs on its own plane.

As pointed out above, the kairic irruptions of sacral "instants" as accomplishments of a sacral tonality of the soul, as discontinuous as they appear to be, are not themselves devoid of interconnective links in the schemata of life. They surge forth at seemingly unpredictable intervals in the intentional schema of natural experience, and their actually standing over against that schema indicates a punctuation in an accomplishment being performed in a hidden network of interconnected progress—a genetic network of "transnatural history" that the soul's progress in sacredness projects. (We may call this history "providential history," a history that in a religious context is the historical unfolding of a covenant between human beings and the Divine).

In the religious perspective, divine interest in human lives, Divine Providence, does not belong to human history. The Kingdom of God is not of "this world." In the perspective of the natural intentional schema of the world, Divine Providence proceeds in a continuity of discontinuous acts.

The sacral logos projects itself through the kairic stirring of states of soul transcending ties to the lifeworld's codes and principles. Our primogenital ties, those of the vital code of sharing-in-life, come to be informed by the human moral sense. These latter run counter to survival values, reaching beyond to the kind of devotion that sacrifices self for others' good. The telos here would not be survival but human communion transcending the finiteness of life and the destruction of all its accomplishments.

In this kairic timing of Divine Providence, we may also understand the interventions of God in worldly affairs, God's "rewarding" and "punishing" human beings right in this world. We may also view the Christian mystery of the messianic Incarnation of the Divine in time in this perspective. In grasping the dynamic of the kairic timing of becoming, we see how two different orders may remain parallel while one yet irrupts into the other at propitious moments, introducing a measure and sense of proportion appropriate to the workings of the level broken into and yet of a different order when it comes to the principles in play. This is particularly helpful in grasping the Son of God's taking flesh to Himself. Here is an utterly unique kairic intervention of the Divine in human affairs.

The timing of kronos and kairos here, while intertwined, proceeds in two different orders: that of human history, and that of salvation history. This constructive distinction calls for a specific modality of freedom, one in which human beings are called by the innermost stirrings of their souls to meditate in action, proportioning their direction and pace within the ontopoietic boundaries of life so that the designs of Divine Providence may be accomplished.

Yet in what order of "sense" does this transformation of the soul occur? What new sense is the logos of life introducing? As noted before, the sacral quest was initiated by a differently oriented logos than that of the ontopoietic unfolding of life in which it comes into play. As was also here brought out, at that point at which surged the moral sense serving the otherwise survival-oriented purposes of the course of life, an essentially counter-oriented swing away from life's egocentric survival concerns and toward consideration of the other as one's other self introduced a transformation in the interactive relationships among human beings as human and not just as living beings of higher life performance. Indeed, while scrutinizing the interrogative modality of the quest, we discover that both the moral sense and the quest for the sense of life fuse to various degrees of intermotivation (for example, the moral sense moves in the quest while dismantling the constructive networks of our creative minds, undermining their motivations and dissolving the links of the purposive-psychological-social network that maintains it). These networks naturally involve the interests, life motivations, cooperative as well as competitive involvements with others. The quest is imbued with our feelings and emotions, which carry it onward at the constructive prompting of the logos of life. "Letting go" of these networks would seemingly open a "void." And it does lead to feelings of disappointment, emptiness, and loss if the reasons for letting go are of a practical vital nature. Yet if the reasons for abandoning strivings proceed from the interrogative line of the sacral quest, no "void" will open; after we acknowledge the validity of our own interests, the well-being of others fills our concern instead. Others' survival, life concerns, pains and sufferings, losses, and need for help now come to the fore. As the progress of the interrogative quest is matched by a concurrent unfolding of the moral sense in the personal frame, the other takes on an ever more significant role in our interior unfolding and growth.

There is an oscillation between the two possible outcomes of the quest: one that stops at nihilism and skepticism and one that leads to advance by following the sacral clue that the interrogative soul discovers at each step and staves off the void with. Each step in the corrosive course of the interrogation of life takes one precisely toward the other: toward an other self, inner source of the next step in the line of experience of the segment of life just dismantled. The transformation of our inner state occurs then in the accomplishment of a new way of relating to the other. This happens in its own timing.

Although the sacral quest takes place within the course of real life, the moves of the spirit that prompt its establishment have their own independent timing. Each of these moves has its own rhythm and cadence of questioning and its own consequential order which projects itself in an unrepeatable series of subjective acts. The transformative moment occurs in an unaccountable step among these acts and affects the entire system of experiencing, changing the nature of our acting within the opening space so that it is free of the congeries of prejudice established in the soul by her past experiences, shifting her away from attention to practical interests and aims and freeing her from their pressures. Thus our inmost beingness opens in solicitude, sympathy, caritas towards others acquiring a lasting interior disposition to come to their aid. As emphasized above this transformative step does not occur among those taken in the vital/natural current of time, with its fleeting events and processes. This transformation is not prompted by the creative network of the logos of life, but by a specific line of advance we have already here called "the sacral thread of the logos of life"; this thread weaves its way from one transformative instance to another, intensifying its action and expanding its reach, working toward the self's complete dedication to the Other.

There is also to be distinguished a third outcome of the sacral quest, one that neither stops at the void, yielding to nihilism, nor advances step by step. Rather, the unfolding moral sentiment unfolds in a kairic spirit a sacral route. This third route intensifies the sacral quest into a metaphysical speculation, one seeking the ultimate sense of life directly, seeking an approach to the Ultimate through a despoliation of the earth-bound soul that binds its innermost to the divine.

While in my previous writings I have very much favored this last route of mystic élan,[10] I have found since in my own quest that the path of moving in tandem with the moral sentiment offers clearer light when it comes to taking further steps. It is this line for conducting the sacral quest that I now take up for inquiry.

To the point, the kairic spirit at work in the transformation of the soul—in forging its "transnatural destiny," as I call it—is both broadly and deeply involved in our sacral transformation through its being twinned with the moral sense as it deepens one's innermost response to another human being. The sacral quest after the sense of life, as I have pointed out numerous times, begins already in some of its aspects within the ontopoietic unfolding course of individual life.

There appears, indeed, to be an entire vast network stretching over and penetrating both the human vital/creative course of the logos of life and the spiritual/kairic accomplishments of the transformative sacral quest. *Mirabile dictu,* this kairic network of transformative steps is in its dynamic and endlessly varying modalities, itself an offspring of the logos of life, which subtends it throughout. It may seem as if the logos of life were almost connatural, and almost involuntarily had layed down a sequence of changeable and contingent, irremediable events that occurred almost spontaneously even while it also engendered an entire system of spontaneous but voluntary actions having a distinct sense, a set of transformative spiritual ways to redeem all the contingency by equally strenuous and continuing effort. Within this network, the crucial factor—the conductor of our quest and its transformative engine participating in the moral sense and the communal nature of life—is the Witness.

6.7. The Witness

I have written extensively already about the witness.[11] Let us now in summary fashion review the course of human existence, for the person involved intimately in the web of existential transactions with others is seeking throughout the course of life to communicate with the other not only in interaction but in deliberation, feeling, in hesitation and personal decision making.

And so we appeal to the personal, societal, interworldly solidarity of humans, draw on similar types of experiences, and seek "objective" but sympathetic judgment—"counsel," yes, but foremostly "understanding" of our plight. We desire that our neighbor be a "witness" to our tribulations and deliberative ponderings on life; we seek his or her felt engagement in our conflictive situations, we seek solace in feeling that our confidant "is with us." All the same, we rarely follow the advice we are given, and when we do, the wisdom of the other frequently does not lead to a proper handling of the matter at hand and when it does, it is usually only an approximate solution and any case is often based on false premises. Although our worldly "witness" shares with us the common log of humanity and has true empathy with us in our concerns, he or she does not and cannot reach the most intimate poignancy of our situation, our concerns, deliberations, pains. Coming as he or she does from a uniquely singular intertwining of life's affairs, it is not possible for our witness to transgress the barriers of individualization and personhood and attain complete identification with us.

The one thing that comes from this is the apprehension that human "witnessing" always fails and that we seek beyond the human witness another witness who could discern intimately our own state within its singular context of situation and experience and who would be up to sharing himself our pains and tribulations and hopes and aspirations to the point of witnessing by his entire solicitude our failings, incertitudes, mistakes and "understanding" not only our good but also our bad intentions and actions. He is expected by us to "understand" it all. This a witness who would be a unique, all-encompassing in understanding, and all-solicitous witness of our soul. This witness would be above the conundrum of life's opacity and its contingent conditions, for none of us can fully address another "earthly" singular human being. In our seeking such a one it is quite clear that we, perhaps unknowingly, are reaching "beyond" to *the sacral witness.*

The promptings and intimations that the soul receives from within to turn to others to guide her, or to monitor her steps, the urge to share her failures or successes with someone who would see all and understand and partic-ipate solicitously in her plight cannot be quieted by another human being. Nowhere in the world is there one to turn to for "affirmation." This urge goes beyond the human frame beyond its limitations. It prompts an elevation of life-bound needs to a point whence the life-confined, concretely inscrutable, and contingent timing of life—whether ontopoietic or kairic—might surpass whatever the vital and creative lines of development the logos of life may offer; for our urge points beyond all human understanding, even that most devoted and solicitous. We seeks a surpassing witness and so reach to the sacral logos to confide our deepest self, offering our innermost for assay— naked, holding back nothing, making no attempt at self-justification. The sacral witness is privy to all human suffering, to all human frailty, to all human moral struggle, all failure, aspiration, and triumph. The sacred witness personifies the sacral logos that overarches the human existential struggle and the sacral quest.

What conditions would a human witness have to fulfill to become capable of this total solicitude and participation in the innermost moves of another person in her "truth"?

6.8. The Paradoxes of the Logos of Life's Sacral Thrust

The life course as well as the personal disposition to react and act, to suffer and rejoice, to submit or revolt, to love and to hate, to value and to despise, all these are grounded in a great registering of minute sensations, sensitivities, feelings, bents, and inclinations, which are in turn the yield of the long labor of life. Individualizing life unfolds from generation to generation gathering special features, dispositions, tendencies in a course as long as the history of the human life story on earth. Differentiations of climate, soil condition, water supply, in short all differentiations, have led to differently nuanced cultures as well as to the histories of societies, into both of which individuals are ingrown, with each profoundly imprinting their sensibilities and valuations— all of which surfaces in the inmost lives of people. To "understand" a given person in the sentient minutiae of its being and to have intimate solidarity with its inward moves calls for a witness to retrace that person's existence and to experience his or her specific routes of both ontopoietic and creative-moral unfolding. It is clear that no human person can meet these demands. The witness that we call upon surpasses concrete humanness then. This is a witness who does and does not belong to the ontopoietic reality of life.

The sacral quest holds a unique position with respect to the survival-oriented timing of the logos of life. It does belong to our temporality because it is the point of spiritual reference upon which the human moral quest is suspended. And it does not belong, because the individualizing sequence of becoming does not apply to it. In its origin, unfolding, and singularization, the sacral quest escapes particularization of any sort. It inheres to the logos of life in that as quintessential element of the concrete human condition it appears within the ontopoietic timing of the life of the individual; but it does not belong to the life course because it does not follow the steps of its timing.

As a matter of fact, the sacral quest is not "in process"; it does not time itself nor is it timed and yet it presents itself within life's timing.

If we consider the kairic timing of the transnatural quest for the ultimate sense of life and the phases of moral/spiritual transformation that follow one upon the other with each significant accomplishment, we see that their timing, while embedded within the stream of ontopoietic life, does not follow that stream's timing. It unfolds according to its own cadences and its own intrinsic law, the law of the moral modulation of our inward beingness. Indeed, it reaches to the very self.

This inner transformation involves not only our life-oriented attitudes' developing new capacities for self-detachment and charitable self-sacrifice for the other, but it also reaches to and involves as well the very core of the self, the dynamic strings that give the pitch for how we feel about ourselves-in-our-beingness: the detachment from life's disturbances, the innermost communion with the rest of living beings, the open horizon of hope for the blessedness of peace in communion with the Witness. We have here transcended with the very self that the ontopoietic life-horizon built as a springboard. But for what?

What is the sense of this new radical reversal of the logos of life, which after having fostered this marvelous freedom to creatively deploy life's virtualities now moves toward the successive weakening, disintegration, and it would seem extinction of this project?

Does the logos of life vanish in this arc from birth and death?

Or perhaps it just "hides" its further path?

To recapitulate, having reached this point, we are presented with three lines of reflection by which to make determinations.

6.8.1. Moral Sense and the Origin of Conscience   First of all, when we consider the main point of our kairic journey we equate the human condition with consciousness and its creative apparatus. Taking place concurrently with their appearance is the emergence and unfolding of the moral sense. The emergence of the moral sense and of conscience places the human being on a "higher" plane, as Scheler expresses it, than that of the "lower" animals. With the appearance of the moral sense a special emphasis is now given communal ties; the vital solidarity of the drove or pack is raised to the plane of a moral responsibility to care for the other, to show solidarity, sympathy, love.

6.8.2. The Radical Conversion of Sense   While the human creative condition and moral sense both develop in ontopoietic time, the quest for ultimate understanding goes in a direction reverse to that of the ontopoietic unfolding of life and works to undo its kairic accomplishments. Its logos goes counter to the trend of the logos of life and yet it belongs to the logos of life as a special thread. On reaching this third movement of the soul, this special thread of the logos—a thread that to distinguish it we will call the "sacral" thread—advances its own timing through the steps of its own kairic accomplishment of the progressive transmutation of the soul.

The quest prompted by the moral sense (a response of a particular sort since the thread of the moral sense is a line advanced by the logos of life) is a mode of becoming but of an absolutely "spontaneous" becoming, one that does not follow a preprogrammed sequence to be accomplished but is a "freely" projected becoming building on the accomplishments of each actor. Indeed, through the moral and entirely freely chosen work of the conscience, the self-enclosed ontopoietic course may be undone and remolded in a free redeeming course. The quest within which this work occurs is the guarantee of this freedom. In contrast to the ontopoietic sequence that gives directions for life's constructive progress, the network of the sacral-kairic thread of the logos of life encourages our confiding the inner self to the Sacral Witness as a beacon for its moral/spiritual support in its dramatic deliberative endeavors. This quest involves decisions that are absolutely free of natural constraints and that fulfill by a Kairic-Sacral motivation.

In this quest the soul intensifies its resolve and sets upon a course of its own. It is a manifestation of a radical conversion of the self. The optimal moment and state of the sacral logos within the human soul seems to mark a borderline between the ontopoietic logos of life and logos' sacral turn toward territory that is beyond the reach of the logos of the vital individualization of beingness. We will come to this point later on. For the time being there is a most significant insight for us to ponder.

6.8.3. The Transnatural Quest Spreads from the Individual to the Community
As the sacral thread within the ontopoietic course of the logos times itself by its moves of accomplishment, there unfolds in its course a singular flux of transformational instants of self-coalescence in temporalizing moves, a network comparable to the nervous system in that it penetrates into every corner/avenue of the soul's constructive progress, molding it in appropriate places in appropriate ways. This timing effects, first, the radical transformation of the complete self. Secondly, and most significantly, the flux that gathers within the transnatural quest of the singular person simultaneously extends deep into the interhuman network of sharing-in-life of human interaction; it spreads into and draws in the motivation of communal ties. The effects flow

from the inspirational force of the logos operative in the moral sense, which translates us from the human interaction level of transactions to the level of human communion. It lifts humanness as such, lifting if from a pragmatic level to one fostering the initiation within the individual of a pilgrimage toward sacralization. Does it reach it? Does it have to reach it in order to maintain its course?

6.8.4. The Communicative Personal Rays of the Logos Present at the Origin of Individuation   That question requires a different type of investigation. For the time being, let us bring out a crucial insight gained from the foregoing, an insight into the "life" of the logos of life.

From the cutting edge of the singularizing-individualizing operations of the logos of life we have moved to the ground in which that individualizing is rooted—opening to view the full expanse of the logos in sharing in life, it being essentially involved in the All.

But when the timing of the vital ontopoietic unfolding is transformed with the kairic sacral transmutation of the self within its communal compass, this grander and sui generis continuum is measurable only through the inner progress of the transformation of the self. These interlaced, intermotivated, partly fusing rays of the logos of life intimate a plurisignificant sense of the logos of life itself, first, in the gist of individualizing ontopoietic temporality, and then within that sequence in the sacral/kairic temporality of the transnatural destiny of the soul. The logos grows in this plurisignificant course and spreads into the innumerable symbolic and sharing-in-life expressions of communal life. Virtually, this pleroma of significance has been present, we can say, from the incipient instant of its self-individualizing unfolding.

6.9. Toward the Completion of Our Itinerary

We ask again, "What is life? From whence does this flux of becoming proceed? And when will it end?" We have defined the "beginning" of life as its self-enacted individualization and have followed its self-individualizing sequence, covering its constructive/deconstructive course to its "end" with life's extinction. And yet if we follow the full ontopoietic course of the logos of life, we find that there is no radical "beginning" of life nor an "end." For one thing, the individualizing sequence transmits the previous individualizing accomplishments forthwith. And then developments that prove to be useless are shed throughout. The essential germ, the logos of life's intrinsic endowment, remains.

We see that it is not without reason that Leibniz—who did not differentiate the various ramifications of life nor outline the logoic progress of ontopoietic growth in the individual monad, and who also did not ponder the ways of ingrownness of becoming, who, in other words, lacked the grounding insights that the ontopoiesis of life provides—in the light of his own evidences stated that the monad does not die, that it only slumbers, waiting to awaken. And, not without reason, he also declared that each individual monad reflects the life of the entire universe. Only in our framework of the logos manifesting itself as the primogenital force prompting and carrying life's becoming do the questions of beingness with which Leibniz was concerned acquire their full sense. They may now be treated along the lines of our revelation of the logos of life.

It seems plausible that life never "finishes." Though using a different frame of reference, science today seems to indicate the same. We gather from this that the interrogative force of the logos of life is pointing us beyond all timing of life, prelife, and manifested reality. *The logos of life, who times itself in its very essence, is an absolute temporality which has no "beginning" or "end."*

The Logos of Life thus belongs to the Fullness of the logos. Hence it is led by the concurrent thread of the transnatural destiny of the soul. Starkly, at the final stage of death, while the breath of life is leaving the disintegrating body, the transnatural quest of the sacral logos comes to the fore. The ultimate question is raised of the provenance of the "models" or *haeccitas* of beingness crystalized bodily in actual existence, that along with the question Leibniz raises of the compossibility of each being with all others to be actualized and then be prompted by their inward force to turn to their depository, their possibility in God's mind.

It is with the disintegration of particular kairic creative projects of life that the reality of the unavoidable decline of the rising arc of the sun of life presents itself to us, as if the creative logos starts to prepare us for death by withholding its impetus and leaving us with novel half steps calling for completion. This slackening, this shrinking of it radiation in the creative kairic sphere is accompanied by a diminution of psychologico-communal sharing-in-life. It seems as if the logoic rhythm and force of projecting life, connatural with the progress of life advancing towards its essential horizon, the "future," contracts over time till the decisive instant at which the breath of life is extinguished and the vitally significant organs of the body disintegrate, as it were abandoned by the ontopoietic drive and the prompting force of the logos that had carried it. Does this mean that the logos of life is extinguished together with its constructive sequence and forces? To the contrary, it seems obvious that the kairic logos, while diminishing the force thrown into the projects of this life has been intensifying its impact on its sacral course; it has been accelerating the sacral transformation of the soul. One could say that it has withdrawn from the earthly, contingent course by deploying more of its forces in sacral timing.

The logos' kairic timing not only arranges life-redeeming moments of kairic sacral accomplishment but also dissociates itself from the logos of life's ontopoietic involvements, leaving them behind. Yet, in the very nature of the kairic accomplishments there remain the ontopoietic relevancies, in that we can still differentiate in them their acquired personal, unique, transnatural nature and their natural life relevancies. The transnatural logos does not simply return to its source. On the contrary, through most intimate communion with the Sacral Witness throughout the destined progress of the life course, that destiny—while now relieved of dependency on the bodily-psychic sphere and its sustenance—carries the mark, the uniquely personal stamp acquired in the flesh, to its union with the sacral Witness on joining the Fullness of the logos. Here, opens an infinite realm of metaphysical specu-lation following the fulguration of the logos in the sacral imagination and dwelling on the logoic intuitions that proceed from kairic communion with the Witness. The kairic transformation in sacrality of the originary initial endowment of the soul suggests numerous lines, paths, for kairic sacred moves and transformations within the logos of life's realm in the Fullness of the logos.

PART SIX

7. THE LOGOS OF LIFE AND THE FULLNESS OF THE LOGOS

7.1. The Timing of the Logos of Life in Its Great Metamorphosis

From our delineation of the career of the logos of life in its temporal progress, we have derived further questions to ponder for the logos of life in its far-reaching radiation spreads its feelers through the entire realm of what we are and what we as human beings endowed with our very peculiar logoic sensibility may envisage. As it appears to us, we humans are essentially paradoxical, having a contradictory innermost orientation. Yet it is through a series of seemingly contradictory/paradoxical turns that the logos of life, availing itself of a profusion of means at its disposal, conducts a line of transformation/transmutation/conversion of sense with which it accomplishes step by step, phase by phase, and finally endows our human existence with the most extraordinary Metamorphosis of sense imaginable.

7.2. The Great Metamorphosis Fulfilling the Ultimate Sense
of the Logos of Life

The logos of life progresses in seemingly fragmentary fashion, and while we as reflecting beings are absorbed in keeping pace with its timing, the logos is all the while, as we have seen, pursuing a coherent task. This is a unique task in that its accomplishment entails its ultimate sense. Availing itself of the profusion of means at its disposal, introducing a series of seemingly contradictory-paradoxcal devices in order to effect every possibility opened to it by its constitutive virtualities, the logos of life conducts a line of trans-formation/transmutation/ conversion of sense with which it projects modes of individual existence. Escalating gradually the transformative sublimation of sense, this fundamental ontopoietic trajectory of kronos timing reaches its peak in the creative Human Condition, and then recedes as the sacral logos prompts and intensifies the creative kairic timing of human existence. That timing in turn, when at its zenith, seems to bring in a reverse move that deconstructs the entire edifice, taking life to the brink of its demise. Not so, not so, for the logos that is seemingly bound up with the progress of the self-individualization of life, reveals itself to have from the "beginning" carried multiple rays of sense, among which was the sacral thread that had been all along accumulating, building, waiting to progressively convert in transformative moves the sense of individual existence.

While loosening the natural creative thrust of life, the logos was intensifying into the sacral vocation of the soul in an absolute metamorphosis of life. Thus the first and last role of the logos of life is accomplished, as it reaches its absolute sense. The transnatural soul now being released from its contingent-temporalizing chains will follow its sacral logos, through identification with its Witness, "into" another sphere of sense.

7.3. Does the Logos of Life Vanish with Death?

Carrying life in stepwise fashion, the logos is not empty-handed. The soul enters that further realm endowed not only with her own accomplishments along her transnatural route but also with everlasting ties with the human network within which those accomplishments were made. Those accomplishments and these ties constitute together the further sacral sphere of the logos of life.

But does the logos of life that carries concretely the poietic individualizing career of a human beingness vanish after having dismantled its natural ontopoietic course? Far from it. As we have intimated throughout, the logos of life prompts itself ever onward in interrogative steps. It continues its task not only in the sacral transfiguration but in prompting individualizing life ever ahead. Its sense lies in the accomplishment of the Great Metamorphosis. Our vanishing from the terrestrial scene of material beingness would seem to indicate its "inferiority" to the creative kairic, sacral—spiritual—threads of transnatural destiny. To judge so would be a hasty conclusion, however. On the contrary, there is a most intimate, congenital translation of sense between the three realms of ontopoietic vital self-individualization, Archimedean creativity, and the transnatural quest. Vital self-individualization, for example, has its life-redeeming counterpart of conscious moral progress, which in turn has its ground in our material embodied beingness. And man's creative powers not only carry life on but also in their emergence at a definitive moments time the evolutive expansion of the logos of life. Not only is the entire transnatural process carried on with the most intimate interdependence with the entire system of embodied beingness but, more importantly, because more basically, the great human drama of the embodiment and the redemption of life finds a dynamic arena for the entire process, a stage that moves and transforms itself.

Embodiment and its postulates as they are given to us in direct intuition point to life's absolute—absolute, because not subservient to any other life. Embodiment contains in its requirements for concrete crystalization in life all the constitutive principles that, radiating as from a center, position it in the universal schema of earth's and the cosmos' energies. Embodiment is the principle constructive device of creation and beingness. Within our orbit of cognition there is incontestable evidence that the coming into being of our universe—its creation—consists in embodiment.

The Logos differentiates itself for the great game of creation-embodiment (incarnation) and then of redemption.

7.4. The Logos of Life, Temporal and Sacral; Transcendent Timing

The constructive project in which the logos of life was ontopoietically engaged has been singularly completed. But this does not mean that the logos of life has vanished together with it. The logos of life's moves are paradoxical, going from one extreme to its opposite, that is, covering the entire range of "possible" constructive (constitutive) directions. Each project of self-individualizing beingness is enmeshed in innumerable existential concatenations with the rest of life's actualizing network. No living being exists organically, vitally, societally, sacrally, etc. by itself. The logos of life operates with an entire network that is centered on the self-individualization of beingness, but which encompasses in its relevancies the entire orbit of our human experience and imagination. Life can not stop at either the death of an individual or the extinction of any group; it is immersed in the entire living network. Of its very nature, as we have seen, the logos of life ever points ahead of its steps. But we must consider first and foremost that the logos of life is a prompting force with shaping devices and a germinal endowment with an immeasurable reservoir of raw material lying on the open horizon. Its searching propulsion advances/prompts from one constructive interrogation to another entailed by the first. This means that as it empties its armory into one individual it continues with its next step an entire transformative process with remaining material, processing it step by step while timing itself, not here in an overt way in manifested reality but at the subjacent ontopoietic prelife level, until with the spark of life what was incipient bursts forth in a novel ontopoietic sequence.

7.5. The Sacral Heavenly Sphere of Life Within the Fullness

Having thrown a glance at the previous data given to direct intuition as the logos of life reveals itself in its proper modalities, we will now see how the logos of life on the wings of sacral imagination offers us the means to further uncover, through conjectural inference, data that will necessarily complete our previously gathered data.

For these conjectures are the very work of the logos. Proceeding from its own evidences about its inner nature, they may be considered as truth, carrying indisputable, apodictic, absolute validity.

Opening what has always been open, the Great Metamorphosis of life, the human soul enters into the field of the sacral rays of the logos of life. There it is that our thirst for infinite understanding, compassion, and harmony with all creation is quenched. Through the infinite magnanimity of the Heavenly Logos, a sublimating sacral ray of the logos of life supplies what is lacking in the individual existential outfit given all the congenital deficiencies responsible for the impairment of life's performance, which is not "our fault." A significant part of the absolute justice we long for in earthly life is the justice of restitution. Compensation for what was missing in vital existence contributes powerfully to the perfect quietude and harmony of sacral life.

Does this mean that the quest of the logos of life, its interrogative constructive advance is satisfied with the Great Metamorphosis and the transition into the field of sacral healing rays? Not so. The logos of life whether ontopoietic or creative, whether life bound or surpassing life with the shedding of its earthly vesture, carries an inner core of intent.

In a two-way reversible course, the sacral logos "breaks" into our real world in a kairic mode, fulfilling an extra-earthly sacrally significant task, so that souls here may participate in the celestial life communicating with the life-redeemed souls in the sacral sphere. There is, indeed, a mediating and constructive streak in the logos of life, one extending beyond its ontopoietic realm and spreading into sacral modalities, a trend with the interrogative intent to bind the souls "above" and those below in growing understanding, love, and harmony, initiating an interactive and emphatic community enduring till the salvation of the sense of life is complete and all is dissolved within the Fullness of the logos.[12]

7.6. The Sense of the Logos of Life Accomplished

Having employed its innermost prompting force in an interrogative mode of advance made through the ontopoietic articulation of a sequence, and this in a constantly sentience-informed advance, the logos of life avails itself of numberless constructive devices, employing all possible means ranging from one extreme to the other and with infinitely diversified and changeable constructive/destructive timing. A discrete continuity is maintained throughout. Ontopoiesis carries its own necessity and opens to the transformative advance of the Great Metamorphosis that completes life's meaning in a transition from temporal life to a-temporality, or better, hyper-temporality.

It is in the temporal accomplishment allowing this transition that resides its very sense. By this transition the sacral soul through its the growing identification with the Witness is prompted together with the interhuman sacral network into the sacral realm Beyond and there the soul is integrated into a network of sacral bonds with past generations.

Carrying life through ontopoietic timing, the creative-kairic networks through an infinite variety of transformative modes of sense transfuse, transform, convert, sublimate the logos of life in its main expressions (ontopoietic, sharing-in-life, creative, sacral) and so reach the culmination of sublimation in the Great Metamorphosis while rejoining the Fullness, within the folds of which life has been all the way.

In brief, it is in its timing that the logos of life reveals its ultimate sense.

8. EPILOGUE

8.1. The Ramifications of the Sacral Quest; in the Two-Way Stream of Communication Between and through Temporal Existence and the Sacral/Heavenly Realm Within the Fullness

In the notion of the "quest" which the human being carries on from his or her inmost beingness through the entire span of the drama of life, there has to be differentiated several essential streaks of logoic interpretation of the interrogating modalities in the sacral dynamisms.

Nothing "happens" at once. An "event" is pregnant with a significance, the fruit of numerous logoic steps forming a knot of constructive coalescence. The logos of life is incessantly "on the go." Thus the sacral quest—as said before here—*is and is not temporal* in numerous ways, depending on its "phase." The logos of life employs, first, the ontopoietic temporality of this world and its interactions. Within that, the progress of the quest occurs in kairic phases and is tied together inwardly by mysterious links of discrete continuity. The various main streaks of the logoic ciphering of the sacral path coalesce various logoic lines in their different temporalities. It seems that the line of the Witness functions like a dynamic massing that gathers into the mainstream all the interrogative byways of the quest. Yet we may distinguish the following essential streamlets that in its progress enter a common pool in the two-way communicative move of the logos of life, which gathers all of its work on its way to the Fullness and sends waves lapping back.

In the two-way participation seen in the processes of the logos of life, of which only the kairic knots of accomplishment/attainment are manifest, the coalescing timings of the various rays of the logos of life/sacral logos are carried by the creative imagination, which when denied reference to ontopoietic frames turns and limns sacral relevancies that are intermediate between the inwardly sacred in the human being and its lodestar. This is not the place to analyze this turn more closely, but just to take cognizance of it.

8.2. Six Ways in Which the Sacral Soul Participates in the Celestial Sphere and That Sphere's Participation in the Soul In Turn

I believe I have substantiated the pervading presence of the virtual and actual sacral logos through the entire spread of becoming/beingness. What reveals itself at the "end" of our life course has actually been present in its work from the outset. The distinct perspectives of "reason" and "faith," seemingly divided by an unbridgeable gap, now appear on the open horizon to be in perfect unity.

8.2.1. The Fulfillment We Seek in-and-Above Temporality We seek the Witness out of our vital frailty, out of our heart's desire to have One to take our side in bearing the injustice and inequities of life. We seek the Witness out of the misery caused by the insoluble entanglements of the dramatic conundrum that is our communal existence. We seek the Witness to ease the insufferable pains of the flesh and psyche, our own and those of others we love; we seek Him to show us mercy despite incorrigible failings. We seek Him to establish fairness by repairing the insufficiencies of our natural endowment and our responsibilities exceeding it; we seek Him out of our unquenchable yearning to surpass all this existence.

8.2.2. All surpassing sphere of fulfillment   It belongs to the schema of the logos of life that we tend toward an all-surpassing sphere of Fulfillment, in which we would find our inadequacies supplied and be in harmony with all creation. In brief, we seek a divine instance as our own measure, as it is circumscribed by the logos of life.

It is thus through the lead of the sacral Witness that we find access to the Heavenly sphere.

8.2.3. Accessing the Plenitude: Self-Denial and Dedication to Fellow Man   As I have unfolded it above, there is a life redeeming line in service to fellow human beings, in forgetting oneself, one's individual, egotistic concerns, for the sake of the other, in short, in abandoning our self-centered life orientation and radiating compassion, charity, love of neighbor. In its culmination our moral sense takes us beyond any sense of "duty" to innermost abandon to the good of others.

Having shed our vital/existential carapace we exult in our sacral transmuted authentic self launched upon a further sublimating course inspired by the sacral logos of life. Our saved authentic self is made heedless of the vicissitudes of earthly existence and can say with St. Catherine of Siena, "All the way to heaven is heaven," and can say even on the day of woe, "May the most just, most merciful, most kind will of God be followed, loved, and forever glorified. Amen."

8.2.4. Participating in the Fullness Through Our Felt Vision of the All Within Our Human Horizon   Thus to our viscera the Divine calls, and we "respond" in our inward vision of the world, life, the existence of all through infinite understanding, mercy, forgiveness, generosity, love. Our vision of our universe is lifted above abysmal suffering to exalted enchantment with all the "gifts" that nature, our Human Condition, and imagination shower upon us.

A transformation sublimates "outward" existence into an inward vision. Existence reborn in grace exults in praise. We feel to made part of the Heavenly, to participate in it already in and through our earthly existence, the gift of an infinite generosity and wisdom.

8.2.5. The Divine Within   We seek the Divine through all the lines of development that the logos projects and which crystalize our very beingness, and which we ourselves prompt through our creative mind as it emits its own logoic rays. Our quest projects not only an interrogative swing outward. In its ahead of itself, outward moves, it also turns its searching gaze inward into its own operational groundwork within the creative mind, within the communal networks of sharing-in-life, into the psyche and the emotional sensorium, into the sentient soul. Carried by a visceral desire to make a contact, to rejoin the source of our true nature, to find it in partaking in the All, the soul peels away one by one all the transient, contingent, arbitrary layers of her beingness, leaving exposed the experience of the despoiled self. That which remains, awaits the All-encompassing, communion with the All-engulfing, the Immeasurable, the encounter with the Divine within.

8.2.6. Awe Before the Immensity of the Creation in Which We Partake; Adoration   The sacral soul on becoming consciously aware of the profusion of rays of the logos that subtend, traverse, and carry it along, stands in awe for the foretaste given just in that realization of belonging to the immeasurable immensity of all creation, which surpasses all possible imagination.

8.3. Heaven's Fullness in Rational Assessment

The entire logoic-experiential/existential thrust of the human cognitive apparatus in drawing upon in its own proceedings is oriented toward assessing the goal to which all our energies tend. To reach that goal even approximately by human means, to come to God "as an idea," is truly unthinkable. The Plentitude of all logoic powers, of the All-unimaginable to our confined to this life mind, truly escapes any inference of the sacral imagination, being the All beyond all. Any attempt to assess the Divine "in se" gets irremediably lost on the way to the immensity of the Infinite, to which we belong as a grain of sand on the shore of a measureless sea.

 To conclude this brief and insufficient sketch of the byways down which the logos of life, ontopoietic and sacral, earthly and transcendent, propels the sacralizing course of human beingness, let us pinpoint that what in the cognitive-intellective perspective of human mind appears to be "folly"—to use the term Erasmus of Rotterdam applied to Christian faith, a term in fashionable use nowadays in the deconstructive wave of thought—to be the greatest human "folly," an absurdity and something impossible for sober reason to accept, is a revelation by the logos of life / sacral logos within our now completed human experience of nothing less than *the reason of all reasons.*

NOTES

[1] Anna-Teresa Tymieniecka, *Logos and Life,* Book 1: *Creative Experience and the Critique of Reason,* Analecta Husserliana, XXIV (Dordrecht: Kluwer Academic Publishers, 1988.)

[2] Anna-Teresa Tymieniecka, "The Life-Force or the Shaping-of-Life?" in *Life–Energies, Forces and the Shaping of Life. Vital, Existential,* Book 1, Analecta Husserliana, LXXIV, ed. Anna-Teresa Tymieniecka (Dordrecht: Kluwer Academic Publishers, 2002.) pp. xv.

[3] Anna-Teresa Tymieniecka, "The Logos of Phenomenology and Phenomenology of the Logos" in *Logos of Phenomenology and Phenomenology of the Logos,* Book 1, Analecta Husserliana, LXXXVIII, ed. Anna-Teresa Tymieniecka (Dordrecht: Kluwer Academic Publishers, 2005.) pp. xiii–xxxviii.

[4] Anna-Teresa Tymieniecka, "The Human Condition Within the Unity-of-Everything-There-is-Alive and its Logoic Network" in *Logos of Phenomenology and Phenomenology of the Logos,* Book 2, *The Human Condition in-the-Unity-of-Everything-there-is-alive. Individuation, Self, Person, Self-Determination, Freedom, Necessity,* Analecta Husserliana, LXXXIX, ed. Anna-Teresa Tymieniecka (Dordrecht: Kluwer Academic Publishers, 2005.) pp. xiii–xxxiii.

[5] Anna-Teresa Tymieniecka, *Impetus and Equipoise in the Life-Strategies of Reason. Logos and Life* Book 4. Analecta Husserliana, LXX (Dordrecht: Kluwer Academic Publishers, 2000.)

[6] Anna-Teresa Tymieniecka, *Logos and Life,* Book 1: *Creative Experience and the Critique of Reason,* Analecta Husserliana, XXIV (Dordrecht: Kluwer Academic Publishers, 1988.)

[7] Anna-Teresa Tymieniecka, "Primogenital Timing: Time Projected by the Dynamic Articulation of the Onto-Genesis" in *Life. Phenomenology of Life as the Starting Point of Philosophy,* 25th Anniversary Publication, Book III, Analecta Husserliana, L, ed. Anna-Teresa Tymieniecka (Dordrecht: Kluwer Academic Publishers, 1997.) pp. 3–25.

[8] Anna-Teresa Tymieniecka, *Logos and Life. The Three Movements of the Soul,* or *The Spontaneous and the Creative in Man's Self-Interpretation-in-the-Sacred,* Book 2, Analecta Husserliana, XXV (Dordrecht: Kluwer Academic Publishers, 1988.) *passim.*

[9] Ibid.

[10] Ibid, *passim.*

[11] Ibid, *passim.*

[12] Through the logos of life we learn that our universe as we apprehend it is relative to the logos of life, which is relevant to us as our measure. The Fullness of the logos is certainly not limited to this one universe and the human measure. Our imagination, a radiation of the logos of life within, points beyond life's earthly frontiers toward infinite universes with their celestial systems.

As to other creations, other universes, our limited mind geared to this universe and its transcendental horizon cannot even envisage these questions. Yet to realize what it means that we as living beings are embodied yields striking insights reformulating classic answers to these questions. Phenomenology of life is accomplishing just that.

REZA AKBARIAN

TEMPORAL ORIGINATION OF THE MATERIAL WORLD AND MULLA SADRA'S TRANS-SUBSTANTIAL MOTION

Abstract: One of the most important consequences of the Trans-substantial motion in Mulla Sadra's philosophy is the demonstration of the temporal creation of the material world. According to this principle, all existents in the world of nature are essentially transformable, and changeable, and all their parts are continually in the process of creation and extinction. So the whole world, which is the sum total of its parts in a sense, with all that exists in it, is created in time and has a temporal contingent entity. That is to say there is no ipseity amongst the personal ipseities except that its non-existence temporally precedes its existence. On the whole, there is no body and material body, be it celestial or elemental, or be it spiritual or physical, except that it is renewal entity renovates and its existence and individuation remains constant.

This principle should actually be deemed as one of the distinctive and prominent characteristics of Mulla Sadra's theorization. It is the key for the solution of many problems, including that of the creation of the world debated for eight centuries before him by the Islamic philosophers and theologians. Mulla Sadra disagrees with theologians who believe the world to have been brought into being in time from utter nothingness. He also rejects the view of al-Farabi and Ibn Sina who only admits the essential origination of the universe and not its temporal origination and the view of Mir Damad about the theory of meta-temporal origination. Mir Damad came up with this idea of (al-huduthal-dahri), which means origination of the world not in time (zaman) nor in eternity (sarmad), but in (dahr) or aeon, and he became celebrated for the exposition of this doctrine. Mulla Sadra rejected this dichotomy of views altogether by pointing to the doctrine of trans-substantial motion

73

A-T. Tymieniecka (ed.),
Timing and Temporality in Islamic Philosophy and Phenomenology of Life, 73–92.
© 2007 Springer.

Key words: Temporal Creation, Trans-substantial Motion, Mulla Sadra, ex nihilo,
              essential newness *(huduth al-dati)*, meta-temporal newness *(huduth
              al-dahri)*, time *(zaman)*, aeon *(dahr)*, eternity *(sarmad)*

The problem of the temporal creation of the material world is one of the
most controversial problems of philosophy, which has always been a topic
of conflict and debate. The assiduous nature of human beings, which drives
them to pursue the origin and the end of the world in which they live, can be
considered as one of the most basic motivators. In addition to having a theological
aspect and being used by theologians as a means to prove the existence of the
Creator of the World, this issue has a philosophical aspect as well.

At the present time the issue of the origin and the end of the world
of existence is under study in scientific fields such as astronomy, physics,
and different views have been asserted in this regard. This issue plays an
important role in Mulla Sadra's philosophy because of two reasons. One is the
issue itself, which has always been a center of attention for philosophers and
religious scholars. The other reason lies in the new outstanding significance
that the issue has found owing to the particular principles of the transcendent
philosophy.

Mulls Sadra makes use of the principle of the trans-substantial motion to
explain a large number of physical and metaphysical problems including the
temporal creation of the world, the relation between permanence and change,
the creation of the world, the creation of the soul, the resurrection of the
body, and various other issues concerning resurrection. This principle can,
therefore be regarded as one of the distinctive and prominent characteristics
of Mulla Sadra's doctrinal formulation.

Concerning the creation of the world a number of contemporary theologians
resort to certain scientific laws such as the second principle of thermodynamics
and the theory of the Big Bang. This kind of reasoning does not escape
criticism either, and the issue of the origination of the world remains a
controversial issue in theology.

Meanwhile, Mulla Sadra adopts a most reliable method for the proof of
the origination of the world and paves the way for theologians to overcome
this problem. He derives this method from the exquisite outcomes of his
innovative theory of motion, trans-substantial motion in the world. This theory
and the creation of the world unveil a reliable link between philosophy and
theology–especially in the world of Islam. Despite futile assertions made by
a few on the incongruity of philosophy and theology, this issue illustrates
the fact that a genuine and resolute philosophical method such as Sadrian
Transcendent Philosophy can be the best supporter of theology.

The philosophical, theological and scientific importance of the issue of the creation of the world on the one hand and the most important and valuable points which Mulla Sadra mentions in this regard on the other hand have urged the author of the present article to select this issue as the theme of this article. It is therefore necessary for the author to give a short definition of origination (huduth) from al-Kindi to Mulla Sadra in the history of philosophy in Islam and a brief account of the difference between them.

1. BACKGROUND

Before Mulla Sadra, Muslim theologians and philosophers trod the path of proving the origination of the world and offered certain reasoning that has been subject to debates and criticisms. However, in the end, they could not achieve this end (i.e. proving the origination of the world) in a desired manner.

In al-Kindi's philosophy, as repeated in many of his treatises entitled *The True and Perfect Primary Agent, as against the Imperfect*, God is the true efficient cause that its action is creation from nothing *(ibda')*. Al-Kindi's account *of* creation *ex nihilo*, brings out vividly his intellectual kinship with the Muslim theologians *of* the ninth century and sets him definitely apart from later Peripatetics. Action in the primary sense, he argued, is a process *of* bringing things forth into being *out of* nothing, and this is God's exclusive prerogative. This is so because God, the Creator *ex nihilo*, **is** the sustainer of all that He has created, so that if anything lacks His sustainment and power, it perishes.[1]

Indeed, the finitude of time and motion is advanced by al-Kindi as a clue to the beginning of the world in time *(huduth)*, and this in turn as the clue to the existence of its author. This argument appears to have drawn upon the historical source of the majority of the scholastic theologians of Islam who were the great champion, in the concept of creation *ex nihilo*, which they opposed to the traditional Hellenic and Hellenistic thesis of an eternal universe as advanced by Aristotle and Proclus.[2] Islamic theologians' argument rested on the thesis that the body of the universe, being finite, cannot be eternal; it was identical with the argument from *huduth*, or *a novitate mundi*.

Given that the world is created by the action of *ibda* in no time, it must be in need of a creator. The world, emanating ultimately from the first cause, is thus dependent on, and connected with, the True One, but is separated from Him by being finite in time and space. In fact, this problem remained one of the important features of Islamic philosophy, and al-Ghazali mentioned it at the beginning of his twenty points against the philosophers in the *Tahafut al-Falasifah*. Al-Kindi, contrary to his great successors, maintained that the world is not eternal. Of this problem, he gave a radical solution by discussing the notion of infinity on mathematical grounds.

After al-Kindi, the *earlier philosophers in Islam, like* Ibn sina, have rebutted the arguments of *al-Kindi* decisively, saying that all the confusion turns on one point, which consists in supposing that, if a thing has a continuous existence into the indefinite past, it has no need of a cause, whereas this is not so. A thing's need or lack of need for a cause pertains to its essence, which makes it a necessary being or a possible being; it has nothing to do with its created-ness in time or eternality.

Where Ibn Sina differs from the theologians is that his conception of creation *ex nihilo* is complementary to the view that the archetypes of the world of creation exist changelessly in the intelligible world and that the world is connected with its divine origin through a permanent hierarchy.

For Ibn-Sina the world is an eternal existent, but since it is in itself contingent in its entirety it needs God and is dependent upon Him eternally. Ibn-Sina's notion of "created-ness" here is intimately bound up with his notions of the possible being and the being necessary of itself. The world is created just because it is both possible and necessary: it is possible by itself, but becomes necessary through its connection with the necessary being. Is this process of creation involving a sudden jump of something from nothing? In short, is *creatio ex nihilo* as understood by the theologians and scholastics possible?

As is well known, *Ibn Sina* believed the world to have had no origination in time but to have been originated beyond time by God, and the world thus being eternal while the *mutakallimun* claimed that the world was created in time, an issue which was discussed in many classical works of Islamic thought such as al-Ghazzali's *Tahafut al-falasifah*.[3] Ibn Sina claimed that if the world were created in time, it would require a change in the Divine Nature which is impossible because God is immutable. The theologians believed that if the world were *eternal* then something eternal would exist besides God and would not even be caused by Him.

Since creation according to Ibn Sina means the necessary emanation of the possible being from the being necessary by itself it is with Ibn Sina a process beyond time in the sense that the category of time does not apply to it. Hence, God and the world are eternal: there arises no question of the temporal priority of the one over the other in the super-celestial realm of the divine, for time yet was not. The divine time indeed is that in which the entire sweep of emanations regarded as an ordered string of specific events is contained in a single super eternal now.

Time according to Ibn Sina, appears only as a phenomenon related to the external aspects of events. God has, however, the logical priority over the world, for He is the ground and the necessary reason for the existence of the world. Though the universe is thus lower in essence and rank, yet as it is now in its determinate form and nature, it is necessary to God. The universe must be conceived either as infinite or finite, both with regard to time and space. Yet it remains true that it is hard to think of a definite beginning of time at a specific moment in the past, which should not have been preceded, by another moment before it. As to the spatial infinity of the universe, we must admit that for the universe to be spatially infinite it is necessary for it to be temporally infinite as well, for an infinite space is a space that takes infinite time to traverse. The conception of an infinite space is thus involved in the conception of infinite time, which is contradicted by that of finite time, but interpreted in the light of their possibility and contingency, Avicenna sets out to describe the process of the generation of the universe.

Mulla Sadra like Ibn Sina disagrees with theologians concerning the issue of *Creatio ex nihilo*. As to the question of creation, Mulla Sadra opposes the simple creation *ex nihilo* of the theologians who believe the world to have been brought into being in time from utter nothingness.

Likewise, he rejects the view of Ibn sina, who only admits the essential origination of the universe and not its temporal origination and believe the world to have been created only in essence or in principio but not in time. "Essential origination" or essential coming-into-being in its strict sense does not imply any concept other than the dependence of the possible existent on something other than itself. In Mulla Sadra's opinion, such a meaning is very far from the actual meaning of origination and it cannot be attributed to the revealed instructions concerning world origination.

"Essential origination" means the existence of a thing being preceded by essential non-existence, or being preceded by parallel non-existence.[4] Both indicate the possibility which inseparably follows the quiddity, namely, the non-requirement of existence and non-existence through itself, as Ibn Sina remarks: "A possible thing in itself is non-existent and by its cause becomes existent."

2. THE TEMPORAL ORIGINATION OF THE CORPOREAL THINGS

But it seems Mulla Sadra is confident that he has performed this important task through the doctrine of trans-substantial motion of matter. After presenting certain premises the main part of which is trans-substantial motion, and after deriving his conclusion about the origination of the world from the above premises he continues as follows.

"I have taught you this method, which no veteran of philosophy demonstrated before me, to prove the temporal creation of the corporeal world, with all the heavens and earths and whatever is contained therein, for it has been proved that the nature which permeates the body and constitutes its matter and form is in its own essence and reality in a state of perpetual change and its Individual existence can not remain the same in two moments of time, let alone be eternal.

On such a basis the world of nature is renewed and recreated at every instance and no aspect of natural creatures is eternal. Every moment a new individual of substances, accidents and natural things is created and no corporeal entity and perpetual existence can be found in this world; corporeal substances are therefore like time and motion, the identity and reality of which is the very renewal (tajaddud) and origination (huduth). Time and motion aren't perpetual or eternal either in their whole or in their parts or either in their universals or in their particulars. Neither are bodily substances, accidents, quiddities and their attributes perpetual and eternal."[5]

Ibn-Sina rejected this idea in his different books and wrote a treatise on the negation of the personal existence of the natural universal. And if it means that with the renewal and the transformation of individuals and referents, terms and essences of a specific essence do not change, and then these are correct words which do not contradict our theory. That is because terms of quiddity by virtue of their unity and individuation they do not have external existence. But the description of eternity and origination is related to individual existents in the external world, and the description of quiddity with such attributes is figurative and in relation to their individuals and referents.

"Thus, the light of the Truth appeared on the horizon of demonstration (burhan) and it became clear that the creatures of the world and of the heavens had no eternity either from the species point of view or from the viewpoint of their individuals and referents, for they all belong to the material world, which is in a state of perpetual change and transformation."[6]

From the aforementioned points we come to the conclusion that origination (huduth) as it has been discussed is a result of trans-substantial motion and is stated to the world of nature, where motion and change go hand in hand. Now we will embark upon the assessment of the proofs of trans-substantial motion in the origination (huduth) of the world. We will then see whether the origination resulting from it is temporal origination or not, and whether it is applicable to all material and natural existence, or whether it denotes the finitude of the world accidents in the past.

Mulla Sadra pointed to the doctrine of trans-substantial motion. This principle can, therefore be regarded as one of the distinguishing features of his doctrinal formulation. "Trans-Substantial motion" (harakah jawhariyah) is an idea which plays a decisive role in the metaphysics of Mulla Sadra, so much so that it is unanimously considered one of the cardinal principles of his philosophical system. It is the basis of his explanation of many of the most difficult problems of traditional philosophy including the temporal creation of the world and the whole meaning of becoming in light of the Immutable and the Eternal.[7]

As is well-known, earlier Islamic philosophers, especially Ibn Sina, had followed Aristotelian natural philosophy in accepting motion *(al-harakah)* only in the categories of quantity *(kamm)*, quality *(kayf)*, situation *(wad')* and place *(ayn)*, all of which are accidents and denied explicitly the possibility of motion in the category of substance. Ibn Sina's main argument was that motion requires a subject that moves and if the very substance of an object changes through transubstantial motion, then there will be no subject for motion. He considered substantial natures and species to be stable and, changeless and argued that since for the occurrence of motion a permanent object is needed so that motion could occur in it, the substantial nature of bodies, which constitutes their substantial identity, is permanent and motion takes place in the above categories of quantity, quality, situation and place. That is to say that the identity of the substantial nature is gradual renewal and becoming, which is identical with the very motion itself. Based on this, motion is the prerequisite for and the analytical accidents of the substantial nature.

Ibn-Sina and some others also hold that unless nature gets changed, it can not cause motion. Yet they maintain that change in nature is caused by external factors like the renewal of its immediate and remote grades in regard to the desired end of natural motions, by the renewal of states in unnatural *(qasri)* motions and the renewal of wills, and by the relative desires of the soul according to ego-centric motivations and desires.

Mulla Sadra chooses to consider substantial movement as a gradual transformation occurring in the inner structure itself of things. He opposed this thesis directly by saying that any change in the accidents of an object requires in fact a change in its substance since accidents have no existence independent of substance, and it is absurd for the accidents, which is, in fact, the manifestation of the existence of the substance, to be separated from it. We can also observe a kind of behavioral coordination and unity among these four-fold moving accidents, which is itself an evidence for their harmony and unity with their essence and substance.

He asserts that there is always "some subject" *(mawdu'un ma)* for motion even if we are unable to fix it and delimit it logically. According to this proof we can establish that the natures of the world, whether spherical or elemental, are changing through their essences and moving with regard to their substances, while their accidents follow them in renewal, and receive any change occurring in the substances, and are unified with them substances in actualization, and move in accordance with the movements of substances. Thus the transformation does not affect the qualities of the world only, but their essences as well.

Every unit considered of a mobile thing is surrounded by two kinds of non-existence, preceding and following, which are both temporal mobiles, because their container is the container of two kinds of existence which encompass the mobile thing from both sides, and these two kinds of existence are mobile. As we already know, the container of mobile things is time. So the existence of that unit is preceded by temporal non-existence; and the same is true of the parts of that unit and the parts of its parts. And the same applies to that which comes next to that unit on both sides, and that which comes next to what comes next.

Thus a thing or substance which is now in a certain ontological state is regarded by Mulla Sadra to be undergoing a continuous and gradual inner transformation until it reaches a new ontological state. The whole process of this inner transformation is in reality a series of annihilations and re-creations by God.

This trans-substantial motion, referring to the existence of the universe below the level of the intelligible and archetypal realities, is not to be, however, confused with the re-creation of the world in every instant as taught by the Sufis.[8] In the Sufi doctrine at every moment the universe is annihilated and re-created. Previous forms return to the Divine Order and new forms are manifested as theophany. That is why this doctrine is called *al-labs ba'd al-khal'a* (literally, dressing after undressing of forms).

In contrast Mulla Sadra's doctrine has been called *al-labs ba'd al al-labs* (that is, dressing after dressing). This implies that the form and matter of an existent become themselves the matter for a new form and that this process goes on continuously as if one were to put on one coat on top of another. All beings in this world are moving vertically as a result of trans-substantial motion until they reach the plenum of their archetypal reality. Each state of this movement contains the forms of its earlier states of existence, while this Tran-substantial movement continues throughout all these stages. It is important to emphasize that Mulla Sadra's dynamic vision of the world in constant becoming, which implies the continuous intensification of the act of *wujud* within a particular being.

For Mulla Sadra, the beings of world are manifestations of the light of *wujud* cast upon their archetypal realities which through the arc of descent *(al-qaws al-nuzul)* bring various creatures into the realm of physical existent. Trans-substantial motion marks the arc of ascent *(al-qaws al-suudi)* through which the ever-increasing intensity of light of *wujud* allows existents to return their archetypal realities in the supernal realm. In this regard there are such things as archetypal realities and the species far from reflecting celestial archetypes, are merely forms generated by the flow of matter in time.

Also for Mulla Sadra, every being in this world has essentially some existential need (*imkan-e faqri*). This statement means that every being in this world, by itself, is but nothingness or "Non-existence". So if any being in the world is left to itself, it immediately moves towards its own denial. Thus, every object can only have a momentary existence, since in the same moment that it has been brought to the domain of existence, its own nature returns it to the domain of non-existence. The point that every being, due to its existential need, is inclined towards its own denial is exactly the very same meaning of mobility and renewal. It is where, according to the theory of Trans-substantial motion, we state that every material entity is changeable in its essence and substance, its existence at every moment is different from its existence at another moment, and the act of perpetual creation is ceaselessly granted by the absolute Divine essence. At the intersection of these two factors, i.e., the existential need of all objects and the perpetual effusion by the absolute metaphysical source, the concept of "new creation" or "perpetual creation" is realized.

This is also the very specific philosophical meaning of "new creation" which is stated in the holy Qur'an "*Bal hom Fi labsen men khalgh-en Jadid*" (Yet are they in doubt with regard to a new creation).[9] The problem of God, on the basis of such a conception of creation, will appear not as a problem but as an objective, evident, and obvious affair which one will face wherever he goes and whatever he sees. God's daily involvement in work is expressed in the best way in the theory of the Trans-substantial motion. The closeness of the Truth to the beings, His dominance over the world, His knowledge over all events, His deep intervention in all affairs, and many problems concerning monotheism and God will receive an explicit meaning in this theory.

Throughout the history of Islamic thought, this concept (new creation) has been interpreted in different ways by many thinkers. One of them is trans-substantial motion as the most genuine philosophical interpretations of the fundamental concept of "creation continua" or "perpetual creation" in the world of Islam. In addition to the atomistic philosophy of the Ash'arites which can be considered as an obvious and purely rationalistic approach to the problem, we are also dealing with Sufis' renewal of ideas which has thoroughly been explained by Ibn Arabi.

The concept of "origination" in Mulla Sadra's philosophy is a consequent of-in fact the same concept as–trans-substantial motion; therefore, it cannot be understood without this concept. This means the origination of a new substance which is exactly the annihilation of another substance.

According to this principle, all existents in the world of nature are essentially transformable, and changeable, and all their parts are continually in the process of creation and extinction. That is to say there is no ipseity amongst the personal ipseities except that its non-existence temporally precedes its existence. On the whole, there is no body and material body, be it celestial or elemental, or be it spiritual or physical, except that it is renewal entity renovates and its existence and individuation remains constant. If these material entities are changing at every moment, at each instance of their being, it is different from what it was before and what it is now was non-existent before *(masbug bil-'adam)*.

The way of reasoning for substantial motion on the origination of the world is explicit, for when motion, and change are inseparable accidents of material nature, according to the principle of that which is changing is created *(hadith)* the origination of the natural world is proved. In other words, nature necessitates change and change necessitates origination *(huduth)*; therefore, material nature necessitates origination. This is along the same lines as the saying 'the need for cause is necessitated by possibility and possibility is necessitated by quiddity; therefore, the need for cause is necessitated by quiddity.z

On many occasions about origination and its relation to trans-substantial motion, Mulla Sadra elucidates the fact that the unity of hyle is not numerical and individual but generic. Thus the combination of matter and form is a kind of uniting combination rather than an inclusive one (merger of two realities knowledgeable to each other). Consequently, when form is temporally originated hyle too, in origination and renewal, is subservient to form. As a result, although as potency in the absolute sense this is a fixed and self-subsistent quality, in view of its special receptacle and potencies, which are subject to change with the alteration of forms, it is changing and originated (hadith). Mulla Sadra's following discourse is in this connection:

"Since the reality of hyle is potency and the reality of the natural form is accompanied by origination and renewal, it takes a special form at every instance and with each form it is attended by a different hyle. That in its turn also has preparedness for another form and thus form has an essential priority over matter and at the same time, by virtue of its specific identity, it is temporally posterior to matter. As a result, both are renewed by virtue of each other without being trapped in being the circle of destruction. We will discuss this problem in our discourse on matter and form."[10]

In connection to Mulla Sadra's above-mentioned discussion He believes that the unity of hyle is a unity of genus rather than personal unity; therefore, hyle has no role of its own. It is rather subservient to the form, just as genus has no role except in relation to differentia.

It is in this context that Mulla Sadra says, "In the world of nature not only forms but also matter is originated in time. "His predecessors believed in the eternity of matter in time and its origination in essence. They believed that forms are originated (*hadith*) both essentially and temporally, but Mulla Sadra says that since materia prima has no role except of being subservient to form, it is originated (*hadith*) both essentially and temporally."[11]

3. TEMPORAL ORIGINATION OF THE WORLD AS A WHOLE

Through the theory of the trans-substantial motion, Mulla Sadra also managed to solve the problem of the origination or pre-eternity of the world, debated for eight centuries before him by the Islamic philosophers and theologians. He believes in temporal necessary being of the universe. In fact, the world is permanently coming into being through the trans-substantial motion and it could be stated that the world is, at any moment, precedent for its non-being. Thus, the whole world as a collection of parts is also temporally contingent because a collection does not enjoy any identity apart from its parts.

Thus in each of the units of the mobile natures there is a non-suitability for the negation of its being preceded by temporal non-existence. And the same is true of the total whole, because the latter has no existence except the existence of the parts, especially as regards the extended things, whether immobile, (e.g., distance) or not immobile (e.g., time), whose parts are equal with each other and with the whole in definition and name. The nature of the whole is the same as that of the parts. And the same is true of the natural universal of the mobile natures, because it has no existence except the existence of the individuals.

On the basis of trans-substantial motion, apart from proving the finitude of events in the past, the first premises of the demonstration on origination is proved. If we look at each referent of material realities, we will see that they are accompanied by renewal and change in both substance and accident and material and form. And the assumption of stillness in material and physical realities is impossible, and it is evident that the entire material events and phenomena have no reality other than their individuals and referents and cannot be presumed to be in a state of stability and stillness. Thus it is true to say that the natural world is in the state of change and in the state of change it is originated; therefore, the world of nature is originated.

So the whole world, which is the sum total of its parts in a sense, with all that exists in it, is created in time and has a temporal contingent entity, because through substantial motion the being of the universe is renewed at every moment or, more explicitly, that the world is created at every instant, so that one can say that the being of the world depends upon its non-being at a previous moment. Where he differs from the theologians is that his conception of creation *ex nihilo* is complementary to the view that the archetypes of the world of creation exist changelessly in the intelligible world and that the world is connected with its divine origin through a permanent hierarchy. The teaching of the Muslim philosophers, which is fully in conformity with that of the Islamic teachings in philosophy, is not only that the world is created in time, but that everything in it will ultimately perish. The only reality which will abide forever is, as the Qur'an has put it, "God's face".

After quoting the proof of those believing in the temporal origin of time and its criticism Mulla Sadra says, "By the grace of God we have proved the fact that each individual of material existents is subsequent to non-existence and eternity in time. We have also consolidated the following two facts: 1. the substances of the natural world in view of their essence are subject to events. 2. What is subject to events in view of its essence and identity is temporally originated; therefore, the whole world of the nature is originated."[12]

And since there is "no whole but through the existence of its parts",[13] "so the world with all its parts, be it the heavenly spheres and stars, or be it simple and complex, is contingent and perishable. And whatever exists in it, at every moment of time, counts as another being and a new creation".[14] It is clear that according to this viewpoint, one cannot assume a starting point for the world, and there is indeed no necessity to assume a starting point because time originates from the world itself. It follows that there was no time before the creation of the world.

4. IS THE WHOLE TIME ETERNAL IN TIME?

In this section it is necessary for us to talk about this issue that although through trans-substantial motion the temporal origination of all material phenomena and realities is explicitly proved, this does not prove the finitude of time and temporal events in the past. That is to say that it does not prove that the world of nature is originated at a certain point and is thereafter in a state of becoming and renewal. This is the same point that Ghazali emphasizes in his criticism on philosophy concerning the origination of the world. He considers philosophers' view concerning the infinitude of the events of the world as discarded and contrary to religious beliefs.

There is no doubt that fragments of time are originated in time, for the criterion of origination in time, which is the subsequence of the existence of a thing to its non-existence in the past, is in accordance with it. This is because the assumption of the whole time necessitates all fragments to be covered by the time and no part to be left without being covered by time. Thus there-is no other time in which the existence of the whole time can be subsequent to its non-existence. Therefore, the presumption of origination in time for the entire time entails contradiction.

Those theologians who believe in the temporal origination of time resort to an estimated (*mawhum*) time. An estimated time is an assumed time which even lacks the source of its abstraction, and one in which only the existence of God is eternal and permanent.[15]

But this justification is invalid. If the estimated time is a mental being and origination (*huduth*) belongs to the qualities of objective realities and external things, and if the estimated (*mawhum*) time, despite having its source of separation, is inconsistent with the principle of the necessary harmony between the abstract concept meaning and its source of abstraction, then how is it reasonable that the eternal and permanent reality should be a source of abstraction of the concept of origination?

On the basis of the theory of trans-Substantial motion, if we look carefully at the proposition the world is temporally originated, we will find out that its subject is not a particular concept and does not enjoy a particular referent. This means that at each moment there is a world that did not exist at the previous moment and is therefore originated. In other words, the said proposition means that any world is originated, according to which judgment of origination acts over the world as a distributive and not a collective whole.[16]

It can be presumed that Mulla Sadra, considering the opinion of the early philosophers who regarded the change and the motion of objects as the most significant issue, and by shifting this change and motion to the essence and the substance of objects, is inclined towards the unification of the issues of "change" and "origination".

Nevertheless, here we need to mention a question about the origination of the world remains to be answered, and that is whether these changes and trans-substantial Originations, as well as the essential restlessness, have a beginning or not and whether or not temporal origination resulting from substantial motion succeeds in demonstrating the origination of the world. Meanwhile, there is no need to assume this beginning in a real or illusory time in order to get involved with the same problems found in theologians' theories. That is because it may be presumed–although with difficulty–that these changes have a non-temporal point of initiation and the reality preceding that point is unknown to us.

Mulla Sadra does not explicitly answer this above question in his al-huduth (*Risalah fi*). But, as it is mentioned since there is "no whole but through the existence of its parts", "so the world with all its parts, at every moment of time, counts as another being and a new creation". So the question when the world was created is an irrelevant and meaningless one. Therefore, the question about the temporal creation of the world is absurd. This question would be meaningful only if there were a flowing time independent of the world, and the world was brought into existence in one of its hours and moments. This question would be reasonable only in case there were a time independent of the world and the world could come into being at a specific moment of this time.

Since it is not so and time is created by matter and is not independent of it, there could be no question about the "time" of creation. But since it is not so, and since time is an offspring of matter, is not independent of it, and comes after and not before it, one con not ask about the time of the creation of the world.

In fact, the whole world is located in "timelessness", the same way that it is located in "placeless-ness". One can not ask where the whole galaxies are located, since when we consider the entire matter; there is no place outside it to determine the location of the world here and not there. The story of time is the same. When there is no time beyond the world, one can not say that the world is at this time and not at another time. Having a time is only applicable to the parts of the world and not to the whole world. Accordingly, it will essentially be a void statement to speak about the temporal contingency and pre-eternity of the world as theologians have been trying to reject or confirm it.

However, we should pay attention to the fact that "temporal origination" in Mulla Sadra's school has a conception other than that of theologians. In this school of thought, "origination" does not mean "the appearance of the world in time" but "the appearance of the world with time". Mulla Sadra disagrees with theologians who believe the world to have been brought into being in time from utter nothingness.

As is well known, Mulla Sadra believed the world to have had no origination in time but to have been originated beyond time by God. He believes that only God is eternal. All else–matter and form, individuals and species, parts and wholes, abstract and material constitutes what called the world and is created in time. He also believes that created-ness in time is a property of the material world, whereas the supernatural worlds are super time and space.

Now, let us see whether the sum of time can be considered eternal in time. The answer is that if the criterion for the eternity of time is that it existed in a time and that an existent was not subsequent to non-existence, then time in its whole may not be eternal in time. This is because no other time beyond the whole time exists in a relation by which we can measure the realization of time. In this connection Mulla Sadra says: "The meaning of the temporal eternality of time is that there has to be no time for the existence of the first thing. On this basis time may not be temporally eternal, for there is no other time for the time."[17]

In the same connection 'Allamah Tabataba'i says: "Temporal origination and eternality are true in the case of temporal qualities such as motion and the moved, which were realized in time. But time itself is not an attribute of temporal origination and eternality in time, for there is no other time for the time with which its existence can be compatible."[18]

Mir Damad who is so outstanding in true Wisdom came up to answer this question by the theory of meta-temporal origination (al-huduth al-dahri), which means origination of the world not in time (zaman) nor in sempiternity (sarmad), but in aeon (dahr), and he became celebrated for the exposition of this doctrine.[19]

Meta-temporal origination or coming-into-being of the world by way of coming into being through "perpetual duration" is like the temporal coming into being, the precedence of preceding non-existence over the existence of a thing by way of separable precedence of it. And the precedence of non-existence[20] and its separable priority is in the "longitudinal" hierarchy,[21] contrary to their state in the temporal coming-into-being; because in the latter case they are in the "latitudinal hierarchy".[22]

According to Mir Damad's view, every existent has for its existence a container or something comparable to it. Thus the container of the mobiles like movement and moving things is time. What is comparable to the container for the luminous non-material things is "Perpetual duration". And the latter is, like those things themselves, simple and devoid of quantity, connection, mobility, and the like. And its relation to time is the same as the relation of the spirit to the body that of governing. And what is comparable to the container for the Truth and His Attributes and Names is "sempiternity".

Mulla Sadra rejected this dichotomy of views altogether by pointing to the doctrine of trans-substantial motion. If the cosmos is changing at every moment, at each instance of its being, it is different from what it was before and what it now was non-existent before (masbug bil-'adam). Therefore, one can accept the doctrine that the world was created from nothing (ex nihilo) while accepting the continuous and uninterrupted effusion(fayd) of the light of Being which is none other than the Divine Light.[23] He thus seeks to provide a philosophical explanation for one of the most difficult of philosophical issues in not only Islamic thought Jewish and Christian thought as well.

The only reality which could precede the existence of time is God who brings the world into being by His creative fiat (al-amr).[24] As a component of the created universe, neither the whole of time nor a part of it could have existed prior to this fiat. Both the sensible and intelligible worlds are subject to continuous permutation and cannot for that reason be eternal.

Now let us go on to say that the statement of Mir Damad that the world is originated on the level of *"perpetual duration"* means that the existence of the material world is preceded by non-existence at the level of perpetual duration, because its existence is preceded by the existence of the world of the souls whose container is the perpetual duration, by way of precedence at the level of *"perpetual duration."*

Thus just as every individual term of the latitudinal hierarchy and every unit of its time are non-existence, for another individual term of the latitudinal hierarchy and for another unit of its time respectively, so every stage in the *"longitudinal"* hierarchy is non-existence, in that stage for another stage of the *"longitudinal"* hierarchy. Just as nonexistence in the latitudinal hierarchy, is actual, so is non-existence in the *"longitudinal"* hierarchy, because the existences are actual, and in the stage of each existence there is non-existence for another stage; rather, each one *is* nonexistence for the other, and each container of existence is itself a container for the non-existence of the preceding one and its associate. And just as the measures of circular movements in this worlds are times, so the extension of the movement of the Sun of the Real Light in the two curves of Descent and Ascent from the axis of the heavenly sphere of the existences of those worlds constitutes Divine Days, as He, Most High, says: "Remind them of the Days of God."[25]

The conclusion is that the existence of the world, in his view, is preceded by the actual non-existence at the level of *"perpetual duration,"* and not preceded by the estimated non-existence *(mawhum)* at the level of time as the Theologians assert nor preceded by the parallel non-existence which is in the stage of quiddity only, as some Philosophers are related to have asserted.

Based on this Doctrine, Mir Damad considered the collection of successive events in the meta-temporal realm of perpetuity *(dahr)* to be sufficient for an infinite regress proof. For this reason, he has denied the possibility of a series of events extending infinitely into the past. If the collection of the links of the regress in perpetuity is sufficient, then one can also deny a series of events extending infinitely into the future.

But the main point is that there is controversy about proofs for the impossibility of infinite regresses produced with links other than true causes, but this is not the occasion to pursue the matter further. For this reason, it is extremely difficult to set up a proof either for the possibility or impossibility of an infinite regress of events, whether extending into the past or the future.

5. CONTINUOUS AND UNINTERRUPTED EFFUSION (FAYD)

Another point to be considered here is that the belief in the origination of the world should not be inconsistent with the continuation of Divine grace and effusion *(fayd)*. Mulla Sadra unanimous with Islamic philosophers concerning the continuation of Divine effusion, in the tenth station of the third journey of his al-Asfar he admits that events and changes lack any beginning. However, based on the theory of trans-substantial motion, he draws our attention to the point that the fact that events have no beginning does not mean that the world is eternal. The reason is that the quality of *"being eternal"* can only be attributed to a constant and continuous subject, and that is nothing but the Creator's essence and effusion. However, nature, which is essential changing and restless, is not marked by any qualification but "origination". Even the matter of this world is not constant so that it can be considered eternal.

On the other hand, most of the philosophers believed in the temporal pre-eternity of the material world, and have given reasons for their own views, including reliance on the above-mentioned principle whose inadequacy has become clear.

Another reason given by them is based on the pre-eternity of divine grace and the absence of stinginess in the higher sources. However, this reason will be useful only in case the possibility of the pre-eternity of the world is proved and its occurrence dependent on divine grace. Hence, those who believe in the temporal creation of the world have tried to prove the impossibility of the pre-eternity of the world, and they have tried to reject the possibility of an infinite series of events extending into the past by means of the invalidity of infinite regresses.

They accept the proofs for the impossibility of infinite regresses only in cases in which the links of the regresses exist simultaneously together and a true ordering exists among them. Therefore, they allow the infinity of successive events and exclude simultaneous events which are not truly ordered from the proofs of the impossibility of infinite regresses.

Mulla Sadra do not adduce any evidence for the eternality of the universe from the universe itself; rather, they approach this argument from the position that God is the Absolutely Effulgent and the Eternally Beneficent—we cannot possibly conceive of His Effulgence and beneficence as limited, as terminating somewhere. In other words, the theistic philosophers have arrived at this thesis that the world is beyond the time through an a priori demonstration, that is, by making the being and attributes of God the premise to the eternality of the universe. Generally, those who disbelieve in God advance the position of the eternality of the universe, but the theistic philosophers say that the very thing non-believers adduce as a reason for God's non-existence is what in their view implies God's existence. The eternality of the universe is a hypothesis to nonbelievers, but it is an established fact to theistic philosophers.

Mulla Sadra asserts that the whole of the physical and even psychic or imaginal universes which extend up to the Immutable or luminous Archetypes are in constant motion or becoming. Were it to be otherwise, the effusion of Being could not reach all things.

One could not possibly talk more forcefully than this on the dependence of the created to the creator and the continual need of the world to a creator. The momentary character of the world obviously reveals its needful character. This indicates that the world is in transition and mobility not only in its appearances and states but even in its very existence and ipseity. And dependence and need have penetrated into the depth of its spirit and have captured its whole existence, which is stated in the holy verse *"koll-o youm-en Hova fi Sha'an"*.[26]

Based on Mulla Sadra's attitudes concerning the origination of the world a synthesis has been made of the two principles of the continuation of the effusion of God and the origination of the world. Mulla Sadra agrees with those earlier philosophers who acknowledge origination in time in the sense of renewed regeneration and the physical transformation of the whole natural world because all bodies enjoy trans-substantial motion and are in a state of change in their nature."And the world is changing not only in its accidents but also in its substances, and every changing thing is originated. And although the world is a single contiguous thing, it is at the same time various worlds. At each instance a new world comes in to belong to the two antecedents and subsequent non-existences. There is no origination in time except that it is subsequent to non-existence, and the world is as such. The whole does not exist except in parts and natural universals do not exist except in particulars, and each particular is subsequent to temporal non-existence.

It may be concluded that although divine effusion does not require any sort of limitation, the bestowal of divine effusion hinges on the capability and possibility of receiving it. Perhaps the material world does not have the capability for receiving pre-eternal and post-eternal effusion. But just as philosophers have not considered limitations on the volume of the world to be incompatible with the extension of divine effusion, its temporal finitude must not be considered incompatible with the constancy of divine effusion.

In general, it may be inferred that Mulla Sadra has tried to propound the issue of origination in two frameworks: of 'hal' (whether) "is the world originated?" and of 'ma' (what) "Basically, what is origination?" and "What can actually be attributed to the quality of being originated?" Mulla Sadra's theory of "trans-substantial motion" in fact paves the way for an answer to these two questions. In this way, there will be a clear and evident answer to the first question, because according to trans-substantial motion, each object–including its matter and form–is obviously originated. Consequently, at each moment we face an entirely new phenomenon. However, as was stated earlier, subsequent to this question, another question similar to the former and within the framework of 'hal' (whether) immediately arises, and that is whether there is any beginning point for successive trans-substantial originations.

Evidently, answering this question involves the same problems that one faces with regard to answering the former question. It may be claimed that the difficulty in acknowledging the origination of the world or its eternity mainly results from the difficulty in the conception of these two origination and eternity. If someone believes in the origination of the world, it is because imagining of the idea of "eternity" and of "infinite time" is difficult for him. And the reason for the one who believes in the eternity of the world is that he cannot imagine "origination" and "finite time".

We may conclude from the preceding points that firstly origination (huduth) is the result of trans-substantial motion of time. This origination is based on change and motion, and change and motion are accompanied by time as the measure of motion. Just as other natural referents and bodies are changing and moving and as that which is changing is subject to origination in time, all substantial bodies and natures are subject to temporal origination. Secondly, this change and origination is universal and is subject to change and generality, and includes matter and form, substance and accident, and every material reality and phenomenon.

NOTES

[1] R. Walzer, "New Studies on al-Kindi," in *Creek into Arabic, Oriens*, (1957); p. 218.

[2] Abu Ridah, *Rasa'il al-Kindi al-falsafiyah*, 2 vols. (Cairo, 1950–1953), "On the Efficient Cause of Generation and Corruption," p. 215.

[3] See al-Ghazali, *Tahafut al-falasifah*, trans. Sabih Ahmad Kamali (Lahore, 1963): p. 13.

[4] "Non-existence" *('adam)* is of two kinds: 1. preceding non-existence *('adam muqabil)* and 2 parallel non-existence *('adam mujami')*. The first is non-existence in terms of time, which does not correspond to the existence of a thing in time. The second is the non-requirement of a possible for either existence or non-existence. This non-requirement is a negative attribute of a possible in itself. This is what is meant by Ibn Sina when he says that a possible thing in itself is non-existent.

[5] *Mulla Sadra, al-Asfar al-arba 'ah, Vol. 3, pp. 61-65, al-Rasa'il, pp. 18, 19.*

[6] *Mulla Sadra, al-Asfar al-arba 'ah, Vol. 3, p. 66.*

[7] See the *Asfar*, 3: p. 80.

[8] See Izutsu, *Creation and the Timeless* Order *of Things: p. 119.*

[9] Qur'an, 50, 15

[10] *Mulla Sadra, al-Asfar al-arba'ah, Vol. 3, p. 63*

[11] *Mutahhari, Motion and Time in Islamic Philosophy, Vol, 1, p. 280*

[12] *Mulla Sadra, al-Asfar al-arba'ah, Vol. 3, pp. 159, 160.*

[13] Mulla Sadra, *al-Masha'ir*, ed. Hanri Corbin, Ketabkhaneh Tahori, 2nd, al-Manhaje.3, *al-Mashair*. p. 64.

[14] Mulla Sadra, *al-Asfar*, Vol. 7, Chapt. 2, p. 297; See: Ibid, chap. 1, p. 287.

[15] *Shaykh Muhammad Taqi Amuli, Al-Fawa'id, Vol. 1, p. 261, Ismailiyyan Institute, Qum*

[16] See al-huduth (Risalah fi), pp. 44–46; also, Sadr al-Din Shirazi, al-hikmnat al-muta'aliyah, vol. 7, pp. 278–285. Here it can be guessed that Mulla Sadra could not accept Mir Damad's theory of meta-temporal origination. For, according to this theory, to attribute the world of matter to be meta-temporal originated", it should be deemed as a collective whole, which is dissolved in another world called meta-temporal. While, according to Mulla Sadra, the world of nature and motions, as a whole, lacks a real collective existence, and thus, is not qualified to be really the subject of one of the descriptions, whether it is "origination" or "eternity", "essential" or "temporal" or "meta-temporal".

[17] *Mulla Sadra, al-Asfar al-arba'ah, Vol. 3, pp. 245*

[18] *Tabataba'i, Nahayat al-hikmat, Tenth Stage, Chapter 5*

[19] See S. H. Nasr, "The School of Isfahan", in Sharif (ed.) *A History of Muslim Philosophy*, 2: 916ff.

[20] "Non-existence" is divided into "temporal non-existence," "non-existence-through-perpetual-duration," and "sempiternal non-existence." Among the latitudinal existents, every stage of existence lacks the properties of another stage and that every lower existence lacks the properties of a higher existence among the longitudinal existents A lower existence in the longitudinal hierarchy lacks the characteristics of the degree of a higher existence, because the lower existence is something caused by the higher. A caused cannot have the characteristics of the degree of the existence of its cause, because the former is nothing but a shadow or a reflection of the latter. But the higher existence in the longitudinal hierarchy does possess the characteristics of the lower, for a cause does not lack the characteristics of the existence of its caused, because the latter is nothing but an outcome of the former.

[21] "Longitudinal," starts from its First Point, which is the Principle of all principles and the End of all ends, then comes the Divine Dimension, then the world of pure Intellects, then the world of souls and finally the world of bodily forms.

[22] "Latitudinal," is meant here as the world of physical bodies, and as a hierarchy in which there is no cause-caused relationship.

[23] For an explanation of Mulla Sadra's views concerning the relation of God and the world see Fazlur Rahman, "The God-World Relationship in Mulla Sadra", in George Hourani (ed.) *Essays on Islamic Philosophy* and *Science* (Albany, 1975): 238–53.

[24] Risalah fi'l-Huduth, pp. 45 f.

[25] Qur'an, *14*, 5.

[26] (Rahman, 29), Mulla Sadra, *al-Asfar*, Vol. 7, Chap. 1, pp. 281–283.

DANIELA VERDUCCI

THE TIMING OF THE ONTOPOIESIS OF LIFE

1. TIME AS PHILOSOPHICAL ENIGMA

That time plays a fundamental role in ontology is the intuition that supports the work, *Sein und Zeit* by M. Heidegger, whose ponderous inquiry, however, was not able to remove the enigmatic character that since antiquity has accompanied the relationship between being and time. Rather, he accentuates it, exhibiting the incapacity to investigate its conversion into *Zeit und Sein* presaged in the work's outline.[1] Thus even after Heidegger, we lack an adequate philosophy for understanding time, and we still find ourselves in the condition described by Augustine of Hippo, who, even while he had awareness of time, no longer knew the answer to what time was, if asked about it.[2]

According to Anna-Teresa Tymieniecka, the being-inside and being-outside of time in comparison with being of traditional ontology, is emblematic of the current dissatisfaction of philosophical aspiration, which since now has been incapable of drawing upon that context of totality and entirety[3] that, "if this be at all possible", reposing in itself and not calling for further justification or explanation, would allow philosophy to advance without delay in its own work of conferring meaning on all the entities that appear bit by bit on the stage of history. In addition, a context of totality and entirety would enable philosophy to avoid always having to delay in devising stratagems for researching reasons-of-being, that the restricted and closed horizon of meaning, at the moment available, does not allow it to find.

It is true that speculative thought to produce systematic totalities of meaning is now viewed with diffidence: since from the end of the XIX century to our days, a critical attitude has prevailed against general theories and systems of philosophy seeking to project an all-encompassing context for every philo-sophical inquiry, because of the fact that illegitimate connections are made between and among various facets of questions. However, even using the hermeneutic methodology in vogue today, it lasts that to find the meaning of a single piece of the "text", it is always necessary to draw upon "deeper" layers of meaning and to enact "a regression through the entire development

A-T. Tymieniecka (ed.),
Timing and Temporality in Islamic Philosophy and Phenomenology of Life, 93–110.
© 2007 *Springer*.

of culture"[4]. Thus not even the methodological updates of the XX century provide philosophy with an adequate context for its progressive development in time: in both speculation and hermeneutics, it remains entangled in the recessive processes of justification or explanation and cannot succeed in unfolding as life would ask it to. The problem of time remains still crucial and unanswered for philosophy, which, not even in its phenomenological inflection with E. Husserl[5] or P. Ricoeur[6], seems able to transform the inscrutability of the relationship between time and being from an objection to ontological inquiry, to the occasion for its in- depth analysis and expansion.

2. A NEW CRITIQUE OF REASON

And yet, it is intrinsic to philosophical intentionality, inaugurated by Taletes in the VII century BC, to constantly measure itself against time: the search for the principle of all things, in fact, continually re-establishes itself because experience constantly presents anew not-yet-known. Philosophy is born with a duplicity built into its structure, by which the stillness, connected with the contact with ontological apexes, lives alongside the dynamism implicated by the processuality of inquiry, which the interrogative pressure from the renewal of experience keeps active and striving to respond to the question: "How must the foundation and the first cause of the totality of the world be constituted so that such a thing, such an essential structure, may be possible?".[7]

In addition, as Anna-Teresa Tymieniecka observes, "the various modes of existence (e.g., reality, ideality, fictive existence, absolute existence)" are fundamentally distinguished from each other on the basis of their relationship with time. In fact, their ontological structure either necessarily requires the reference to time, as in the case of real existence, which is subject to change and action, or they reject it as incompatible with their own nature, as it happens for ideal existence, which does not entail the possibility of change.[8]

But, on the other side, in practical philosophy and religious philosophy, which reflect on cultural-social life and the specifically human vocation of searching for a personal transcendent destiny, what comes to sight first is not so much time, as life.[9]

Along with Nietzsche and with Scheler[10], Anna-Teresa Tymieniecka holds that it is the traditional philosophy of being which represents an inadequate context for understanding time, and that the moment has come to set out upon "a new critique of reason"[11], given that

no longer can the notion of being function as a principle of the principle which sustain what-there-is. The principle, rather, is "beingness", which is what individualizes something and through which, as through a vehicle, life expands.[12]

Also in the sphere of the phenomenological exploration of the 1970s, Anna-Teresa Tymieniecka issued calls to search for a new ontological-metaphysical horizon, able to meet the demands of the changed episte-mological and social context after Husserl, Scheler, Heidegger, Ingarden, Sartre, and Merleau-Ponty; but, above all, for an inquiry that would penetrate further deeply than these thinkers had. It meant achieving the Husserlian aspiration of a phenomenology as *philosophia prima* and at the same time to victoriously accept the challenge issued in the 1950s by Alfred Tarski. The great mathematician and convinced neopositivist, in fact, doubted that phenomenology could overcome "the pragmatic test" and demonstrate its "universal validity", taking position as the discriminating and inescapable reference on the terrain of "the issue of theory and practice". In that period, the question of the human as well as technical value of philosophy for cognition and praxis, even though it is "one that strikes at the knot of all the great philosophical questions we have inherited from two and a half millennia of tradition", arose above all in terms of the relationship between the inspirational role phenomenology has played in the human sciences and in the empirical and hard sciences, and philosophy's ability to maintain, as *philosophia prima*, the *status* of universal reference. In particular, the question was: "Is philosophy, in its new familiarity with concrete knowledge, losing his status of universal reference – of 'first philosophy'?".[13]

Anna-Teresa Tymieniecka responded to this demanding question, producing the "phenomenology of phenomenology" that Husserl had left incomplete, even though "other levels of rationality, towards the revelation of various perspectives of the logos" had come to light following his inves-tigation, rooted in pure intellectual reason. However, they were underesti-mated, or even ignored by the first generations of phenomenologists[14] who for this reason failed to attain the goal of endowing phenomenology with an "absolute cognitive ground".[15] In this context many students and experts of phenomenology demanded it be improved, and thus arose the radical exigency, "to follow the progress of the method in order to inquire into its very logos and its yieldings".[16] To do so, Anna-Teresa Tymieniecka subjects phenomenology itself to a "reduction", but one that goes "in another way" and represents "a different track" than "that of a 'last' trascendental reduction of transcendentality, of transcendental constitution as such" proposed by E. Fink and approved by Husserl, in the *Sixth Cartesian Meditation*.[17]

In fact, this entails, on the one hand, escaping the trap in which Husserl was caught, "by [his] identifying the intentionality of consciousness with cognition"[18]; and on the other, revealing "the ultimate nature of rationality in all of its modalities"[19] that is, "to unearth the universal logos and solve the quandry that puzzled Husserl, the impossible situation of the subject's constituting the world and being simultaneously an objective element of it".[20]

The new way of proceeding has a "conjectural" character, consisting in advancing step by step in the search for "what led to the Logos' being posited within the gigantic schema of dynamic reality",[21] dealing with the questions starting from their original way of appearing[22], rather than turning to speculation, in which Hegel was masterful[23], and postulating the logos as response to the multitude of questions that arise from the cosmos and from the enigmatic nature of the human being. "Conjecturing", one seeks to subject to verification precisely the intuition by which the logos would find its most suitable manifestation not so much on the level of absoluteness and of ideal, a-temporal rigor, as in the disorderly richness of contingent experience, where the process of self-building of life takes place, producing the growing differentiation of its forms.[24] The methodological wager is that "in the conjecture itself is contained an essential element of foothold of its surging, a logoic instance, as well as anticipation of the answer point of logoic destination".[25] In effect, the conjectural dynamic of thought, in the degree to which it espouses C. S. Peirce's indication that "we may gain access to reality only if the observation of philosopher/agent takes into account the fact of that observation"[26], exalts the continuity of life and spirit, and of nature and humanity, giving logoic expression to the poieticity of life self-individualizing itself and equally, allowing traditional "foundational philosophy" to accommodate the present "novel existential situation of human beingness within the network of life, nature, earth, cosmic forces that throws new light on reason". [27]

The intuitive-conjectural incursion conducted in this way through the "inventive powers" proper to the living human[28] has succeeded: A.-T. Tymieniecka has pushed as deeply as the most primitive level of being and has attained the proto-ontological position in which being itself auto-generates and regenerates, manifesting itself as a living spring of a logos that is "ontopoietical" in the degree to which it gives reasons for all things neither statically nor extrinsically, but following the intimate constructiveness of the cosmos, that is, "the constructive entanglements of life's spontaneities, dynamisms, forces in their radiating relevancies for the system of life and cosmic forces in which the logos flourishes".[29]

Thus a new key has been found to open the gate separating nature and culture, following the road that, as recounted by ancient mythology, human genius had already traced when it opened "the Pandora's box of natural forces and their operational rules resulting in the inventive outburst that then upset the equilibrium of vital and existential forces". In fact, "by taking the investigation of the creative/inventive virtualities of the human being as the starting point of philosophy, rather than the cognitive act, we enter into the heart of the ontopoiesis of life in which both nature and culture are situated".[30]

The identification of such a logos, at once living, human and ordering, and therefore pre-ontological and proto-ontological, inasmuch as ontopoietic, is also innovative from the point of view of the enigma of time: in fact, the new logical context finally enables examination of the ancient problem of *kronos* and *kairos*[31], breaking "the timeless pattern of surrender to nature" and rendering inadequate the millenary equilibrium of life between nature and human beings, and between the gifts of nature and their use by living beings.[32]

3. THE HUMAN CREATIVE CONDITION

The success of such an approach has received an absolutely essential contribution from A.-T. Tymieniecka's research beginning in the 1970s, through which she reopened access to the life for the constituting transcendental consciousness and, on the basis of the "conscious-corporeal" experience (*Leib-bewusst*), reflexively went beyond the essential "givenness" of the constitutive genesis of objectivity, in the direction of its "inner working as the locus whence eidos and fact simultaneously spring", in the conviction that "not costitutive intentionality but the constructive advance of life, which carries it, may alone reveal to us the first principles of all things".[33] From this new theoretical position, Tymieniecka has been able to demonstrate that the function of individualizing constructivity, which oversees the evolution of life, determining its growing specialization and complexity, finds its culminating expression in the stage of development marked by the appearance of man, the living being endowed with *Imaginatio Creatrix*.

The creative function, guided by its own telos, generates *Imaginatio Creatrix* in man, as the means, par excellence, of specific human freedom: that is, freedom to go beyond the framework of the life-world, the freedom of man to surpass himself.[34]

Thus, when life reaches the level of the human creative condition, it no longer limits itself to reproducing itself, but in the acts of life of man always engages in "self- interpretation-in-existence"[35], giving rise to new and previously unimaginable forms of life that are congruent with and adequate for the becoming being of life, of which only man possesses "the cipher".[36] For this reason, man is radically the bearer of the metaphysical exigency: in fact, in order to orient the virtualities in his possession in the direction of positive realization, he needs to find the reasons of "beingness" and to draw upon the principle of being, through which he confers on creations the indispensable character of humanly adequate 'objective' form, that makes them graspable and usable. Of crucial importance at this point is the fact that being, so spontaneously set into play, does not limit itself to maintaining the importance of the "indispensable essential factor of all beingness", in the sense of classical metaphysics, inasmuch as it "concerns beingness in its finished, formed, established or stabilized state". Rather, to the degree in which it appears in the acts of the human living, being manifests itself as "the intrinsic factor of the constructive process of individual becoming". This means that, since "becoming is a process in its own advance, in qualification" and since the individual "remains always in the process of becoming", that is, continually proceeding toward "something that is not yet"[37], being, involved in the human creative acts from which becoming proceeds, acts as intrinsic stabilizing anticipator of the acquiring and transforming of form characterizing the natural evolution of the individual life. In this sense, compared to all other givennesses, that of man within his world is not simply comparable to a "process-like nature", but expresses a specific temporal type of constructivism, which furthermore is not reduced to what is developed during life, nor does the human being operate only as "meaning-bestowing-agent", producing its life-world, as Husserl proposed. Man begins before to "create according to being" (= ontopoiesis), because:

... his [man's] very life in itself is the effect of his self-individualization-in-existence through inventive self- interpretation of his most intimate moves of life.[38]

A.-T. Tymieniecka has thus overturned the classic phenomenological priorities, introducing what C. S. Peirce called "the primary reality of philosopizing, its firstness: the reflective agent, who is self-organized and self- regulating".[39] He is independent of anything else because of his creative act with the fulgurating force of *Imaginatio creatrix*. This is presented as the Archimedean point of the human enterprise, instead of the intellective intentionality of the objectifying constitution.[40] The ensuing unveiling of the Logos of Life, as the intrinsic factor of life's origination and unfolding in innumerable rationalities, opens the pristine field of life to an ontopoietic investigation. The phenomenology/ontopoiesis of life is therefore opened as the ultimate level of reason: a primordial ontology, that brings innumerable novel insights, included the possibility of a new conception of time.

4. TIME AND ONTOPOIESIS

The re-integration of ontology into the original triple matrix of becoming, in which a) the human creative condition b) the self- individualization of life's being and c) the existential tentacles revealing the unity-of-everything-there-is- alive[41] all interact, also requires that time and temporality be torn out of their undue inscrutability and, inasmuch as they are placed back into the orbit of the being- life, the logos of which is revealed, that they be re-accepted into a structure of meaning able to comprehend them wholly. Now, time appears as "the main artery through which life's pulsating propensities flow, articulating themselves, intergenerating".[42] In fact, when consciousness takes on, as the Archimedean point for the beginning of research, not "the epistemic perspective", but the "creative/poietic perspective", the peculiar one to human creative condition, "the ordering of living beingness is unveiled at its core, qua the primogenital exfoliation of the logos of life". The phenomenology/ontopoiesis of life establishes itself "at the level of generation", where the becoming of living existence encounters "the constitutive epistemic-presentational manifestation".

In the arteries of becoming, these same beingnesses in their generative phases, as much of expansion as of deterioration and in the existential interchange with the vital enigmas of other beings, show themselves to be resident in the primogenital function of life: the self-individualization of beingness. This self-individualization of the living beings is sustained by the forces and dynamisms that now have become accessible, inasmuch as they are received, distributed and/or rejected by the operative nucleus of the "ontopoietic sequence", which comes on stage "with each life commencing" and acquires awareness with human life.[43] The conscious reflection, that is able to listen to this ontopoietic *logos* of life, can thus enter safely into the labyrinth of the living being, following the weave of self-individualization that life itself produces and that reveals, if one follows its "existential tentacles", the "unity-of-everything-there-is-alive". In such a conscious unfolding of the logos of life as ontopoiesis, the consideration of time is enormously deepened: the subjective and objective aspects of time are no longer isolated and the infinite succession and the infinite duration are no longer so distinct; time and temporality, no longer absolutized, once again find themselves located in their original and primogenital position, in that genuine unitary perspective that was lost speculatively and that now has been regained.[44]

"Life times itself!"[45], such is the discovery that the logos of life communicates to consciousness, when the latter gains awareness that it is a living being. The secret of the "ontopoietic unfolding of life", "the ultimate generation of beingness-in-becoming" has by now been revealed: "ontopoietic becoming times its advance at each and every one of its steps".[46] In this way, also "the universalizing and objectifying of movement, change and becoming that humanity has for millennia assumed in various ways as a means by which to regulate the flow of human existence amid confluence and interaction, yields a universally valid order of life's course, one accepted by all and one that assumes 'time' as 'real', whereas[...] it is just a hypothesis".[47]

"The grand, infinitely complex, flexible artery-in-progress of the constructive advance of life", which is time, encompasses "its relevant cosmic links" and "its reach for a portal to the transcendent aspirations of the human being". For this reason, we can now discover time

amid all the infinitely changing modalities with which the simplifying human mind categorizes the innumerable ways in which processes, events, functional units, etc. advance life (*chronos*) toward its nodal points of accomplishment (*kairoi*), as well as amid the specific circumstancial, as well as the essential, strivings (and the crowning significance of their accomplishment) at the very heart of the poiesis of life.[48]

With striking intuitive and conjectural capability[49], A.-T. Tymieniecka attains, in her phenomenology of life and of the human condition, or in her theory of the ontopoiesis of life, just such a new and broadened perspective on philosophy and meaning[50], in which "kronos" and "kairos", which elude ontological and scientific categorization, offer themselves in their originary modality.

A.-T. Tymieniecka acknowledges that Aristotle was the one who located the physical body and the notion of time "in the same time-motion and space-soul context": he saw time immersed in the physical processes, and generating itself with them[51], but could not detach it from the soul.[52] In fact, time consists of "now moments" that, involving a "before" and an "after", while they number the movement, require that there be "someone" to measure or count the space of time[53], and the soul represents such an "indispensable synthesizing principle for the measurement of time".[54] So indispensable that later Leibniz, even though he was a good Aristotelian and forcefully proposed both the monad as the crucial factor of life in the world, and the *vis viva* as the motor of intra-mundane nature, did not see fit to name it in the spatial-temporal matrix of every-possible-world.[55]

In the perspective of the phenomenology of life, the entire Aristotelian reflection on time is assumed and reinterpreted. In fact, on the one hand, the physical world here is inserted with full rights into that of life, while on the other hand, the ontopoietic horizon representing the most recent achievement of the *logos* of life[56], "reposes in itself, without turning to further points of reference".[57] In the revision of the meaning of time within the new vital context, A.-T. Tymieniecka draws from a neutral and universal concept of motion, which, however, already in Aristotle is seen very soon as oriented toward constructive movements in the cosmos and toward movements of life that are constructive and goal-oriented.[58] Already in the consideration of physical movement, "time and motion remain in reciprocal relation to each other when it comes to measurement"[59], conforming to the Aristotelian indication in *Physics*, 220b 14–22: "we measure not only motion by time but also time by motion, because they determine each other mutually: because time determines motion of which is the number and movement determines time". In the interpenetration of time and movement, there emerges a reference to the measurer; if it is the soul that measures, then there emerges the question of the criterion with which it operates. Does the soul create the measure? Or does it simply bring to completion the operation of measuring and counting? Perhaps the soul itself is time that creates its numbering? The question is not resolved by the idea of the soul "as an intellectual observer"; rather, it requires interpreting the soul as the "integral factor of all that moves, that is, of living beings and the life-processes in which they are entangled" and explaining its role in the "processes and progress of life, of 'coming to be and passing away'"[60].

At this point, A.-T. Tymieniecka's conception of life as self-individualizing-in-existence plays a fundamental role: in fact, according to this perspective, "it is through a crucial specific existential/ontological device that differentiates all life from non-life, that is, through the inward/outward oriented central 'agency' of the individualizing beingness, that life's ontopoietic processes are carried out"; therefore, it turns out phenomenolog-ically that we are not dealing with a "universal or universalised" generic motion, but with the specific movement of the *Bios*, which numbers time. This confirms the Aristotelian vision that assigned to each living being a soul, like "a system of articulation with a glimmering of consciousness". Leibniz also observed that even from the simplest forms of life, the soul shows that it possesses a capacity for synchronization.

However, in the ontopoietic context of life, it emerges that the soul does not only play "a counting role": it does not merely observe the temporal succession; rather, exercising "a living function" of organizing, articulating and dynamically operating, the soul introduces distinct phases into the temporal process and acts as "an articulator of motions into their successive, concurrent and telic knots, a configurator of phases and culminating-points of accomplishment".[61] In the degree to which we can avail ourselves of the meaning horizon of the ontopoiesis of life, we can proceed beyond Aristotle and Leibniz and grasp the soul, that gathers all the life-processing functions and through them articulates the constructive progress of life, as the concrete principle of life itself, as promoting through life's functioning the movement through which time is numbered. The soul, which Tymieniecka has conceived of as

a stretching over the entire territory of the self- individualizing processes of life, comprises then all the being's circuits of energy and forces, all stirrings, moves, operations, and processes, from the simplest vital ones, through those psychic and gregarious ones orchestrated by the entelechial principle of vital significance, up to the emergent Human Condition, which with its creative orchestration ushers in freedom and the specifically human significance of life.[62]

Correspondingly, in the degree to which the soul is identified as the concrete principal of life itself, it also turns out that

time, being originally and primordially coeval and congenital with the constructive deployment of life, and hence to be distinguished among the relevancies, both those cosmic and those abstractly rational, participates in two lines of a combined strategy of life, and hence has one twofold modality, that of *kronos* and *kairos*.[63]

5. KRONOS AND KAIROS

However, if time and movement are functions of a progress that constructs life and if time appears in the crystallization of the motility proper to the vital functioning, then we can no longer identify temporality principally with succession, as has happened till now. In the constructive phases in which life crystallizes itself, in fact, that is, in the phases of generation, of growth, of fruition, of decline, and of extinction, in measuring the interval of time it is not enough to identify "a direct cause-effect nexus in which the lapse of time is to be apprehended as a sequence in which each occurrence or event would have a clearly traceable cause and be in turn the cause of the next occurrence, change, transformation". "The vital process of *bios* do not proceed through we can only abstractly distil from the entanglements of the functions which carry them on"! On the contrary,

the ontopoietic course of life proceeds through **the confluence** of numerous operations, processes, moves, stimuli and it is this confluence to perform the transformative or sensoro- motor operations. This confluence itself crystallizes in a multiple *motio*. Hence it crystallizes in time, which lends it a "moment" of fulfillment, the measure of the step onward in the process of growth or decline.[64]

In order to measure the interval of time in the ontopoietic course of life, it is therefore necessary to use the modality of "**confluence**". In fact,

each constructive advance of individualizing life (e.g., the opening of the petals of a flower, the rise of the sap of a tree in early spring, the cross pollination of flowering plum trees effected by insects . . .) is a result of a bundle of results – of numerous operations and processes, **each of them crystallizing segments of time that flow together to work a change,** a transformation, a moment of constructive progress.

Consequently, whether or not consciousness registers it, "life–bios–is timing itself. It measures itself, and thus its temporal spread by its natural constructive advance in the cyclic cosmic order".[65] It is not time that orders; time is not added to the construction factors from outside. The movements of the vital operations that begin in the latent organic forces, emerging from other apparently not organic forces, or movements of a virus that enters in a cell to reproduce itself, all these temporally regulate themselves from within and their advance marks and measures the temporal process itself. In this way, the measure of movement—of organic/sensorial/psychic movement and that of time that crystallizes in it—springs from the movements within the sentient and living soul of the living being.

On the other hand, this crystallization, universally constructive/destructive of time, takes place in virtue of the more radical self-constructive tendency of life, that expresses itself in a self-individualizing progress, supported by an "entelechial principle of life", from which emanates an "entelechial framework" that, like a pre-existent model in the germinal state, presides over the constructive advancement of life toward self-realization. In this ontopoietic unfolding, every juncture of development and every step forward participates in a broader construction, in an interwoven and interconnected network that flows from different functional sectors but in which all the parts cooperate with each other. Each operative confluence, which constitutes a segment of the constructive advance, is constructive because, even while it is not taken for granted, it appears oriented by a final principle, toward a successive stage that has been prepared as a task to bring to completion with respect to the previous stages of the process.[66] This positive and constructive deployment of the operative moments to the point of confluence is what determines in temporality the arrival of the "propitious moment"[67] that is to be understood as "the confluent moment of the constructive mode".

In conclusion, if we identify "the long winding operations and processes of timing" with the notion of "kronos", we subject them to the simplifying effect of the impartial observation of human intelligence, which reduces time to succession or continuity of happenings and events. In order to grasp "istances of 'kairos'", we must focus on "the mulitifaceted timing of the constructive achievements that punctuate life's progress". Thus if kronos indicates the order and the sequence of life, moments of kairos are "life-constructive fulfilments marking ontopoietic progress, and their occurrence within the play of favourable and contrary conditions". Starting from these experiences of living temporalization, we also deal with the complicated problem of cosmic time and mechanical temporality.[68] Since we have no evidence of "movement timing itself" in the cosmos, we approach these moves and processes as "stripped-down versions of the timing of life" and so posit for it an abstract line of succession, seeing only lifeless mechanical motion. In this way, we reach both cosmic time and the time of mechanical movement, and equally, the uniform abstraction "of all of time's qualitative life-coordinates" in the measurement of time with the hourglass, the clock, and the metronome. "We empty the prototype of living time of all its genetic content, leaving a mere skeleton".[69]

6. HUMAN HISTORY

The reign of *Bios* is coextensive with temporalization itself, placed as it is between the two extremes of the need for the constructive entelechial principle and of the chance of the external conditions of the unfolding of the principle. Kronos and kairos are the arteries of life and take form in this oscillation.

A gradual change intervenes in this situation in the moment in which the animal species emerge, in the course of evolution, in the complexity of their forms and their growing "flexibility", in adhering to the internal request and the external offerings to oppose adversities and seize opportunities. This flexibility reaches its culmination in the emergence of a new category of life, that of human freedom. In fact, it is between freedom and arbitrariness that human self-individualization oscillates. The timing of life's self-unfolding, its self-interpretative course, here undergoes several transformations, with time as *kairos* coming into its own. *Kairos* here assumes original, uniquely significant roles with respect to the specifically human significance of life, its projecting of new avenues, history, and the personal quest for transcendence.

In effect, it is in the crystallization of the human creative condition that the entelechial decodification, up to this point relatively rigid, of the law of life in the progressive unfolding of the species in evolution, attains the flexible, inventive, incessantly transformable progress of the "free will" or of the imagination of the human being. In this way, *kronos* and *kairos* take on new modalities and new roles. Temporalization itself passes through the innumerable interrogatives concerning the entire sphere of human life in its universality: freedom, coercion, arbitrariness, order and disorder, monotony and revolt, peace and crisis in personal and social life. On the one hand, there are still the regular and daily activities and gestures, while on the other, there is the incessant flow of aware and personal psychic life, made up of stimuli, sensations, emotions, motivations, and conscious acts, all variably linked together. The process of human self-individualization defines itself by striving for accomplishment: tasks, goals, and ideals, projected inventively by the human creator emerge, in fact, as the fruit of the creative human re-orientation in the surrounding world and thus pose themselves in contrast to the organic and vital sensorial movements constructive of life that were previously given.[70] Thus, even though due credit should be given to the progress of the evolution of the species from the entelechial flexibility to the exercise of freedom, at the point in which the creative orchestration of the specifically human emerging function establishes itself, the crystallization of the creative function in the human condition remains the principle example of the emergence of the unique temporalization that is the *kairos*.[71] Within the new creative functional orchestration, in which human will seems to rise on the wings of the *Imaginatio Creatrix* above all natural urges, we see introduced "the primordial moves of the human spirit", "the thrust toward the other", "the will to undertake" and lastly "the deliberative inventive quest". These functions activate themselves in the sphere of the evaluative framework, that installs the human creative condition in the esthetic, moral and intellectual perspective and open to the specifically human evaluation of life. In addition, these factors of the human dynamic operate in the limits that the world of life projects in structures and rules: thus the human being, while striving to always go beyond, because of the creative push, maintains his creative and inventive drive in the open but not absolutely unlimited confines of the human, following a direction that it fundamentally finds within the confines of the system of life itself.[72]

With the advent of the human condition, we witness the emergence of an extraordinary sphere of expansion of the work of self-individualization and self-interpretation toward the interior and toward the exterior of the living being. However, interior life, the life of experience and consciousness, manifests a temporalization of its own, because *kronos* and *kairos* become more acutely defined in our sensations, feelings, thoughts, and judgements and in their concatenations. In particular, temporalization of the interior aware self-interpretive course inserts itself in the model of *kronos*, inasmuch as the acts not only succeed each other, but in the proceeding, form new modalities of experience that can also be seen as monotonous. But, "when animated by hidden inner stirrings toward ventures, projects and aspirations that are to be actualised in the external realm of life, inward acts acquire the "exciting" rhythms of kairic striving for accomplishment".

It is thus that the experience of human life in its interiority and in its external activity are transported by two connected arteries: in fact, they are marked by *kronos*, "the everyday tacit carrying on of repetitive assignments for life's maintenance" and by the "kairic rhythms of urgency, promise, expectation, ecstatic hope, and final attainment of goals". These achievements require the right proportions, the right measures, the right occasions, and advance in the creative and constructive progress of peoples, social groups, cultures, and nations.[73] Also on the level of the history of human society there is therefore an advance of both *kronos* and *kairos*: it proceeds through the succession of daily affairs, regular tasks, and goals, while indispensable daily progress is marked by the realizations of *kairos*.[74] In the sphere of such a socially lived human temporality, there arises "fabulation", "the response of imagination that is triggered by the urge to understand, a response that goes further than the factual timing of reality". It is launched "narrating" real events and continues "telling stories, myths, and sagas" that transmit "ancestral wisdom".[75] This fabulation, or imaginative temporalization of life by human beings, finds place for the profundity of the personal being of each, and from here emerge "the communicative networks of sharing-in-life".[76]

University of Macerata
Translated by Sheila Beatty–University of Camerino.

NOTES

[1] Cf.: M. Heidegger, *Sein und Zeit*, § 8, in: *Gesamtausgabe*, hrsg. V. F. W. Herrmann, Bd. II, Klostermann, Frankfurt am Main 1977. English transl. by J. Stambaugh, *Being and Time*, State University of New York Press, Albany 1996. P. Chiodi, in the Introduction to the italian edition of *Sein und Zeit* (*Essere e tempo,* Longanesi, Milano 1970, pp. iii–iv), also underlines the doubly incomplete character of the work, which not only lacks the second, historical part, converging in any case in other Heideggerian inquiries (for instance: M. Heidegger, *Der Begriff der Zeit. Vortrag vor der Marburger Theologenschaft–Juli 1924*, hrsg. von H. Tietjen, Niemeyer, Tübingen 1989), but above all lacks the third section of the first part, in which he should have discussed the problem of the meaning of being in general, conclusive in terms of the issues of "the problem of the being of Dasein" and of "the problem of the meaning of the being of Dasein", dealt with in the first two sections. To pursue this topic further, see: A. Fabris, *Essere e tempo di Heidegger. Introduzione alla lettura*, (*Being and Time of Heidegger. Reader's Introduction*) Carocci, Roma 2000.

[2] Cf.: A. Augustinus, *Confessiones*, in *Corpus Christianorum. Series Latina XXVII*, ed. L. Verheijen, Turnhout 1981, l. XI, 14: "Quid est ergo tempus? Si nemo ex me quaerat, scio; si quaerenti explicare velim, nescio". In this regard: J. Quinn o.s.a., *The concept of time*, Augustinianum, Roma, 1965. L. Ruggiu (ed. by), *Filosofia del tempo*, (*Philosophy and Time*) Mondadori, Milano 1998. L. Ruggiu, *Tempo e anima in S. Agostino*, (*Time and the Soul in S. Augustine*) in: L. Perissinotto (ed. by), *Agostino e il destino dell'Occidente*, (*Augustine and the Destiny of the West*) Carocci, Roma 2000, p. 79–118.

[3] The theme of the whole is of Hegelian origin. Cf.: G. F. W. Hegel, *Phänomenologie des Geistes*, in *Gesammelte Werke*, hrsg v. W. Bonsepien und R. Heede, Bd. XI, Meiner, Hamburg, 1980. Tr. by J. B. Baillie, *Phenomenology of Mind*, Harper & Row, New York, 1967, *Preface*,

§ 20: "The truth is the whole". Recently the paradigm of philosophy as type of entire and integral knowing has been set back into play in Italy in the ambit of the philosophical school that through G. Bontadini descends to V. Melchiorre and his students, including F. Totaro. Cf.: F. Totaro, *La tensione all'intero e le ragioni del filosofare*, (*The Tension of the Whole and the Reasons for Philosophizing*) in AA. VV., *Lo statuto epistemologico della filosofia*, (*The Epistemological Statute of Philosophy*) Morcelliana, Brescia 1989, pp. 182–188. Id., *Interalità dell'essere, prospettiva e misura della prassi*, (*The Wholeness of Being, Perspective and Measure of Praxis*) in G. Nicolaci – P. Polizzi, *Radici metafisiche della filosofia. Scritti per Nunzio Incardona*, (*Metaphysical Roots of Philosophy. Writings for Nunzio Incardona*) Tilgher, Genova, 2002, pp. 161–168. Id., *Per una metafisica dell'inattuale. Riflessioni di un discepolo della prima ora*, (*For a Metaphysics of the Non-Current. Reflections of a First Generation Disciple*) in: F. Botturi, F. Totaro, C. Vigna (ed. by), *La persona e i nomi dell'essere. Scritti di filosofia in onore di Virgilio Melchiorre*, (*The Person and the Names of Being. Writings of Philosophy in Honor of Virgilio Melchiorre*) Vita e Pensiero, Milano 2002, vol. I, pp. 205–219. Id., *Etica dell'essere persona e nuova cittadinanza*, (*Ethics of Being a Person and New Citizenship*) in: F. Botturi (ed. by), *Le ragioni dell'etica. Natura del bene e problema fondativo*, (*The Reasons of Ethics. The Nature of the Good and the Problem of Foundation*) Vita e Pensiero, Milano 2005, pp. 41–64.

[4]   Cf.: A.-T. Tymieniecka, *Life's primogenital timing. Time projected by the dynamic articulation of the ontogenesis*, in: "Analecta Husserliana", L (1997), p. 3. Even in the sciences, the regressive temptation is always lying in ambush, even though camouflaged in progressivism. Cfr.: J. Barbour, *The end of time. The next revolution in physics*, Oxford University Press, Oxford 2000.

[5]   E. Husserl dedicated numerous studies to the theme of time, some still unpublished. Cfr.: E. Husserl, *Zur Phänomenologie des inneren Zeitbewusstseins (1893–1917)*, ed. by R. Boehm, in: "Husserliana" 10, Nijhoff, Den Haag 1966. Id., *Texte zur Phänomenologie des inneren Zeitbewusstseins (1893–1917)*, ed. by R. Bernet, "Philosophische Bibliothek", LXVII, Meiner, Hamburg 1985. Id., *Die Bernauer Manuskripte über das Zeitbewusstsein*, 1917/1918, ed. by R. Bernet and D. Lohmar, Dordrecht, Kluwer 2001. In addition: G. Brand, *Welt, Ich und Zeit. Nach unveröffentlichen Manuskripten E. Husserls*, Nijhoff, Den Haag 1965. M. C. Franza, *Fenomenologia e tempo* (*Phenomenology and Time*), Edizioni dell'Ateneo, Roma 1982.

[6]   Cf.: P. Ricoeur, 1: *L' intrigue et le récit historique* / 2: *La configuration dans la récit de fiction* / 3. *Le temps raconté*, Editions du Seuil, Paris 1991.

[7]   M. Scheler, *Erkenntnis und Arbeit*, in: *Gesammelte Werke*, ed. by M. Scheler and M. Frings, Francke, Bern-Munich 1960, VIII, "Die Wissensformen und die Gesellschaft", p. 208. Cfr. also: D. Verducci, *Il segmento mancante. Percorsi di filosofia del lavoro*, (*The Missing Segment. Itineraries of the Philosophy of Work*) Carocci, Roma 2003, p. 51.

[8]   Tymieniecka, *Life's primogenital timing*, cit., p. 3.

[9]   *Ibidem.*

[10]   We refer to the convergence of Nietzsche and Scheler on the idea of a "God in becoming" that substitues the static God of traditional theism. Cf.: G. Cusinato, *Katharsis. La morte dell'ego e il divino come apertura al mondo in Max Scheler*, (*Catharsis. The Death of the Ego and the Divine as Openness to the World in Max Scheler*) ESI, Napoli, 1999; Id., *Scheler. Il dio in divenire*, (*Scheler. The God in Becoming*) Messaggero, Padova 2002. Such progress in the theological conception also entails advancement in the comprehension of time. Nietzsche proposes the expression "God in becoming" in § 238 of *Human, All Too Human*, treating it as a hypothesis to verify. Cf.: F. Nietzsche, *Menschliches Allzumenschliches I*, in: *Nietzsche Werke. Kritische Gesamtausgabe*, ed. by G. Colli and M. Montinari, IV$_2$ 1963. Tr. by R. J. Hollingdale: *Human,*

All Too Human, Cambridge University Press, Cambridge 1986. Scheler, in part IV of *Idealismus-Realismus* (in: *Gesammelte Werke*, cit., IX, "Späte Schriften", 1975, pp. 245–253), commenting on *Sein und Zeit* of Heidegger, demonstrates that he has attained the notion of dynamic eternity set within becoming, hence on the level of absolute or ethical time and in contrast to physical, quantifiable time. Cf.: M. Scheler, *Schriften aus dem Nachlass. Band II: Erkenntnislehre und Metaphysik*, in: *Gesammelte Werke*, cit., XI, 1979, pp. 207, 208, 213–214.

[11] This is the intent with which A.-T. Tymieniecka begins the publication of the 3 volumes of the series *Logos and Life*. They are: Id., *Logos and Life. Creative Experience and the Critique of Reason*, Book 1, "Analecta Husserliana", XXIV (1988); Id., *Logos and Life. The Three Movements of the Soul*, Book 2, "Analecta Husserliana", XXV (1988); Id., *Logos and Life. The Passions of the Soul and the Elements in the Onto-poiesis of Culture*, Book 3, "Analecta Husserliana", XXVIII (1990). Cf. in addition: Id., *The Creative Experience and the New Critique of Reason*, in *Japanese Philosophy*, "Analecta Husserliana", VIII (1979), pp. 205–229.

[12] Tymieniecka, *Logos and Life. The Passions of the Soul. . .*, cit., p. 9.

[13] A.-T. Tymieniecka, *The pragmatic test of the ontopoiesis of life*, in: "Analecta Husserliana" LXXXIV (2005), p. xiii.

[14] A.-T. Tymieniecka, *The logos of phenomenology and the phenomenology of logos*, in : "Analecta Husserliana" LXXXVIII (2005), p. xiii.

[15] Ibid., p. xiv.

[16] Ibid., p. xv.

[17] Ibid., p. xiv. Cfr. : E. Fink, *Sixth Cartesian Meditation: The Idea of a Transcendental Theory of Method*, tr. R. Bruzina, Bloomington: Indiana University Press, 1995. R. Holmes observes that "the work was written as a continuation of Husserl's five *Cartesian Meditations*: the *Sixth Cartesian Meditation* was drafted by Eugene Fink and then worked on and critiqued by Husserl. It is subtitled *A Transcendental Theory of Method* and was intended–as R. Bruzina, *Introduction* to Fink, *Sixth Cartesian Meditation*, cit., pp. xlviii–xlix notes–to show that the methodological question in phenomenology, in the 'radical self-reflection' that phenomenology puts into practice, the question of the nature of the move back to the *beginning* beyond which questioning cannot go, is ultimately going to involve the central substantive difficulty of the nature of the difference and identity between human and transcendental subjectivity, between the subjectivity that lives and subsists with the world and the subjectivity that constitutes the world and all in it. This is a question of how a phenomenologist can explicate a subjectivity that both belongs in the world and yet constitutes objectivity and its world. Fink's answer is to the effect that to explicate the sense of world and subjectivity within it (again from the translators introduction) "requires a dimension of reflective analysis in phenomenology that works beyond the strict limits of the intuitional giving of something in its very self [*Selbstgebung*]" (*Ibid.*, p. lviii). That is, it seems to require we violate the fundamental principle of phenomenology to not accept "any judgment as scientific *that I have not derived from evidence*, from 'experiences' in which the affairs and affair-complexes in question are present to me as *they themselves*" (E. Husserl, *Cartesian Meditations: An Introduction to Phenomenology*, tr. D. Cairns, Dordrecht: Nijhoff Publishers, 1977, p. 13)", R. Holmes, *The sixth Meditation*, in: R. Feist and W. Sweet eds., *Husserl and Stein*, Washington D. C., RVP, 2004, Chapter 3. Cfr. G. van Kerckoven, *Mundanisierung und Individuation bei Edmund Husserl und Eugen Fink : die sechste cartesianische Meditation und ihr Einsatz*, Würzburg, Königshausen & Neumann, 2003.

[18] Tymieniecka, *The logos of phenomenology. . .*, cit., p. xxxv.

[19] *Ibidem.*

[20] Ibid., p. xv.

[21] A.-T. Tymieniecka, *Impetus and Equipoise in the Life Strategies of Reason*, "Logos and Life", Book IV, Dordrecht: Kluwer Academic Publishers, 2000/ "Analecta Husserliana", LXX (2000), p. xxxiv.

[22] Tymieniecka, *Life's primogenital timing*, cit., p. 4.

[23] Cf.: G. Rametta, *Il concetto di tempo: eternità e* Darstellung *speculativa nel pensiero di Hegel* (*The concept of time: Eternity and Speculative* Darstellung *in Hegel's Thought*), F. Angeli, Milano 1989.

[24] Tymieniecka, *Impetus and Equipoise*, cit, p. 98.

[25] Ibid., p. xxxiv.

[26] Ibid., p. 14. The reference is to C. S. Peirce, *Evolutionary Love*, in: M. R. Cohen (ed. by), *Chance, Love and Logic. Philosophical Papers by the late Charles S. Peirce*, New York, Harcourt: Brace & Co., 1923.

[27] Tymieniecka, *Impetus and Equipoise*, cit., p. 99.

[28] Ibid., p. 100.

[29] Ibid., p. xxxiv.

[30] Ibid., p. 102.

[31] Tymieniecka, *Life's primogenital timing*, cit., p. 4.

[32] Tymieniecka, *Impetus and Equipoise*, cit, p. 99.

[33] A.-T. Tymieniecka, *Tractatus Brevis. First Principles of the Metaphysics of Life Charting the Human Condition: Man's Creative Act and the Origin of Rationalities*, "Analecta Husserliana" XXI (1986), p. 3.

[34] A.-T. Tymieniecka, *Logos and Life. Creative Experience...*, cit., pp. 25–26.

[35] Ibid., p. 7.

[36] Tymieniecka, *Impetus and Equipoise*, cit., pp. 13–22: "The Ciphering of the Inner Working of Life and the Full Manifestation of the Logos of Life"; "The Primal Ciphering of the Logos of Life"; "The Creative Vision and Ciphering".

[37] M. Kronegger-A.-T. Tymieniecka (ed. by), *Life. The human quest for an ideal*, in: "Analecta Husserliana", XLIX (1996), p. 15.

[38] Ibid., pp. 4–5.

[39] Tymieniecka, *Impetus and Equipoise*, cit., p. 14.

[40] A.-T. Tymieniecka, *Die phänomenologische Selbstbesinnung* (I), in: "Analecta Husserliana", I (1971), pp. 2–7. In this regard: D. Verducci, *Anna-Teresa Tymieniecka. La trama vivente dell'essere*, (Anna-Teresa Tymieniecka. *The Living Weave of Being*), in: A. Ales Bello e F. Brezzi (ed. by), *Il filo(sofare) di Arianna. Percorsi del pensiero femminile nel Novecento*, (*The Philo(sophizing) of Arianna. Itineraries of FeminineThought in the Twentieth Century*) Mimesis, Milano 2001, pp. 66–68. Cfr. anche: D. Verducci, *The Human Creative Condition Between Autopoiesis and Ontopoiesis in theThought of Anna-Teresa Tymieniecka*, in: "Analecta Husserliana", LXXXIX (2004), pp. 4–5.

[41] Tymieniecka, *Life's primogenital timing*, cit., p. 5.

[42] Ivi, p. 4.

[43] Tymieniecka, *The pragmatic test of the ontopoiesis of life*, cit., p. xxiii.

[44] Tymieniecka, *Life's primogenital timing*, cit., p. 5.

[45] Tymieniecka, *Logos' timing of Life – Fabulating history*, in: "Analecta Husserliana" XC (2005), p. xiii.

[46] *Ibidem.*

[47] *Ibidem.*

[48] Tymieniecka, *Life's primogenital timing*, cit., p. 4.

[49] Cf.: D. Verducci, *To reason as living men. Conjecture as the inferential supporting framework of the human condition according to the meta-ontopoiesis of Anna-Teresa Tymieniecka*, in: *Phenomenological Inquiry*, 27 (2003), pp. 63–76.

[50] Cf.: A.-T. Tymieniecka, *The first principles of the Metaphysics of Life*, in: "Analecta Husserliana", XXI (1986).

[51] Aristotle, *Physics* III, 201.

[52] Aristotle, *Metaphysics* 1071b 7.

[53] Aristotle, *Physics* IV, 223a 27. See also: E. Cavagnaro, *Aristotele e il tempo. Analisi di Physica, 4, 10–14* (*Aristotle and the time. Analyse on Physics, 4, 10–14*), Bologna, Il Mulino 2002.

[54] Tymieniecka, *Life's primogenital timing*, cit., p. 5.

[55] Ibid., p. 6.

[56] Cf.: A.-T. Tymieniecka, *The Ontopoiesis of Life as a New Philosophical Paradigm*, in: "Phenomenological Inquiry" 22 (1998), pp. 12–59.

[57] Tymieniecka, *Life's primogenital timing*, cit., p. 4.

[58] Ibid., p. 6.

[59] Ibid., pp. 6–7.

[60] Ibid., p. 7.

[61] *Ibidem*.

[62] Ibid., p. 8.

[63] *Ibidem*.

[64] Ibid., p. 9.

[65] *Ibidem*.

[66] Ibid., p. 10.

[67] Ibid., p. 11.

[68] See also: S. Toulmin-J. Goodfield, *The discovery of time*, Harmondsworth, Penguin 1965.

[69] Tymieniecka, *Life's primogenital timing*, cit., p. 12.

[70] Ibid., p. 13.

[71] Ibid., pp. 13–14.

[72] Ibid., p. 14.

[73] Ibid., p. 16.

[74] Ibid., p. 16.

[75] Tymieniecka, *Logos' Timing of Life...*, cit., p. xvii.

[76] Ibid., p. xviii

SECTION II

MICHAEL F. ANDREWS

EDMUND HUSSERL: THE GENESIS AND ORIGIN OF TIME

1. INTRODUCTION

The phenomenological interpretation of time requires a special task, inasmuch as it has no particular "entity" for its theme. The theme of temporality, phenomenologically speaking, of course, is transcendental phenomenology, that is, the structure of every condition of possibility of knowing. Consequently, the question of the origin and genesis of time, which appeared in various forms throughout Husserl's thirty-year project (roughly, from 1900–1930), is primarily concerned with apprehensions of time. These are the lived experiences in which the temporal in the Objective sense appears. Right from the start, however, we need to be clear about the proper object of our investigation. By the origin and genesis of time, Husserl does not mean Objective time as such. He is clear on this point, especially in his 1905 lectures, later published as *The Phenomenology of Internal-Time consciousness*: "One cannot discover the least trace of Objective [that is, chronological or "cosmic" time] through phenomenological analysis. The 'primordial temporal field' is by no means a part of Objective time."[1] The question that haunts our inquiry, then, is the following: Does the phenomenon of time give us the totality of the structure of its being? Or does the origin and genesis of time lead us towards apprehending that the whole of time in principle can *not* be secured? In other words, how might Husserl's description of the origin of time expose the basic structure of every possible experience? In what sense does a description of the genesis of time necessitate a return to the phenomenological data of which everything that is experienced consists phenomenologically?

2. THE QUESTION OF TIME AS THE SUBJECT OF HUSSERL'S WORK

Husserl himself articulated this paradox in various ways throughout his professional career. From as early as the *Logical Investigations* to as

113

A-T. *Tymieniecka (ed.)*,
Timing and Temporality in Islamic Philosophy and Phenomenology of Life, 113–127.
© 2007 *Springer*.

late as his famous *Encyclopaedia Britannica* article, the problem of the
genesis and origin of time remained central to Husserl's thought. Even the
question of phenomenological psychology and its relationship to transcendental phenomenology should be seen in relation to the problem of the genesis
of time. This is especially so in light of the context of contemporary discussions amongst many German intellectuals in the early decades of the twentieth
century. We may note, for example, Einstein's publication of the theory of
general relativity in 1915 alongside Husserl's introduction to transcendental
phenomenology in *Ideas*, first published just two years earlier. In *Ideas*, of
course, Husserl attempts to grapple with the problem of time in light of the
transcendental structure of consciousness. In the *Encyclopaedia* article as well,
written over the course of five successive drafts between early September
1927 and February 1928,[2] Husserl again investigates the theme of transcendental phenomenology by way of "the phenomenology of the perception of
Bodies." In this essay, Husserl notes that the phenomenological reduction
"reveals the Phenomena of actual internal experience," an obvious reminder
of his theory of internal time consciousness first promulgated in his 1905
lectures.

In contrast to psychological time, phenomenological time reveals all
of the essential Forms constraining psychical existence. Because transcendental phenomenology is a more mature theory of the *a priori*, eidetic
phenomenology stands as the *sine qua non* of psychological phenomenology.
Empirical objectivity includes all transcendences, including the lived and
experienced content of Objective time and Objective space. Hence, a
phenomenological description of the genesis and origin of time must begin
by placing a bracket [*epoché*] around the Objective world of real things and
events. Husserl's dogged emphasis (from post-1913 *Ideas* onward) concerning
the necessity of the transcendental reduction thus heralds a bold return
to several problems that were left unresolved in his earlier 1905 lectures
concerning internal time-consciousness.

It is my argument that *Ideas* and the *Encyclopaedia* article, along with the
1905 lectures on internal time-consciousness, betray a vast ocean of complex
insights with which Husserl was continuing to wrestle long after he was
first introduced to the problem of the origin of time by Brentano. In his
lectures on internal time-consciousness, Husserl first described the analysis of
time-consciousness as "an age-old crux of descriptive psychology and theory
of knowledge." Turning first to Book XI of St. Augustine's *Confessions*
and then to Brentano's unpublished analyses, Husserl tellingly likened the
problem of time as involving the most "extraordinary difficulties, contradic-

tions, and entanglements."[3] It is to Husserl's phenomenological explication of the genesis and origin of time that grounds the focus of our inquiry.

3. THE EXCLUSION [*AUSSCHALTUNG*] OF OBJECTIVE [*OGJEKTIVEN*] TIME

Early in his 1905 lectures, Husserl states that his overall task is to present a phenomenological (as opposed to merely psychological) analysis of time-consciousness. At the outset of his project, Husserl thus makes an important distinction between "phenomenological time" and "objective" (or "cosmic") time. On the one hand, objective time includes all temporal distinctions, namely, all material and mental things with their physical and mental properties. Objectivity entails everything that exists in the empirical sense and which can be qualified by chronological measurement. This encompasses the whole of our experience, including events, relations, situations, spatial and temporal forms of appearances, sensory data, etc. Because Objective time includes individual Objectivity in general, Husserl notes that temporal Objectivity is constituted in subjective time-consciousness and, therefore, belongs in the context of empirical objectivity.

On the other hand, the phenomenological content of lived experiences of time—what Husserl calls *Zeiterlebnisse*—necessitates the exclusion [*Ausschaltung*] of every lived experience, including lived experiences of the perception and representation [*Vorstellung*] of time itself. What Husserl means by phenomenological time, then, is a necessary form or process that in effect binds experiences with experiences. Following Brentano, Husserl designates "phenomenological time" as a living stream of experience [*Erlebnis*]. However, although every temporal and spatial experience must be constituted in terms of comprising both a beginning and an end, the stream itself remains always intact.

Let us take, for example, an experience of "joy." While the phenomenality of the experience-itself can be bracketed and investigated in light of its eidetic structure, nevertheless the stream of conscious experience remains always intact. Experiences of joy rise and dissipate depending on many factors, for instance, duration, intensity, and quality. But whereas psychologism naively takes the object of joy as a given entity, that is, as the more or less presupposed point of departure for every inquiry, we need to take into consideration the constitution of the object by which joy (and every other experience) is constituted. The subject of our inquiry, then, is not the empirical experience of joy (or sadness, or whatever), but the immanent time of the flow of consciousness.

What Husserl seems to propose is the notion that internal time consciousness *itself* presupposes the immanent flow of that which makes all experience possible in the first place, namely, phenomenological time as the transcendental structure of all conscious activity. Hence, the living stream of experience [*Erlebnis*] *endures* apart from all temporal signs and data, regardless of how such temporal data is perceived or sensed. What changes is not the phenomenological datum through whose empirical apperception the relation to Objective time is constituted, but, rather, the appearance of duration, intensity, and quality as such. What remains constant, then, is the immanent time of inner experience:

> What we accept... is not the existence of a world-time, the existence of a concrete duration, and the like, but time and duration appearing as such. These, however, are absolute data which it would be senseless to call into question. To be sure, we also assume an existing time; this, however, is not the time of the world of experience but the *immanent time* of the flow of consciousness.[4]

The problem of the genesis of time is stated for Husserl in terms of immanence, and is not limited to his 1905 lectures. The problem resounds as well almost ten years later in Husserl's "discovery" of the transcendental Ego in *Ideas*. As temporal being, every experience is an experience of the pure, or transcendental, Ego. Therefore, the possibility exists that the Ego may direct its pure personal glance to this experience or to that experience, it may grasp it as really being, or as enduring in phenomenological time. Nevertheless, what gets posited as a result of the transcendental reduction's exclusion of Objective time is what concerns the essential being of the object under scrutiny. According to Husserl, the discovery of the transcendental reduction functions as a sort of anticipatory hermeneutic. The world does not merely appear. Rather, the world must be apprehended by consciousness through an interpretive act. In fact, it is the very act of interpretive apprehension that constitutes the world *qua* "world."

Whereas the theory of intentionality describes how the world is given *qua* world, it does not adequately account for how time is a process or operation by which things get constituted at all. In effect, every experience comes to consciousness in two ways. First, consciousness grasps every possible or actual experience under the rubric of temporal succession. This means that the experience is constituted on account of the total unity of the temporal stream of consciousness that makes such experience possible in the first place. Since the feature of this stream is to be carried off into an object, every experience *qua* experience is constituted by an essentially self-contained organization of experiences. This means, however, that not only the object *but the temporal stream of consciousness-itself* is a constituted unity, a process. There is no "identity pole" around which temporal succession is tied or strung along. All there is, is the process, or flux, or stream of inner experience.

Second, experiences are grasped under the rubric of simultaneity, and this raises the question of the "essence" of time. No experience simply falls out of the sky in a neatly wrapped package. Rather, the meaning (and, hence, the experience) of every experience is constituted by a present moment of experience that has about it a fringe of experiences that transcends the primordiality of the Now-form of the absolute present. This fringe of experiences cannot be wholly separated from the primordial experience itself. Why not? According to Husserl, this is because the fringe of experiences is *itself* the condition of possibility of the coming-into-presence of the Now. Following Brentano's lead, what Husserl seems to be saying is that temporal unities of experience constitute the one primordial fringe of the pure Ego, that is, its total primordial Now-consciousness. As Husserl notes, the question of the essence of time leads back to the question of the "origin" of time, now grasped according to its greater implications:

The question of the origin is oriented toward the primitive forms of the consciousness of time in which the primitive differences of the temporal are constituted intuitively and authentically as the originary [*originären*] sources of all certainties relative to time.... With this last question we are asking about the primordial material of sensation out of which arises Objective intuition of space and time in the human individual and even in the species. We are indifferent to the question of the empirical genesis. What interest us are lived experiences as regards their objective sense and their descriptive content . . . We are concerned with reality only insofar as it is intended, represented, intuited, or conceptually thought. With reference to the problem of time, this implies that we are interested in lived experiences of time.[5]

4. THE TEMPORAL CHARACTER OF PERCEPTION

In order to investigate the *a priori* genesis or origin of time, we must bring an investigation of the essential constitution of time-consciousness to bear on the content of every act and apprehension. In *Ideas*, Husserl notes that every experience that enters as an object into the focus of possible reflection possesses the particular temporal character of the Now-form, described above. Otherwise, no object could be given or taken *qua* object *qua* consciousness. This is what Husserl really means by intentionality, namely, that what is "given" to experience is a purely immanent description of what is given in inner intuition or inner experience. Intentionality characterizes consciousness in a "pregnant" sense of the term. It describes the whole stream of experience as a single stream of consciousness, a unity of one consciousness.

Intentionality is a manifestation of a unique peculiarity of experiences, it necessitates that every conscious act is a consciousness *of* something.

Similarly, every perceiving is a perceiving of something and every judging is a judging of something. Whether valuing, wishing, acting, hoping, etc., the stream of lived experience constitutes the unity of such a radical process. In this way, we may define the origin of time as a return of the conscious stream to itself. In terms of transcendental phenomenology, this means that the pure (or transcendental) Ego is not an object at all, but rather the totality of perceptions. Since the pure Ego may even include objects whose "reality" has been suspended, the traits of the consciousness of this pure Ego must be true in *any* world, whether real or imagined.

Of course, Husserl does not allude to an ego, whether pure or empirical, at all in his lectures on internal time-consciousness. In this sense, we might say that Jean-Paul Sarte is closer to the earlier Husserl than the later Husserl is to himself. For Sartre, the ego is a pure fiction; as a unity, the ego is transcendent. But for the later Husserl, that is, the Husserl of the post-1913 *Ideas*, the ego is not transcendent, but transcendental, whereas the world is transcendent. For the later Husserl, the pure Ego may best be described as "pure" and not empirical. It constitutes, therefore, the fundamental structure of every field of observation. The transcendental Ego is an act of pure reflection; the pure Ego is *a priori*.[6]

Of course, once Husserl introduces his discovery of the pure Ego into the phenomenological description of constitution, the implications concerning the problem of the genesis of time become all the more staggering. Let us look at some of the main points of Husserl's analysis in more detail. As transcendental, the Ego is a ray of retention that passes through a series of acts and perceptions. The relationship between Ego and object is therefore unbreakable. On the one hand, the transcendental Ego constitutes the unity of all conscious acts, it constitutes a subject-oriented stream of internal time-consciousness. Yet on the other hand, the object that appears in its unity appears only through an object-oriented analysis. Hence, the knower-in-act cannot be separate from the known act. In effect, Husserl makes a medieval (Aristotlean) distinction here, saying that *noesis–cogitatio* is distinct but inseparable from *noema–cogitatium*. Transcendental phenomenology explores ways in which objects are constituted in consciousness. Even more, the question of the genesis of time sheds light on how the essence of experience is constituted as a process or unitive stream of internal time-consciousness.

Finally, we approach the heart of the problem concerning the origin and genesis of time, according to Husserl's phenomenological description. "Cosmic" time anchors movement, it measures the process by which objects are mediated in, through, and of, Objectivity. Phenomenologically speaking, however, "cosmic time" is merely a chronological rendering of consciousness, it measures the "before" and "after" on the Objective world of events and occurrences.[7] But "phenomenological time" is entirely different. In phenomenological time, there are not individual objects (whether real or imagined) at all. All there "is" in phenomenological time, is the metaphorical "flux" of successive points of actuality from which springs every "now." The question of the origin of time thus leads to a radical understanding of the meaning of transcendental phenomenology, namely, the genesis of internal time-consciousness. In every act of experience we discover an immanent content. But this content is neither a pole of identity nor a temporal Object. What Husserl is describing here is a radical process or flux of absolute subjectivity. This unitive stream of experience is a condition of possibility of every lived experience of actuality.

And herein lies the great paradox concerning Husserl's account of the genesis and origin of time. How can that which is truly transcendental be self-constituted and, at the same time, self-constitut*ing*? What is truly transcendental must have as its source what is ultimately and truly absolute, namely, subjective time-consciousness. But insofar as subjective time-consciousness shows itself in the fore-structure of every experience, it stands in direct opposition to the possibility of ever being grasped in its wholeness. The phenomenality of time requires that it be given as a whole in its totality, that is, given completely, infinitely. But the "whole" of time is precisely what in principle can never be given.

5. THE EVER-FRESH "NOW"

Upon further analysis, it appears that, for Husserl, the subject or "form" of internal time-consciousness is not a subject (properly speaking) at all. Rather, it is a radical process, or apprehension, or flux, or totally unity of the temporal stream. The goal or task of this process, according to Husserl, is infinite. Hence, since the task of internal time consciousness includes "seeing" the entire world of real or imagined phenomena Objectively, so, too the process-itself is infinitely given according to infinite multiplicities of perspectives. Consciousness *qua* consciousness is an infinite flow of acts and perceptions. At the same time, however, this infinite flow is not chaotic, but ordered. Such temporal ordering means that consciousness *qua* consciousness is oriented around a particular "Now-point." This "Now" serves as the primordial originator by which the world (whether real or imagined) emerges into meaning.

The origin of time, therefore, may be described in the phenomenological sense as a temporal constitutive flux, an *absolute* subjectivity. Furthermore, the givenness of such radical orientation can be said to form *itself* into a temporal unity; hence, the origin or genesis of every unity of experience is always a new "present-Now" from which springs the "Now" at every horizon. This new "just-Now" is the protension of the anticipated "present-Now" that emerges-into-being even as the "Now" falls into retention. Consequently, for Husserl the "ever-fresh Now" that constitutes the unity of experience is *never* static. On the contrary, the genesis of unity of experience is constituted by a constant flowing into and out of the phenomenological "ever-fresh Now" that can not be equated with Objective time because it is never naturally experienced.

According to Husserl, the genesis and origin of time must account for both change *and* duration. In terms of change, we might say that phenomenological time lacks the one thing that it seeks, namely, the fullness of its own interior experience. This "lack" is what Husserl terms "apprehension." According to Husserl, temporal duration lacks the "just-Now" that every "Now-point" seeks. Through the processes of protention and retention, internal time consciousness posits every constituted phenomenon as a unity of inner experience. Paradoxically, however, this unity of inner experience collapses the "just-Now" under its own weight. As a transcendental structure of experience, the "just-Now" ceases to be "just"-Now at the precise orientation-point that the "ever-present-*Now*" apprehends its own coming-to-be. Consequently, a trace of the "just-Now" is retained in every unitive experience of the living stream. But this trace is no longer "just-Now." It constantly gives way to the coming-into-presence of a *new* "just-Now," it apprehends coming-to-be as a change in temporal orientation. Without change there can be no living stream of experience. Yet, what is experienced in the living stream is a radical, transcendental process of unitive subjectivity. What endures in phenomenological time, then, is the inner experience of infinitely changing perceptions of phenomena.

The stream of living experience constitutes the world through the guise of protention and retention. But whereas the transcendent is given to consciousness, the transcendent is not transcendental. Or, perhaps another way of saying this: Internal time is pre-reflective, that is, internal time is constituted; whereas consciousness of internal time is reflective, hence, constitut*ing*. What Husserl seems to be driving at is the notion that the origin of phenomenological time makes possible conditions of perception and, at the same time, violates these conditions by constituting the *stream-itself* as the bearer of every condition of possibility. Phenomenological time is not constituted by a collection of "before-" and "after-" points. Phenomenological time does not change; it *endures*. It apprehends a content even as it is experienced, but certainly not in an empirical sense.

Let us take, for example, my nine-month old daughter. Phenomenologically speaking, an infant is not governed by the god *Chronos*. In fact, for an infant, chronological time has little (if any) meaning whatsoever. An infant cries when he or she is hungry, not because it is "time" for dinner, but because she *is* hungry. That is, she cries because she *is hunger*. Hunger is not something an infant has or feels or emotes, it is something an infant *is*, phenomenologically speaking. At the precise moment hunger hits, the body contorts, knees kick, the voice screams, tears flood, blood rushes to the face, etc. None of these activities are constituted as the result of a careful and reflective process of complex mental deliberations. For an infant, therefore, hunger is not so much constitut*ed* as it is *constitutive*.

In a similar fashion, melody, too, is constitutive. Let us take for example, this time, my daughter's favorite nursery rhyme, "Itsy-Bitsy Spider." As an infant, my daughter does not "understand" the words to the song she hears, she does not "appreciate" the clever rhyming scheme or "grasp" any particularly complex metrical syntax. Yet, the melody captivates her. It "has" her, so to speak, under its spell. The melody pulls her and lulls her into experiencing a new state of heightened awareness concerning the world that surrounds her. Rather than my daughter constituting the melody in terms of its having a particular rhythm or cadence, the melody—with which she is, for the most part, completely unfamiliar—constitutes *her*. She giggles as the spider "crawls up the water spout." Yet, she has no conceptual framework to understand what concepts like spiders or water spouts or "up" or "crawls" truly entail. For her, the melody is not constitut*ed* but constitut*ing*. My daughter giggles and grabs at my fingers, she squeals and slaps her hands, her whole body bounces and shakes as this melody announces that something "new" is about to arrive.

I think this serves as a fairly good example of what Husserl is attempting to describe by way of his phenomenological analysis of the origin of time. Because melody is a non-spatial Object, it is most closely related to time. Husserl even describes how sound is *timely*, for instance, when any one note dies away, it always "dies" in conjunction with the anticipation of the appearance of a new note:

When, for example, a melody sounds, the individual notes do not completely disappear when the stimulus or the action of the nerve excited by them comes to an end. When the new note sounds, the one just preceding it does not disappear without a trace; otherwise, we should be incapable of observing the relations between the notes which follow one another. We should have a note at every instant, and possibly in the interval between the sounding of the next an empty [*leere*] phase, but never the idea [*Vorstellung*] of a melody.... [E]ach presentation is naturally joined a continuous series of presentations each of which reproduces the content of the preceding but in such a way that the moment of the past is always attached to the new.[8]

Each preceding note falls into retention, and earlier notes are forgotten as they flow-off into silence. But in order for a melody to make sense, that is, in order for a melody to *be a melody* rather than, say, a cacophony of noise, each note that is forgotten must also, at the same time, remain somehow "present" in an objective unity. In other words, for Husserl, extension or duration is not merely a matter of presentations of tones simply persisting in consciousness. Paradoxically, the notes that slip into the past must, at the same time, persist, that is, constitute, the present. Otherwise, instead of listening to a melody, all we would experience are a "chord of simultaneous notes or rather a disharmonious jumble of sounds such as we should obtain if we struck all the notes simultaneously that have already been sounded."[9] Each note "gives way" to silence in the apprehension of the perceived next note; yet each former-note lingers long after it ceases to be. In so doing, retention anticipates the present, it engenders a new "fresh-Now," it apperceives a continuity of varied quality and intensity through a harmonious flow of protention and retention. The "giving way" is retained in the memory of the living-Now.

6. THE ACT OF APPERCEPTION: ANTICIPATION AND DURATION

Phenomenologically speaking, "anticipation" entails a constitutive part of every experience. Take, for example, the hushed concert hall in the few minutes preceding a musical performance. As the lights dim, the audience falls silent. The silence, however, is quite deafening, in that the silence is filled with anticipation in conjunction with the expectation of what-is-to-come. Strictly speaking, this coming-to-be of a "future-Now" *is* nothing at all, it "is" not. What is phenomenologically given is only the absolute appearing of the "ever-fresh Now." Nevertheless, the Now always arrives under the apperceived appearance of protention and retention. What is involved in this appearance? In a succession: a "now" appears and, in unity therewith, the trace of a "past" and a "future."[10]

In a similar way in which the unity of consciousness encompasses the present and the past through retention, so, too the unity of consciousness encompasses the present and the future via protention. *Nota bene*, however, that the unity of consciousness does not deflate the past (or future) into the present. Otherwise, the temporal moment "past" must, in the same sense as the element "red" that we actually experience, be a present moment of lived experience—"which, of course, is an obvious absurdity."[11] For Husserl, such unity of consciousness posits a phenomenological datum, though he is clear to point out how his own analysis at this juncture raises important objections against Brentano's inability to distinguish (on this same point) between act and content. Consequently, what Husserl calls "the temporal moment" must be understood, phenomenologically speaking, through the "supervention" of a moment, that is, through that which is apperceived or interwoven with (what Husserl calls) the running-off [*Ablauf*] of other contents, qualities, intensities, etc.:

We see, therefore, that it is no use to have an analysis of time-consciousness which will make the intuitive temporal interval comprehensible solely through the continuous gradation of new moments which somehow are pieced to or melted away from those moments of content which constitute the temporally localized objective entity [*Gegenständliche*]. To put it briefly, the form of time is itself neither the content of time nor is it a complex of new content added to the time-content in some fashion or other.[12]

Let us return, again, to the previous example noted above. Although the moment of silence in the concert hall before which the orchestra begins to play is empty, nonetheless that moment is fully pregnant with anticipation. The "empty present" anticipates the "sound" of what is to-come, along with what-just-was. Paradoxically, retention and protention are mutual, co-constitutive, transcendental elements of the ever-fresh Now. In effect, this means that all transcendent apprehension and positing [Setzung] must be excluded or bracketed in order to take "the sound" as a hyletic datum. "It begins and stops," Husserl writes, "and the whole unity of its duration, the unity of the whole process in which it begins and ends, 'proceeds' to the end in the ever more distant past."[13] But what does Husserl mean by this sinking back into "the ever more distant past?" For Husserl, I "hold" the sound in "retention," and as long as the retention persists; the sound "has its own temporality." In other words, what Husserl is describing is a kind of apperception, that is, the way that immanent-temporal Objects [*Zeitobjekte*] are given or "appear" in a continuous flux. From the point of view of the flux of consciousness, the same sound which is heard now is *past*, its duration expired. Points of temporal duration recede, sound "vanishes into the remoteness of consciousness."[14]

During this whole flux of consciousness, the inner stream of consciousness is aware of one and the same sound as enduring, as enduring through a course of successive Now's. The "future-Now" is therefore always, already antici-pated as a constitutive element in every unity of duration. However, although a trace of the "not-yet" is anticipated, this anticipation does *not* define the living-Now. The futural "not-yet" is *felt*, it is constitutive, it is a condition of possibility of experience; but it is not yet present to the same degree that the "ever-fresh now" constitutes the flux of the immanent temporal Object. St. Paul, as well, speaks of immanent things in his Letter to the Colossians. There, St. Paul calls the things of the Present Age "only a shadow of what was to come."[15] The messianic structure of the anticipated future of the Coming Age already has its roots in the present moment: *today* is the day of salvation. For St. Paul, the future is not-yet, but it is not *wholly* not-yet. Constituted through a structure of apperception and anticipation, the "not-yet" appears as a constitutive event. The future constitutes the present by properly orienting the "ever-fresh now" towards what is infinite and transcendent, *viz.*, towards a future beyond the grasp of the Present Age. Similarly, retention and protention co-constitute the present moment by properly orienting the "ever-fresh now" as a temporally localized objective entity [*Gegenständliche*]. Phenomenologically speaking, protention and retention engender the transcendental flow of inner experience.

This dual experience of protention and retention, that is, the experience of anticipation and duration (both backward and forward-facing), is *constitutive* in the sense that it anticipates the structural "present" of every just-Now experience. As an apperceptive structure, anticipation has already begun to transform the Present Age. But such apprehension is merely a shadow, a trace, a pregnant pause *before* the orchestra actually arrives on the scene. In a similar way to St. Paul, Husserl, too, acknowledges that the present moment is full of pregnancy. The present-Now anticipates the "not-yet" that has not quite arrived (but is already keenly anticipated) and, at the same time, retains a trace of what just-was-but-no-longer-is. Otherwise, every just-Now would be *all that there is*, resulting in the complete loss of both experience and intelligibility. In effect, Husserl is saying that internal time-consciousness marks the transcendental origin and genesis of time and meaning. Hence, the absolute-Now (phenomenologically speaking, that is), can be justified only by bracketing the structure of cosmic time. But insofar as the nature of Objective time is violated, what we discover is the eidetic structure of consciousness, that is, a continuous flow or process of protention and retention. Without internal time-consciousness, there can be no before and after, since there would be no flow of apperception. Objective time, therefore, is a psychological habit, it is structured in terms of the natural attitude. Intentionality, then, does not break temporality down. Rather, it takes "temporality" as a whole, a unity, a totality, and it explicates, unfolds, opens-up everything that is implicit in it.

According to Husserl's descriptive analysis, intentionality explicates the just-Now, it makes intelligible every note and every letter by anticipating what came before and what follows in the stream of inner experience. Without protention and retention, all that there would be is non-sense, since even "nothing" is a concept constituted from the stream of inner experience. (This is why Husserl notes that the truly absolute subject, the single "thing" that alone will survive the destruction of the world, is internal time consciousness.)[16]

These formal, synthetic rules of protention and retention engender the origin and genesis of phenomenological time. Without them, inner time-consciousness would not be able to constitute vast fields of multiple acts into a unitive experience of intentional Objectivity.

CONCLUSION

Throughout our discussion, it has been important to note that the ever-fresh Now is not an atomic particle or an isolated moment like a frame in a reel of old film. Rather, the living-Now is a process, a pure flux that constitutes the co-relation between what is immediately past (retention) and what is immediately to come (protention). Husserl calls this principle of temporal constitution "transitivity," meaning that "to every time belongs an earlier and a later."[17] This essential unity of retention and protention constitutes a melting, or blending, of part into part. Consequently, each retention contains something of a retention...of a retention...of a retention..., etc., just as each protention anticipates or apprehends a fringe of what is not-yet but what is about-to-be. What is about-to-be and what-just-was form a cohesive unity of experience that constitutes the living stream of inner experience.

The question concerning the origin or genesis of time has now taken us full circle, to an understanding that the unity of inner time consciousness constitutes the whole realm of the multiplicity of acts and experiences. This inner unity, however, is not a pure flux that will eventually result in chaos. Rather, the flux is governed by formal and synthetic rules. The most important rules of internal time-consciousness are those of retention, protention, and anticipation. In effect, it is only through internal time consciousness that the whole world is opened-up to us *qua* world, as opposed to the mere "temporal" description of the unfolding of Objective things in the natural attitude. In effect, Husserl's question concerning the origin of time raises as well the meaning of the transcendental structure of knowledge. How are meaning, sensibility, and knowledge of objects constituted or built up? In other words, to what extent does the question of the origin of time, which includes the possibility of experience, necessitate, at the same time, "a return to the phenomenological data of which all that is experienced consists phenomenologically?"[18]

Inner-time consciousness engenders a unitive flux of inner experience. This "unity," however, is not a thing, not an identity pole, not a *res*. The flow of this stream is constitutive, it constitutes a horizon in which the intentionality of objects belongs. Thus, the tree stands outside my window, it constitutes its appearance for me, it presents itself in unity and harmony. But we can only reach Objective harmony about what we see by agreeing that "what" we see is there, present, before us. Consequently, what Husserl discovers *via* his reduction to phenomenological time is the contingency of all things.

Hence, by Objectivity Husserl means "authentic" experience, i.e., the intuitive and ultimately adequate standard for evaluating experience. "The question of the origin," Husserl argues, "is oriented toward the primitive forms of the consciousness of time in which the primitive differences of the temporal are constituted intuitively and authentically as the originary [*originäreen*] sources of all certainties relative to time."[19] In other words, the question of the origin and genesis of time has nothing to do with psychological or psychical states of empirical persons, as with psychologism and nativism. On the contrary, what Husserl discovers by analyzing the origin and genesis of time is phenomenological time, that is, the *a priori*, lived experience of pre-reflective consciousness.

For Husserl the origin of time is constitutive, its pure flow *constitutes* time through an historical genesis of inner experience. In his 1905 lectures Husserl first described the origin of time as a process or flux or living stream that constitutes consciousness via apperceptive "traces" of protention and retention that lie on the fringe of every ever-fresh Now. But by the time *Ideas* was published in 1913, Husserl had begun to move away from these earlier realist leanings. Now, he began to describe the genesis of time in terms of transcendental phenomenology, more specifically, in relation to the laws of consciousness in which the flow or stream of internal time gets constituted. Whereas Husserl in his lectures of 1905 argued that internal-time consciousness is pre-reflective (that is, constitu*ted*), he later begins to shift his analysis in the 1910's to say that consciousness of internal time is reflective (that is, constitu*ting*). This shift in Husserl's description of the origin of time is emblematic of the more controversial shift in Husserl's emergent view concerning the scope and goal of the transcendental project itself (say, from 1905-1915). In effect, the development of Husserl's analysis of the genesis of time reflects his own growing interest in transcendenta Idealism.

Seattle University

NOTES

[1] Edmund Husserl, *The Phenomenology of Internal Time-Consciousness*, ed. Martin Heidegger, trans. James Churchill (Bloomington, IN: Indiana University Press, 1964), pp. 24.

[2] With only slight revisions, the fourteenth edition of Husserl's *Encyclopaedia Britannica* article remained in print from 1929 to 1974. Please see, "The History of the Redaction of *The Encyclopaedia Britannica* Article," Thomas Sheehan, *Edmund Husserl Collected Works VI*. (Dordrecht: Kluwer Academic Publishers, 1997), pp. 36–37.

[3] Husserl, pp. 2122.

[4] *Ibid.*, p. 23.

[5] *Ibid.*, p. 28.

[6] Of course, for Husserl there are not two egos. There is only one ego, which can be described either *empirically*, that is, as embodied, enfleshed, existing in the world, or *purely*, that is, as the pure idea of what the thing is, if it should ever appear.

[7] This is a fascinating topic in itself, based, in part, on Aristotle's own elucidation of temporality in terms of "past" and "future." In effect, Husserl is saying that consciousness must remember the event in order for the event to have significance. Otherwise, there would be merely change and not "time" in the proper phenomenological sense of which we are speaking here.

[8] Husserl, pp. 30–31.

[9] *Ibid.*, p. 30.

[10] For a more detailed description of this subject, please refer to *The Phenomenology of Internal Time-Consciousness*, p. 36ff.

[11] Husserl, p. 38.

[12] *Ibid.*, pp. 39–40.

[13] *Ibid.*, p. 44.

[14] *Ibid.*, p. 45.

[15] Colossians 2:16–17.

[16] For more details of this discussion, please refer to Section 83 of Husserl's *Ideas*.

[17] Husserl., p. 29.

[18] Ibid., p. 27.

[19] *Ibid.*, p. 28.

SEYYED MOHAMMED KHAMENEI*

TIME, TEMPORAL, AND TEMPORALITY

The issue of time and temporality has always been among the important philosophical topics occupying the minds of great thinkers in the course of history. It is also considered an important subject in Islamic philosophy and different ideas have been propounded in this regard.

In order to study the issue of temporal things, we must first begin with a definition and study of time itself. It appears from the history of philosophical thought and human cultures that the cognizance of time and its definition has a long record. For instance, in the ancient Iran, centuries before the outset of philosophical discussions in Greece, they believed in 'Zirwan', the goddess of time, and considered her the first and the eternal and pre-eternal existence, as well as the creator of the world. Greek philosophy was also influenced by this idea later. We understand from some of Plato's words that he viewed time as being eternal and pre-eternal like God, Himself, or, in other words, he held that time was created simultaneously with the world (and the heavens) and would be annihilated with the annihilation of the mortal world.[1]

After Plato, in the light of his naturalist and mechanical view of creation, Aristotle introduced time as the product of the circular and continuous motion of the first sphere (the mother sphere). He maintained that this motion was imposed upon it from the outside and, thus, demonstrated the existence of a creator. It is said that, before him, Archytas of the Tarentum (the Pythagorean philosopher, 440–360 BC) believed in the same idea.[2] However, without referring to the spheres, he considered time the effect of motion. As we know, Plato, too, held that the world of Ideas is unchanging while the material world is prone to change and motion and, naturally, enjoys time. Perhaps, his view of time is, in fact, the continuity of Pythagoreans' ideas in this regard.

Although stoics did not believe in an essence for time either, it seems that their definition of time as 'an entity coming into existence between the beginning and end of the world is, in fact, the same as Pythagoreans' definition stating that time is the result of the changes and motion in the world.

* Persident of Sadra Islamic Philosophy Research Insitute (SIPRIn).

A-T. Tymieniecka (ed.),
Timing and Temporality in Islamic Philosophy and Phenomenology of Life, 129–136.
© 2007 Springer.

Plotinus believed in the stability of the One and the Intellect, but maintained that the Universal Soul (the third essence) was in change so that it could be the source of the origination of the existents and events in the world. He considered time the continuity and extension of the soul's life.

Most Muslim philosophers regarded time as the effect of the motion of a thing (or things) whose essence was fixed but enjoyed a rotary or spatial motion. Normally, they equated it with the first sphere and, thus, were in agreement with Aristotle in this regard.

A few Muslim philosophers considered time an absurd issue. Some of the Christian theologians and philosophers of the Middle Ages believed in the existence of two types of time; namely, material time and spiritual time.

From among the European philosophers of the Renaissance period, Newton, too, believed in two types of time: pure and mathematical time and relative time. Some have interpreted Descartes' statements in this regard as indicating that he viewed time as a form of thought. Some others have also said that, in line with Aristotle, he considered time a product of motion.

From among the philosophers of the modern era, Kant and Heidegger's theories of time are more famous than those of others. Kant defines time as an apriori experience belonging to man's inner and mental nature and as a mental mould granting a system to sensibles (in his view crude entities) and consolidating them.

Heidegger believes that time and existence are connected to and inseparable from each other. This view is similar to what *Ishraqis* (Illuminationists) and Abualbarakat, the Islamic philosopher, and some other Iranian philosophers said in this regard.

On the whole, early philosophers are divided into two groups concerning their theories of time:

The first group consists of those philosophers who abstract time from the accidental and sensible motion of objects or things. They believe that true time is merely limited to the 'moment' or 'present'.

The second group consists of those philosophers who abstract time from the linear motions and changes due to the motion of the fluid and changing quiddity of objects or things and consider it a mental issue.

According to Islamic philosophy, concerning its relation to time, motion is of two types:

1) instantaneous motion (*harakat-i tawassutiyyah*), whereby the 'present' moment is considered the true time and the continuous and conjunctive line of moments of time are viewed as abstractions existing in the mind;

2) continuous motion (*harakat-i qat'iyyah*), whereby the true time is considered the collection of points, states, and moments of the motion

of the moving object. This motion is drawn as a single line. Here the 'moment' or the 'present' is considered an abstract and mental issue.

Most Islamic philosophers believe that instantaneous motion is the criterion for the truth of time; however, some of them, e.g., Mir Damad and Mulla Sadra, hold that the criterion here is the continuous motion.

The difference between the above two theories is revealed in this classification. Almost, all the thinkers who regard time as being originated in the external and horizontal motion of objects believe that instantaneous motion is real and that continuous motion is abstract. In contrast, those who abstract time from the fluid quiddity of the moving object hold that it is the instantaneous motion which is objective and real.

* * *

1. TIME AND TEMPORALS

Any temporal thing is an entity enjoying time, and such temporal entities are the very material and corporeal existents which are assumed to be in motion. Therefore, unmovable and fixed entities or, in other words, disengaged (abstract) existents are not prone to time and belong to the timeless world.

One of the important subjects in Islamic philosophy is 'the timeless world' (in contrast to the physical and material world). Thus, here, existents are divided into two general groups: temporal or changing existents and non-temporal or unchanging existents.

Plato's Ideas are of the type of time-less existents, and the world of these Ideas must be regarded as the world of unchanging and timeless things. This theory has been, more or less, accepted in Islamic philosophy through some justifications and interpretations.

This issue has no place in modern western philosophy. For example, according to the common tradition in the Renaissance period, Heidegger considers time as being limited to existence and existent (Dasein) and holds that being is purely concomitant with and necessitated by time. However, in his eyes, being is not an object and, thus, is not 'temporal'.

Heidegger believes that the non-temporal presence of existence is impossible; therefore, we can conclude that he does not regard non-temporal things as being in existence, and that for him the world is limited to the material world.

However, Islamic philosophers maintain that there are, at least, two worlds: material and non-material or temporal and non-temporal worlds. Some thinkers, such as Mir Damad (Mulla Sadra's master, deceased in 1041 AH, 1631 AD) believed in the existence of three worlds. This is because the non-material and non-temporal world is divided into two real and independent types, namely, perpetual duration (*Dahr*) and everlasting (*Sarmad*).

The world of perpetual duration abounds in existence, enjoys stability, and is lacking in motion, change, and, as a result, time. It reminds us of Plato's world of Ideas. This world has come into existence through God's sudden making and creation (such a making is called 'innovation' in Islamic philosophy).

The everlasting world is hypothetical and limited to God. [3] Neither do time and motion bear any meaning in this world, nor is there a direct relation between it and the material and temporal world. The making and adminis- tration of the material world is done by the everlasting world.

Mir Damad refers to these three worlds as three receptacles. In his view, the material and temporal world is surrounded by the everlasting world, exists in it, and obtains its existence from the everlasting world gradually, that is, with time. While being stable and non-changing, the everlasting world, itself, is the source of change and the perfectional motion of material existents. On the other hand, the everlasting world, itself, is surrounded by a higher world, the world of perpetual duration, and is the origin of the sudden and innovative coming into existence of existents and their manifestations in the world of perpetual duration from pure non-existence into non-temporal existence. Accordingly, the everlasting world (or the hypothetical receptacle) is pure stability and merely stands in a making relation to stable and unchanging things (the world of perpetual duration).

Following Ibn Sina, Mir Damad analyses these three types of beings: If we evaluate the relation of these three worlds with time, we will face three different situations.

1. Being in the world of matter, which is being in time.
2. Being in the world of perpetual duration, which is being 'with' time rather than 'in' it, i.e., this being surrounds time.
3. Being in the everlasting world, which is a pure and stable being, bears no relation to time, and is free from any kind of change or transformation. Here, the stable and timeless is related to the stable and timeless.

Mir Damad interpreted the idea of another philosopher called Abualbarakat (5th Hijri century, 11th Christian century), who held that time is the measure of existence, on equal terms with his own theory.

According to Mir Damad's theory, temporal existents qualified with motion and change merely refer to those existents that exist in the receptacle of time, i.e., this very external world of ours. Their main property is change and moving towards perfection. Nevertheless, this very world, together with its motions and free from limits of time, is like a single point and a stable and non-moving phenomenon in the world of perpetual duration from which it attains its existence. By placing the world of perpetual duration between the world of matter and God, Mir Damad intends to solve the problem of the relation between the pre-eternal and eternal, on the one hand, and with the originated, on the other.

According to Plato,

"The Creator intended to turn the world into an eternal living thing; however, since it could not be everlasting, and since the conformity between the pre-eternal and the originated (the unchanging and the changing) was impossible, He created a moving image of eternity (the material and temporal world). Thus time and the world have been created with each other and will also be annihilated with each other".[4]

From among all the ideas and theories given on time and temporal things, Mulla Sadra's philosophical theory (979–1050 AH, 1571–1640 AD) is the firmest and most logical of all. First, he harshly attacked Ibn Sina and Aristotle's Peripatetic theory stating that the essence of things is fixed and that the motion of point is realized in four categories out of Aristotle's ten-fold categories. Then he demonstrated that, as an essential characteristic, motion flows in the nature and our material world principially, and that quantitative and qualitative motions are the cause of their trans-substantial motion. He also proved that their motion originates in their own essence and nature rather than in the outside, and that motion is an essential attribute, like moisture for water.

Therefore, any body, due to its essence and substance, enjoys a state of becoming, renewal, and incessant perfectional change which is intertwined with its being. If motion is denied to matter, it will be annihilated.[5]

In Mulla Sadra's view, the existence of all material existents is in flux and never remains at a fixed point; therefore, it passes through various points in the course of its motion and divides the line of motion into the prior and the posterior, and the beginning and the end. As a result, time, which is the collection of the very points of the line of motion of bodys' natures, originates in the motion of the substance of those objects. Moreover, time is nothing but the measure of trans-substantial motion.[6] We divide this time into 'moment' and 'present' and assume that it is real. Time is abstracted from motion, but from one in the essence of nature rather than from anything else.

Unlike Mir Damad, who attributed the existence of the changing world to the everlasting world and stable everlasting existents, Mulla Sadra believes that the becoming of nature and, as a result, time is the effect of a direct act of 'Divine emanation' that is related to the type of creation of existents.

In Islamic philosophy, creation is limited to a few types, the most important of which are sudden creation and making out of pure non-existence or 'innovation' and gradual creation from another thing following temporal non-existence. This is called 'creation'.

Both kinds of creation originate in divine theophany. The creation of non-material existents is merely the result of a perfect theophany, while the creation of material existents is the result of frequent and continuous theophanies or permanent and successive emanation.

In other words, the story of creation can be retold as follows: Possible existents have been created in two types:

First, there are existents that have attained an existence deserving their quiddity all at 'the same time' and lack potentiality. In other words, they await no more perfection and are actualized. They have suddenly come into existence and attained their real and permanent place in the world of being. Such existents, which are called disengaged intellects and souls by Peripatetics, are not temporal.

Second, there are existents whose attaining their real and main place in the world of being requires traversing a long way and leaving a number of levels behind. Any level of their ontological perfection leads to another potential perfection, and with every step and at each level a little is added to their existence and perfection, until they reach their final point and ultimate perfection and settle down in the threshold of their 'real place in the world'.

The passage through each level - which turns the imperfect material existent into a 'perfect and actual existent', the transient into a 'perfect and actual existent', and the transient and suspending quiddity into a real and ultimate one - can be called an 'event'. This perfectional journey of material existents is the very change and renewal of nature and the incessant and permanent Divine emanation that exists in the nature of matter and is absent in immaterial existents.

Time, which is the product of this renaissance and renewal of nature and the trans-substantial motion of objects, can be considered the very measure of the Divine and incessant emanations. Likewise, the renaissance and the trans-substantial motion of bodies can be likened to the 'beats of existence', an existence that oozes from God's Knowledge and Will and from His Infinite and Pure Existence. Through relating the flowing, time-generating, and material existents to the Divine emanation, Mulla Sadra rejected the existence of the world of perpetual duration.

The critical point here is that, according to Mulla Sadra, the trans-substantial motion of matter (and in its mystic sense, the incessant theophany and arrival of emanation) is never disjunctive. Thus one can never say that the object of motion (or emanation) changes at every moment, and that the first moving or object (A) is other than the second moving (B). Rather, we must say that at all points of the trans-substantial and continuous motions, there is only one object and one moving thing that moves following a conjunctive line. In this way we can abstract a mental and rational phenomenon called 'time'.

Accordingly, the entire world of nature moves towards the final point on a straight line in its trans-substantial motion and creates an event at each moment. We call the collection of these events 'history' and the continuous line of motion of nature 'time'. In other words, the entire world is the continuous theophany of the Creator (or the very Pure Existence), and time is nothing but the mathematical and quantitative interpretation of the Divine Emanation.[7]

Mulla Sadra poses the theory of the trans-substantial motion of nature and its relation to metaphysics based on firm philosophical proofs in his well-known book, *al-Asfar*, and discusses all of its aspects.

If we cast a glance at the history of the theory of time and motion in philosophy, we can find some similarities between Mulla Sadra's theory in this regard and the related philosophical theories in ancient Iran and the ideas of Heraclites, Plotinus, and St. Augustine, who were all in a way influenced by the Iranian Illuminationist (*Ishraqi*) philosophy.

Plotinus's theory, which introduced time as a product of the creating motions of the Universal Form, is, in a way, in conformity with Mulla Sadra's theories of emanation and trans-substantial motion. This is because, unlike the Peripatetics' view of spherical motions, the soul's motions do not belong to the category of quantity and, rather, belong to the category of 'act'. They consist of the gradual creation of the essence of objects and events and lead the material quiddities towards their ultimate perfection. This, itself, requires motion, instability, and the continuity and permanence of trans-substantial motion. The reason is that if the 'Universal Soul' had created all material objects from the very beginning in a complete, actual, and non-potential form, they would have naturally enjoyed stability and been needless of motion and, as a result, of time. Thus history would have never come into existence.

The writer believes that Plotinus's theory is the continuity of Heraclites's and the idea of the continuity of the world, which Aristotle has disfigured and metamorphosized. The idea of the continuity of the world of matter is in conformity with the theory of continuous emanation.

St. Augustine's (354–430 AD) statement in his *Confessions* and his idea of the relation of time to the soul can be considered as having been inspired by Plotinus (203–270 AD). They had failed to look at the depth of this issue in Europe in the Middle Ages; however, it seems that, through being inspired by this theory, they divided time into material time and spiritual (soulish) time. The spiritual time was pre-eternal and fixed and the material one was changing. This is similar to Faydh's theory in this regard.

They assumed the existence of a copulative time between the two types that could rationally mediate between the originated and pre-eternal times (or between origination and pre-eternity) and called it *aevum*.

* * *

Mulla Sadra's theory of trans-substantial motion is not only related to emanation or metaphysics but also grants a specific philosophical and scientific clarity to the issue of time and temporal things (world events) and reveals the truth and mechanism of history and social and natural changes following a philosophical approach. It also demonstrates the mode of existence of natural existents, which, according to his theory of trans-substantial motion, is a systematic collection of successive events, and its relation with history or the developmental journey of the soul and the intellect (Hegel failed to demonstrate and grant a logical form to this issue).

NOTES

[1] Timaeus, B 38.

[2] Simplicius (500), *Commentary on Aristotle's Physics*.

[3] Other Islamic philosophers use the term 'everlasting world' in a more general sense and do not limit it to God.

[4] Plato, *Laws*.

[5] Mulla Sadra, *al-Asfar*, vol. 3, Sayyed Mohammed Khamenei, *Treatise of Mulla Sadra's Transcendent Philosophy*.

[6] Time is an abstract and mental issue. However, if we don not measure it in terms of amount and numbers, and since amount, itself, is an external thing, time will appear like an objective entity.

[7] Mathematics and numbers represent the demonstrative and explanatory aspect of the realities of nature or physics. This relation might have been intended by those who claim that, in Pythagoras's view, number is the origin of the world.

NADER EL-BIZRI

SOME PHENOMENOLOGICAL AND CLASSICAL
COROLLARIES ON TIME

"The seemingly uneventful and motionless moment when our future steps into us is so much closer to life than that loud and accidental moment of time when it happens to us as if from outside" (Rainer Maria Rilke; 8th letter to the young poet Franz Xaver Kappus; August 12, 1904, Flädie, Sweden)

I

In the *Kritik der reinen Vernunft* (*Critique of Pure Reason*)[1] Immanuel Kant argued that space and time were subjective *a priori* "forms of pure intuition" (*Raum und Zeit als Formen der Anschauung*). Moreover, he grasped time as being the ground for understanding the physical properties of things and the formation of concepts about them, as well as founding motion in arithmetic, which is based on counting in a temporal sequence (*Die Zeit begründe physikalische Begriffe wie Bewegung und Veränderung, außerdem die Arithmetik, weil man nur in zeitlicher Folge zählen könne*). On his view, time is not empirical nor is it determined from any specific experience; it is not what exists in itself nor is it inherent in things as an objective determination (A31, 33; B 47, 49). This critical thesis had far reaching consequences on the unfolding of transcendental idealism and theories of time that were mediated by reflections on subjectivity and inter-subjectivity, without entailing a homogenization of time as being single-dimensional; namely as a mere succession, like what is implied by the Kantian tradition.

The unfurling of phenomenology in its classical early Husserlian formative systems consisted in part of being a revived "neo-Cartesian" response to the prevalent neo-Kantianist doctrines that were dominant in the 19th century; particularly within German philosophical *cum* academic circles. After all, one could note that Edmund Husserl picks up the project of transcendental philosophy from where Descartes fails to continue.[2] This consequently left an

137

A-T. Tymieniecka (ed.),
Timing and Temporality in Islamic Philosophy and Phenomenology of Life, 137–155.
© 2007 *Springer.*

imprint on the development of phenomenological accounts of transcendental subjectivity and their determination against the intentional horizons of time (using in this regard *analytic tools* in reference to the workings of temporality in terms of the so-called: "*protentions*" and "*retentions*").

While the "notion" of time occupied a relatively focal function in the maturation of Husserl's phenomenological tradition, its most radical determination from a metaphysical viewpoint was articulated in Martin Heidegger's fundamental ontology as elaborated in his influential tract: *Sein und Zeit*.[3] The Heideggerian existential analytic of *Dasein* (*existenziale Analytik des Dasein*) was itself elucidated against the horizon (*Horizont*) of time with its triple *ekstasis*. Moreover, the *temporocentric* inclination in Heidegger's thinking assimilated his conception of spatiality (*Räumlichkeit*) to temporality (*Zeitlichkeit*; in distinction from *Temporalität*); that being the case until he confessed in his 1962 seminar: "*Zeit und Sein*",[4] that his attempt in section 70 of *Sein und Zeit* to derive spatiality (*Räumlichkeit*) from temporality (*Zeitlichkeit*) was "untenable".[5] Further accounts of the centrality of time (*le temps*) emerged through prolongations of phenomenology within French intellectual coteries; as for instance it was expressed in Emmanuel Levinas' views on *Otherness* (*l'autre*; *l'altérité*; *autrui*) and their ontological-ethical bearings.[6]

The elaboration of phenomenological conceptions of time continued to be articulated from within theories of subjectivity and inter-subjectivity; be it in the Husserlian sense or in the Heideggerian "corrective" account of *Da-sein* ("*being-there*", as opposed to being a *subject/self*),[7] or through Maurice Merleau-Ponty's consideration of *le corps propre* (body-subject),[8] and Levinas' meditations on the relation (if not conflation) between *le temps* (time) and *l'autre* (the other). These philosophical developments, within the so-called "Continental" modern intellectual history, were dramatically contrastive with the dominant 20th century techno-scientific objectifications of time; without entailing that their theories were *incommensurable*, in spite of their conceptual divergences.

II

Following conceptual patterns that are in part akin to Henri Bergson's speculative rethinking of time in reference to an experiential inner-sense of temporality, namely as: *la durée*,[9] which contrasted with "time in nature" (and was ultimately advanced as a fragile and rather *scientifically* unsuccessful response to Einstein's theory of relativity), the phenomenological thrust in philosophy also interiorized *time* and de-homogenized its conception, in an attempt to surpass prevalent objectifying scientific explications of its nature in terms of its concretized and quantifiably measurable *external* manifestations in the physical reality. However, a conception of time based on an internal consciousness of temporality seemed to be confronted with the difficulty of accounting for beings in an "externalized reality" that are experienced and cognized as being subject to "generation and corruption"; hence as being inherently *temporal*.

A contemporary of Heidegger, the 20th century philosopher and mathematician, Hans Reichenbach offered rigorous analytic interpretations of the epistemological implications of Einstein's theory of relativity, particularly in reference to the question concerning time.[10] The "scientific philosophy" of this founder of the "Berlin Circle" (namely the society: *Die Gesellschaft für empirische Philosophie*) can be described as a logical empiricism, or a neo-positivism *qua* logical positivism, which did not reject the verifiability principle, but refined it in reference to a conception of "coordinative definitions" (whereby a definition is coordinated with a real given object, and hence its arbitrariness is limited by the objectivity with which it is coordinated). Of such definitions, he included notions related to the uniformity of time, to temporal simultaneity and the causal ordering of the flow of time.

According to Reichenbach, philosophy assesses the results of the science of its age and tests their epistemic consequences; hence highlighting their theoretic refutability, rather than solely focusing on proving them. On his view, the reality of time pointed to a relational concept that is derived from the epistemological *cum* logical analysis of Einstein's theory of relativity and its causational presuppositions. He also concerned himself with the derivation of a *metric* of time, and the establishing of the epistemic grounds for accepting the coordinative definition of physical simultaneity in synchronized (congruent) clocks that are located at distant places from each other. This idea reflected Einstein's revelation of the relative reality of timing that is determined in reference to the motion *cum* speed of spatial travel and the actions of gravitational forces ("Warped" time entails that different clocks run at differing rates in different places in reflection of the geometry of the four-dimensional *SpaceTime*).[11] For instance, the time needed for a signal, which may even be traveling at the speed of light (hence: a lighting signal), to transmit from one time-locality to another has to be figured in the computing of simultaneity between two clocks located at these distant and separated localities for them to be synchronized (namely, to realize a successful and accurate time-coordination at great spatial distances). A more familiar observation regarding time-delay between the occurrence of a distant event and the signals we receive from it is experienced with a stormy sky, whereby the signal of the flash of *lightning*, which travels at the speed of light from a distant cloud, is visually transmitted to us before the slower auditory signal from that same cloud that reaches us as a *thundering* sound. Ultimately, the uniformity, homogeneity, and absoluteness of quantifiably objective time are not substantiated. Time is relational and relative, as the hypothetical situation of the case of an interstellar traveler at high speed shows. After all, according to the theory of relativity: if a traveler is transmitted between stellar systems (namely vast distances in space) at high velocity (hypothetically tending towards approximating the speed of light), then this voyager will age much slower than someone who does not travel. A similar observation is made regarding the motion at subatomic miniscule-microscopic scales, as well as with actual watches/clocks. In all of this, the ordering of time is patterned in a sequential causal process, yet, unlike a mechanical grasp of causality, time is essentially directional in the sense of being irreversible.

Arguing for the need to develop a "scientific philosophy" that accords with the developments of science in the 20th century, and that surpasses the "errors" of speculative philosophy, Reichenbach emphasized that the method-ological requirements of this novel turn in philosophizing necessitates an epistemological and logical analysis of the dominant physical theories of his age; namely Einstein's mathematical-physical theory of relativity, and its associated non-Euclidean geometries. According to him, the old philosophy, which was speculative, absolutist, rationalist, and driven by picturesque system-building ended in its highest form with Kant's thought, which reflected the dominant Newtonian physics of his era and its supporting Euclidean geometry, whilst not holding truisms anymore.

Based on Reichenbach's arguments, speculations in modern philosophy are expressions of "the old system", and are utterances of *historians* rather than philosophers. To eschew the shortcomings of precedence, and in correspon-dence with the science of the age, research on time ought to be mediated by an epistemological and logical analysis of mathematical-physical theories, along with the empirical testing of their consequences. Unlike the philoso-phers of the phenomenological traditions, Reichenbach suggested that a turn to the history of philosophy/science in the effort to *philosophize* in the 20th century is philosophically and scientifically inconsequential, if not even futile and confusing. According to his reductive strictures about the rigor of methods, one could state that a philosophical inquiry about time that is not conducted from the standpoint of an epistemological and logical analysis of contemporary mathematical-physical theories is incoherent; or amounts to no more than *idle talk* from the perspective of a scientifically-based theory of knowledge. In contrast with the thrust of this line in thinking, the philoso-phers of the phenomenological traditions (particularly of the Heideggerian variation) endeavored to secure the "autonomy of philosophy" from science, with a particular emphasis on the subtle but significant distinction between *thinking* (namely, as a response to: *what calls for thinking*) and scientific analysis and research; proclaiming that "science *does not think* like thinkers do". The *truth* of *thinking*, as un-concealment *qua* revealing, is thus distinguished from the truth of science that is purportedly pictured as being that of "correctness" and "correspondence".

III

In connecting with the history of philosophy, particularly in its early-modern systems, Husserl believed that the seeds of transcendental thought were to be found in Descartes' turn to the *ego cogito*, despite the structuring of the Cartesian *Meditations* as a form of "psychology". Moreover, in reception of Kant, Husserl celebrated the grasp of time as a "form of intuition", even though he argued that the Kantian critical thinking "constructed" transcendental subjectivity rather than furnished an adequate method (*epochè* or "phenomenological reduction") by virtue of which it could be properly accessed. And yet, Husserl elaborated some of the Kantian directives, by endeavoring to investigate cognition and consciousness in reference to "*a priori* intuitions".

While Husserl's appeal to precedence in articulating his research remained auxiliary with respect to his system-building of phenomenology as a *science* of the sciences, the engagement with the history of philosophical thought, in rethinking *philosophy*, found its most pronounced expressions in Heidegger's poignant (yet controversial) critique of classical ontology; and principally in his polemical attempts to reconnect with the metaphysical legacies of the Ancient Greeks, and the Pre-Socratics in particular.

In an effort to contrast his grasp of *Zeit* with classical (Greek-Latin) conceptions of *khronos* and *tempus*, in terms of an existential analytic of *Dasein* against the horizon of temporality, Heidegger objected to what he proclaimed as being "vulgar" (*vulgär*) notions of time as attested in the works of principal metaphysicians like Plato, Aristotle, Augustine, and Hegel. In consequence, he believed that an authentic grasp of *Zeit* (time) depended on the maturation of "fundamental ontology" in the elucidation of the *Seinsfrage* (namely referring to the Heideggerian effort in *Sein und Zeit* to elucidate the question of being, and of its meaning in particular, in reference to the ontological difference between *das Sein* and *das Seiende*).

In generalized terms, the phenomenological differential variations in rethinking temporality call upon us to distance ourselves from the authoritative techno-scientific conceptions of time, even by way of "bracketing" our "natural attitudes" and received opinions, or by "suspending" our judgments (to reflect herein on the phenomenological sense of *epochè*). Furthermore, such phenomenological efforts tended on certain occasions to mediate their reflections on time by way of evoking selected authors and constellations of texts in the history of philosophy; and this matter is manifest primarily in Heidegger's critique of classical ontology. It is in this sense that our inquiry will partially deviate from directly focusing on "phenomenology" in the following two sections, in order to present some principal pointers and directives regarding classical corollaries on time in the history of philosophy and science, which might further inform our approach to modern phenomeno-logical speculations about temporality and their metaphysical entailments.

IV

Classical concepts of time confronted philosophers with perplexing and uneasy paradoxes. Some wondered whether time was altogether nonexistent,[12] while others doubted the reality of its divisibility into parts by arguing that the *past* ceased to be, that the *future* does not yet exist, and that the *present* as a moment/now that is without magnitude is not a real part of time.[13] In addition, it was unclear whether time progressed smoothly or proceeded by way of discontinuous and divisible leaps. Although inquiries about the nature of time were essentially integrated within physical theories of motion (*kinesis*; *metabole*), their cosmological and metaphysical bearings had impacted philo-sophical and theological speculations about creation and causation.

In Plato's *Timaeus* (37d; 38a)[14] time (*khronos*) was pictured as a moving image (*eikona*), which came into existence with the generation of the heavens, and that imitated (*mimoumenon*) eternity (*aiona*) by circling round according to number (*arithmos*),. In the earliest systemic philosophical investigation of the essence and existence of time, which was contained in Aristotle's *Physics* (219b3-4; 220a25-b20; 222b20-23),[15] *khronos* was defined as the [measuring] number (*metron*) of a continuous (*sunekhes*) motion (*kinesis*) with respect to the anterior (*proteron*) and the posterior (*husteron*). Rejecting the claim that time was the movement of the whole (*holos*) Aristotle argued that the circular, uniform, and continuous motion of the celestial sphere (*sphaira*) acts as the measure (*metron*) of time (*Physics*, 223b21). Moreover, the Aristotelian conception of *khronos* had affinities with the notion of *ekstatikon*, as the mode of undoing beings, which is implied by change *qua metabole* (*Physics*, 222b; *Metabole de pasa phusei ekstatikon*).

Aristotle's theory subsequently received numerous responses by Neo-Platonist and Hellenist exegetes (grouped in the monumental: *Commentaria in Aristotelem Graeca*).[16] For instance, Damascius argued that time was a simultaneous whole, while Plotinus grasped it as the changing life of the soul (*Enneads*, 3.7.11–13).[17] As for Simplicius, he defended the thesis of the eternity of the world against doubts raised by the grammarian John Philoponus who adopted a Christian doctrine of *creatio ex nihilo*. As for the author of the *Confessiones*,[18] Augustine of Hippo, he noted that *tempus* (time) was created when the world came to be, while affirming that the existential reality of time is grounded in the present (*praesens*), which in itself is what tends not to be (*tendit non esse*), given that only eternity was stable (*semper stans*). On his view, temporality is marked by *distensio*, namely dilatation or extension (*étirement, écart*; *Confessiones* XI, sect. 23). Based on a belief in the linear directionality of time, from Genesis to Judgment, Augustine argued that the *presence* of *past* things was preserved in memory, the *presence* of manifest (*present*) things was confirmed by perception, and that the *presence* of things *future* was highlighted by expectation. Accordingly, the reality of time depended on an *anima* (soul) that remembers, perceives, and anticipates events; partly echoing Aristotle's claim in the *Physics* (218b29-219a1-6, 223a25) that *khronos* required *psukhe* (soul) or *psukhes nous* (intellect) to compute its *arithmein* (numbering).[19]

V

The reception and adaptive assimilation of the Greek conceptions of time, within the mediaeval Islamic civilization,[20] varied in their levels of adherence to the sources. While philosophers (*al-hukama'*; *al-falasifa*) of the Peripatetic and Platonist tradition tended to find innovative prolongations of the views of the Ancients within monotheistic outlooks on time, dialectical theologians (*al-mutakallimun*; i.e. the exponents of *kalam*) tended in general to object to some of the bearings of these "pagan" doctrines, and consequently developed novel onto-theological accounts regarding eternity, perpetuity, and temporality.[21] However, conceptions of time and its measurement within the history of ideas in Islam were not restricted to the doctrines of the philosophers and the theologians, rather, accomplished investigations in this regard were also conducted in classical traditions in science and mathematics that built on the legacies of the likes of Euclid, Archimedes, Ptolemy, Apollonius of Perga, and Heron of Alexandria, as well as referring to Plato and Aristotle.

The research in geometry, arithmetic, algebra, astronomy, optics and mechanics in the mediaeval Islamic civilization (principally: 9th–14th century

CE),[22] offered solid foundations for the design, construction, and perfection of time-measurement devices and instruments, including astrolabes,[23] sundials, water-clocks (*cum* automata) and compasses. These investigations assisted also in devising the theoretical *cum* geometric rudiments for the design of optical lenses in catoptrics and dioptrics (respectively: the sciences of reflection and refraction),[24] which were of great value for later developments in the observations of astronomy in reference to the motions of the heavenly spheres and their cycles, culminating through the history of applied-optics in Galileo's telescope. The applications of this research assisted in timekeeping for religious purposes,[25] or to support studies in meteorology and concrete determinations of timing in navigation.

Ishaq Ibn Hunayn's (fl. 9th century CE; Baghdad) translation of Aristotle's *Physics* (*al-Tabi'a*) secured the transmission of the Aristotelian conception of *khronos* (*al-zaman*) into Arabic, which subsequently inspired variegated emergent philosophical interpretations of time in the history of ideas in Islam. For instance, al-Kindi (d. ca. 873 CE) held that *al-zaman* (time) had a beginning and an end, and that it measured motion according to number (*Tempus ergo est numerus numerans motum*), while al-Farabi (Alfarabius; d. 950 CE) and Ikhwan al-Safa' (The Brethren of Purity; fl. 10th century CE, Iraq)[26] affirmed that time resulted from the movement of the created celestial sphere (*al-falak*). As for Abu Bakr al-Razi (Rahzes; d. 930 CE), he claimed that the *dahr* (perpetuity) was absolute (*mutlaq*), while construing *al-zaman* (time) as being a flowing substance (*jawhar yajri*) that is bound (*mahsur*) as well as being associated with the motion of *al-falak*.

In *Kitab al-hudud*, Ibn Sina (Avicenna; d. 1037 CE) defined *al-zaman* (time) as that which resembles the created being (*yudahi al-masnu'*), and acts as the measure of motion (*miqdar al-haraka*) in terms of the anterior and the posterior (*al-mutaqaddim wa al-muta'akhkhir*). He also noted that *al-dahr* (supra-temporal duration) resembled the Creator (*yudahi al-sani'*) insofar that it was stable throughout the entirety of time. Moreover, in the *Isharat wa'l-tanbihat*, he linked time to physical inquiries about motion, and in *'Uyun al-hikma*, he construed it as a quantity (*kammiyya*) of motion that measures (*yuqaddir*) change, and whose perpetuity (*dahr al-haraka*) generated temporality.[27]

Time also played a notable role in *Kitab al-manazir* (*Optics*; *De aspectibus* or *Perspectivae*)[28] of the polymath al-Hasan Ibn al-Haytham (Alhazen; d. ca. 1040 CE) who argued that the propagation of light rays was subject to time, and consequently inferred that the velocity of light (*al-daw'*) was finite despite being immense in magnitude. He moreover held that acts of visual discernment and comparative measure (*al-tamyiz wa'l-qiyas*) were subject to the passage of time even if not felt by the beholder, as well as cautioned that, if the temporal duration of contemplative or immediate visual perception fell outside a moderate range it resulted in optical errors. In addition, he listed *al-zaman* as one of the known entities (*ma'lumat*) while taking duration (*mudda*) to be its essence (*mahiyya*) and the scale (*miqyas*) of its magnitude (*miqdar*) and quantity, which become knowable by way of the observational methods of the science of astronomy in reference to the motion of the celestial sphere (*al-falak*).

Moreover, the 10th century mathematician Abu Sahl Wayjan Ibn Rustam al-Quhi (d. ca. 1000 CE) sought to geometrically establish the possibility of an infinite motion in a finite time (*fi al-zaman al-mutanahi haraka ghayr mutanahiya*); opposing in this the philosophical *communis opinio* of his age, which followed the doctrine advanced in Aristotle's *Physics* (Book VI, 7, 238a20–37). Accordingly, al-Quhi showed that if the arc of a given semicircle can be traversed in a finite time, its projected motion on an infinite branch of a hyperbola, which tends to infinity, is likewise covered in a finite time. His demonstration appealed to optics in assuming that the propagation of light in this projection was instantaneous; hence that the motion on the arc of the semicircle and that on the branch of the hyperbola were simultaneous; whilst taking the former to being uniform and considering the latter as being variable and unbound in its accelerating speed along the infinity of the hyperbolic curve.[29]

Opposing the views of the Peripatetic (*masha'i*) philosophers in Islam, the exponents of *kalam* (dialectical theology) articulated alternative conceptions of time that rested on physical theories inspired by Greek atomism.[30] Time was grasped by the *mutakallimun* (the dialectical theologians; mainly the *Mu'tazilites* of Basra in Iraq) as being a virtual (*mawhum*) phenomenon of changing appearances and renewed atomic events (*mutajaddidat*), whereby a discrete moment (*waqt*) replaced the concept of a continuous *zaman*. For instance, Ibn Mattawayh (a disciple of the Mu'tazilite Chief *Qadi* of Rayy: 'Abd al-Jabbar; both fl. 10th–11th century CE) held in his *Tadhkira fi ahkam al-jawahir wa al-a'rad* (*Treatise on Substances and Accidents*) that: accidents (*al-a'rad*) do not inhere in substances (*al-jawahir*; namely the atoms) for even a moment (*la yujab lubuthuha abadan*); given that God recreates the world continually. Motivated by this *kalam* physical theory, though resisting its thrust, al-Nazzam (Ibrahim Ibn al-Sayyar; d. 845 CE) believed in the divisibility of particles *ad infinitum*, which entailed that a spatial distance with infinitely divisible parts requires an infinite time to be crossed unless its traversal proceeded by way of leaps (*tafarat*); echoing in this the Stoic views regarding the Greek notion of *halma* (leap).

In doubting the doctrine of the eternity of the world in *Tahafut al-falasifa* (*The Incoherence of the Philosophers*),[31] Abu Hamid al-Ghazali (d. 1111 CE) attempted to show that duration (*mudda*) and time (*zaman*) were both created. Furthermore, he argued that "the connection between what is habitually (*bi'l-'ada*) taken to be a cause and what is customarily taken to be an effect was not necessary", given that observation only shows that they were concomitant/concurrent. Consequently, he proclaimed that the ordering relation of an antecedent cause with a consequent effect does not necessarily rest on an irreversible directionality in time. In defense of causation, Ibn Rushd (Averroes; d. 1198 CE) argued in *Tahafut al-tahafut* (*The Incoherence of the Incoherence*) [32] that al-Ghazali's "refutation of the causal principle" entailed an outright rejection of reason (*'aql*), while asserting that the eternal (*al-qadim*) was timeless and that the world was subject to the workings of a continuous *zaman*. However, Ibn Rushd may have misread al-Ghazali's thesis by mistaking "the rejection of a necessary connection between what is habitually taken to be a cause and its effect" with a "refutation of causation" outright. After all, al-Ghazali's doubts regarding the "necessary connection between cause and effect" reflected his belief in the existence a "contingent" sense of causation that embodied an inherent "habitual" course of nature, with which corresponded a deeply entrenched human "custom" of knowing natural phenomena through *seeming* causal connections. Hence, al-Ghazali's causation is "habitual" rather than "necessary", and this does not readily entail a refutation of the causal principle as much as showing its contingent character, wherein it is *believed* that Divine Volition breaks the habitual course of nature (and of causation) under exceptional circumstances; known in religious terms as "miracles" (like when Abraham was thrown in the fire and did not burn; *Qur'an* [21:69]: "*O Fire! Be thou coolness and peace on Abraham*").

Furthermore, in affirming the truth of Genesis, Moses Maimonides (Musa Ibn Maymun; d. 1204 CE) asserted in *Dalalat al-ha'irin* (*The Guide for the Perplexed*)[33] the belief that time was created, given that the celestial sphere and its motion on which it depended were both generated. And, although speculations about time continued with scholars of the caliber of Fakhr al-Din al-Razi (d. 1209 CE), Ibn 'Arabi (d. 1240 CE), Mir Damad (d. 1631 CE), and Mulla Sadra (d. 1640 CE), or with European Latin counterparts (like luminaries of the station of Thomas Aquinas, Duns Scotus, Robert Grosseteste, and Roger Bacon) the elucidation of its uncanny reality remained inconclusive and its quotidian familiarity was perplexingly enigmatic.

While the classical traditions in science and philosophy of the Ancient and
Mediaeval scholars (in the transmission of knowledge within the Greek-
Arabic-Latin lineage) tended not only to connect the discussion of conceptions
of time with physics and psychology (*De anima* treatises), but more essentially
with theological bearings of cosmology, and even religious mysticism, the
developments that started to unfurl in the Renaissance began to place more
emphasis on the *physical-mathematical* imports of reflections on temporality.
This state of affairs culminated in the deliberations of early-modern science
and philosophy with the principal thinkers of the age (mainly the 17th century)
of the aptitude of Galileo, Descartes, Huygens, Leibniz, and Newton.

The radical philosophical turn to the *foundational* character of subjectivity
in view of effecting equipoise with this physical *cum* scientific and mathematical penchant in inquiring about time, its essence and existence, found
its poignant expression in Kant's positing of time as an *a priori* form of
intuition. Since that philosophical *revolution* took place, idealists *cum* ratio-
nalists tended in general to align themselves with a subjective mediation of
conceptions of time in contrast with realist, empiricist, or positivist inclinations that aimed at systematically inquiring about time in the context of
scientific theories of physics, whilst seeking observational verifications of
their empirical consequences. It is in this sense that contemporary speculations
about time in phenomenology and Continental (European) philosophy tended
in general to adopt lines in thinking that contrasted with (Analytic) philosophy
of science and modern scientific theories of physics about time. It is with
this spirit that phenomenological attempts to rethink the classical conceptions
of time were principally mediated by ontological and ethical speculations as
respectively embodied in the legacies of Heidegger and Levinas.

Heidegger noted in *Begriff der Zeit* that: "*Dasein* is not in time, but is *time*
itself".[34] In further accentuating the intended meaning behind this proposition,
he emphasised that "*Dasein* is not [only] *time*, but is *temporality* itself".[35]
The mortal *Dasein*, is temporal in being "*futural*"; given that it is running
ahead to "the most certain yet most indeterminate past", namely its own
death. Furthermore, as highlighted in *Sein und Zeit*, *Dasein*'s being-in-the-
world (*In-der-Welt-sein*) is a mode of being-toward-death (*Sein-zum-Tode*).
The existential *Angst* from nothingness impresses itself on our being in its
most burdening form in solitude and away from the distracting immersions in

quotidian pursuits. Everydayness rather carries an alienating and estranging flight from *death*, as well as a comforting tranquillization about its unsurpassable eventuality. Death is the *"possibility as impossibility"* that arrests and terminates all possibilities.

As Sartre commented in *L'être et le néant*,[36] in reference to Heidegger's *Sein und Zeit*: death is the *"possible"* [yet certain] annihilation of all my existential possibilities. In being-ahead-of-itself *Dasein* projects its own potentiality-to-be as being-toward-an-end. In picturing itself as *no-longer-being-there-in-the-world*, and hence of being lifted from experiencing its own death, *Dasein* would still take dying upon itself as being essentially its own. A constant unfinished quality lies in the constitution of *Dasein*, for, as long as it is a being, it has not yet attained its wholeness (*Gänze*). It is in loosing its being-in-the-world *qua* its being-there by death that *Dasein* reaches its *existential plenitude*. From this perspective, Heidegger's analytic of *Dasein* suggests that time is rather closed off by the *"futural"* past as ending in death; and hence as being finite, despite the centrality of "openness" in the Heideggerian later writings.[37]

Heidegger's reflections on the temporality (*Zeitlichkeit*) of *Dasein* were articulated as a critique of classical conceptions of time. He thus wondered: "how does time show itself in everyday circumspect care (*Sorge*)?" On his view, the existential meaning of the "clock" turns out to be "making present" (*Gegenwärigen*) of the moving pointer (*Zeiger*;[38] namely the mechanism of quantifying time and its measurement, which originated from the *pendulum* principle). What shows itself in this temporal "making present" is public (*qua* objectively present) "time" that is countable as well as counted. According to Heidegger's critical reading of the history of metaphysics, the conceptual source of this classic grasp of time is to be found in Aristotle's *Physics* (Book *Delta*, 11, 219b1, *et seq.*), which resulted from a "natural" (and ontologically *forgetful*) understanding of being (*Sein*) that is "oblivious" of the *Seinsfrage* (the question of being). This conception of time renders the counted "now" (*Jetzt*) *present in motion*. World-time (*Welt-Zeit*) is thus a *present* "now-time" (*Jetzt-Zeit*); namely: an uninterrupted and irreversible temporal succession of "now-moments" that are objectively present in their flight. Each "now" is present as the "same", as well as disappears when another "*now*" dawns or arrives, being already and always: *no-longer*.

In being self-forgetful in its everyday quotidian preoccupations, *Dasein* is oblivious of its authentic and constitutive "futurality" due to its absorption within "public-time". And yet, *Dasein* is aware of the fleeting time from the knowledge of its own mortality and existentially dissolving passing away.[39] The present of *Dasein* arises from its future as being-ahead-of-itself in being-toward-death. Thrown and abandoned to its worldliness, *Dasein* falls prey to "world-time" in taking care of it. *Dasein* "awaits" with anticipation its *future*, it "retains" with recollection its own *past*, and "makes *presence*".

Even though, in *Sein und Zeit*, Heidegger judged Augustine's conception of time as being "vulgar", his reflections on *Dasein*'s "awaiting" with anticipation its *future*, "retaining" with recollection its *past*, and "making *presence*", seem to echo Augutine's view that: the reality of time depended on an *anima* (soul) that remembers, perceives, and anticipates events (given that: the *presence* of *past* things was preserved in memory, the *presence* of manifest given things was confirmed by perception, and that the *presence* of *future* things was highlighted by expectations). As if it were the case that an existential analytic of *Dasein* sufficed to distinguish Heidegger's utterances from those of Augustine, even though they designated a similar state of affairs. The abstract conceptual distinction between both thinkers is drawn in terms of the use of differing appellations *cum* signifiers in accounting for time; Heidegger's notion of "*Dasein*" is arguably established on phenomenological grounds that *bracket* (to use a Husserlian parlance) the classical Augustinian conception of *anima* (*qua* soul). However, Heidegger's version of a "phenomenological reduction" does not fully validate the claim that his transcribing of Augustine's utterance within an analytic of *Dasein* successfully distinguishes his voice from that of his predecessor; hence continuing with arguable boldness to critically assess Augustine's views as being "vulgar", while not convincingly showing how his own *echoing* utterances were more sound.

Nonetheless, despite these shortcomings, and in view of illustrating Heidegger's account of time in reference to an existential analytic of *Dasein*, we could assert (without adopting his views) that, in busily losing itself in what it is taken care of by its inauthentic mode of everyday preoccupied being, the "irresolute" mortal *Dasein* loses its own time. However, in its being as care (*Sorge*), *Dasein* is always already disclosed as temporal *qua* "futural". The existential analytic of *Dasein* hence proceeds from the standpoint of temporality and the explication of time as the transcendental horizon of the question of the meaning of being.

As authentic potentiality-for-being-a-whole, *Dasein* accomplishes its fullness in death. After all, *Dasein* does not exist as the sum of the momentary realities of experiences that succeed each other and disappear (*Sein und Zeit*, section 72). The "*between* birth and death" already lies in the being of *Dasein*. Being born, *Dasein* is already dying in its being-toward-death. Moreover, as care (*Sorge*), *Dasein* is that "*between*" itself (*Zwischen*) as "self-opening *middle*" (*Mitte*).[40] Ultimately, authentic being-toward-death, that is the finitude of temporality (rather than its eternity and perpetuity), is the ground of the historicity (*Geschichlichkeit*) of *Dasein*. This "fundamental ontological" elucidation of time and temporality in reference to *Dasein*, away from dominant modern techno-scientific definitions, finds another parallel expression in the writings of Levinas, which nonetheless were critical of Heideggerian leitmotifs. While *Dasein* is not within time but is "*Zeit*" itself (hence Heidegger's "time" appears as being *finite*), Levinas' rethinking of *le temps* in reference to *l'autre, autrui, l'Autre*, or *l'altérité* reflects time as being *infinite* (thus, in a single turn in thinking towards "*infinity*", Levinas ambitiously endeavoured to disprove Heidegger's temporal "finitude" as well as attempted to refute Hegel's processional *cum* dialectical accomplishment of "totality" in the "Notion", the "Absolute").

VIII

Levinas stated that the essential theme of his own philosophical research is the "de-formalisation [*mettre en scène*] of the notion of time".[41] Based on this penchant in thinking, he held that death (*la mort*) grants us the possibility of rendering our finite time *meaningful* by way of making it a "*time*" dedicated in essence to others (*autrui*);[42] this insight was furthermore seen by him as being the ethical ground for the *realities* of sacrifice, love, parenting, or devotional worship, and, through which living acquires its multi-layered signification.[43] In the face of death, the human subject stands dispossessed of command in a passive relation with what is uncanny; hence, loosing mastery in front of an *otherness* (*altérité*) that is unknowable in its privation.[44] An-*other*-within-the-same announces its *presence* as self-transcendent *absence*. In the face of death a readiness is pronounced in mortality as: "*me voici!*" ("Here I am!"), which itself marks the "*Adieu*" (as "Farewell") of being essentially a self-abandoned dying "*à Dieu*": "To God".

   With Levinas, time is not closed off but is rather revealed as "*openness*" to the "mystery of death", as a future that is refractory to thought (namely, a *future* as *avenir* [*à venir*] instead of the prolongation of the present as *le futur*).[45] Time relates to the absence in the infinite horizon of the future. The finite mortal being, in standing "face-to-face" with the other,[46] enters into an "unsymmetrical" and "un-reciprocal" ethical relation with otherness by way of the infinity of time that is announced by the *future* opened up through death (*L'avenir que donne la mort*);[47] given that death never *presences*.[48] The mortal being faces infinitude in its own temporality through being destined to dissolution in a movement toward God.

While Heidegger's response to techno-scientific conceptions of time and their reflection of classical precedence, was mediated by way of an "ontological-phenomenological" elucidation of the question of being (*Seins-frage*) in terms of an existential analytic of *Dasein* against the horizon of temporality, Levinas' interrogation of dominant "formalised" notions of time was intricately articulated in terms of an "ethical-phenomenological" impetus in modern thought that rested in part on novel (and arguably "apologetic")[49] speculations in "onto-theology".

While Heidegger and Levinas may have enriched reflections on time by attempting to rethink this notion from within a critique of the metaphysics of presence, their phenomenological efforts were still confronted with challenges rising from the methodologies of research in phenomenology. This is particularly the case when their efforts in attempting to think about time as a "phenomenon" paradoxically illustrate how temporality is hardly *phenomenal*; and, in consequence, that: time is not readily a given of intuition. It is in this sense that Heidegger's reflections on time and temporality resonated with his challenging and intricate meditations on *Ereignis* (the event of appropriation; or as recently rendered with some unease as: "en-owning"), which points to the "*temporalizing* of time".[50] Time is thus not a being, and in its constant passage it is not temporal. In reflections on the *Phänomenologie des Unscheinbaren* (*The phenomenology of the unapparent*; *La phénoménologie de l'inapparent*) Heidegger uttered: *Es gibt Zeit*, as: "there is time": "it gives time" (hence, echoing the saying: *Es gibt Sein*, as in: "there is": "it gives *being*"); and finding resonance with Levinas' "*il y a*", where time is the *hypostasis*; hence: "*il y a le temps*". And yet, albeit the efforts made in phenomenological research in view of elucidating the question concerning the essence and existence of time (a matter that furthermore baffles scientific theorists), this formidable riddle remains hitherto unsolved.

University of Cambridge, UK

NOTES

[1]   Immanuel Kant, *Kritik der reinen Vernunft*, ed. Raymond Schmidt (Hamburg: Felix Meiner 1956); Immanuel Kant, *Critique of Pure Reason*, trans. Norman Kemp Smith (New York: St. Martin's Press, 1965).
[2]   See: Rudolf Bernet, Iso Kern, and Eduard Marbach (eds.), *An Introduction to Husserlian Phenomenology* (Evanston, Illinois: Northwestern University Press, 1993), p. 66.
[3]   Martin Heidegger, *Sein und Zeit* (Tübingen: Niemeyer, 1986).
[4]   Refer to the seminar: *Zeit und Sein* (*Time and Being*) as presented in: Martin Heidegger, *Zur Sache des Denkens* (Tübingen: Nieymeyer, 1969).

[5] I have discussed this matter elsewhere in: Nader El-Bizri, "*ON KAI KHÔRA*: Situating Heidegger between the *Sophist* and the *Timaeus*", *Studia Phaenomenologica* IV (2004), pp.73–98. See also: Françoise Dastur, *Heidegger et la question du temps* (Paris: Presses Universitaires de France, 1990); Dominique Janicaud. *Chronos: Pour l'intelligence du partage temporel* (Paris: Grasset, 1997).

[6] To avoid conceptual confusions, it is worthy to note that the appellation "phenomenology" is applied in this inquiry to a variety of philosophical 20th century European traditions in thinking (German/French in particular), rather than restricting this designation to Husserlian research. It is in this sense that Heidegger, Levinas and Derrida are presented as being thinkers who offered prolongations of phenomenology, or who have been impacted in their intellectual formation by phenomenological methods of investigation.

[7] Heidegger deploys the coined term "*Dasein*", which points to existence in classical German philosophical usage, in view of differentiating his discourse from theories of subjectivity and inter-subjectivity of the Husserlian and Cartesian traditions, and in view of stressing the mode of existing of the "human being" as that of being-in-the-world (*In-der-Welt-sein*); namely as "being-there" (*Da-Sein*). At times, Heidegger attempts to introduce a nuance between "*Dasein*" and "*Daseyn*" (with a shift from "*Sein*" to the more archaic German "*Seyn*") in his later writings or notebooks.

[8] Mainly as noted in: Maurice Merleau-Ponty, *Phénoménologie de la perception* (Paris: Gallimard, 1945).

[9] As Bergson puts it: "*Le temps qui ne dure pas n'est pas mesurable*"; see: Henri Bergson, "*Durée et simultanéité*", in *Mélanges* (Paris: Presses Universitaires de France, 1972), p. 102.

[10] I refer the reader to the following tract: Hans Reichenbach, *The Rise of Scientific Philosophy* (Berkeley: University of California Press, 1951), pp. 144–156. This study, which was composed by Reichenbach as part of his popular later writings, expands on his dense and technical reflections on time and space in reference to Einstein's theory of relativity, as these were principally elucidated in his earlier masterful work: *Philosophie der Raum-Zeit-Lehre*, 1928.

[11] I refer the reader to the following selection of studies that reflect on the philosophical and epistemological entailments of Einstein's theory of relativity and on more recent developments in theories of time in physics: Peter Galison, *Einstein's Clocks, Poincaré's Maps: Empires of Time* (New York: W. W. Norton, 2003); Lisa Randall, *Warped Passages: Unravelling the Universe's Hidden Dimensions* (London: Allen Lane, Penguin Books Ltd., 2005); Lewis Marder, *Time and the Space Traveller* (London: Allen and Unwin, 1971).

[12] This classical thesis was echoed by the 20th century philosopher J. M. E. McTaggart, and more recently seconded by Michael Dummett; see: J. M. E. McTaggart, *The Nature of Existence* (Cambridge: Cambridge University Press, 1927), chapter 33; Michael Dummett, "A Defense of MacTaggart's Proof of the Unreality of Time", in *Truth and Other Enigmas* (London: Duckworth, 1978). Both differ in this regard from Reichenbach's affirmation of the reality of time based on his analytic *cum* epistemic inclination to advocate the physics of his age; namely, Einstein's theory of relativity.

[13] The *present* as a *moment/now* is "without magnitude" like it is the case with the mathematical point in Euclid's *Stoikheia* (*The Elements*). One could even hold that the microscopic miniscule quantification of an *atomic* time-unit like a *Khronon* would not restrict our imagining of its further divisibility.

[14] Plato, *Timaeus*, trans. R. G. Bury, with parallel Greek text (Cambridge, Mass.: Harvard University Press, 1999).

[15] Aristotle, *Physics*, ed. W. David Ross (Oxford: Oxford University Press, 1998).

[16] See: Philoponus, *Corollaries on Place and void*, with: Simplicius, *Against Philoponus on the Eternity of the World*, trans. David Furley and Christian Wildberg (London: Duckworth, 1991); Simplicius, *Corollaries on Place and Time*, trans. J. O. Urmson (London: Duckworth, 1992). I also refer the reader to: Richard Sorabji, *Time, Creation and the Continuum* (Ithaca: Cornell University Press, 1983).

[17] Plotinus, *Enneads*, trans. Arthur Hilary Armstrong, with parallel Greek text (Cambridge, Mass.: Harvard University Press, 1966–1967).

[18] Augustine, *Confessions*, ed. James O'Donnell (Oxford: Clarendon Press, 1992).

[19] I have investigated related topics in: Nader El-Bizri, "Avicenna's *De Anima* between Aristotle and Husserl," in *The Passions of the Soul in the Metamorphosis of Becoming*, ed. Anna-Teresa Tymieniecka (Dordrecht: Kluwer Academic Publishers, 2003), pp. 67–89.

[20] I undertook this thematic deviation, from focusing on modern phenomenological reflections on time, to addressing classical corollaries on this subject in the history of science and philosophy in the mediaeval Islamic civilization, in view of elucidating the diversity of serious intellectual historical endeavors to solve the paradoxes of conceptions of time and temporality. The focus on mediaeval Islamic thought offers highlights of classical concepts of time that gave expression to prolongations of Greek speculations in this domain, as well as acted as a ground for later developments in the history of science and philosophy, as manifested in the variations of European mediaeval and Renaissance scholarship, and through them in the developments of the 17th century. Moreover, this *turn* towards a brief survey of research on the essence and existence of time in the history of ideas in Islam is a reflection of the lines of inquiry that are grouped under the covering title of this volume of the Kluwer Academic Publishers *Dialogue between Islamic Philosophy and Occidental Phenomenology Series*, to which this chapter humbly belongs.

[21] I have discussed this elsewhere in: Nader El-Bizri, "Time (Concepts)", in *Medieval Islamic Civilization: An Encyclopedia*, ed. Josef W. Meri (New York–London: Routledge, 2005), Vol. II, pp. 810–812.

[22] One could mention herein the polymaths: Muhammad Ibn Musa al-Khawarizmi (the father of algebra; d. 850 CE), the Banu Musa (Sons of Musa Ibn Shakir; fl. 9th century CE, Baghdad), Ya'qub Ibn Ishaq al-Kindi (d. 873 CE), Thabit Ibn Qurra (d. 901 CE), Abu 'Abd' Allah al-Battani (Albategnius; d. 929 CE), Ibrahim Ibn Sinan (d. 946 CE), Abu Sa'd al-'Ala' Ibn Sahl (d. 1000 CE), Abu Sahl Wayjan Ibn Rustam al-Quhi (d. 1000 CE), Abu al-Hasan 'Ali Ibn Yunus (d. 1009), Ahmad Ibn Muhammad Ibn 'Abd al-Jalil al-Sijzi (d. 1020 CE), Abu 'Ali Ibn Sina (Avicenna; d. 1037 CE), al-Hasan Ibn al-Haytham (Alhazen; d. ca. 1040 CE), Abu Rayhan al-Biruni (d. 1048 CE), 'Umar al-Khayyam (d. ca. 1129 CE), Ibn al-Razzaz al-Jazari (fl. 13th century CE), Nasir al-Din al-Tusi (d. 1274 CE), and Kamal al-Din al-Farisi (d. 1320 CE).

[23] Astrolabes could not have been developed and perfected unless great accomplishments have been made in the domain of spherical geometry, given that they presupposed a careful and accurate projection of the forms that are on curved *cum* spherical surfaces unto rectilinear planar surfaces.

[24] For instance, 10th century research on anaclastic (refractive) curves as sections in conics (parabola, hyperbola, ellipse, convex and bi-convex curves) offered geometrical models for optical studies in catoptrics and dioptrics in view of perfecting lenses, as manifest in the works of Ibn Sahl, al-Quhi, and al-Sijzi, with extensions of their findings in the investigations of Ibn al-Haytham and Kamal al-Din al-Farisi. This mathematical research involved the introduction of motion in geometry, which was not admissible by the Greeks, and hence allowed for further applications and theoretical prolongations of Euclidean geometry, and facilitated the maturation of the study of geometrical transformations, not only in reference to figures, but to their spatial relations and congruence as well.

[25] Time measurement (*tawqit*; *mawaqit*) is central to the determination with accuracy of the timings of the decreed five daily prayers in Islam, and in supporting the observations in astronomy for demarcating the beginning of the fasting month of *Ramadan* and its ending with the start of *'Id al-fitr*, which depend on a developed coordinative system to compute time in the lunar cycle, with its temporal shifts with respect to the solar calendar and seasons.

[26] Ikhwan al-Safa', *Rasa'il Ikhwan al-Safa' wa Khullan al-Wafa'*, ed. Butrus Bustani (Beirut: Dar Sadir, 1957).

[27] Ibn Sina, *Kitab al-hudud*, ed. A.-M. Goichon (Cairo: Institut français d'archéologie orientale du Caire, 1963); Ibn Sina. *al-Isharat wa'l-tanbihat*, ed. Sulayman Dunya (Cairo: Dar al-ma'arif bi-misr, 1957–1960).

[28] Ibn al-Haytham, *Kitab al-manazir*, ed. Abdelhamid I. Sabra (Kuwait: National Council for Culture, Arts and Letters, 1983); Alhazen, *The Optics*, trans. Abdelhamid I. Sabra (London: Warburg Institute, 1989).

[29] See: Roshdi Rashed, *Geometry and Dioptrics in Classical Islam* (London: al-Furqan Islamic Heritage Foundation, 2005).

[30] See: Alnoor Dhanani, *The Physical Theory of Kalam* (Leiden: Brill, 1994).

[31] Abu Hamid al-Ghazali, *Tahafut al-falasifa (The Incoherence of the Philosophers)*, trans. Michael Marmura, with parallel Arabic text (Provo, Utah: Brigham Young University Press, 1997).

[32] Ibn Rushd, *Tahafut al-tahafut*, ed. Muhammad 'Abid al-Jabiri (Beirut: Markaz dirasat al-wihda al-'arabiyya, 1998).

[33] Moses Maimonides, *Dalalat al-ha'irin (The Guide for the Perplexed)*, trans. M. Friedlander (New York: Dover, 1956).

[34] Martin Heidegger, *Begriff der Zeit, Gesamtausgabe, Band 64* (Frankfurt am Main: Vittorio Klostermann, 1924); pp. 6–8, 10–14, 16–20.

[35] We find an analogous thesis, which does not belong to the Heideggerian tradition, but rather offers prolongations of Hegelian concepts, in Kojève's view on history as implied by his statement: "*La présence réelle du Temps dans le Monde s'appelle donc Homme. Le Temps est l'Homme, et l'Homme est le Temps*"; see: Alexandre Kojève, *Introduction à la lecture de Hegel* (Paris: Gallimard, 1947), p. 370.

[36] Jean-Paul Sartre, *L'être et le néant* (Paris: Gallimard, 1943), pp. 594–5.

[37] One could add herein that Openness (*Offenheit*) belongs to the family of Heideggerian appellations that point to *spatiality* and emplacement like: the clearing (*Lichtung*), the open (*Offene*), the rift (*Riss*), the threshold (*Limen*), cleavage (*Zerklüftung*), the between (*Zwischen*), region (*Gegend*), making room (*Einräumen*), and giving space (*Raumgeben*). And yet, Heidegger's reflections on *Zeit-Raum* accentuated his belief in the co-entanglement of space and time, as well as pointed to their "equiprimordiality" in his later thinking. I have discussed this matter elsewhere in: El-Bizri, "*ON KAI KHÔRA*", op. cit.

[38] Heidegger, *Sein und Zeit*, op. cit., section 81.

[39] As Janicaud thoughtfully noted in his meditations on the lived experiencing of temporality and aging: "*Vieillir, c'est renoncer peu à peu aux jeux insouciants, au plaisir sans arrières-pensées, aux illusions sans mesure. C'est même oublier qu'on croyait pouvoir reculer la frontière du possible grâce à d'insondables réserves d'avenir*". See: Janicaud, *Chronos*, op. cit., p. 240.

[40] Martin Heidegger, *Beiträge zur Philosophie (Vom Ereignis), Gesamtausgabe, Band 65* (Frankfurt am Main: Vittorio Klostermann, 1989).

[41] Emmanuel Levinas, *Entre nous* (Paris: Bernard Grasset, 1991), p. 263.

[42] It is perhaps worthy noting in this context that the "giving of time" beyond any accounts of exchange was explored with labyrinthine and uneasy speculations in: Jacques Derrida, *Donner le temps* (Paris: Galilée, 1991).

[43] Emmanuel Levinas, *Totalité et infini* (La Haye: Martinus Nijhoff, 1974), p. 208.

[44] Emmanuel Levinas, *Le temps et l'autre* (Paris: Presses Universitaires de France, 1991), pp. 57–9.

[45] Levinas, *Le temps et l'autre, op. cit.*, pp. 83–4.

[46] As Levinas affirmed: "*La relation avec l'avenir, la présence de l'avenir dans le présent semble encore s'accomplir dans le face-à-face avec autrui*"; see: Levinas, *Le temps et l'autre, op. cit.*, pp. 68–69.

[47] Levinas, *Le temps et l'autre, op. cit.*, p. 68.

[48] As Levinas puts it: "*La mort n'est jamais un présent …si tu es, elle n'est pas; si elle est, tu n'es pas*"; see: Levinas, *Le temps et l'autre, op. cit.*, p. 59.

[49] One would evoke herein the thematic distinction between Levinas' *philosophy* and his Rabbinic and Talmudic writings as for instance illustrated in some of his works, like: Emmanuel Levinas, *Quatre lectures Talmudiques* (Paris: Minuit, 1976); Emmanuel Levinas, *Du sacré au saint. Cinq nouvelles lectures Talmudiques* (Paris: Minuit, 1977).

[50] Heidegger, *Zur Sache des Denkens, op. cit.*, pp. 20–24.

SECTION III

MĪR DĀMĀD ON TIME AND TEMPORALITY

Mīr Muḥammad Bāqir Dāmād al-Ḥussaynī Isterābādī, (1491A.H.) known
also as "*Ishrāq*" (Illumination)[1], "*mu'alim al-thānī*" (Second Teacher-the first
being Aristotle) and "*Sayyīd al-afāḍil*" (Master of the Learned)[2] is the founder
of the "School of Isfahān" and one of the most celebrated philosophers of the
Safavid era. Mīr Dāmād who did much of his studies in Mashhad studying the
Shifā' and *Ishārāt* of Ibn Sīnā continued his studies in Qazwīn and Kashān.
It was Isfahān however where he spent most of his prolific life composing
numerous works and training such students as Sayyīd Aḥmad 'Alavī and Mullā
Ṣadrā.[3] Mīr Dāmād who died in Najaf, like many other Muslim philosophers
of the School of Isfahān made an attempt to bring about a rapprochement
between Peripateric's (*mashshā'is*) notion of the createdness and eternity of
the world and that of the theologians (*mutikallimūn*).

Mīr Dāmād's *magnum opus* is a work known as *Qabasāt ḥaqq al-yaqīn
fī ḥuduth al-'ālam* (Fire of the Truth of Certainty Regarding the Createdness
of the World).[4] Mīr Dāmād chooses the word *Qabasāt* based on the Quranic
verses [7:27 & 9:20] to mean particles of fire. It is in this work, one of
the most difficult examples of Islamic philosophical treatise that Mīr Dāmād
discusses the question of time and its relationship to the eternity (*qidam*) and
createdness (*huduth*) of the world. *Qabasāt* is divided into ten chapters each
one called *Qabas*, and each *Qabas* consists of smaller parts called *wamīḍ*
(lightning). The choice of the title of this work as well as chapters and sections
clearly indicate Mīr Dāmād's interest in Suhrawardī and his school of *ishrāq*.
In fact, the connection between Mīr Dāmād and Suhrawardī is made even
more clear not only by the title of his numerous works such as *Jazawāt*
(Ecstacies), *Ufuq al-mubīn* (The Clear Horizon), and *Mashāriq al-anwār* (The
Orient of Light), but also by the fact that he is one of the few philosophers
who accepted Suhrawardī's principality of essence (*aṣālat al-māhiyyah*).[5]

Before a discussion concerning the nature of time and temporality according
to Mīr Dāmād, it is imperative that something about the structure of *Qabasāt*
be said. In the first *Qabasa*, different types of createdness and division of
existence is discussed. Second *Qabasa* deals with three types of intrinsic

A-T. Tymieniecka (ed.),
Timing and Temporality in Islamic Philosophy and Phenomenology of Life, 159–165.
© 2007 *Springer.*

priority and posterity and third *Qabasa* is a discussion on two types of distinctive posterity (*taqadum al-infikākī*). Fourth and fifth chapters are less significant as far as the concept of time is concerned but in the sixth *Qabasa* the relationship between time and motion are discussed. This chapter which is unparalleled in depth and complexity of language, undertakes a discussion on the concept of finitude and *ad infinitum* as it relates to existent beings as opposed to integers. The following chapters treat a variety of issues which are not particularly relevant to our discussion here. Therefore, in a general sense it can be said that our discussion on the concept of time is primarily based on chapters one, two and nine even though references will be made to other chapters.

For Mīr Dāmād, time can be divided into three ontological domains or divisions, *Sarmad* (transcendental), *Dahr* (eternal) and *Zamān* (temporal). His views on eternal createdness (*hudūth-i al-dahrī*) according to some is a rendition of Ibn Sīnā's view on the problem of createdness and eternity of the world and according to others it is a clarification and response to the inherent problems of Ibn Sīnā's views on the subject matter. Mīr Dāmād is particularly sensitive to Ibn Sīnā where he discusses divisions of time and its relationship to eternity and createdness into three categories:
1. The relationship between immutable to immutable (*Sarmad*).
2. The relationship between immutable to changeable (*dahr*).[6]
3. The relationship between changeable to changeable (*zamān*).
Ibn Sīnā seems to have conflicting views on this since he identified *dahr* as that which is with time but is not of time, a kind of frozen time which dominates *zamān*.[7] Mīr Dāmād begins by opposing the traditional view of the philosophers in general and Ibn Sīnā in particular who has argued that the problem of eternity on both ends are insoluble and can be equally proven and refuted (*jadalat al-ṭarafayīn*).[8] Ibn Sīnā's concept of essential createdness, Mīr Dāmād argues, is eventually reduced to a mere linguistic difference between God and the incorporeal substances since the latter's existence is not created in the real sense of the word. In order to preserve the transcendental nature of God, Mīr Dāmād maintains, a real *hudūth* is required (he calls this *hudūth fī matn al-a'yān*).[9]

An accurate understanding of Mīr Dāmād's view on time and the question of *hudūth and qidam* requires a thorough understanding of such figures as Abu'l Barakāt-i Baghdādī, Ibn Sīnā and Suhrawardī, but that is a discussion which is beyond the scope of this work. What we do surmise from *Qabasāt* is that for Mīr Dāmād, time can be divided into three ontological domains or divisions, *Sarmad* (transcendental), *Dahr* (eternal) and *Zamān* (temporal). *Sarmad* can be viewed as the domain that belongs exclusively to the Necessary Existence and therefore no existent, be it corporeal or incorporeal may enter this domain. Compared to this ontological domain, all that lies below it be it corporeal or incorporeal is therefore non-existent since their existence is contingent and not necessary. That which is contingent has a shadow existence and while it has its own ontological level of reality, it nevertheless is non-existent when it is compared to *Sarmad* and therefore can be called *'adam al-sarmadī* (transcendental non-existence). This non-existence which is intertwined with the ontological fabric of all other domains makes them to be existent from one aspect, and non-existent from another one. *Sarmad* therefore is a timeless time, an entity that transcends time. As Rūmī the Persian mystical poet said:

> In the timelessness, where there is Divine Light, Where is the past, present or the future.

Next is the ontological domain of *Dahr* where all incorporeal beings reside. These incorporeal intelligibles which have been referred to by different names such as Plato's forms or archetypes, Ibn 'Arabī's *a'yān al-thābitah*, Suhrawardī's *Arbāb al-anwā'* or *rab al-naw'* act as an intermediary between *sarmad* and the ontological realm below it.

Dahr is not extant and is therefore indivisible, it is non-existent from the aspect of *Sarmad* but existent from the perspective of the inferior ontological domain called *zamān*. *Zamān* for Mīr Dāmād is the ontological domain where all existent beings reside and is inclusive of those corporeal entities which undergo change and are subject to generation and corruption. Mīr Dāmād distinguishes between *zamān* and *dahr* by telling us that existent beings are within time (*fī'l-zamān*) whereas they are concommitent with *dahr* (*ma'al-zamān*).[10]

T. Izutzu an eminent scholar of later Islamic philosophy argues that there is another interpretation of *sarmad, dahr* and *zamān* which Mīr Dāmād himself may have recognized and alluded to in the *Qabasāt*.[11] Contrary to the previous interpretation, this view offers a more dynamic relationship between the three ontological realities as well as in and of themselves. Accordingly, the Absolute or *sarmad*, despite its simple existence, contains certain individuations or particularities (*ta'ayyun*) which can be actualized. T. Izutzu describes this as divine essence which through its attributes is particularized and thus there is a dynamic relationship between the essence of the Absolute and its attributes which are its inherent particularization. It is precisely the mutual relationship between the essence of the Absolute and its attributes which according to Izutzu, is what Mīr Dāmād calls *sarmad*. *Sarmad* here is not an absolute ontological reality but a relationship between two unchangeable phenomena which from the aspect of *zamān,* it appears contradictory but from above remains valid. From the same perspective, *dahr* is the relation between the archetypes which are unchangeable and *zamān* which is subject to change and therefore this ontological relationship is one of relativity.

For the three categories of time, *sarmad, dahr and zamān*, it is *dahr* which for Mīr Dāmād is the philosophically significant issue and one which he thinks is the key to the understanding of the problem of creation and eternity of the world. The concept of *dahr* according to Mīr Dāmād solves the following problem: There are those philosophers who believe in the eternity of the world by arguing that even though the world may have been created, but since it has always been co-eternal with God, it is therefore eternal and its createdness has no beginning in time. To put it differently, since God is the eternal cause which has always been there, the effect must have always been there. This coeternality in time however does not mean ontological equality with God since God is ontologically prior to its effect. Many Peripatetic philosophers in particular Ibn Sīnā base their argument on this basis and state that since existents came from non-existence and because their existence is contingent upon God, they should therefore be regarded as a non-existence. This concept which I have alluded to before is traditionally referred to as *ḥudūth al-dhātī* (essential createdness). It is as an alternative to this concept that Mīr Dāmād puts forward in his theory of *ḥudūth al-dahrī*.

Mīr Dāmād argues that the world of existent beings is created not because its existence is prior to this type of non-existence, namely *'adam al-dhātī* (essential non-existence) for this is a conceptual understanding of causality. The type of createdness Mīr Dāmād advocates is of a different type, namely a "real one" since it follows a real non-existence as opposed to an essential non-existent (*'adam al-dhātī)*. This priority and posteriority is not in the domain of time but it is in *dahr,* that is, it is a non-existence that is neither essential (*dhātī*) nor temporal (*zamānī*) but is eternal (*dahrī*).

Eternal non-existence is therefore real non-existence since *dahr* is not extant, linear or in a state of influx. It is not clear why Mīr Dāmād states that ontologically, *dahr* is non-existing in the sense that its existence is contradictory to an actualized existence. Therefore, he says this is different than essential non-existence(*'adam al-dhātī*) of existent beings where existence is incompatible with but is not contradictory to an actualized existence. Since *dahr* transcends time and is non-existent, Mīr Dāmād tells us that the only way to be cognizant of it is through a mystical mode of knowledge (*kashf wa shuhūd*) while a person is in a deep state of meditation.

Mīr Dāmād appears to be arguing that coming into being and perishing is not only an integral part of *zamān* but is somehow related to the ontological domain of *dahr*. Mīr Dāmād's perceptive observation of *zamān* sees *dahr* within it as well as by arguing that *zamān* is in a state of continuous change and influx and therefore cannot *"be"* (*wujūd*) in the authentic sense of the word. In a sense it is *Not*, rather than *is* and this simultaneous existence and non-existence for Mīr Dāmād is indicative of the non-existence of *zamān* and the existence of *dahr*.

Sayyid jalāl al-Dīn Ashtiyānī, one of the most eminent contemporary Muslim philosophers criticizes Mīr Dāmād's view as being more rhetorical than substantial and argues that the concept of *hudūth al-dahrī* is a reformulation of essential createdness (*hudūth al-dhātī*) of Ibn Sīnā.[12] He furthermore maintains that whatever Mīr Dāmād wanted to elaborate upon using the concept of *hudūth al-dahrī*, can also be explicated by Ibn Sīnā's *hudūth al-dhātī* and goes so far as to say that Mīr Dāmād's *hudūth al-dahrī* is really *hudūth al-zamānī*. As Ashtiyānī states:

> If [Mīr Dāmād] wants to refute eternality of what is not God, refutation of the eternality of time is impossible. Therefore, we should abandon the effort to prove the createdness of time (*hudūth al-zamān*) and accept a type of *hudūth* .... This is precisely *hudūth al-dhātī* or something of this kind which may be called by another name.[13]

Ashtiyāni's criticism is strictly Ibn Sīnīan in that he identifies any *hudūth* with the notion of time. *Hudūth* of any existent being, Ibn Sīnā says is posterior to its *'adam* and therefore *'adam* is an indirect cause of existent beings. Also, *hudūth* and *'adam* are contradictory and thus for *hudūth* to occur, *'adam* should vanish.

Mīr Dāmād might accept part of this argument and refute a section of it. He admits the contradictory nature of *wujūd* and *'adam* but states that it has no bearing on the question of time. *'Adam* and *wujūd* are not necessarily contradictory when it comes to existent beings since to be contradictory requires that they be at the same time. For example, A and ∼A cannot be at the same time but their occurrence at two different times is possible and not contradictory. In other words, *wujūd* and *'adam* can be contradictory in time but when and where this contradiction fades away is in *dahr* where posterity and priority are ontological. It is precisely the conceptual nature *of hudūth* (*mantiqī, 'aqlī, i'tibārī, dhihnī, bi'l-martibat al-'aqliyyah*) and not its reality which is troubling to Mīr Dāmād. A real *hudūth* must be independent of God in the real sense of independence which Mīr Dāmād identify as when a cause creates an effect and in this sense, God is the ultimate cause of creation.

There are primarily two problems with the theory of *hudūth al-dahrī*. First, despite the complex and sometimes verbose and repetitious nature of his argument, Mīr Dāmād does not succeed in achieving his original objective, that is to separate in a real sense the transcendental reality of *sarmad* and that of *dahr*. This lack of success is not due to the weakness of his argument but is deeply rooted in the ontological structure of Mīr Dāmād's philosophy. As Mullā Ṣadrā realized, reconciling the principle that states "from One emanates only one" (*al-wāhid layusader ila'l-wāhid*) with bestowing independence upon the reality of anything except God, ultimately fails. Mīr Dāmād has made a noble attempt to bring about a rapprochement between the notion of real *ḥudūth* which he thinks the realm of *dahr* makes possible, and Ibn Sīnā's notion of *ḥudūth al-dhātī*. This attempt despite the sophistication of the arguments involved in my opinion fails.

The second objection is one that is equally valid for Ibn Sīnā and Mīr Dāmād, both of whom in my opinion have disregarded a subtlety when they claim that *'adam* precedes *wujūd*. Let us analyze this further. If *'adam* precedes *wujūd*, then in order for *wujūd* to become *mawjūd*, *'adam* should become *ma'dūm* so *mawjūd* can come into being. In order for *'adam* to become *ma'dūm*, it must be something such that it can become *ma'dūm*, and this is contradictory to the very definition of *'adam*. So the very notion of *'adam* is as problematic as *wujūd* and one that is not entirely clear either in Ibn Sīnā or Mīr Dāmād.

The other alternative is that *'adam* does not precede *wujūd*. The first problem that arises is that if *'adam* did not precede *wujūd*, then *wujūd* must have always been there. If we identify *wujūd* with God then this problem is solved but we have also sided with the eternity of the world as stipulated by *mashshā'is*. If we don't identify *wujūd* with God, then we have the problem of co-eternality of *wujūd* with God and that is even a bigger problem. In short Mīr Dāmād's perspective of *ḥudūth* in general and *ḥudūth al-dahrī* in particular rests upon the notion of *'adam* preceding *wujūd* and if this axiom itself is problematic, so is his conclusion. The irony of it is that to the extent which *Qabasāt* is understandable, Mīr Dāmād does not address the problematic nature of the above truth claim but rather, he offers a solution to the question of eternity and createdness of the world on its basis.

To summarize the foregoing discussion, it can be said that Mīr Dāmād wants to restore the createdness of the world in the real sense of creation and not as Peripatetic philosophers have explicated. The philosophers notion of creation is based on essential creation (*ḥudūth al-dhati*) which implies priority and posterity in the essential sense of the word such as the posterity of number three to two. This Mīr Dāmād says, is not real *ḥudūth* and he argues that real *ḥudūth* is possible and necessary only where and when the created and creator stand in a causal relationship. This is made possible according to him, within the ontological realm of *dahr*.

Mīr Dāmād's view on time is a much neglected area of scholarship both because of the difficulty of his language and the complexity of his philosophical concepts. His contribution to Islamic philosophical tradition however is enormous since his grand synthesis of various notions of time not only provides the reader with a compendium of Islamic philosophers' view on time but offers a middle ground between the peripatetics and that of *mutikallimūn* on the problem of eternity and createdness of the world.

Mīr Dāmād's classification of time provides a rich venue for a comparative study between his notions of time and some of the Western philosophers such as Heidegger. The relation between Being and time in the Qabasāt which has been all but ignored remains a fascinating area of study.

Mehdi Aminrazavi
University of Mary Washington

NOTES

[1] Mīr Dāmād's psudoname in his collected works of poetry is "Ishrāq". See *Diwān-i ash'ār,* ed. Sayyid Ahmad, MS.347 of 4771, Mashhad, Imām Riḍā Library.

[2] *Sayyid al-Afāḍil* (The Master of the Learned), is a title that Hājj Mullā Hādī Sabziwārī has bestowed upon him. See *Gharr al-fra'iḍ* known also as *Sharh-i manzumah,,* Tehran: McGill Univ. Press, 1348, p.112.

[3] His title as "Dāmād" meaning in persian "groom" is due to the fact that his father married the daughter of 'Ali ibn 'Abd al-'Ali also known as Muhaqiq-i Kirkī and therefore Mīr Dāmād is the grand son of this notable figure. For more information on his life and thought see the following works: Musavi M. Behbahani, *Hakim-i Isterābād,* Tehran: Tehran University Press, 1377. Introduction to the *Qabasāt,* ed. M. Muhaqiq, Tehran: Tehran Univ. Press, 1367, S.A. Mousavī Behbahanī, "Mīr Dāmād, falsafah wa sharh-i hāl wa naqd-i āthār-i uo", majillay-i maqālāt wa barrasihāy-i nashriyyah daneshkadeh ilāhiyāt wa ma'arif islami, V.3–4, 1349.

[4] *Qabasāt,* ed. M. Muhaqiq, Tehran: Tehran Univ. Press, 1367.

[5] It is note worthy that the connection between Mīr Dāmād ends the *Qabasāt* by the prayer of light. See *Qabasāt,* p.483.

[6] *Qabasāt,* p.8–9 & 18–19.

[7] *Ibid., p.9.*

[8] See Ibn Sīnā, *Shifā, al-mantiq:al-jadal,* ed. Ahmad F. Al-Ahwani, Cairo:1385, p.76.

[9] Henry Corbin suggests the term "événement eternal" which is close to the Greek term used by Proclus and conveys the real meaning of this term.

[10] Mīr Dāmād elaborates on this Ibn Sīnīan notion in the *Ta'liqāt.*

[11] Tushiko Izutsu, Intr. to *Qabasāt,* ed. M. Muhaqiq, Tehran, Tehran Univ. Press, 1367, p.112. for more information on Mīr Dāmād's intellectual thought see H. Corbin, "Confessions extatiques de Mīr Dāmād" in *En islam iranien,* tome IV. Paris, 1972, pp.9–53.

[12] S.J. Ashtiyānī, *Muntakhabāt-i az āthār-i hukamāy-i Iran,* Tehran: De L'institute Franco-Iranien, 1350, p.8–9, 40–43.

[13] Ibid., p.15.

MASSIMO DURANTE

HISTORICAL AND MESSIANIC TIME:
THE STRUCTURE OF SUBJECTIVITY
AND THE QUESTION OF JUDGEMENT

Dann sind wir auf der Erde erwarten worden. Dann ist uns wie jedem Geschlecht, das vor uns war, eine schwache messianische Kraft mitgegeben, an welche die Vergangenheit Anspruch hat.

Über den Begriff der Geschichte, Walter Benjamin

Le prophète assume la révélation qui lui fait ressentir l'apparition du transcendant [...]. Mais, adopté par Dieu, il est, de plus, introduit avec lui dans l'affrontement du non-transcendant, dans une position de conquête à l'égard du temps, dans une histoire.

Prophètes et prophéties, André Neher

1. INTRODUCTION: HISTORICAL AND MESSIANIC TIME

A study of the *superlative* in philosophy would be fruitful and is long overdue. Once the word *realis* was conceived, the concept of the superlative was needed as Thomas Aquinas sought the *ens realissimum*. The word *realis* derives it meaning not only from the things it applies to, but also from the superlative which it tends towards. In Kant's attempt to understand the *sublime*, he needed the superlative to conceive the idea of sublime as a feeling of *attraction* for that which is *absolutely great*. The absolutely great is in fact defined as that "beyond which no greater is subjectively possible"[1]. Again, once Heidegger sought to conceive the possibility of a *certainty* that is not founded on the object, he not only conceived death as that certainty but as the certainty *par excellence*, the certainty from which all other certainties descend[2]. These examples serve to illustrate that once we are confronted with the philosophical question of the status of messianic and historical time, the concept of the superlative is required. Why is this so? Because in thinking about messianic and historic time we ask ourselves what is *most essential* to us *as* temporal beings, what is *most essential* to our lives *as* temporal existences. If one does not take into consideration the full meaning of the

167

A-T. Tymieniecka (ed.),
Timing and Temporality in Islamic Philosophy and Phenomenology of Life, 167–193.
© 2007 *Springer*.

superlative, part of our conception of messianic and historic time would be definitively lost. In messianic and historical time the pivotal relation to what is essential (to what is *most essential*) is conceived in a different way: *this difference is precisely – this is the thesis of the present paper – what distinguishes messianic from historical time*. What is, therefore, most essential to us in historical time? In the messianic time? In historical time, what is most essential to us is by definition what we cannot be indifferent to, i.e., what makes a difference to us. It thus becomes the guiding principle or idea for the époque which asserts it. Philosophy of history would be impossible without the possibility of referring to the notion of *idea*, whose philosophical construction is in it a compendium of any philosophy of history. The notion of idea is, in our view, the key notion for understanding a philosophy of history, since it is not possible to account for historical time viewed in its progression or, at least, in its tension, towards the future, without being able to manifest a vision itself of history. This vision or idea becomes the guiding principle of this progression or tension towards the future. It also raises the most difficult problem that any philosophy of history should be able to account for: that is to say, at what point one can affirm that the *idea* has been *realised*. The tension between the idea and its realisation is the tension that animates any philosophy of history and, at the same time, brings into question the immanent statute of its guiding principle. Since realising an idea means to assign to the idea a real object, the idea always transcends the real object which intends to realise it and fulfils the program of the ideal guiding principle of history. We should keep in mind in the course of our reflection this first consideration: the immanence of any philosophy of history is always transcended from within, in virtue of its own logic or construction. In historical time, therefore, what is most essential is this idea or vision, which defines the difference and transcends at any time the historical object that is meant to realise it. For this reason, this idea or vision is none other than the manifestation itself of being (in the forms of truth, identity, etc.). Therefore what is most essential in historical time is the *manifestation of being*. Naturally, it does not follow from this that what does not belong to history does not also belong to being; it only means that it does not belong to the manifestation of being. This is the reason that motivates within a religious perspective the idea of a final Judgement.[3] What, therefore, is most essential to us in messianic time? In messianic time what is most essential to us is the idea of *salvation*. This idea transforms existential time into a *value*, which has to be lived, endorsed and asserted, since in it and through it, something, even existence itself, is placed radically at risk. Historical time differs from the messianic time, since in historical time what is most essential to us is the manifestation of being, which is "always already saved".[4] In messianic time, what is the most essential is no longer to be part of the manifestation of being, but to be saved. This idea of salvation concerns, as we will see further on, existence *as* a whole. In a certain sense, a manifestation is still needed, but it is no longer the manifestation of being, but the manifestation of a sign,[5] which may guide us on our journey towards salvation. It remains true that, as the sign demands a manifestation, it also requires a concept of history: in this sense, the journey towards salvation is never entirely dissociated from the history of salvation. But salvation is required because of the concreteness of the historical dimension in a sense other than the one required by the manifestation of being: the danger, the risk, whose existence as a whole is exposed to and which we have to be saved from is always encountered within history and, thus, it is in the very horizon of history, that the *value* of the existence opened to salvation is at stake, it is lived, endorsed and asserted. Messianic time is dominated by the thought of salvation, which transforms existence into a *value*: this value does not concern, in this perspective, something which belongs to existence, which *is* in the existence, but the existence as a whole. Since this value concerns existence as a whole, it also affects what transcends the existence as such and allows us to perceive existence in its wholeness. As we shall see in the present essay, this consideration constitutes the basis of the central moral dimension of messianic time, since in this dimension the moral character of an action is realised in the action, but is measured in relation to the existence as a whole[6] as well as to what transcends existence (and not only in relation to what exists as a given datum). To resume what we have said above, *the concept of historical time is that which concerns the manifestation of being, while the concept of messianic time is that which concerns salvation, which transforms the whole existence in a value which has to be endorsed and asserted*. Historical time is, thus, an *ontological time*, whose temporal forms are based on being (the past being intended as what *is no longer*, the present as what *is* and the future as what *is not yet*): past and future are based on the present of being (*is*) and they represent the negative account (*no longer*; *not yet*) of the positive dimension of the present. Messianic time can be thought of as a *conditional time*, which is based on the eventuality of the coming of the Messiah: the future (we could say the same thing of the past) is not based on the positive account of the present. And this is the case, not because the coming of the Messiah is uncertain (one is sure that he will come), but because the coming of the Messiah never coincides with his simple presence: "If it happens that to the question 'when you will come?' the Messiah answers, 'Today', the answer is certainly impressive: so it is today! It is now and always now. There is no need to wait, although to wait is an obligation. And when is it now? When is the now which does not belong to ordinary time, which necessarily overturns it, does not maintain but destabilizes it?"[7]. This means that even the presence of the present is thought of beginning with the idea of condition; even the present is, in itself, conditioned by something else that transcends the presence of present. The main difference, as we will see throughout our study, resides in this fact: in ontological time the presence of the present is based on the idea of *identity* (hence past and future are intended as modifications of the present); in the messianic time the presence of the present is based on the idea of *transformation* that the realisation of a condition requires (hence past and future are never assured since they take part in this transformation). The relation to the possibility of the coming of the Messiah (to the *future*) is, for the self, the fact of endorsing a transformation that is required by a condition, in whose realisation the whole of existence is measured: this means that the coming of the Messiah is an event meant to transform all of life. Phrased differently, the entire sequence of events, which life consists of, is altered by this event.

2. THE MEANING OF SALVATION WITHIN EXISTENCE

In our view, Emmanuel Lévinas has been, of all 20th century philosophers, the one who has penetrated most deeply into the relation between historical and messianic time, and whose conception of messianism comes closest to the spirit of Hermann Cohen's thought on the subject in the ethical terms in which it is formulated.[8] In particular, Lévinas' meditation on messianism is one of the most important attempts to understand the notion of salvation in the sphere of human existence. In this essay, we will argue that Lévinas' reflections on this subject can account for the distinction between historical and messianic time. We have already sketched this out in the first paragraph: this distinction may also serve, on the other hand, as a guiding theme in the interpretation of Emmanuel Lévinas' philosophy. Lévinas reflection on messianism[9], which was influenced by the rabbinic tradition[10], begins with Walter Benjamin's critique of nineteenth-century philosophical theories of history based on a conception of time according to which history is interpreted as a linear, continuous progression of time. According to these theories of history, time is understood as a chain of events that reveals the meaning of history. History is interpreted as the progressive manifestation of raison or of meaning (that is to say of being), not only because raison is immanent to the becoming of history (as the eternal counterpart of becoming) but also because the final event (viewed as a logical consequence[11] in the chain of events which make up history) has a specific role: it is a recapitulation of history. This final event, which is still logically part of the plan of history, justifies the study of historiography and transforms history into a narration, in a version of history, which is, according to Benjamin, the one told by the victor[12]. This means – more importantly – that the final event mainly coincides with a victory or a defeat, i.e., a conflict, since history is, as it has been noticed[13], and as Thucydides put it, a narration of wars, that is to say of conflicts deeply rooted in human nature. In this perspective, Benjamin is aware of the fact that the final event in the concatenation or chain of events is not only a recapitulation of history, but also an implicit judgement brought on human beings by the course of history. According to Benjamin's conception of history[14], which is strongly entrenched with Marx's philosophy of history, a man inexorably judged by the course of history is fundamentally alienated. He is alienated in the sense that he no longer possesses his own time: he is defrauded by his own time, to which he is no longer capable of assigning a human meaning. Benjamin protests that a man becomes, in this way, a function of the judgement brought forth by the course of history: in this perspective human subjectivity becomes a part of the manifestation of being. Man's life receives meaning according to the place and the role the course of history assigns to it. Benjamin's critique of any philosophy of history based on a linear, homogenous conception of time (which turns out to be close to an ontological representation of time) is fundamentally moral in nature. The interesting point of Benjamin's critique is its moral nature and this is the reason why Hannah Arendt and Emmanuel Lévinas refer to his work in their reflections. In particular, the most interesting point of Benjamin's critique is the problematic relation between freedom and responsibility established in a philosophy of history based on the progressive conception of time as a chain of events. If a human being cannot stand against the course of history, by judging the chain of events that claims to absorb and cancel his individual standing, his freedom is indeed limited. As Lévinas points out, through a radicalisation of this point, freedom consists precisely in the possibility of judging history[15]. In this perspective, Benjamin's attempt to defend the concept of freedom, which, as we shall see later on, requires the reference to the messianic tradition, is motivated pragmatically by the intent to ensure a larger role to human responsibility in the construction of subjectivity and to place the idea of moral consciousness on a more solid footing. What is, in fact, moral consciousness if it is only the a posteriori affirmed and proclaimed consciousness of evil?[16] Lévinas' moral philosophy is to be conceived as an attempt to provide this question, which arises in Benjamin's meditation on history, with a philosophical answer. This answer, which requires a renewal of the idea of subjectivity, is intended to overturn the melancholic[17] acceptance of the course of events, which this conception of moral consciousness is based on. Both Benjamin and Lévinas are aware of the fact that all traditional human constructions, such as the kingdom of justice, begin with a revolt of the soul. In this perspective, which is precisely that one of Lévinas, several important considerations concerning the critical conception of historical and messianic time have already been suggested by Benjamin. According to the German philosopher, the coming of Messiah entails interrupting time, i.e., interrupting the representation of time viewed as a homogenous and progressive succession of events. This interruption – which is a pure eventuality in the sense that all events receive their meaning and logic by this event – is not an event that belongs to a chain or concatenation of events: it overturns the logic governing this succession or concatenation of events, on whose continuity historical time seems to be based[18]. This interruption – once more, according to a long-standing tradition, the idea of individual is based on the notion of instant, that is to say an instant that does not belong to a succession of instants but has an absolute meaning – is an event (which has the temporal form of an instant[19]) that occurs within existence. Even tough it occurs in the horizon of existential life, it does not receives its meaning by what already exists; on the contrary, it constitutes a form of criticism over what exists since it transcends existence in virtue of its absolute dimension. It transcends human existence, not only because the coming of the Messiah is an event that we cannot understand in exclusively secularised terms, as it has been properly noticed[20], but also because this event requires, on the part of the human being, a transformation of the self as an act of absolute freedom, which is inconsistent with the idea that subjectivity is a mere moment or manifestation of being. This transformation is firstly interpreted by Lévinas as a revolt against the melancholy that stems from the mere acceptance of a succession of events intended as an accomplished fact determined by those in power; secondly, this transformation implies the interruption of this presumed succession or concatenation of events in virtue of the individual standing of the moral agent; thirdly, this individual standing requires from the soul, from the moral consciousness, an action through which subjectivity structure itself in the response to a pure eventuality, which is thought beginning with the eventuality of the coming of the Messiah. For Lévinas, the realization of messianic times depends, therefore, on a reaction of the conscience when it is confronted with a condition that surpasses and transcends it, but which also invites it to act. We should emphasize, in this perspective, a quotation made by Lévinas himself: "If you return to Me, I will return to you"[21]. This "if" establishes, according to our interpretation and understanding, a different conception of time: on the basis of this conception, the future – which assumes a particularly important role in the shaping of messianic temporality – is conceived not in an ontological perspective (as differed present) but in relation to the eventuality of this condition ("if"), which cannot be envisaged or calculated on the basis of the present. This condition requires, thus, absolute freedom of conscience. A problem subsequently arises which delineates historical (ontological) from messianic time. How is this absolute freedom to be reconciled with being, on the one hand, and with the requirement to assume responsibility for others, on the other hand? Being and responsibility should be rethought on the basis of this conditional dimension: this is the moral basis of Lévinas meditation on messianism. It requires, as we shall see, that one establish a precise relation between freedom and subjectivity. This conditional time – a concept of time thought in terms of the eventuality of the event, whose possibility entails a transformation of the soul – is the philosophical legacy of the messianic tradition of the 20th century. This conception of time also implies a different representation of being. If one ceases to think of being as emerging all at once within presence, the extension of time in which being emerges presupposes the notion of an interval, which alone renders visible the duration of being. Duration is no longer understood as something permanent but as a continuation across a point of rupture. Instead of the proclaimed continuity on which historical time is intended to be based on, messianic time is tied up with the idea of a continuation across a point of rupture. One would not be able to understand the essence of messianism without this idea of rupture or interval or distance between the word that announces the coming of the Messiah, that is, the realization of messianic times, and the salvific event that stems from the coming of the Messiah, that is, the realization of the kingdom of justice on earth. In our opinion, the meaning of salvation within existence set forth in the philosophical tradition of messianism is deeply entrenched with the meaning of this interval of time, i.e., with the idea of continuation across a point of rupture. How should one conceive the rupture which structures the interval of time and which enables one to distinguish the gesture in which being emerges – the occurrence of being, its verbal dimension – from the essence that emerges, from the word, which is its expression? How should one conceive the chiasm between gesture and speech, which is brought about by the discontinuity of time? It is necessary to reverse the ordinary connection between action and words, to conceive the eventuality of a word which announces the gesture of being, the possibility of a depth between the word and the action, where the gesture of being, the res gestae, history express themselves and thus submit themselves to judgment. This reversal expresses indeed the structure of messianic temporality, which represents a rupture with the linear sequence of time that is strictly based on the correlation between origin and end. This rupture, which invests moral conscience and structures the self, makes it possible to judge history where the occurrence of being seems to reach its conclusion and emerge as a totality. According to the messianic perspective, being does not produce and manifest itself within a representation of time to which all of history corresponds: if there is a judgment, this judgment is not the one set forth by the tribunal of history; history itself will be subject to a judgment for the plain reason that the coming of the Messiah does not corresponds to a presence in the line of the succession of time but to an event which is addressed above all to the moral conscience. The secularization of messianic categories (for instance, the idea of judgment) is likely to disguise the meaning of these categories, since in the process of secularization, these categories were given a meaning based on an ordinary conception of time (founded on the priority of the present over other forms of temporality), which is not the conception of time of the messianic tradition. In particular, the idea of future as it is conceived in messianism does not cover the idea of future based on the priority and centrality of present. In this perspective, future is only a modified form of present: it is a prediction based on the account of a past event. Of course, this representation is not alien to Judaism and messianism. However, it is not the concept of future that can account for the idea of revelation or redemption or for the coming of the Messiah. As Lévinas notices with reference to Rosenzweig[22], here the concept of time is to be de-formalized, that is to say, time is to be conceived not as an intuitive understanding of a priori form, but, understood beginning with a relation or conjuncture between events, namely the coming of the Messiah and the transformation of the soul which this event requires as a condition ("if"). In this way, messianic time introduces a different conception of freedom that stems from precisely this transformation of the soul confronted to the idea of salvation, on whose terms, as we shall see further on, subjectivity is to be redefined. According to the messianic conception of time, a human being can be defined free not in relation to the status, either determined or undetermined, of an act (as in the ontological tradition), but in so far as he perceives that, in relation to an act (for instance a choice), something is radically placed at risk. As Lévinas has rightly emphasized, the requirement of absolute morality is that of absolute freedom. But this requirement also opens the possibility of immorality, i.e., that of evil. It is precisely in terms of the idea of evil that subjectivity is, in our opinion, defined in modernity: the two Talmudic traditions, in their attempt to define the meaning of messianism in terms of the relation between the idea of salvation and that of history, build their reasoning on the idea that the conception of evil affects and, therefore, characterizes human subjectivity. The notion of evil is inherent in the assumption behind both the supra-historical and the intra-historical idea of salvation. According to messianism, a human being is not free in the sense that he can knowingly choose between good and evil, since he always chooses (his own) good; he is free in the sense that, in responding to evil, he determines, through responsibility for the evil, the sense in which he perceives himself as free, that is to say, the sense in which he conceives his own existence as something of value placed at risk. We shall thus explore in the next paragraph the issue as to how these two traditions of messianism imply a specific conception of evil: saying that subjectivity is constituted in response to evil, by the responsibility we assume for evil does not mean that evil has priority over good; it means, on the contrary, that freedom is mystery and that one can learn this mystery only through responsibility. In other words, we act in a responsible manner, we bear a responsibility, on the assumption of freedom; but we can define ourselves free only in relation to what we can assume responsibility for. We will come back on this point later on.

3. THE MESSIANIC PERSPECTIVE: TWO TRADITIONS

In this paragraph, we will describe two Talmudic traditions which account for the interpretation of messianism – more precisely of the idea of salvation – in its relation to the concept of history. The analysis we will conduct in this paragraph is particularly relevant in political and legal philosophy. Within modernity – at least beginning with Kant – history is meant to realise the idea of law. History progressively manifest how men transform a social community into a political one, i.e., into a state; it involves how institutions are created and develop; how citizens tend to resolve conflicts in a political and legal manner and how rights are progressively asserted and defended, etc. All the conceptual apparatus – ideas, categories, etc. – which serve to found the political and the legal community impinges on a long tradition of both political and legal philosophy. However, this is not the only case. For instance, many political and legal categories and ideas come from the secularisation of theological one[23] – whose conceptual apparatus is a point of reference of many conceptualisations[24]. In fact, this process of secularisation has been influenced by the messianic tradition greatly. We cannot describe this point in full detail. Suffice it to say that the consideration of the secularisation of theological categories and ideas constitutes the critical horizon within which our present analysis is to unfold. It is important not lose sight of this horizon, since the problem does not involve, in our view, choosing, as an explanation, the idea of secularization over the idea of the legitimacy of modernity[25]; but rather to understand to what extent the process of secularization can really capture the specificity of messianic time. To phrase it concisely (and we will return to this point in greater detail later on in this essay), it is evident that the notion of *future* which results from the process of secularization derives from the ontological conception of time (future is nothing else than a *differed present*). It does not involve a conception of future as an *unpredictable event or possibility* that requires a transformation of the soul. This point must eventually emerge, however, from our analysis of the supra-historical and intra-historical idea of salvation. As Lévinas pointed out,[26] two Talmudic traditions can explain the messianic idea of salvation: Rabbi Yochanan's intra-historical tradition, according to which salvation and thus the attainment of good are conditioned by the human freedom and the personal moral action; Rabbi Schmouel's supra-historical tradition, according to which salvation and the attainment of good are *not* conditioned or, in more precise language, are conditioned by an *external* event which transcends the human being – an event that nevertheless operates within the sphere of human existence. These different traditions presuppose and suggest two different representations of a moral subject and of the development of man's moral conscience. According to the first tradition, the moral agent's conscience is precisely the tight link between human freedom and the moral action that achieves the good. There is a deep unity, rooted in moral conscience, between freedom (*the world of ends*) and the moral action (*the world of means*), which is reflected in the conscience, i.e., it is a modification of the conscience. The moral agent is such because its action is a manifestation of a good that is already written in the moral conscience: human action is, in virtue of the unity of the conscience, a *sign* of freedom and self-consciousness. It is consequently the condition for the sign to appear. Human action constitutes or modifies the fabric of history since it makes it possible to represent history as a unified world of ends. In this perspective, history has a moral standing in so far as the world of ends is a product of the freedom of human conscience. According to the second tradition, human transcendence is the horizon in which the link between human freedom and the achievement of the good is placed. Human action is no longer understood as self-consciousness but as a separation from the self, which remains subject to transcendence. As separation from the self, human action is not a sign of freedom, but the *trace* of the responsibility for the separation that it has instituted. In this perspective, history, which this separation institutes,[27] has a moral standing in regards to the responsibility assumed by the moral agent in relation to the order of separation determined by the will. Will is no longer viewed as the expression of freedom but as a separation from itself: in order to achieve the good, the moral agent has to act, but its action is made possible by the very fact that the will places something outside of itself, that it is separated from itself. There is no pre-written end in history on which the act of will or the subject's action is based. If will and action are necessary to achieve the good (this is the extent to which Lévinas subscribes to the first tradition), they do not suffice to determine the plan of history. This means that the moral agent becomes a subject not because he attributes, from the very outset, the world of ends (the universe of moral freedom) to the conscience; but because he becomes subject to the responsibility that comes from the order of separation, i.e., the will separated from itself. This responsibility is not measured in relation to the present (of will or consciousness) but in relation to becoming, namely to the interval of time linking the future to present, in an *unpredictable fecundity* (this is the extent to which Lévinas subscribes to the second tradition): "L'histoire n'est pas une éternité simplement diminuée et corrompue ni l'image mobile d'une éternité immobile; l'histoire et le devenir ont un sens positif, une fécondité imprévisible; l'instant futur est absolument neuf, mais il faut pour son surgissement l'histoire et le temps".[28] Future is not part of a general definition of time. Future has an autonomous status: it is viewed as a tense and not as a mode of time. On the basis of this conception of time, i.e., of future, history and becoming can have a positive meaning, according to which future is not only the expression of the negativity of time, but an *unpredictable fecundity* that can determine the renewal of time and, therefore, of the responsibility fixed in advance in relation to the ends that the conscience sets out to achieve. Lévinas summarizes the meaning of the intra-historical and supra-historical traditions in these words: "Les deux thèses de Rav et de Schmouel apparaissent maintenant plus clairement: ils témoignent d'une alternative fondamentale: ou bien c'est la morale, c'est-à-dire l'effort des hommes, maîtres de leurs intentions et de leurs actes, qui sauvera le monde, ou bien il y faudra un événement objectif qui dépasse la morale et la bonne volonté des individus".[29] This basic alternative, whose meaning has been clarified above in relation to the development of the moral conscience, leads us to consider the core of messianism: the question of *salvation* as well as of the structure of the recognition of *signs* leading to salvation. On the basis of the intra-historical and supra-historical tradition, we have understood that the development of the conscience and of the moral subject sensibly differs according to the tradition considered. This difference does not create an opposition, but it suggests that the recognition of signs is made possible by human activity (intra-historical dimension) that places itself, however, within the interval of time that separates word from action and the action from the achievement of the good, within a transcendent reality that awakens and renews the conscience of human freedom (supra-historical dimension). According to Lévinas, human beings are always involved in the never-ending tension between these two traditions of messianism: the moral subject has to assume the responsibility for acts of peace and justice, but this responsibility, which determines the individual action, is not in turn determined by a prior decision based on self-consciousness; this kind of responsibility is intimately linked with the event of the transcendence of time, i.e., with the autonomy of future that defines the separation of the self, of the will separated from itself. This never-ending tension between the two traditions of messianism can also characterise the issue of salvation according to a perspective that, beginning with the status of the moral action, concerns the metaphysical question of evil: this question is decisive in the modernity if one is to account for the notion of subjectivity (of the moral subject). We cannot expound this point fully, but, in our view, the notion of moral subjectivity arose in the modern age from a philosophical reflection on the nature of evil, and in particular, beginning with Leibniz' theory of metaphysical evil, which comes about from the finite nature of human being, i.e., from the fact that man is a *creature*.[30] What we retain from this conception, as a sign of modernity, is the idea that the limited, finite condition of human being, as a creature, is given *metaphysical* status which, in the above perspective, becomes a *general* principle capable of explaining human existence. We will return to our main point concerning the relation between the idea of salvation and that of evil according to Lévinas messianic philosophy: "Pour Rabbi Eliezer, si le mal corrompt l'être au point d'exiger une médication, la guérison ne peut pas être obtenue du dehors, comme une grâce. Sur un être corrompu – l'acte extérieur n'a plus prise. Rien ne peut pénétrer dans un être qui par le mal s'est fermé sur lui-même. Il faut qu'il se ressaisisse lui-même pour être guéri de l'extérieur. Précisément, *parce que le mal n'est pas simplement un égarement, mais une maladie profonde de l'être, c'est le malade qui est le principal et le premier ouvrier de sa guérison*".[31] The conception of evil together with that of sin is decisive if one wishes to understand the logic of salvation in either the messianic or political-legal tradition (e.g. jus-naturalism). To cite a few examples, both the conception of "state of nature" as opposed to the idea of a "civil society" and that of criminal punishment are based on a particular representation of evil (in its relation to the moral agent). If evil has power over the individual to the degree that it affects not only his or her behaviour but also the conditions that determine his or her behaviour, i.e., the inner life of the human being, then salvation can not be achieved without a radical change capable of transforming the individual's inner life. The more this change is interpreted as a manifestation of the inner life of an individual, that is to say, the more it comes from within and not from an external cause, the more it will be viewed as a radical and true change. If, on the contrary, evil, conceived as a mistake, comes from the worldly behaviour and conduct of the human being, then repentance and salvation are susceptible to an external intervention. According to the first conception of evil, the individual aspect of moral consciousness is stressed: the transformation required by the coming of the Messiah is an inner transformation of the self, which the self is called to accomplish of his own accord. As in a longstanding tradition of legal and moral thought, law is to be internalised: human behaviour is legitimized only when the moral agent finds within himself the motives for his actions. This means that the conditions for the kingdom of justice are the expression of an inner order, i.e., the writing of the inner life that accounts for the human freedom and truth. According to the second conception of evil, the collective standing of moral consciousness is stressed: the transformation effected by the coming of the Messiah is a transformation of the self from the outside, which the self is meant to realise by acting within a community. In this perspective, the moral agent no longer needs to do away with the *angelic* interpretation of the Torah:[32] law cannot be internalised, since it in fact accounts for our inter-subjective relation with an external order which cannot be violated or appropriated by anyone.[33] Again, both of these conceptions of evil are necessary to account for Lévinas' interpretation of ethical messianism and messianic time as a description of the constitution of the moral subject, i.e., of a moral subjectivity. In this perspective, Lévinas conceives an idea of Messiah as a construct of subjectivity requiring a redefinition of the inner self. The transformation of the self required by the coming of Messiah (the coming of the Messiah is *this* transformation that opens the self to the responsibility for the other) defines the principle of constitution of the individual subject in his individuality, since the possibility of salvation always concerns the human being *individually*. Salvation has a *conditional* dimension in that it requires such a transformation or movement of the self confronted with suffering or evil. The promise of salvation is therefore addressed to the free agent who does not depend on the external order. This freedom of the self, which is the very condition for salvation, does not consist only in the affirmation of the conscience against suffering or evil, but also in a different conception of the inner self or subjectivity. Subjectivity is no longer understood as a pure identity, i.e., the ability to remain the same over a period of time, but as an ipseity, i.e., the ability to enter into a relation with what the self is not, with what the self cannot assume or dispose of, namely the transcendent. This construction of subjectivity is built upon a conception of time derived from the specific conception of messianic time as conceived differently from the historical one.

4. THE STRUCTURE OF SUBJECTIVITY: RESPONSIBILITY AND FREEDOM

In our view, if the idea of time is conceived beginning from the process of its own temporalisation (*Zeitigung*), i.e., from the meaning that time assumes when it is thought of in relation to concrete conjunction of events of human existence,[34] then the idea of subjectivity differs according to the process of temporalisation which is endorsed either in historical or in messianic time. In the historical conception, as we have stressed, time is thought of within the horizon of being (ontological conception of time) since it serves its own manifestation. It is therefore in this horizon that it acquires meaning for the human person. Subjectivity is constituted and understood, in this perspective, as a moment or reflection of the manifestation of being: the human being is defined by the part he plays in this manifestation. To put it differently, if in the ontological perspective subjectivity is laden with the idea of self-development, of self-recognition during self-development, this idea of recognition is entirely dominated and guided by the process of manifestation of being, within which the subject recognizes himself as a reflection (the historical moment) of this manifestation. In the messianic conception, as we have suggested, time is conceived within the horizon of salvation (a conditional conception of time is manifested), since existence as a whole is placed at risk. It is in this horizon that time acquires a meaning for the human person: the formalization of the meaning of time is, therefore, the (condition of the) founding of the moral consciousness. As we will see in this paragraph, subjectivity requires the founding of a moral consciousness. It is thus founded and understood in response to the ethical question which man is called to face. The interpretation of messianism to which we subscribe is the one that refuses both a personal and a political conception of Messiah, intended as a force that intervenes within history to change the human course of action. According to Lévinas interpretation, the personal and ethical standing of the Messiah consists in the invitation to human beings to intervene within history and to assume a responsibility for the suffering of one's fellow man. This responsibility is personal and *historical* (this is the intra-historical interpretation of messianic time, to which Lévinas is faithful). However, it is measured in relation to the becoming of the other, which is no longer based on the present of the self. It *transcends* the horizon of time in which the self wishes to define and limit his own responsibility (this is the supra-historical interpretation of messianic time, to which Lévinas is also faithful). Responsibility is no longer based on the autonomy and identity of the self ensured by the continuity of time: in the messianic perspective, the logic of becoming (the incessant passage from being to not-being) is surpassed by the idea of the coming of the Messiah, which qualifies time in terms of a *discontinuity*. This discontinuity is a fragmentation of time, which is no longer viewed as a fall from being, as a pure negativity, i.e., a negation of what is or has been; the fragmentation of time is, thus, based on a different conception of future, which is no longer understood as the agent of negation but as an event that is susceptible to self-transformation. This is so because it invites the self to affirm itself in response to this event or transformation. It is clear that the self may remain silent, completely closed to the coming of Messiah, to the event of the other: absolute freedom is required of the self so that it may be open to this event. This is the reason why the advent of the Messiah defines a *conditional* conception of time. The Messiah advent is, in a certain sense, on which we insist, conditioned by the self's response. This response is necessarily free: both the extreme of morality and the extreme of immorality require an absolute freedom,[35] which is inconsistent with the rigid ontological conception of time. Yet, this absolute freedom is meant to be inconsistent as well with a kind of a moral responsibility that exists before the present and emergence of the self's autonomy. How may freedom and responsibility be reconciled? It is necessary to envisage that this conditional conception of time presides over the constitution of the moral conscience and, hence, to the constitution of subjectivity in moral terms. To do this, we have to go back to the idea of messianism and, more specifically, of messianic time. In the messianic perspective, we believe that the relation between word and action is overturned: the word does not intervene *a posteriori* to explain us the consequences of an action, the mystery of the world that has been achieved by the course of human actions. The word (that is to say rationality) is not an *a posteriori* explanation and justification of what has been produced within history. The word does not intervene to unveil a mystery. The messianic word proclaims what still has to be accomplished: freedom and, thus, responsibility are no longer measured in relation to a deterministic conception of freedom, i.e., in relation to the idea of determination. Freedom is not judged, in the messianic perspective, with regards to the quality of an action, that is to say by establishing to what extent the action may be said to be determined or free (the word comes after the action); freedom is judged with regards to a risk at which the moral consciousness is placed and that gives a particular value to existence. Freedom and responsibility are, therefore, measured, in the messianic perspective, in relation to a quality of consciousness, which is a form of vigilance over this risk or sign of salvation. Since this risk or sign of salvation (the word comes before the action) transcends the present of the self, this vigilance is a relation of the consciousness with the messianic time, whose future conditional event is a form of human transcendence. Consciousness is open to transcendence: the human being understands that something (which is his existence as a whole) is radically placed at risk, that is to say that is evaluated in moral terms and that this moral evaluation depends on the self's relation to the other, whose suffering is already the Messiah's suffering. In this sense, this extreme vigilance over the other qualifies the messianic consciousness in moral terms. This quality, which qualifies the consciousness, also qualifies time, not as a modality of consciousness (as a modification) but as a mode of transcendence. Vigilance is a quality not because it is a modality of consciousness but because it is open to transcendence. That is to say, *it lives in the depths between word and action, which is the structure itself of messianic temporality*. Messianic conception of time, at least according to Lévinas interpretation, not only overturns the logic of the teleological representation of history but it also overturns the ontological understanding of time. In the messianic perspective, the word announcing the essence of being is never contemporaneous with the event of being. The word is, instead, the relation with the human being, the moral consciousness, who receives this word or sign and asserts it in the community. This existence is structured by the transcendence of the word that comes across it and opens the human being to the infinite dimension of a word always to come, to the communication between the human finitude and the infinite. We have already stressed this point: the messianic conception of temporality structures the moral consciousness, the inner self who is open to the exteriority of the other, that is to say to the transcendence of the infinite. This means, contrary to a longstanding interpretation, that messianism is not laden with a teleological representation of time, based on the idea of an end of history, as Lévinas pointed out: "[...] le judaïsme n'apporte donc pas une doctrine d'une fin de l'histoire dominant la destinée individuelle. Le salut n'occupe pas un bout de l'histoire – sa conclusion. Il reste à tout moment possible". The temporal conception of salvation is crucial in understanding messianism. Salvation is *at every moment possible*: the coming of messianic times structures consciousness on the basis of a different conception of time that is no longer based on the idea of consciousness understood as a presence to itself. This different conception of time opens the consciousness to a form of temporality, which is no longer founded on the priority of the presence and does not coincide with the totality of history. If salvation remains *at every moment possible* for the human consciousness, then human consciousness must remain open, *at every moment*, to salvation: that means that human consciousness is no longer conceived as something determined beforehand according to the historical dimension, to the logic of becoming, which claims to determine every moment or instant of time. The notion of duration stemming from the messianic conception of salvation (which is, at every moment, possible) is a way of conceiving the freedom of consciousness in relation to historical determinations. Duration is not a continuum based on the permanence of being or on the homogeneity of time. Duration is a relation with something (which is not a thing) transcending the dimension of historical determinations and ensuring, in this sense, the freedom of consciousness (we will see this more clearly in the following paragraph). As a corollary to this, as pointed out earlier, the realisation of messianic time does not depend entirely on the human action, in the sense that the messianic conception of time (and salvation) confronts the human being to something he cannot simply dispose of or appropriate: *the constitutive dimension of the human being is that of a certain openness to a form of otherness that remains beyond his control.* We are here confronted with the deepest meaning of the notion of salvation, that is to say, the idea of possibility. If the coming of the Messiah remains at every moment possible, it is precisely because the human being is always open to this possibility, which also implies that human beings do not have power over this possibility. The very essence of possibility resides in the fact that one possibility must leave another possibility unaltered, free to be a different or contrary possibility or even to realise itself. The coming of the Messiah requires absolute freedom, or in other words, such a possibility leaves unaltered the possibility that the Messiah will not come. To put it differently, the Messiah will not come for those who are not capable of recognising him (*there are those who say that the Messiah has already come*). This possibility becomes possible *if and only if* a transformation of the self occurs: *if*, in other words, subjectivity is constituted in the response to this possibility. Remaining in the messianic perspective, the essence of subjectivity is freedom, but at the same time subjectivity is constituted by the response. Such response is already a responsibility, according to Lévinas, for the word announcing the coming of the Messiah. That is to say, in the response or in the responsibility for the otherness of the other who asks to be freed of his own suffering. What does this means? How can responsibility constitute the essence of subjectivity, which is freedom? Freedom is a mystery that as such cannot be determined. Freedom can only be testified by the responsibility we assume for the other: in other words, we are free always and only in relation to what we assume responsibility for. It is responsibility that lets us perceive our own freedom, teaching us what the value of freedom is to us. We clarify, in relation to the structure of subjectivity, what we have already said regarding the concept of existence: messianism is characterised by the fact of transforming existence into a value, which has to be asserted in the perspective of salvation. This value is, from the point of view of the self, what Lévinas calls *man's personal vocation*:[36] the response to the other's plea for help. It is only within such a response (which requires a transformation of the self) that the condition of the coming of the Messiah is, to put it in this way, *realised*. This conditional dimension, to insist yet again on this point, which expresses the peculiarity of messianic time, is the destiny of the word announcing the coming of the Messiah: this word, when put in the future form (*it is sure that he will come*) cannot reach anyone if it does not rely on the response, ever individual and personal, from the person who receives this word and asserts it within the community. It is only within such a response, or responsibility, that moral consciousness and the subjectivity of the subject can be constituted and emerge. In this perspective, subjectivity is not the result but the experience of a transformation: subjectivity consists precisely in the response to the other (which also means to be responsible for the other), that is to say to go, beyond oneself, toward something which is not brought forth by one's will, which is out of reach. The possibility of salvation resides, thus, in the moral consciousness; but this possibility exists only if the moral consciousness emerges, if subjectivity recognises itself as something open to what is other than itself, to an otherness which remains out of reach, impossible to be appropriated by the consciousness: this is the meaning of the *transformation* required by the coming of the Messiah. This impossibility to be appropriated by the consciousness is what Lévinas calls the *infinition of the infinite*, that is to say the idea of duration of messianic time (*the coming of the Messiah remains at every moment possible*), which awakens one's consciousness confronting him or her with what the consciousness is not, to what radically surpasses it.

5. ETHICS TOWARD RELIGION: INFINITY AND GOD

If, in the historical notion of time, subjectivity emerges as a moment in the manifestation of being, then, in the messianic conception of time, subjectivity is constituted by responsibility understood as the prism through which we can look at the question of freedom. The ethical conception of messianic time consists precisely in the building of the moral conscience: human freedom has a concrete content because it is confronted with a *condition* that does not depend on any historical process or on the logic of becoming in which freedom belongs to a retrospective glance, which determines the degree of determination of any human action. In the latter perspective, the idea of value is identified with what has real existence, to effectiveness, to the positive existence with respect to what has been determined. In the former perspective, namely the messianic perspective, the idea of value, in which the existence as a whole is transformed, is identified with what is possible (*the coming of the Messiah is at every moment possible*), to what transcends the existence itself and confronts the existential conscience with what the conscience is not, i.e., with the otherness of the other. This possibility is a judgement pronounced on the effectiveness of existence, which is no longer justified in itself and by itself, since we figure out the possibility of another existence: as we have pointed out, the essence of possibility lies in the question whether or not it leaves another possibility unaltered. This possibility, which is precisely that of salvation, is suspended in a condition, in a conditional structure of time, the coming of the Messiah, in which all of existence is placed at risk. That is to say, it requires an act of freedom from the self. This act of freedom is already a response to this condition: the possibility of the coming of the Messiah leaves unaltered the possibility that the Messiah will not come. This means that it is only within the response that the condition of the response is realised. If the Messiah is the guiding idea of history (according to Hermann Cohen[37]), or at least of the history of salvation, the realisation of the idea, namely the ethical responsibility toward the other, is always transcended by the idea, the otherness of the other, which is the *condition* for the moral conscience to emerge. The idea always transcends its realisation (which is witnessed, from another point of view, by the relation between Moses and Aaron); in other words, history is transcended from within: salvation requires acknowledging a sign, the sign of Messiah, but this sign (whose manifestation implies the history of salvation) does not belong to any immanent dimension, since the presence of the Messiah is not a presence in the ontological sense, but a possibility transcending the immanence of history. History is not, from the messianic point of view, a totality of meaning which is recomposed: it is precisely the *non-indifference* toward the otherness of the other, whose breaking through or plea for help, modifies the logic of becoming and *overturns* the representation of history as a chain or succession of events. The moral consciousness is not the record of what has already happened and has an effective existence: if this is the case, morality would be nothing more than that of the strongest or, to put it differently, the moral consciousness would be reduced to the simple awareness, the passive witness, of the evil which has already occurred. Moral consciousness is a revolt against this idea of a passive witness to the power of the strongest: moral consciousness cannot simply be the condemnation of evil but it must be somehow laden with the idea of good. Good is not viewed, in the messianic perspective, as a substance or a set of norms but instead as something which has a relation with salvation. It is because all of existence has been transformed into a value by the messianic conception of time that the good directly affects moral conscience. We are confronted here with the most difficult problem of the present reflection: what is the meaning of salvation, in the existential and ethical perspective of messianism, when salvation is to be thought of in relation to the good? In the historical conception of time, the manifestation of being is already the achievement of the good, since being, as we have pointed out, does not need to be saved: its own manifestation is its adventure and its reward. But what is said about the human existence when confronted with the idea of salvation? Salvation does not mean, in this perspective, merely surviving one's life; it does not mean life after death, since, here, the meaning of salvation is sought within the horizon of human existence. Salvation does not mean either the fact of being saved from damnation or evil: in this perspective, good has no priority over evil, since it is still merely thought of as the absence of evil. We should try to attach a positive meaning to salvation in order to understand existence as a value to be endorsed and asserted as the good. If the manifestation of being is based on the correlation between positive and negative that gives us the meaning of the becoming, then the idea of salvation, i.e., the coming of the Messiah, has to be thought of as something beyond the correlation between the positive and the negative. Concerned with the meaning of existence, salvation points out that there is something which survives any negation, that there is something positive which does not receives its meaning by any correlative negation, i.e., which transcends the logic of opposition between the positive and the negative. How can something, which is not even a thing, survive negation? How can it have a positive meaning, which is not tied up with its negative dimension, which transcends the logic of becoming? How can one experience this form of transcendence or, to put it differently, how can the self transcends itself without being alienated by his own transcendence?[38] If we claim to be able to conceive the self as *separate* from transcendence, then the idea of transcendence turns out to be contradictory. The self cannot transcend itself and remain the same self throughout the experience of transcendence: if it remains the same, then the self hasn't experienced transcendence. If the self is modified, then the self who has experienced transcendence is not the same as the initial self. But this is the case if we conceive self and transcendence as separate, as if the self was always already predetermined in subjectivity when confronted with transcendence. The idea of transcendence ceases to be contradictory if we think transcendence as a constitutive dimension of the self: subjectivity is, in this perspective, understood as the experience of the transformation of the self, which is open to the experience of transcendence. Transcendence is no longer an alienation of the self if it ceases to be understood as the content of an experience of an already predetermined self. Transcendence is to be thought of as the constitutive dimension of human subjectivity: *subjectivity is always the experience, and not the result, of the transformation of the self confronted with the otherness of the other, a possibility leaving unaltered all other possibilities.* A human being is defined by the fact of being capable of an infinite transcendence; but being capable of an infinite transcendence means, as Lévinas says, having the idea of God: "L'idée de l'Infini [...] conserve pour la réflexion le nœud paradoxal qui déjà se noue dans la révélation religieuse. Celle-ci, liée d'emblée dans sa *concrétude* à des obligations envers les humains – idée de Dieu comme amour du prochain – est 'connaissance' d'un Dieu qui, s'offrant dans cette 'ouverture', demeurait aussi absolument autre ou transcendant. La religion ne serait-elle pas le concours originaire de circonstances – qui ne doit pas être pour autant jugé contingent – où l'infini vient à l'idée dans son ambiguïté de vérité et de mystère?".[39]

Università di Torino, Italy

<h2 style="text-align:center">6. REFERENCES</h2>

Michael Bernard-Donals – Richard Glejzer, *Between Witness and Testimony: The Holocaust and the Limits of Representation*, Suny, New York, 2001.

Maurice Blanchot, *The Writing of the Disaster*, University of Nebraska Press, Nebraska, 1986 (original edition, *L'écriture du désastre*, Gallimard, Paris, 1980).

Hans Blumenberg, *The Legitimacy of Modern Age* [1966], The MIT Press, Boston, 1985.

Leonardo Casini, "Ambiguità del nichilismo", in *Per la filosofia. Filosofia e insegnamento*, Anno XXI, n. 62, sett.-dic. 2004, pp. 51–70.

Fabio Ciaramelli, *Transcendance et éthique*, Ousia, Bruxelles, 1989.

Hermann Cohen, *L'éthique du judaïsme. La vocation universelle d'Israël*, Paris, Cerf, 1994.

Massimo Durante, "Mélancolie et messianisme. L'infinition de l'infini' comme horizon du jugement", in *Cahiers d'Etudes Lévinassiennes*, n. 4, 2005, pp. 49–85.

Didier Franck, *Dramatique des phénomènes*, Paris, Puf, 2001.

Marcel Hénaff, "Don cérémoniel, dette et reconnaissance" in Marco Olivetti (Ed.), *Il dono e il debito*, Cedam, Padova, 2004.

Immanuel Kant, *Critique of Judgment*, Indianapolis, Hackett Publishing Company, 1987.

Gottfried Wilhem Leibniz, *Discours de métaphysique suivi de Monadologie et autres textes*, Paris, Gallimard, 2004.

Hartmut Lehmann – James Van Horn Melton (Eds.), *Paths of Continuity: Central European Historiography from the 1930s to the 1950s*, Cambridge University Press, Cambridge, 2003.

Emmanuel Lévinas, *L'au-delà du Verset*, Editions Minuit, Paris, 1982.

Emmanuel Lévinas, *Totalité et infini. Essai sur l'extériorité*, Paris, Le livre de poche, 1992.

Emmanuel Lévinas, *Emmanuel Lévinas. L'éthique comme philosophie première*, Le Cerf, Paris, 1993.

Emmanuel Lévinas, *Dieu, la mort et le temps*, Grasset, Paris, 1993.

Emmanuel Lévinas, *Transcendance et intelligibilité*, Labor et Fides, Genève, 1996.

Karl Löwith, *Meaning in History: Theological Implications of the Philosophy of History* [1949], University of Chicago Press, Chicago, 1957.

Michel Löwy, *Walter Benjamin. Avertissement d'incendie*, P.U.F., Paris, 2001.

Patrick Nerhot, *Questions phénoménologiques suivi de lectures freudiennes*, Paris, L'Harmattan, 2002.

Stephane Mosès, *Au-delà de la guerre. Trois études sur Lévinas*, Paris, Éditions de l'éclat, 2004.

Adriaan Peperzak, *The Quest for Meaning. Friends of Wisdom from Plato to Lévinas*, Fordham University Press, Fordham, 2003.

Dan Sperber, *Le symbolisme en général*, Hermann, Paris, 1974.

Franco Todescan, *Le radici teologiche del giusnaturalismo laico*, Giuffré, Milano, 3 vol., 1983–2001.

Franco Todescan, *Itinerari critici dell'esperienza giuridica*, Giappichelli, Torino, 1991.

Franco Todescan, *Etiamsi daremus: studi sinfonici sul diritto naturale*, Cedam, Padova, 2003.

NOTES

[1] Immanuel Kant, *Critique of Judgment*, Indianapolis, Hackett Publishing Company, 1987, p. 107.

[2] See, for instance, what Emmanuel Lévinas (*Dieu, la mort et le temps*, Grasset, Paris, 1993, p. 18) says on this point: "Ma relation avec la mort ne se limite pas quant à elle à ce savoir de seconde main. Pour Heidegger (cf. Sein und Zeit), elle est certitude par excellence. Il y a un a priori de la mort. Heidegger dit la mort certaine au point de voir dans cette certitude de la mort l'origine de la certitude même, et il refuse à faire venir cette certitude de l'expérience de la mort des autres".

[3] See Emmanuel Lévinas, *Totalité et infini. Essai sur l'extériorité*, Le livre de poche, Paris, 1992.

[4] To refer to the expression of Aristote quoted here, in this perspective, by Sergio Givone and recalled by Leonardo Casini, "Ambiguità del nichilismo", in *Per la filosofia. Filosofia e insegnamento*, Anno XXI, n. 62, sett.-dic. 2004, pp. 51–70, quotation p. 62.

[5] We take, here, the meaning of sign in the perspective of Dan Sperber, *Le symbolisme en general*, Hermann, Paris, 1974, quoted by Marcel Hénaff, "Don cérémoniel, dette et reconnaissance" in Marco Olivetti (ed.), *Il dono e il debito*, Cedam, Padova, 2004, p. 24, note n. 14: "[...] cet aspect central n'épuise pas la question du symbolisme que l'on peut résumer ainsi: un symbolisme est un dispositif d'éléments sensibles présentant des valeurs différentielles qui ne vise pas à signifier quelque chose mais à la réaliser; cela concerne aussi bien un système algébrique qu'un rituel de guérison, une danse de masques que de formes de politesse. Son ordre est celui de la valeur, non de la signification, de l'opération non de la signification". In the messianic perspective the sign, the symbol, has this statute: it is a value that is meant to realise what it announces (at variance with the historical conception of time where it is the manifestation of being).

[6] We borrow this idea, tough from a different perspective, from Bernard Williams, *Moral Luck: Philosophical Papers: 1973–1980*, Cambridge University Press, Cambridge, 1981.

[7]   See Maurice Blanchot, *The Writing of the Disaster*, University of Nebraska Press, Nebraska, 1986, p. 142. See also the original edition, *L'écriture du désastre*, Gallimard, Paris, 1980, pp. 214–215: "Le messianisme juif (chez certains commentateurs) nous laisse pressentir le rapport de l'événement et de l'inavènement. Si le Messie est aux portes de Rome parmi les mendiants et lépreux, on peut croire que son incognito le protège ou empêche sa venue, mais précisément il est reconnu; quelqu'un, pressé par la hantise de l'interrogation, lui demande: 'Quand viendras-tu?' Le fait d'être là n'est donc pas la venue. Auprès du Messie qui est là, doit toujours retentir l'appel: 'Viens, Viens'. Sa présence n'est pas une garantie. Future ou passée (il est dit au moins une fois, que le Messie est déjà venu), sa venue ne correspond pas à une présence". See also, p. 215: "L'appel non plus ne suffit pas; il y a des conditions – l'effort des hommes, leur moralité, leur repentir – qui sont connues; il y en a toujours qui ne sont pas connues. Et s'il arrive qu'à la question: 'Pour quand ta venue?', le Messie réponde: 'Pour aujourd'hui', la réponse certes est impressionnante: c'est donc aujourd'hui. C'est maintenant et toujours maintenant. Il n'y a pas à attendre, bien que ce soit comme une obligation d'attendre. Et quand est-ce maintenant? Un maintenant qui n'appartient pas au temps ordinaire, qui nécessairement le bouleverse, ne le maintient pas, le déstabilise, surtout si l'on se souvient que ce 'maintenant' hors texte, d'un récit de sévère fiction, renvoie à des textes qui le font à nouveau dépendre de conditions réalisables – irréalisables: 'Maintenant pour peu que tu me prête attention, ou si tu veux bien écouter ma voix'".

[8]   See Hermann Cohen, *L'éthique du judaïsme. La vocation universelle d'Israël*, Paris, Cerf, 1994, "L'idée de Messie", pp. 71–89.

[9]   We have argued this interpretation of Lévinas reflection on messianism in a precedent study. See in this perspective, Massimo Durante, "Mélancolie et messianisme. L'infinition de l'infini' comme horizon du jugement", in *Cahiers d'Etudes Lévinassiennes*, n. 4, 2005, pp. 49–85, in particular the first paragraphe: " Mélancolie et messianisme. L''Angelus Novus' de Walter Benjamin". On the same perspective see Stephane Mosés, *Au-delà de la guerre. Trois études sur Lévinas*, Paris, Éditions de l'éclat, 2004.

[10]   Emmanuel Lévinas, "Textes messianiques", in *Difficile liberté*, Paris, Le livre de poche, 1997, pp. 89–90, note 1.

[11]   For the philosophical critique of the idea of a necessary consequence in a retrodictive reasoning see Patrick Nerhot, *Questions phénoménologiques suivies de lectures freudiennes*, Paris, L'Harmattan, 2001, pp. 127–130.

[12]   See Walter Benjamin, *Selected Writings*, Volume 4: 1938–1940, ed. Michael W. Jennings & Howard Eiland, Cambridge: Belknap Press of Harvard University Press, 2002, *Theses on the Philosophy of History*, n. VII: "The nature of this sadness stands out more clearly if one asks with whom the adherents of historicism actually empathize. The answer is inevitable: with the victor. And all rulers are the heirs of those who conquered before them. Hence, empathy with the victor invariably benefits the rulers. Historical materialists know what that means. Whoever has emerged victorious participates to this day in the triumphal procession in which the present rulers step over those who are lying prostrate".

[13]   See on this point Arnaldo Momigliano, *The Classical Foundations of Modern Historiography*, Cambridge University Press, Cambridge, 1992.

[14]   See Walter Benjamin, *Selected Writings*, Volume 4: 1938–1940, cit., *Theses on the Philosophy of History*. On Walter Benjamin's concept of history see recently, Michel Löwy, *Walter Benjamin. Avertissement d'incendie*, P.U.F., Paris, 2001.

[15]   See Emmanuel Lévinas, *Entre nous. Essai sur le penser-à-l'autre*, Le livre de poche, Paris, 1998, p. 41: "Le monde humain est un monde où l'on peut juger l'histoire. Pas un monde

nécessairement raisonnable, mais où l'on peut juger. L'inhumain, c'est être jugé, sans qu'il y ait personne qui juge. Affirmer l'homme comme un pouvoir de juger l'histoire, c'est affirmer le rationalisme".

[16] See on this point, Adriaan Peperzak, *The Quest for Meaning. Friends of Wisdom from Plato to Lévinas*, Fordham University Press, Fordham, 2003, pp. 193–194.

[17] See note n. 12. You may see Massimo Durante, "Mélancolie et messianisme. L''infinition de l'infini' comme horizon du jugement", cited. See also on this perspective Michel Löwy, *Walter Benjamin. Avertissement d'incendie*, cited.

[18] See, for instance, in this perspective, Karl Löwith, *Meaning in History: Theological Implications of the Philosophy of History* [1949], University of Chicago Press, Chicago, 1957, in particular what he says of Burckhardt's conception of history, p. 21: "And yet there is some kind of permanence in the very flux of history, namely, its continuity. This is the only principle discernible in Burckhardt's *Reflections on History*, the one thin tread that holds together his observations after he has dismissed interpretations by philosophy and theology. The whole significance of history depends for Burckhardt on continuity as the common standard of all particular historical evaluations. If a radical crisis really disrupted history's continuity, it would be the end of a historical epoch, but not a 'historical' crisis". On this point see, Hartmut Lehmann – James Van Horn Melton (eds.), *Paths of Continuity: Central European Historiography from the 1930s to the 1950s*, Cambridge University Press, Cambridge, 2003, p. 373.

[19] See Walter Benjamin, *Selected Writings*, Volume 4: 1938–1940, cit., *Theses on the Philosophy of History*, n. XVIIb: "Every second of time [is] the narrow gate through which the Messiah may enter". On this point see also with interest, Michael Bernard-Donals – Richard Glejzer, *Between Witness and Testimony: The Holocaust and the Limits of Representation*, Suny, New York, 2001, p. 45: "Like the disaster, the historical event (the full and present moment) and the human action and utterances taking place that bring it to consciousness (voices raised in lament, horror, and chastisement) take place out of historical time, not in the utterances themselves, but in the moment between the occurrence and the utterance. Each moment, preceding historical time, is 'the strait gate through which the Messiah might enter' (Benjamin, "Theses", 264)".

[20] See on this point Gershom Scholem, who stands against the idea that messianism can be reduced to a vague form of humanism, *The Messianic Idea in Judaism: And Other Essays on Jewish Spirituality*, Schoken Books, New York, 1971.

[21] Emmanuel Lévinas, "Textes messianiques", in *Difficile liberté*, Paris, Le Livre de Poche, 1997, p. 112: "Quatrième argument enfin qui rend le débat dramatique: pour la première fois, la particule *si* figure dans le texte cité: *Si vous revenez à Moi, Je reviens à vous*. L'exigence de la moralité absolue est une exigence de liberté absolue. Et par conséquent une possibilité d'immoralité. Que se passera-t-il en effet si les hommes ne reviennent pas à Dieu? Il se passera ceci: le Messie ne viendra jamais, le monde sera livré aux méchants et la thèse des athées – de ceux qui estiment le monde livré à l'arbitraire et au mal – triomphera." We translate the point cited.

[22] See Emmanuel Lévinas, "Diachronie et représentation", in *Emmanuel Lévinas. L'éthique comme philosophie première*, Le Cerf, Paris, 1993, p. 467: "Mais nous avons cherché le temps comme dé-formalisation de la forme, la plus formelle qui soit, de l'unité du *je pense*. Déformalisation dont Bergson, Rosenzweig, Heidegger ont ouvert la problématique à la pensée moderne, en partant, chacun à sa manière, d'un concret plus 'ancien' que la forme pure du temps: liberté de l'invention et de la nouveauté (malgré la persistance de l'imagine kinétique du courant) chez Bergson; conjoncture biblique 'de la Création, de la Révélation et de la Rédemption' chez

Rosenzweig; 'auprès des choses', *Geworfenheit* et *Sein-zum-tode* (malgré l'ex, encore kinétique des extases) chez Heidegger".

[23] For a deep account of this question see Franco Todescan, *Le radici teologiche del giusnaturalismo laico*, Giuffré, Milano, Volume: 3 1983–2001. See also of the same author, *Itinerari critici dell'esperienza giuridica*, Giappichelli, Torino, 1991, and, *Etiamsi daremus: studi sinfonici sul diritto naturale*, Cedam, Padova, 2003.

[24] See on this point the classical text of Karl Löwith, *Meaning in History: Theological Implications of the Philosophy of History*, cit., p. 28: "[…] moderns elaborate a philosophy of history by secularizing the theological principles and applying them to an ever increasing number of empirical facts". For a criticism of Löwith's thesis you may see Hans Blumenberg, *The Legitimacy of Modern Age* [1966], The MIT Press, Boston, 1985, p. 44: "What mainly occurred in the process that is interpreted as secularization […] should be described not as a *transposition* of authentically theological contents into secularized alienation from their origin but rather as the *reoccupation* of answer positions that had become vacant and whose corresponding questions could not be eliminated".

[25] See for this idea Hans Blumenberg, *The Legitimacy of Modern Age*, cited.

[26] See Emmanuel Lévinas, "Textes messianiques", in *Difficile liberté*, cit., pp. 95–98.

[27] See Emmanuel Lévinas, "Le moi et la totalité", cit., pp. 38–39: "La volonté ne tient donc pas toute la signification de son propre vouloir. Sujet libre de ce vouloir, elle existe comme jouet d'un destin qui la dépasse. Elle comporte, par son œuvre, une signification imprévisible que lui prêtent les autres en situant l'œuvre détachée de son auteur dans un contexte nouveau. Le destin ne précède pas cette décision, mais lui est postérieur : le destin, c'est l'histoire. La volonté entre dans l'histoire parce qu'*elle existe en se séparant d'elle-même* : tout en voulant pour elle-même, elle se trouve aussi avoir voulu pour les autres. Aliénation qui ne doit rien à l'histoire, qui institue l'histoire, aliénation ontologique".

[28] See Emmanuel Lévinas, "Textes messianiques", in *Difficile liberté*, cit., p. 101.

[29] See Emmanuel Lévinas, "Textes messianiques", in *Difficile liberté*, cit., p. 107.

[30] See Gottfried Wilhem Leibniz, *Discours de métaphysique suivi de Monadologie et autres textes*, Paris, Gallimard, 2004, p. 204: "On voit bien cependant que Dieu n'est pas la cause du mal. Car, non seulement après la perte de l'innocence des hommes le péché originel s'est emparé de l'âme, mais encore auparavant il y avait une limitation ou imperfection originale connaturelle à toutes les créatures, qui les rend peccables ou capables de manquer." And also pp. 290–291: "Mais la substance *limitée* enveloppe la négation de quelque réalité. La substance absolue est Dieu, la substance limitée est créature, par exemple Moi".

[31] Emmanuel Lévinas, "Textes messianiques", in *Difficile liberté*, op. cit., p. 109.

[32] See Emmanuel Lévinas, "Le pacte", in *L'au-delà du Verset*, Editions Minuit, Paris, 1982, pp. 98–99: "*La lutte de Jacob avec l'Ange, c'est cela aussi: surmonter dans l'existence d'Israël l'angélisme de la pure intériorité.* […] Mais, vous savez, l'Ange n'est pas le sommet de la créature: être purement spirituel, il ne réalise pas la condition que présuppose la vie selon la Thora: il n'a ni à manger, ni à prendre, ni à donner, ni à travailler, ni à ne pas travailler le Shabbat! Principe de générosité, mais rien que principe. La générosité comporte une adhésion, certes. Mais l'adhésion au principe ne suffit pas et comporte une tentation, appelle à l'attention et à notre combat. […] *Le Talmud est la lutte avec l'Ange*".

[33] See Gershom Scholem, *The Messianic Idea in Judaism: And Other Essays on Jewish Spirituality*, cited.

[34] See Emmanuel Lévinas, *Entre nous*, cit., p. 263: "Mon thème de recherche essentiel est celui de la déformalisation de la notion du temps. Kant le dit forme de toute expérience. Toute

expérience humaine revêt en effet la forme temporelle. La philosophie transcendantale issue de Kant emplissait cette forme de contenu sensible venant de l'expérience ou, depuis Hegel, conduisait dialectiquement cette forme vers un contenu. Ces philosophes n'ont jamais exigé pour la constitution de cette forme même de la temporalité une condition dans une certaine conjoncture de 'matière' ou d'événements, dans un contenu sensé en quelque façon préalable à la forme. La constitution du temps chez Husserl est encore une constitution du temps à partir d'une conscience déjà effective de la présence dans son évanouissement et dans sa 'rétention' et dans son imminence et son anticipation – évanouissement et imminence qui déjà impliquent ce qu'on veut bâtir, sans même que soit fournie aucune indication sur la situation empirique privilégiée à laquelle ces modes d'évanouissement dans le passé et de l'imminence dans le futur seraient attachés. Ce qui paraît dès lors remarquable chez Heidegger, c'est précisément le fait de poser la question de savoir quelles sont les situations ou les circonstances caractéristiques de l'existence concrète auxquelles la passation du passé, la 'présentification' du présent et la futurition du futur – appelées *extases* – sont essentiellement et originellement attachées. Le fait d'être sans avoir eu à le choisir, d'avoir affaire à des possibles toujours déjà entamés, sans nous – extase du 'd'ores et déjà'; le fait d'une emprise sur les choses, auprès d'elles dans la représentation ou le connaître – extase du présent; le fait d'exister-à-la-mort – extase du futur. Voilà, à peu près, car la philosophie est plus sage, l'ouverture heideggérienne."

[35] See *supra* note n. 21.

[36] See Emmanuel Lévinas, "Textes messianiques", in *Difficile liberté*, cit., p. 127: "Le judaïsme, tendu vers la venue du Messie, dépasse déjà la notion d'un Messie mythique se présentant à la fin de l'histoire pour concevoir le messianisme comme une vocation personnelle des hommes".

[37] See Hermann Cohen, *L'éthique du judaïsme. La vocation universelle d'Israël*, cit., "L'idée de Messie", pp. 71–89.

[38] See Didier Franck, *Dramatiques des phénomènes*, P.U.F., Paris, 2001, p. 160: "Le problème est celui de la conservation du moi dans la transcendance, de la subjectivité du temps ou encore, cela revient ici au même, de la victoire sur la mort".

[39] See Emmanuel Lévinas, *Transcendance et intelligibilité*, Labor et Fides, Genève, 1996, p. 22. See also pp. 21–22: "Mais que peut-on chercher sous la pensée d'autre que de la conscience ? Quelle est enfin cette pensée recherchée – ni assimilation de l'Autre au Même, ni intégration de l'Autre au Même – et qui ne ramènerait pas tout transcendant à l'immanence et ne compromettrait pas la transcendance en la comprenant? Il y faudrait une pensée qui ne soit plus bâtie comme relation : de pensant au pensé, dans la domination du pensé, une pensée non astreinte à la rigoureuse correspondance entre noèse et noème, non astreinte à l'adéquation du visible égalant la visée à laquelle il aurait à répondre dans l'intuition de la vérité ; il y faudrait une pensée où ne serait plus légitime la métaphore même de *vision* et de *visée*? Exigence impossible ! A moins qu'à ces exigences ne fasse écho ce que Descartes appelait l'idée de l'infini en nous – pensant au-delà de ce qu'elle est à même de contenir, dans sa finitude de cogito". And also pp. 28–29: "Que l'idée de l'infini, dans sa passivité, puisse être entendue comme le domaine de l'incertitude d'une humanité préoccupée d'elle-même et incapable d'embrasser l'infini et où le fait d'être frappé par Dieu ne serait qu'un pis-aller de la finitude, c'est probablement la méconnaissance de l'originalité irréductible de l'altérité et de la transcendance et une interprétation purement négative de la proximité éthique et de l'amour, l'obstination de les dire en terme d'immanence, comme si la possession ou la fusion – idéal d'une conscience intentionnelle – épuisait l'énergie spirituelle. Que la proximité de l'Infini et la socialité qu'elle instaure et commande, puissent être meilleures que la *coïncidence de l'unité*, que la socialité soit de par sa pluralité même, une excellence irréductible, même si on ne peut pas le dire en termes de richesse sans retomber dans l'énoncé de la misère ; que la relation ou la non-indifférence à l'autre ne consiste pas, pour

l'Autre, à se convertir au Même, que la religion ne soit pas le moment de l''économie' de l'être, que l'amour ne soit pas un demi-dieu – c'est certainement cela aussi que signifie l'infini en nous ou l'humanité de l'homme comprise comme théologie ou l'intelligibilité du transcendant". On the idea of transcendence in Lévinas' philosophy see Fabio Ciaramelli, *Transcendance et éthique*, Ousia, Bruxelles, 1989.

ABDUL RAHIM AFAKI

THE HISTORICALITY OF LINGUISTIC SIGNS AND THE AHISTORICALITY OF MEANINGS: THE ROLE OF DIVINE NEOLOGISMS IN THE MAKING OF ISLAMIC-ARAB TRADITION

How is the divine word to affect the human life-world? This is the question that has made me attract towards the currents both of Western and Islamic hermeneutics. Both of these currents are rooted in man's endeavor to interpret the divine Scriptures as objectively as possible, for the objectivity of the *ahistorical* divine meaning can cleanse the subjectivity of the *historically* evolved human discourse. In case of Western hermeneutics, the ahistoricality of divine meaning undid its cleansing effect as soon as the orientation of Western civilization started to be identified by the Enlightenment. Since then on, the focal point of Western hermeneutics has been the historicality of human discourse rather than the ahistoricality of the divine word. But the case of Islamic hermeneutics is a little different. Right from the out set, Islamic hermeneutics has never been able to discard itself from the ahistoricality of divine discourse. It has rather been revolving around the Qur'ān as an absolute source of the divine meanings. Muslims all over the world believe that these meanings not only direct an individual to lead a pious life but they also guarantee the transformation in man's collective life-world. So the orientation of man's interest in understanding the divine word is not simply determined by his urge to the personal piety but mainly by his intent of interpreting the divine meaning in relation to his life-praxis (shared with others) so that it may be transformed accordingly. Thanks to my primary interest in the divine meaning-human praxis relationship, I have made an attempt in this paper, benefiting from certain notions of Western hermeneutics, to interpret the transformation of pagan-Arab tradition into Islamic-Arab tradition. The transformation was realized through the development of Qur'ānic hermeneutics as a triadic complex of the divine revelation, the human life-form and the language. On this complex triadic scale, keeping the Western hermeneutical

195

A-T. Tymieniecka (ed.),
Timing and Temporality in Islamic Philosophy and Phenomenology of Life, 195–221.
© 2007 *Springer.*

discourse in background, we shall see how the pagan-Arab tradition was transformed into Islamic-Arab tradition through the two-dimensional impact of the Qur'ān and the Prophet. What the role of the Prophet Muhammad was in this development. How the companions and their successors contributed to that development both as the transmitters of the Islamic heritage and the practitioners of the Prophetic hermeneutics.

1. LANGUAGE-LIFE COMPLEX AND PAGAN-ARAB TRADITION

One of the most significant cultural facets of the pre-Islamic Arab life-world was its inhabitants' extreme pride of being Arab. This pride was mainly due to the language they spoke, as they called all of the non-Arabs *'ajam* one of whose connotations is *a'jamu* that means 'one who has got an obscurity in his tongue,' or 'one who cannot express one's own words with eloquence and clarity.'[1] There were two forms of expressions through which the pre-Islamic Arabs could manifest the eloquence with perfection namely *al-khatabah* (the oratory) and *ash-shi'r* (the poetry). One should not take both of them as merely the two literary forms rather they were to encompass the whole tribal life-form of the Arabs on the plane of language. They were the manifestations of their *hurrīyyah* (freedom) and *furūsīyyah* (chivalry) which required the glibness (*dhalāqah*) of tongue, the purity (*nasā'ah*) of style, the elegance (*anāqah*) of dialect (*lahjah*) and the spontaneity of intuition (*talāqat al-badīhah*). [2]

Owing to their chivalric and tribal life-form, the Arabs were sentient and self-esteemed as well as the men of courage and sense of honour. All of these characteristics of their specific mode of life were objectivated in their poetry and oratory. One's pride of belonging to a particular tribe, the race of honour and bravery among the tribes, interest based political tensions and oppositions between the tribes, diplomatic relationships between the tribes and their chieftains were the routine states of affairs in the chivalric life form of the Arabs. In view of these states of affairs, one can understand how much significant the role of a poet and an orator would be in that form of life. Therefore, the Arabs, in the pre-Islamic era, 'used to discipline their youth both in poetry and oratory since their childhood, as they desired them to be either an orator to give support to the tribe or a poet to give rise to the reputation of the tribe.'[3] That is, both poets and orators were to play the heroic role in the making of the chivalric tradition of the Arabs. On the one hand, they had to objectivate the meanings of courageous and heroic chivalric deeds of their fellow-tribal men in the form of verses or statements. On the other hand, they had to do this in the most effective way in order to make them perfectly convincing for all. That's how the poets and the orators safeguarded the whole pagan culture on the plane of language; and the generation after generation, the transmission of the culture through language took shape of a tradition. This all encompassing role of Arabic language as a medium through which the chivalric culture of the Arabs was developed into a tradition simultaneously closes down and opens up the possibility of aptly responding to the question: How was the pagan-Arab tradition transformed into an Islamic-Arab tradition?

It seems to close down the possibility of responding to the question aptly if one wholly and solely refers to certain contemporary proponents of Western hermeneutics like Gadamer, Habermas and Apel. At the same time it opens up the possibility if one refers, realizing the limits of fruitfulness of Western hermeneutics, to the Prophetic hermeneutics based upon the Qur'ān and its life-oriented interpretation by the Prophet, which we call the *Sunnah*.

2. LIMITS OF FRUITFULNESS OF WESTERN HERMENEUTICS IN INTERPRETING THE TRANSFORMATION OF ARAB TRADITION

Setting Western mind's face against the enlightenment prejudice regarding the concepts of tradition and authority, Hans-Georg Gadamer explores the possibility of philosophizing tradition positively. Moreover, both Jürgen Habermas and Karl-Otto Apel extend their efforts in making it philosophically viable to interpret one tradition in relation to another. I do not wish to reject every possibility for the fruitfulness or instrumentality of Western hermeneutics, but rather I tend to realize the limitations of this fruitfulness in interpreting the transformation of the pagan-Arab tradition into the Islamic-Arab tradition.

Take for instance Gadamer's philosophical hermeneutics which justifies the evolvement of all mind-set of an individual as 'prejudices', both legitimate and illegitimate with respect to his affiliation with a specific tradition. In this paradigm, it is unlikely for an individual to transcend the historically or traditionally given prejudices while understanding or interpreting some text like tradition itself. However, one can be able to cleanse the illegitimacy of one's prejudices in an hermeneutical situation by referring to the effective historical consciousness which is always available in the guise of tradition. The tradition is not, according to Gadamer, a dead past, instead, it is a living continuity, a flow of 'effective-history' which encompasses not only the past but also the relevant present. It is the 'effective-historical consciousness' that has given rise to the human sciences as they are and as well as to the social structure as it exists. It is in the living process of tradition that we acquire our prejudices and fore-meanings regarding a text, and again the text is to speak of the tradition that has already objectivated in it. This is what Gadamer calls 'hermeneutical situation,' that is, 'a situation in which we find ourselves, with regard to the tradition that we are trying to understand.' 'Effective-historical consciousness is the consciousness of the hermeneutical situation' that makes us realize that we are not standing outside the situation 'and hence are unable to have any objective knowledge of it.'[4] Instead, we are always within the situation and the 'illumination' of it is a task which 'cannot be completely achieved,' as we exist as historical beings and all of our knowledge 'proceeds from what is historically pre-given.' The concept of situation is essentially concerned with the 'concept of *horizon*' as explored by Gadamer. The hermeneutical situation, as shown above, determines the limits of the possibility of understanding the tradition in which we always find ourselves. 'The *horizon* is the range of vision that includes everything that can be seen from a particular vantage point.'[5] Moreover, one's horizon makes one know 'the relative significance of everything' that is included within the horizon whether it is 'near or far, great or small.' When one acquires a horizon, one becomes able 'to look beyond what is closed at hand-not in order to look away from it, but to see it better within a larger whole and in truer proportion.'[6] If we relate the notions of situation and horizon to that of prejudices, we can say that it is our prejudices that, on the one hand, determine the hermeneutical situation in which we find ourselves. On the other hand, 'they constitute... the horizon of a particular present, for they represent that beyond which it is impossible to see.'[7] As the hermeneutical situation, as discussed above, is determined by the effective-historical consciousness the operation of prejudices in the horizon of present is a continuous process. The significant aspect of this operation of the prejudices in an hermeneutical situation or within a horizon of the present is the encounter with the tradition which relates the horizon of the present to the historical horizon. 'Understanding... is always the fusion of these horizons.' It means that in the process of understanding, the historical horizon is projected to be fused with our present horizon and so it is no more there to be 'solidified into the self-alienation of a past consciousness.'[8] It implies a hermeneutic circle in which the tradition becomes a larger whole which determines all of our prejudices, and again the prejudices are necessary conditions to understand the tradition itself as a continuous flow that encompasses all past and present horizons. In this framework of philosophical hermeneutics, no experience of understanding can take place outside the continuum of tradition, that is, the historicity of tradition is inevitable if one attempts to interpret some text on the essential ground of one's prejudices.

Drawing upon Gadamer's philosophical hermeneutics and the later Wittgenstein's language/life complex, Habermas construes his hermeneutical approach to the empirical-analytical sciences of action in the pragmatist framework of the rules of inquiry as the rules of social action rather than the rules of grammar. In view of the model of translation from a foreign language to one's own primary language, Habermas makes it possible for an individual to transcend one cultural tradition or one set of rules of grammar, but in relation to the other. Habermas opines that the cleansing of human reason is attained through the transition between two languages or traditions. That is, the translation from a foreign to one's primary language is not a mutual communication through the correspondence between two sets of grammatical rules, as an ordinary language is not like the language of calculus where the meanings are fixed with the application of rules. Instead, in case of an ordinary language translation one always requires to interpret the meaning appropriating it within one's own tradition which is different from the foreign one from which the meaning was imported. This is a sort of the fusion of horizons of the two traditions which enables one to make the meaning understandable in one's own life-world which is at first linguistically foreign and unintelligible. According to Habermas, when one learns an ordinary language, one masters the rules of that ordinary language grammar in terms of 'socialization... in a cultural life form.' One's mastery of a particular set of grammar rules, restricting one to the limits of one language game, simultaneously opens up to one the possibility of transcending the rules. This self-transcendence through language can be grasped by the help of foreign-language-learning model. The learning of foreign language presupposes 'the mastery of at least one language' in advance which Habermas calls 'primary language'. One's mastery of the primary language not only makes it possible for one to understand something within the structure of one grammar but it also makes foreign language intelligible. This transition between languages is a cleansing process for human reason. According to Habermas:

"Reason, which is always bound up with language, is also always beyond its languages. Only by destroying the particularities of *languages*, which are the only way in which it is embodied, does reason live in *language*. It can purge itself of the residue of one particularity, of course, only through the transition to another."[9]

One can fully grasp the notion of translation and its relationship with understanding in the paradigm of foreign language. As long as one understands something in a foreign language one does not need to translate it into one's own primary language. But when one confronts some 'problematic' in understanding something, one has to appropriate that foreign language expression through translation. So '[t]ranslations are only necessary in situations where understanding is disturbed.'[10] The notion of translation is not only concerned with the problematic understanding in the transition of one language to another but it may also arise between the two partners of a conversation within the limits of one language. Both of the partners following the same rules of grammar communicate each other in two ways: First, they understand one another in general; and second, one of them is to make oneself understandable in a given instance. The rules of grammar, according to Habermas, 'not only make consensus possible; they also include the possibility of setting situations right in which understanding is disturbed.'[11] In order to avoid the disturbance in understanding each other's viewpoint the partners of a dialogue must play the role of the interpreter which is tantamount to the role of translator as already discussed regarding the transition between the native and the foreign language.

Here Habermas demarcates the limitations of Wittgenstein's notion of language game and Gadamer's explication of the hermeneutical problem. Owing to the limitations of his notion of 'language game as a form of life' Wittgenstein restricts his concept of understanding to 'the virtual recapitulation of the training through which native speakers are socialized into their own form of life.' The limitation of Wittgenstein's concept of understanding is, according to Habermas, due to his inability to differentiate between 'learning one's mother tongue' and one's 'mastering a foreign language.' This inability leads Wittgenstein to a very limited concept of translation 'as a transformation in accordance with general rules.' This concept of translation is devoid of its pointing to a 'productive accomplishment to which language always empowers those who have mastered its grammatical rules: assimilating what is foreign and thereby developing one's own language system.' This is what one can experience in everyday life situations in which the dialogue partners must first find a "common language" as a result of having mutual understanding in the model of translation.[12] Criticizing Wittgenstein, Habermas refers to Gadamer's notion of the hermeneutical problem. Learning a language, for Gadamer, is not a real form of understanding, as one masters a language 'by living in it' without following the model of translation. The act of real understanding is deeply concerned with the hermeneutical problem which has no relevance with 'the correct mastery of language,' rather it arises when two partners have a dialogue through the medium of language. That is the situation in which the interlocutors follow the model of translation to make their conversation intelligible for one another.[13]

Habermas equates translation with tradition. The dialectical mediation as it takes place between two languages or two cultural life forms through the process of translation also comes to happen between two generations or epochs in the continuation of traditions. That is to say, tradition, like translation, is a medium through which 'languages reproduce themselves' by 'a bridging of the distance between the generations.'[14] There is a part-whole relationship, according to Habermas, between one's learning a language as a socialization in a cultural life form and in the making of a tradition. Habermas insists on inducing hermeneutical dimension in the Wittgensteinian notion of 'the practice of language games.' As a small unit of tradition one's mastery of a language game grammar is not only grounded on one's learning 'the conditions of possible consensus' but in addition also on one's understanding how to negotiate in the 'conditions of disturbed consensus.' Haberms appreciates Wittgenstein's deviation from positivism by bringing to awareness the fact that one cannot master the grammatical rules on the symbolic plane of language itself. Instead, one can learn the rules in the cultural life form. At the same time he criticizes Wittgenstein for his positivistic shortcomings of neglecting the hermeneutical aspect of mastering the rules of grammar. Wittgenstein's language game is, for Habermas, a sealed and 'opaque' bundle of rules which allows nothing to pass through and so the practice of the game is an ahistorical mechanism. Habermas, opting the hermeneutical dimension of language from Gadamer, transforms language from a 'monadically sealed' oneness into a 'porous' unit which is developed hermeneutically and historically in the making of tradition. For him, '[l]anguage exists only as something traditional, for tradition mirrors on a large scale the life long socialization of individuals in their language.'[15] The ahistorical mechanism of the application of grammatical rules in an 'identical way', as Wittgenstein expounds, reduces the dimension of intersubjectivity of language communication to the 'intersubjective validity' of the rules. This rule application mechanism transforms an ordinary language into a formalized language like the languages of calculus that have the monodological opaque structure as mentioned above. The reconstruction of the monadological structure of language game grammar through the application of grammatical rules is devoid of the hermeneutical characteristic of dialogue and intersubjective communication. In a formalized language structure, strictly logical connections which determine the application of grammatical rules cannot permit intersubjective communication, as 'the perfect order' of the formalized language is absolutely devoid of the element of 'ambiguity' or 'disturbed understanding.' In this regard, '[o]rdinary languages are imperfect and do not ensure lack of ambiguity' therefore, 'the intersubjectivity of communication in ordinary language is continually interrupted.'[16] This discontinuity in the intersubejctive communication can be compensated through hermeneutic understanding. The porous structure of ordinary language permits the situations of disturbed consensus wherein the individuals following grammatical rules intersubjectively attempt to negotiate the disturbance through the historical process of hermeneutic understanding.

The process takes the form of a dialogue between the individuals. The dialogue filling the hermeneutic gape between the individuals eradicates 'the breaks in intersubjectivity'; and at the same time it also establishes 'the delicate balance between separation and union in which the identity of every self must engage.'[17]

As compared both to Gadamer and Habermas, Apel's response to the problem of historicism, one's distancing from his own tradition due to one's engagement in a dialogical mediation with a foreign tradition, is a little complex. Apel advices a non-Western contemporary man to construct a philosophy of history in order to address the problem of historicity characterized as the crisis of break with his tradition due to the inevitable adoption of the Western technical-industrial form of life. This philosophy of history should be both hermeneutic and scientistic in character. Its hermeneutic character may help one interpret the linguistically handed down heritage of one's own and the foreign tradition, while the scientistic character may help one explain the remnants of traditions which are given linguistically undocumented. This binary function of interpretation and explanation, according to Apel, makes the philosophy of history aptly address the problem of historicism which the contemporary non-Western man is facing.

According to Apel, the non-Western men's inevitable adoption of 'the European technical-industrial form of life and its specific foundations' force them to distance themselves from their own tradition. This emergent crisis of break with tradition which Apel calls 'the problem of historicism' cannot be resolved, he argues, 'solely by hermeneutic reflection', rather along with it they must also 'achieve a quasi-objective, historical-philosophical system of reference.'[18] They must most preferably seek a 'philosophical and scientific orientation' to mediate a hermeneutic understanding both of their own and foreign, particularly the western, 'traditions of meaning by sociological analysis of those economic and social orders' which they belong to.[19] Furthermore, there are always certain limitations and contradictions faced by the interpreter in order to understand the texts of temporally and spatially distant cultures. In the course of history, human beings have always been unable to have a transparent and lucid understanding either of their 'intentions' and 'motives' behind their actions or of at least their conceptions of meaning that are objectivated in the linguistic documents like historical and literary works. They have always been and still are unable to put the full and pure expressions of their intellectual 'convictions' and 'intentions' in the linguistic texts and so the major part of their history remains in the natural and actual forms of life. When an interpreter is to mediate the tradition he finds a huge 'barrier to understanding' due to the 'contradictions which are determined by the intermeshing of sense and nonsense, intended actions and naturally determined reactions.'[20] Here one can understand why Apel does not find merely an hermeneutic reflection enough to mediate tradition. Instead, he puts emphasis on undertaking a philosophy of history that seeks to integrate both hermeneutic and explanatory sciences. The hermeneutic side of the philosophy of history is concerned with the interpretation of those motivations and intentions of life that can be understood by the drive of 'the hermeneutic interest in intersubjective agreement.' Whereas the explanatory scientific side of the philosophy of history may deal with those 'factually contingent factors of human history' which are unable to rise to the level of intersubjective agreement because they are not 'subjectively transparent but are merely factually effective and can only be analyzed by means of a quasi-objective explanatory science.'[21]

With the dialectical mediation of hermeneutic and explanatory methods Apel incorporates the critique of ideology through the model of psycho-analysis. Drawing from his notion of the 'partial suspension of hermeneutic communication' Apel equates the critique of ideology with the technique of psychotherapy further relating to the mediation of explanation and inter-pretation. In a discourse between people, according to Apel, one party does not take the intentions of the other 'seriously hermeneutically', rather 'distances himself from the other objectively as a quasi-natural entity.' He no longer attempts to create the unity of language in communication, but rather seeks to evaluate what the other person says as the symptom of an objective situation which he seeks to explain from outside in a language in which his partner does not participate.'[22] This is what Apel calls 'the partial breakdown of hermeneutic communication in favour of objective method of acquiring knowledge' and which he further equates with the situation wherein a psychotherapist treats his neurotic patient. The breakdown of hermeneutic communication is to have an analogical relation to 'the break with tradition' as we have already discussed as the problem of historicism. Responding to this problem Apel proposes to explore a philosophy of history that must, on the one hand, unify both hermeneutic and scientistic methods and, on the other, 'adopt the objective distantiating cognitive role of a psychother-apist regarding 'the behaviour and meaning claims of what has been handed down [through tradition] and of contemporaries.'[23] The hermeneutic method of historical explanation emphasizes that 'the objective context of events as a result of historical reconstruction is mediated through an understanding of the intentions of participating human beings' whereas the scientific explanation of history attempts to mediate the causes behind the events 'by method-ological analysis of objective, operating factors of which the responsible actors are not at all conscious as meaningful motives.'[24] Apel considers 'the quasi-objective cognitive achievement of the behavioral sciences' as an ideal form of scientistic explanation to be incorporated into his proposed method of philosophy of history. His cognitive model opts a mid-way between the methods mentioned above by realizing a connection between 'the quasi-natural causal process of a specific mode of societal practice and the neurotic symptoms of individuals in this society.'[25] This proposal takes the form of a psychoanalytic-psychotherapeutic model as a critique of ideology, as it, on the one hand, analyzes human history to diagnose the ailment of the social sciences, and on the other, cures the ailments by therapy of the society. The guiding cognitive interest of this model, Apel argues, 'corresponds to the life-a priori of a psychosomatic self-diagnosis and self-therapy of mankind.'[26]

All of these three paradigms of contemporary Western hermeneutics seem to work within the historicity of one or more traditions. The historicality as essentiality of these paradigms limits their benefits for one who tends to interpret the transformation of a historical continuum or tradition through a text which is ahistorical in character. This is the case of the transformation of the pagan-Arab tradition into Islamic-Arab tradition through the divine mode of the Qur'ān. In order to interpret this transformation one, therefore, will have to explore an hermeneutics, which may incorporate the ahistorical or the divine with the historical or the mundane. That's what I shall do in what follows, yet I shall have no hesitation in grafting certain concepts of Western hermeneutics on my hermeneutical approach, which is rooted in the Qur'ān and the Prophetic life-praxis, that is, the *Sunnah*.

3. THE REVELATION-LIFE-LANGUAGE TRIAD AND THE TRANSFORMATION OF ARAB TRADITION FROM PAGAN INTO ISLAMIC

The orientation of the pre-Islamic (*al-jāhilī*) tradition, as we have discussed above, was linguistic and the main contributors to that culture were the poets and the orators. The manifestations of the Arab sentiments, regarding their pride of affiliation with their language, show that the most eloquent from among them was considered to be the most dignified. This is very famous that Labīd ibn Rabī'ah, one of the poets of the Seven Suspended (*ashāb al-mu'allaqāt as-sab'*), was prostrated by the attendants of the *'Ukkāz* Festival[27] due to the eloquence of his *qasīdah* (ode) which was thereafter hung up in the *ka'bah* on account of its merit. He is reported to abandon poetry after embracing Islam owing to the unsurpassable eloquence of the Qur'ān.[28] In addition to the linguistic orientation of the pagan-Arab tradition one more significant element of their culture is that all of the Arabs in the pre-Islamic era were not homogenously polytheists. There were instead certain people from among them who were monotheists. They were originally the offspring of Ishmael, the son of Abraham and so there was an underlying consciousness of monotheism in their culture. We shall further substantiate these two points while discussing the rise of the Prophetic hermeneutics in what follows.

The linguistic orientation of the development of pagan-Arab tradition guaranteed an intersubjective meaning context of Arabic language wherein the Prophet was succeeded in making the Arabs understand the word of God. That's the reason why the Qur'ān was revealed onto him in the language that was being shared between him and his original public, that is, the chivalric and pagan Arabs. The Qur'ān says:

"Verily this is heedfully revealed from the Lord of the worlds. The Trustworthy Spirit came down with it, in the perspicuous Arabic language (*bi lisān 'Arabī mubīn*), to thy heart so that thou mayest be from amongst the cautioners (*al-mundhirīn*). . . . Had we revealed it to any of the non-Arabs, and had he recited it to them, they wouldn't have believed in it." (*Shu'arā'* 26:192–199)

The Qur'ān explains that if it had been revealed in a language other than the language shared between the Prophet and the original addressees, the pagan Arabs, they would have never convinced by it. For, the intersubjective meaning context established through the pagan-Arab tradition was given as to the Prophet and the pagan Arabs at the plane of Arabic language. It would, therefore, be unlikely for the Prophet to convince the Arabs through interpretation of any text other than the Arabic one. The Arabic language shared between the Prophet and his original addressees would be a precondition of all understanding and interpretation of the Qur'ān construed either by the Prophet, his companions, their successors, or any other individual or group belonging to any epoch throughout the history of Muslims.

The traditionally given meaning context of Arabic language, being comprised of Arabic signs and symbols and their corresponding meanings, was neither subjective nor objective. The language-as-traditional-meaning-context had been intersubjectively developed by the Arabs in their unique life-world. The Qur'ān was revealed in the perspective of that meaning context through the signs and symbols of Arabic language whose meanings were prejudged or "prejudiced" by the Arabs with reference to their tradition. This prejudiced meaning, on the part of the Qur'ān, was a misunderstood or misinterpreted meaning of a linguistic symbol with reference to its traditional use in the pagan Arab life-world. Besides, as we have mentioned above, the pre-Islamic life-world was not homogenously pagan or polytheist (though predominantly to be so), rather there were certain monotheistic elements out there in that culture, which reflects that there was a plausibility of misunderstanding regarding the traditional meanings of a linguistic symbol. The polytheist-monotheist dichotomy of meanings of a linguistic symbol might have always been there in that culture to give rise to the misunderstanding. Had the only source of meanings been the traditional life-language complex, it would have been impossible for an individual to cleanse the misunderstandings from his culture. He could instead cleanse his own reason as per the historical predominance of tradition. But the transformation of pagan-Arab tradition into Islamic-Arab tradition shows that there is a source of meanings which is far more stronger than that of the historicality of tradition. This is an ahistorical and divine source which we call the Qur'ān, which bestowed on the Prophet the neologisms of meaning along with his ability of hermeneutic praxis to realize that ahistoric neologisms in the historic life-world. The Prophet started his hermeneutic praxis to realize the ahistoric-divine neologisms in the historically predominantly polytheistic life-world of the Arabs with the treatment of the most fundamental religious-linguistic symbol, Allāh.

The symbol of Allāh, as it was used in the pre-Islamic Arab world, was to have a particular meaning but the Prophet shared its use with the Arabs through a different divine neologism. Allāh is originally *al-ilāh* the proper noun with *alif* and *lām*, as Zamakhsharī mentions, which means 'any god whether true (*haqq*) or false (*bātil*) but predominantly true ones ... However, the word Allāh with the deletion of *hamzah* is specifically used for one true Deity rather than any other god.'[29] The Arabs, despite the fact that they were polytheists, did not give status to any of their several gods equivalent to that of Allāh. 'They worshiped several gods other than Allāh under the yoke of their misbelief that they being close companions of Allāh might support them in order to become close to Allāh.'[30] The Qur'ān describes their belief regarding their several gods in the verse 3 of *Sūrah* 39:

"We only serve them in order that they may bring us nearer to Allāh" (*Zumar* 39:3)

Owing to the divine neologism of the same linguistic symbol of Allāh, the Prophet established the Islamic conception of *tawhīd* (oneness of Allāh) both by using that word in the language and by practicing its new meaning being cleansed from all polytheistic attachments to it. He added instead certain theistic connotations in terms of many attributions (*sifāt*) to, and explanations about the symbol in order to Islamize or Qur'ānize it. The Prophet, through the divine neologisms, attempted to eliminate the prejudiced misunderstandings of his original addressees regarding the traditional meaning of the linguistic symbols by the way of a dialogic-hermeneutic process. The dialogue between the Prophet and his addressees was realized on the plane of language given to both of the parties through tradition. His addressees were equipped with the prejudiced and misunderstood meanings of the traditional linguistic symbols while the Prophet was the bearer of the divinely revealed neologisms of the same symbols. This is the most significant aspect of the dialogic-hermeneutic process that the neologisms were not to bring the new symbols with the new meanings rather the divinely appropriate meanings for the old traditional symbols which were being used with the mundanely corrupt meanings in the pagan-Arab life-world. There were two horizons: the first was the mundane-historical horizon of tradition which was given to both the parties engaged in the dialogue in terms of language-life complex of the Arabs. The Second was the divine-ahistorical horizon of the Qur'ānic neologisms corresponding to the first through the same complex. The fusion of the two horizons, to use Gadamer's phrase, was realized when the Prophet made them fuse together through his hermeneutic praxis. The fusion of the divine or ahistorical and the mundane or historical horizons through the Prophetic-hermeneutic praxis gave rise to the understanding between the two parties regarding the use of traditional-linguistic symbols in terms of the Qur'ānic neologisms. This is the uniqueness of the Prophetic hermeneutics that it convinced the pagan Arabs to come into the fold of Islam through the fusion of the divine and the mundane horizons on the plane of the language-life complex. The Prophetic hermeneutics, by introducing the neologisms for the religiously significant traditional-linguistic symbols, not only developed the tradition further but meanwhile it also guaranteed the cleansing of the tradition culturally, socially, ethically and politically from all of the pagan or non-Islamic attachments to it.

The Prophetic hermeneutics was absolutely objectivist in character. The Prophet's engagement in the dialogic-hermeneutic process was not self-intended. He was instead divinely determined to not only deliver the word of Allāh to his addressees but to make them understand it through an appropriate interpretation of it as it is mentioned in the Qur'ān:

"And we have sent down unto thee the reminiscence (adh-dhikr) so that thou mayest explain clearly to the people what is sent for them and that they may give thought." (Nahl 16:44)

The Prophet did not deliberate to be engaged in the dialogic-hermeneutic process with the fellow Arabs. It was bestowed upon him instead to communicate the divine word revealed unto him from Allāh in terms of the traditionally given linguistic symbols that had already been in use in the pagan-Arab life-world. It's the twofold givenness of the traditional linguistic symbols and their divine neologisms that determined the role of the Prophet as an absolutely objectivist interpreter of the Qur'ān. He was not supposed to amalgamate anything in the dialogic-hermeneutic process by his own without the divine sanction. That's the reason why the Prophet's hermeneutic praxis in terms of his sayings and acts, being different from the divine revelation though essentially related to it, is collectively called *Sunnah* as a source of Islamic teachings complementary to the Qur'ān. The significance of the *Sunnah* as a source of Islamic teachings is justifiable owing to the role of the Prophet as an absolutely objectivist interpreter of the Qur'ān.

Muslims all over the world have generally been conceiving Islam as a combination of the divine knowledge and the human praxis. The Qur'ān as a Word of God is a sort of theory that precedes and determines the human life that is a praxis. The Qur'ān was revealed onto the Prophet throughout the twenty-three years of his carrier as a prophet and he realized that Word of God through his act throughout the course of the same period. The Prophet was an interpreter par excellence who was restricted not only to the plane of theory while interpreting the Word of God. Instead, he made his community understand the Word by realizing it on the plane of life-praxis as well. The Word-act correspondence or the revelation-life correspondence took the form of a theory-practice combination to be manifested at the highest level in the life of the Prophet. That's why Muslims without any exception submit so strictly to the Prophet to purify their souls to lead a good life according to the teachings of Islam. That is to say, 'all words of purity (*al-Kalim aT-Tayyab*) mount up to God with the anchor of the good deed (*al-'Amal as-Sālih*)' (*Fātir* 35:10) and in order to reach that height one is to strictly follow the Prophet. For it is the Prophet who is 'soul' to the mortals from amongst themselves to 'purify their souls' by 'educating' them according to the Word of God (*Baqarah* 2:129 & 151) and then this purity (*tazkīyyah*) leads them to a good communal life.

This twofold model of Islam was realized by the Prophet with all of its deep rooted impact on the Arab culture through Arabic language. It is the language which provided the Prophet with the platform in order not only to communicate the appropriate meaning or neologism of *al-kalim at-tayyab* to the Arabs but to make it practically prolific on the level of *al-'amal as-sālih* in their life-world. Arabic language, therefore, became the precondition of the Prophetic hermeneutics to realize the functionality of the theory-praxis model in the early Islamic social order. Owing to his role as an interpreter in the early Islamic community, the Prophet was to use Arabic language in order to address all problems of understanding the Qur'ān that might distance the life (praxis) from the revelation (theory). The companions of the Prophet were to constitute the communication community (to use pragmatists' phrase).[31] A community wherein the individuals were fully capable of grasping the divine neologisms which the Prophet communicated to them on the plane of Arabic language shared in the community as an historical continuum of tradition. They were the most brilliant and outstanding interpreters of the Qur'ān after the Prophet, for they were the direct addressees of the Prophet. They shared all process of understanding and interpreting the Qur'ān with the Prophet. They were to understand the Word of God, which was revealed in their language, in the perspective of those meanings which were constituted in their own cultural life-form. They strictly followed the Prophet's acts by applying their understanding of the revelations which had already been enlightened through their communication with the Prophet. The intellectual-hermeneutic talent of each of the companions was the most significant element to determine his or her position in the community established by the Prophet. From among the companions Abū Bakr is considered to be the closest to the Prophet and so the highest in the rank after the Prophet. It is so because he was extraordinarily outstanding in understanding and interpreting the Qur'ān along with its application to the human life. For instance, when he heard the Prophet reciting the verse:

"Today I have perfected for you your religion (Dīn), I have completed my blessing upon you, and I have chosen for you Islam as a religion." (Mā'idah 5:4)

Abū Bakr is reported to realize[32] on account of his deep understanding of the verse that the Prophet's life would soon come to an end with this final revelation which completed the Divine message. In addition, one should not forget that it was also Abū Bakr, who with his absolute conviction, shared with the Prophet the understanding of the very first verse revealed onto the Prophet when there was no other man on the surface of the earth to be so privileged by the Prophet. The companions' outstanding ability of understanding the Qur'ān and its application to life was guaranteed by the presence of the Prophet in their community on the two-fold plane of intellect and act or of theory and praxis. The two-fold conviction of the companions helped the Prophet establish a unique culture which was characterized by an amazing balance between intellect and act on the ground of his own life-model manifested as an absolute balance between the Divine revelation and the human action. The culture of balance between intellect and act or revelation and life was made to flourish by the Prophet himself throughout the Arab peninsula. The companions not only adopted that culture with absolute devotion and extreme dedication but they transmitted it both temporally and spatially. Their achievements in this two-fold transmission of their culture to the other parts of the world and to the successive historical epochs were to shape the Islamic tradition characterized as intellect-act harmony. But, as we have seen above, this tradition was developed on the essential plane of Arabic language, so it should more appropriately be called Islamic-Arab tradition rather than Islamic tradition. They not only maintained the Prophetic legacy of balancing between intellect and act but transmitted it to their successors (*Tāba'īn*) and through them to their successors (*Taba' tāba'īn*) with an obligation they strictly bound to (*sabīl al-mū'minīn*) as the Prophet was bound to communicate it to them. The Qur'ān says:

> "O Apostle! Communicate hath been sent to thee from thy Lord. If thou didst not, thou wouldst not have communicated His message." (*Mā'idah* 5:67)…"And we have sent down unto thee the message so that thou mayest explain clearly to the people what is sent for them and that they give thought." (*Naḥl* 16:44)

The departure of the Prophet from the early Islamic society was not to end the functionality of the Prophetic hermeneutics. He delivered that hermeneutical heritage to the companions, and their total submission to the Prophetic sayings and doings in leading their life was to guarantee the further development of the heritage. The end part of verse 44 of *Sūrat an-Naḥl*, that is, *la'allahum yatafakkarūn* (they may give thought), which have cited above, reflects that when the Prophet interpreted some verse of the Qur'ān he at that moment made the companions learn how to reflect on the Qur'ān in order to have an appropriate understanding of it. It is the deep rooted impact of this Prophetic culture, flourished and transmitted further by the companions to their successive generations that the people of those generations could never transcend from harmonizing their life with the divine message. The level of the harmonizing, although very high, was not tantamount to that of the companions, for those people were to adopt that culture from the companions while the companions were to submit to the Prophet for the same purpose. All academic and intellectual endeavors of those generations were encompassed by their passion of attending the unique lectures offered by the companions in different parts of the Islamic world. The lectures were not on any topic other than the Prophetic way of interpreting the Qur'ān and its realization in his lived experiences. These lectures concerning the Prophetic balance between intellect and act as offered by the companions and attended by the successors were the foundation stones of Islamic intellectual tradition, which we called Islamic-Arab tradition. In this regard, the companions' successors living in the different regions of the Islamic state developed different schools of the Islamic tradition of intellectualism. In the outset, there arose three schools namely the *Makkī* school, the *Madanī* school and the Iraqi school of the Qur'ān exegesis being affiliated with three of the most learned companions of the Prophet namely 'Abd Allāh ibn 'Abbās, Ubaī ibn Ka'ab and 'Abd

Allāh ibn Mas'ūd respectively.[33] These three schools were not different in their entirety with respect to the character of Qur'ānic interpretation as three of the companions construed it, rather they were different in name due to the fact that they were developed in three different regions of the Islamic state by the three different companions. Furthermore, the most significant factor in the making of this intellectual tradition of Qur'ānic hermeneutics was the fact that whatever the companions delivered to their successors was not purely their own understanding of the Qur'ān, but rather they transmitted how the Prophet intellectualized and activated according to a verse while interpreting it. For instance, interpreting the 14th and 15th verses of *Sūrat al-A'lā* (Chapter 87):

"That will prosper who purifies himself and refers to the name of his Lord and offers prayer." (*A'lā* 87:14–15)

the Prophet is reported by Jābir ibn 'Abd Allāh to say that here the word prayer (*salla*) referred not only to offering prayer but to formally establishing it five times a day.[34] That is the way the Prophet made his companions learn how to relate the revelation to life. If one relies only on the Qur'ānic verse in order to understand how to offer prayer overlooking the hermeneutic aspect of the Prophetic praxis in this regard, he cannot understand the appropriate meaning of it.

However, the establishment of these three schools does not imply that the companions other than the three, whose names are mentioned above, were not better interpreters of the Qur'ān. Suyūtī (d.1505/911) in *Itqan* and Zarkashī (d.1391/794) in *Burhān* listed the names of ten companions who were famous for their exegetical talent. The list includes the four caliphs (*al-Khulafā' al-arba'ah*), Ibn Mas'ūd, Ibn 'Abbās, Ibn Ka'ab, Zayd ibn Thābit, Abū Mūsā Ash'arī and Ibn Zubayr.[35] There were thousands of reports concerning the Prophet's sayings and doings that many of the companions were to deliver to the successors to build up the Islamic tradition of intellectualism manifested on the plane of language as the revelation-life harmony or the intellect-act balance. The total submission to the Prophetic way of interpreting the Qur'ān leads the companions to shape the early phase of the tradition of Qur'ān exegesis. The tradition was grounded upon the essential relationship between the divine revelation and the Prophet's further response to it in terms both of his acts and sayings in order to make his companions understand it. Then by delivering those Prophetic acts and sayings to their successors, the companions further developed the tradition of Qur'ān exegesis.

Owing to the role of the Prophet as the interpreter par excellence of the Qur'ān, as well as the role of his companions as the immediate communicators of his hermeneutic acts and sayings to their successors, there arose the tradition of *tafsīr bi'l-ma'thūr* (traditionist exegesis). One of the first objectivist-scholarly attempts regarding the inscription of the Prophetic acts and sayings was one made by 'Abd Allāh ibn 'Amr ibn 'Āṣ. In view of his extreme devotion to following the Prophet in order to lead a pious life he was specially permitted[36] by the Prophet to register his sayings whenever he opportuned to do so.[37] Ibn 'Amr's compilation was famous as *aṣ-Ṣaḥīfat aṣ-Ṣādiqah*, but unfortunately the manuscript did not survive to be preserved for the later scholars. Like Ibn 'Amr many other companions are also reported to note down the Prophetic sayings but none of the manuscripts was to survive to authenticate its existence except the reports from the later sources which show that they existed in the earlier days of Islam. In this regard, I partly agree with Zarqānī who says:

"The prophet and his companions were highly learned as far as the Qur'ān and its sciences are concerned. They were to know the Qur'ān more than what the later scholars could know of it. But their scholarly knowledge was not construed as a discipline of learning. It was not composed in the form of a book, as they simply did not require it to compile as a record in the face of the Qur'ān."[38]

The word *ma'thūr* is a term used in *Ḥadīth* literature and it literally means 'some *ḥadīth* of which some people give information to some other people; something which the successors (*khalaf*) transmit from the predecessors (*salaf*).'[39] Therefore, *tafsīr bi'l-ma'thūr* is a type of Qur'ān exegesis that an exegete can construe by juxtaposing the transmissions from the earlier exegetes. This is the type of Qur'ān exegesis that Ibn Khuldūn (1332/732-1406/808) named as *tafsīr naqlī* (traditionist exegesis) which is based upon the traditions or exegetical remnants (*āthār*) received from the predecessors including the companions and their successors.[40] *Tafsīr bi'l-ma'thūr* seems to be characterized as an objectivist exegesis of the Qur'ān. For, if one has to interpret the Qur'ān, it seems, as the term *ma'thūr* implies, that one has to refer to mainly the two sources (*ma'khadh*), the traditions from the Prophet and that from his companions without amalgamating one's own hermeneutic thought with it. But the hermeneutic state of affairs has never been as simple as it seems to be. Let us see how the objectivist cognition of the traditions is hindered through certain hermeneutic problems.

The first source of Qur'ān exegesis, which Zarkashī calls *an-naql 'an rasūl Allāh* (the tradition from the Prophet of Allāh) has never been absolutely objectively found as an indubitable and true source. Instead, Zarkashī advices us to be 'prudent (*ḥadhar*) from the weak (*aḍ-ḍa'īf*) and the fabricated (*mawḍū'*) traditions which are many in number.'[41] That's the reason why Imam Aḥmed ibn Ḥanbal admonished his addressees from the fabricated exegetical traditions. He said:

"Three types of books have no basis (*uṣūl*) namely *al-maghāzī* (the traditions concerning the Prophet's wars), *al-malāḥim* (the reports concerning the clashes between the companions) and *at-tafsīr* (the traditions concerning the Qur'ān exegesis)."[42]

Zarkashī, referring to the student researchers of Ibn Ḥanbal, further explains that by this Ibn Ḥanbal means that all of the traditions concerning the Qur'ān exegesis, the Prophet's wars and the companions' clashes are not baseless rather only those which have no 'authentic unbroken links' (*asānīd ṣiḥāḥ muttaṣilaḥ*).[43] It implies that every proponent of *tafsīr bi'l-mā'thūr* should be very well versed in all of the *ḥadīth* sciences (*'ulūm al-ḥadīth*) so that he could testify the authenticity of the given tradition referred to the Prophet. This is the only way to safeguard *tafsīr bi'l-mā'thūr* from the blending of the fabricated traditions. Otherwise one has to find some other way out in order to solve this hermeneutic problem like adopting the method of *tafsīr bi'r-ra'y* (exegesis by one's personal opinion) at the expense of the way of *tafsīr bi'l-mā'thūr*. That is to say, this hermeneutic problem may lead one from objectively given tradition (or objectivity) to subjective opinion (or subjectivity) as a source of interpretation.

In addition to the Prophetic traditions the other basic sources of *Qur'ān* exegesis are the adoptions from the sayings of companions (*al-akhdh bi qawl aṣ-ṣaḥābī*), the derivations (of meaning) from the common language (*al-akhdh bi muṭlaq al-lughah*), and the adoptions from Judaic-Christian traditions (*isrā'īlīyyāt*).[44]

According to Zarkashī, the second source of Qur'ān exegesis is the saying of the companions, as its hermeneutic status (*manzilah*) is determined by its being referred (*marfū'*) to the Prophet. The unbroken link of a companion's report to the Prophet is a significant element for the justification of authenticity of the report. In this regard, Zarkashī, referring to Abū 'l-Khatṭṭab-*the Ḥanbalite*, notes that without the unbroken tradition link a companion's saying does not seem to be authentic (*ḥujjah*) in itself, as without that link it is plainly a companion's personal opinion (*ar-rā'y*). But if it is not only a companion's personal opinion rather something referred to the Prophet, then it will be taken as a part of the tradition (*ar-rawāyah*) which makes it authentic.[45] That is, the objectively given tradition link of a companion's saying to the Prophet is to make the saying authentic. Otherwise in case when a companion's saying is simply a subjective viewpoint without any reference to the Prophet the authenticity will be lost. For in this case the objective givenness of tradition link is replaced by the subjective construing of the meaning which cannot be convincing without some sound hermeneutic underpinning. Here Zarkashī mentions the names of three companions, 'Alī, Ibn 'Abbās and 'Abd Allāh ibn 'Amr ibn 'Aṣ as the most celebrated exegetes of the Qur'ān from amongst the companions in the sense that most of the Qur'ān exegesis have traditional citations with their references. The same doctrine of traditional link may be extended for the reference to the sayings of the successors of the companions in order to interpret the Qur'ān in view of the traditions. In this regard, Zarkashī gives names of certain exegetes from amongst the successors including Ḍaḥḥāk, Saʿīd ibn Jubayr, Mujāhid, Qatādah, Abū'l-ʿAlīyyah ar-Riyāhī, Ḥasan Baṣrī, Rabīʿ ibn Anas, Muqātil ibn Sulaymān, ʿIkramah and ʿAbd Allābh ibn Zayd ibn Aslam etc..[46]

So an exegete, who is to compile a *tafsīr bi'l-mā'thūr*, may come across at least two types of transmissions made by the companions. First, he may derive some hermeneutic viewpoint from a companion which is authenticated by the objective givenness of its tradition link to the Prophet. Second, he may derive from a companion some subjectively construed meaning of a Qur'ānic verse or word supported by his own hermeneutic justification. The former is called *at-tafsīr bi'r-rawāyah* (exegesis by the tradition) which is by and large objectivist in nature, whereas the later is called *tafsīr bi'd-darāyah* or *bi'r-rā'y* (exegesis by the personal knowledge or opinion) which seems to lead one toward subjectivism. However, to the traditionist exegete, who is referring to the companions for Qur'ān exegesis, both are objectively given. It depends on the exegete how he deals with that givenness. If he accepts the tradition as it is given to him, he will be an objectivist in his approach to the tradition. But if he prefers one on the other owing to his own *dirāyah* or *rā'y*, then he will be a subjectivist. One should note here that this is the subjectivism-objectivism distinction with respect to an exegete's acquaintance with the tradition. Nevertheless, the subjective-objective distinction with respect to the hermeneutic approach toward the meaning of the Qur'ān will have a different orientation. This is justifiably possible that an exegete attempts to interpret a Qur'ānic verse with the help of some objectively given tradition concerned with that verse but still finds that the connotation of the objectively given tradition is different from the objective meaning of the verse. In that case, the exegete will have to interpret the verse or the tradition subjectively in order that the objective meaning of the verse may be safeguarded by its compatibility or deviation from the given tradition. That is to say, either *tafsīr bi'l-mā'thūr* or *tafsīr bi'r-rā'y* may have the blends of both objectivism and subjectivism at the same time.

Although Zarkashī mentions Arabic language, as we have seen above, as one of the basic sources of Qur'ān exegesis, I shall explain the role of language in a relatively larger context. For, I do not consider language as only a source of interpretation rather, as I have already mentioned above, it is a precondition of all acts of understanding and interpretation in its being a platform of the development of tradition as an historical continuum. In what follows we shall see what the role of language had been in the binary development of Qur'ān exegesis in terms of *tafsīr bi'l-mā'thūr* and *tafsīr bi'r-rā'y*.

As a proponent of *tafsīr bi'l-mā'thūr* one is to submit to the traditions (*āthār*) comprised of the sayings and acts of the Prophet and his companions as the essential sources of Qur'ān exegesis. The ideal possibility of this hermeneutic traditionism is one that is characterized by the self-effacement attempted by an exegete in order to cognize the objective meaning of the Qur'ānic verses in the light of traditions. That is, the exegete is to minimize as much as possible the impositions of his own subjective judgments as regards the meaning of the verses. This process of self-effacement is obviously different from that expounded by Emilio Betti.[47] The Bettian process of self-effacement is to enable an interpreter to harmonize himself with the text by overcoming his prejudices whatsoever. For a Qur'ān exegete, who is to compile a *tafsīr bi'l-mā'thūr*, the situation is not so simple, rather he confronts a double hermeneutical problematic. On the one hand, he is given the Qur'ān as an objective reality full of meanings, which may help him lead a pious life. On the other hand, an equally objectively significant reality is there in the form of the Prophetic traditions being an absolutely true interpretation of the Qur'ān. The former is absolutely and purely indubitable as an objective reality being revealed onto the Prophet from Allāh in the same form as it is nowadays commonly found as a book. But the later is reported to have been hugely blended with the highly dubitable traces of misleading traditions passed through the course of about two and a half centuries of one-to-one transmissions concerning the sayings and acts, from the Prophetic era to the epoch of the first compilers of *tafsīr bi'l-mā'thūr*. As compared to the former, the cognition of the latter is far more serious a problematic for one who intends to interpret the verses through the traditionist drive. To this double hermeneutical problematic the Bettian notion of self-effacement is not an appropriate solution, one instead needs a double hermeneutical solution. That's what exactly the early Muslim Qur'ān exegetes realized. On the one hand, they laid foundations of the sciences of traditions (*'ulūm al-ḥadīth*) in order that the true traditions may be cleansed from the blended ones. On the other hand, they, in the face of the self-effacement to objectively cognize the truth of traditions, referred to their subjective attempts of finding some meaning context other than the one-to-one transmission of traditions. This attempt leads them toward *tafsīr bi'r-rā'y*. In order to activate their subjective opinion they found a huge meaning context in the form of language as a medium of all historical givenness to them and as a precondition for all possible acts of interpretation. *Tafsīr bi'r-rā'y*, whose major meaning-context was the language of the Arabs, might rarely be found separate from *tafsīr bi'l-ma'thūr*, whose main thrust was tradition. Instead, both were commonly found as complementary to each other in a full-fledged Qur'ān exegesis as Ibn Khuldūn mentions in *Muqaddimah*:

"This kind of Qur'ān exegesis [linguistic exegesis] rarely appears separately from the first kind [traditionist exegesis] while the latter is essentially purposed. The former (linguistic exegesis) was to appear only after the language and the related sciences (linguistics) had become crafts. However, it has now predominated (the latter) in some of the (Qur'ān) exegeses."[48]

But at some other place in *Muqaddimah*, Ibn Khuldūn seems to opine differently regarding the instrumental role of Arabic language. He, differentiating the two kinds of Qur'ān exegesis, says:

"It should be known that the Qur'ān was revealed in the language of the Arabs [*bi lughat al-'arab*] and according to their rhetorical methods [*asālīb balāghatihim*]. All Arabs understood it and knew the meaning of the individual words and composite statements...He [the Prophet] used to explain unclear statements (in the Qur'ān) and...[t]he men around him [*aṣ-ṣaḥābah*], thus, became acquainted with (the subject). They knew why individual verses had been revealed, and the situation that had required them, directly on (Muḥammad's) authority...

...The (explanations) were transmitted on the authority of the men around Muḥammad and were circulated by the men of the second generation after them on their authority. They continued to be transmitted among the early Muslims, until knowledge became organized in scholarly disciplines and systematic scholarly works were written...

...The linguistic sciences ('*ulūm al-lisān*) then became technical discussions of the lexico-graphical meaning of words, the rules governing vowel endings (*i'rāb*), and style (*balābghah*) in (the use of) word combinations. Systematic works were written on these subjects. Formerly, these subjects had been habits with the Arabs. No recourse to oral and written transmission had been necessary with respect to them. Now, that (state of affairs) was forgotten, and these subjects were learned from the books of philologists. They were needed for the interpretation of the Qur'ān, because the Qur'ān is in Arabic and follows the stylistic technique of the Arabs [*minhāj balāghatihim*]." [49]

One may find oneself a little confused while reading the two citations from Ibn Khuldūn's *Muqaddimah*, as, in the first citation he applies the condition that the linguistic exegesis of the Qur'ān was developed 'only after the language and the related sciences (linguistics) had become crafts,' whereas in the second citation he discusses the linguistic exegesis with respect to the Arabic language as something traditionally practiced by the Prophet, his companions and the generations thereafter. But in my view it is not as confusing as it seems to be in the first sight as we shall see in what follows.

Drawing upon the two citations from Ibn Khuldūn, one may infer that there have been two different roles of Arabic language in the excavation of Qur'ān exegesis. The twofold role of Arabic language is determined by its twofold use: first, the use of Arabic as a conventional language as it was spoken, read and written by the Arabs following the rules of grammar given to them historically-conventionally. Second, the use of Arabic as a set of rules and laws as it was learned to be practiced mostly by the non-Arabs by cognizing the technicalities of the rules of grammar again grounded upon the cultural life-form of the Arabs. The later is the sense of language in which it is to be taken as a set of philological principles and grammatical rules explored on the symbolic plane of linguistic signs though the relevance of these signs with the Arab life-form cannot entirely be omitted. However, the network of grammatical rules becomes hard enough to lessen the historic-hermeneutic concern of language in the exegesis. These two uses of Arabic language are the two different ways of practicing it regarding its users' specific interest of understanding the Qur'ān and the *Sunnah*. In either case the language is not simply a source of interpretation as both Zarkashī and Suyūṭī believe, it is instead a basic precondition for every act of understanding and interpretation of the Qur'ān and the *Sunnah*. Nevertheless, as a meaning-context the language may also be taken by one, like Zarkashī and Suyūṭī, as a source of interpretation. But unlike the reports concerning the sayings of the Prophet, the companions and their successors, the language is not to provide certain explanations for the verses of the Qur'ān. It is instead to provide a platform for the intersubjective constitution of meanings in terms of the linguistic signs as the instruments for the mediation of meanings in the background of Arab tradition. Again it is through language that those meaning constitutions were transmitted to the successive generations or epochs in the making of the tradition of Islamic intellectualism in terms of *tafsīr* and *ḥadīth*.

CONCLUSION

Under the influence of the enlightenment dictates, Western hermeneutics shifted its focus from the Bible to the general sort of texts more concretely related to the human situation like a piece of art, a work of literature and a social issue etc. The distancing of the human life-from from the divine text caused Western hermeneutics to shift its interests from addressing the divine-human relationship to focusing the texts emerged in the socio-historical order. This shift of interest from divine to mundane led the enlightenment mind to antagonize tradition as something stagnant that might be an obstacle in the way of progress.

In the contemporary scene of Western hermeneutics, Hans-Georg Gadamer not only criticizes the enlightenment's critique of prejudice as having a 'negative value' but he has also deviated from the enlightenment in expounding his notion of tradition. He conceives tradition as a living

continuum rather than a dead past. It is a temporal flow that affects everything comes into the way of historical development. It is the continuity of
tradition that affects consciousness to hold prejudices regarding the interpretation of a text. And against the objectivity of tradition one can find
the legitimate subjectivity of one's prejudices. Drawing form Gadamer, both
Jurgen Habermas and Karl Otto Apel have also made attempts to explore the
possibilities of dialogue between two different traditions. I have drawn fruit-
fully from the contemporary Western hermeneutics in order to interpret the
transformation of Arab tradition from pagan into Islamic. In this interpretation
I have found various notions of Western hermeneutics, like the hermeneutical concern of the historicality of text, the conventionality of language, the
dialogue between two traditions, the fusion of horizons, the text-life-language
triad, the imposition of meaning onto or the derivation of meaning from the
text etc., to make a graft on the tradition of Islam. Although the graftage
has been found highly fruitful, I have not overlooked the limitations of that
fruitfulness.

Interpreting the transformation of Arab tradition from pagan into Islamic, it
has come into light that although the three contemporary Western hermeneu-
ticians namely Gadamer, Habermas and Apel endorse the intercultural and
intertraditional dialogic process of understanding, they do never transcend the
historicality of interpretation. However, the rise of Islamic-Arab tradition is
aptly interpreted by the adjustment between the historicality and the ahistoricality or more appropriately between the historically and traditionally given
linguistic signs and the divinely revealed meanings. One should note here that
I have made this adjustment possible by grafting certain notions of Western
hermeneutics on certain facets of Qur'ānic hermeneutics.

The development of Islamic-Arab tradition is grounded upon the construing
of the Prophetic hermeneutics characterized by the theory-praxis model of the
Qur'ān and the *Sunnah* respectively. The Prophet was divinely determined to
interpret the Word of God absolutely objectively[50] not only by his own words
but by his deeds as well. The Prophet was to realize the theory-praxis model
of Islam with all of its deep rooted impact on the Arab culture through Arabic
language. It is the language which provided the Prophet with the platform in
order not only to communicate the appropriate meaning or neologism of *al-
kalim at-tayyab* to the Arabs but to make it practically prolific on the level of
al-'amal aṣ-ṣāliḥ in their life-world. So the communication community of the
companions understood the neologisms which were revealed in their language,
in the perspective of those meanings which were constituted in their own
cultural life-form. The companions not only adopted that divinely oriented
culture with absolute devotion and extreme dedication but they transmitted

it both temporally and spatially. Their achievements in this two-fold transmission of their culture to the other parts of the world and to the successive historical epochs were to shape the Islamic tradition characterized as intellect-act harmony. But, as we have seen above, this tradition was developed on the essential plane of Arabic language, so it should more appropriately be called Islamic-Arab tradition rather than Islamic tradition. They not only maintained the Prophetic legacy of balancing between intellect and act but transmitted it to their successors *(Tābaīn)* and through them to their successors *(Taba' tāba'īn)* with an obligation they strictly bound to *(sabīl al-mū'minīn)* as the Prophet was bound to communicate it to them.

University of Karachi, Pakistan

NOTES

1 Ibn Manẓūr, *Lisān al-'Arab (Language of the Arabs)*, Volume IX, corrected by Amīn Muḥammad 'Abd al-Wahāb & Muḥammad aṣ-Ṣādiq al-'Ubaydī, Beirut, Dār Iḥyā' at-Turāth al-'Arabi, 1999/1419, p. 67

2 az-Zayyāt, Aḥmad Ḥasan, *Tārīkh al-Adab al-'Arabī (History of the Arabic Literature)*, Beirut, Dār al-Ma'rifah, 2002/1423, p. 19

3 Ibid.

4 Gadamer, H-G, *Wahrheit und Methode (Truth and Method)* trans. G. Barden and W.G. Doerpel, New York, Crossroad, 1975, pp. 268–269

5 Ibid., p. 269

6 Ibid., p. 272

7 Ibid.

8 Ibid., p. 273

9 Habermas, Jürgen, *Zur Logik der Sozialwissenschaften* (On the Logic of the Social Sciences), trans. by Shierry Weber Nicholsen & Jerry A. Stark, Cambridge, Polity Press, 1988, p. 144

10 Ibid., p. 145

11 Ibid.

12 Ibid., pp. 145–147

13 Ibid., pp. 145–146; also see Gadamer, H-G, *Wahrheit und Methode (Truth and Method)* trans. G. Barden and W.G. Doerpel, New York, Crossroad, 1975, pp. 346–347

14 Habermas, Jürgen, *Zur Logik der Sozialwissenschaften* (On the Logic of the Social Sciences), trans. by Shierry Weber Nicholsen & Jerry A. Stark, Cambridge, Polity Press, 1988, p. 148

15 Ibid., pp. 148–149

16 Ibid., p. 150

17 Ibid., p. 151

18 Apel, Karl-Otto, *Transfromation der Philosophie (Towards a Transformation of Philosophy)*, trans. Glyn Adey & David Frisby, London, Routledge & Kegan Paul, 1980, p. 66

19 Ibid.

20 Ibid., p. 68

21 Ibid.

22 Ibid.

23 Ibid., p. 69

[24] Ibid.

[25] Ibid., p. 71

[26] Ibid., p. 72

[27] Islāhī, Amīn Ahsan, *Tadabbur-e-Qur'ān* (*Reflection on the Qur'ān*), Volume I, 7th Reprint, Lahore, Fārān, 1997/1417, p. 14

[28] Ibid., also see az-Zayyāt, Ahmad Hrasan, *Tārīkh al-Adab al-'Arabī* (*History of the Arabic Literature*), Beirut, Dār al-Ma'rifah, 2002/1423, p. 54 and Nicholson, R.A., *Literary History of the Arabs*, Surrey, Curzon Press, 1993 (originally published in 1907), p. 119

[29] az-Zamakhsharī, Abū'l-Qāsim Mahmūd ibn 'Umar ibn Muhammad, *Al-Kashshāf 'an Haqā'iq Ghawāmid at-Tanzīl wa 'Uyūn al-Aqāwīl fī Wujūh at-Tā'wīl* (*The Searchlight on Realities of the Obscured Revelations and Essences of the Words in the Expressions of Interpretation*), Volume I, 3rd Reprint, arranged, verified & corrected by Muhammad 'Abd as-Salām Shāhīn, Beirut, Dār al-Kutub 'Ilmīyyah, 2003/1424, pp. 15–16

[30] Islāhī, Amīn Ahsan, *Tadabbur-e-Qur'ān* (*Reflection on the Qur'ān*), Volume I, 7th Reprint, Lahore, Fārān, 1997/1417, p. 47

[31] See the second section of this paper particularly the discussions Habermas's and Apel's philosophical thoughts. Both of them owe to the pragmatists to use the notion of communication community.

[32] Haykal, Muhammad Husayn, *The Life of Muhammad*, trns. by Ismā'īl Rāgi al-Fārīqī, Karachi, Dār al-Ishā'at, 1989, p. 487

[33] az-Zarqānī, Muhammad 'Abd al-'Azī m, *Manāhil al-'Irfūn fī 'Ulūm al-Qur'ān* (*The Fountains of Cognition in the Qur'ānic Studies*), Volume II, Beirut, Dār al-Fikr, 1988/1408, pp. 19–22

[34] as-Suyūtī, Jalāl ad-Dīn 'Abd ar-Rahmān ibn Abī Bakr, *Al-Itqān fī 'Ulūm al-Qur'ān* (*The Mastery in the Qur'ānic Studies*), Tehran, Dār Dhawī al-Qurbā, 2001/1422, Volume II, p. 402

[35] Ibid., p. 372

[36] Ibn 'Amr along with some of the other companions was specially permitted to record the prophetic sayings, as during the early days the Prophet prohibited the writing of his speech acts lest the writers might not mix up his sayings with the revelations. See Dr. Subhī as-Sālih (d.1986), *'Ulūm al-Hadīth wa Mustalahuhu*, Qum, Manshūrāt ar-Radī, 1362/1943, pp. 7–11 including footnotes. In this regard, there is a famous *hadīth* reported by Abu Sa'īd al-Khudrī according to which the Prophet said: "Do not write from me. One who writes from me anything other than the Qur'ān, it will be disastrous for oneself. However, there is no problem if you narrate from me. But one, who deliberately tells a lie narrating me, will occupy his seat fro the hellfire." See Imam Abū 'l-Hussayn Muslim ibn al-Hajjāj al-Qushayrī an-Nīsāburī, *Mukhtasar Sahīh Muslim*, Beirut, Dār al-Kutub al-'Ilmīyyah, 1419/1998, p. 670

[37] According to Dr. Hamidullāh (1908–2002), with the permission of the Prophet, Ibn 'Amr used to register whatever he heard from him without discriminating his moods of pleasure and anger. Some of the companions criticized Ibn 'Amr on this. So he went to the prophet and directly asked him: "O Messenger of Allah, may I write down whatever I hear from you?" The prophet replied: "Yes." Ibn 'Amr further asked: "Even when you are pleased, even you are in anger?" Thereupon the prophet, pointing to his mouth, further replied: "By Allah, whatever issues from this is verily right and truth." See the English translation by Dr. Hamidullāh of Abū 'l-Khayr Ahmad ibn Ismā'īl al-Qazwīnī, *Kitāb as-Sard wa 'l-Fard fī Sahā'if al-Akhbār*, Islamabad, Pakistan Hijra Council, 1411/1991, pp. 7–8

[38] az-Zarqānī, Muhammad 'Abd al-'Azīm, *Manāhil al-'Irfān fī 'Ulūm al-Qur'ān* (*The Fountains of Cognition in the Qur'ānic Studies*), Volume II, Beirut, Dār al-Fikr, 1988/1408, p. 28

[39] Ibn Manzūr, *Lisān al-'Arab* (*Language of the Arabs*), Volume I, corrected by Amīn Muhammad 'Abd al-Wahāb & Muhammad aṣ-Ṣādiq al-'Ubaydī, Beirut, Dār Ihyā' at-Turāth al-'Arabī, 1999/1419, p. 69

[40] Ibn Khuldūn, 'Abd ar-Rahman ibn Muhammad, *Muqaddimah Ibn Khuldūn* (*Ibn Khuldūn's Preface to History*), Beirut, Dār al-Kutub al-'Arabī, 2001/1422, p. 407 & *The Muqaddimah: An Introduction to History*, Volume II, trans. Franz Rosenthal, London, Routledge & Kegan Paul, 1967, pp. 444–445

[41] az-Zarkashī, Badr ad-Dīn Muhammad ibn 'Abd Allāh, *Al-Burhān fī 'Ulūm al-Qur'ān* (*The Demonstration in the Qur'ānic Studies*), Volume II, Beirut, Dār al-Kutub 'Ilmīyyah, 2001/1422, p. 173

[42] Ibid.

[43] Ibid.

[44] All of these sources of Qur'ān exegesis were mentioned by Zarkashī except the last one which Ibn Khuldūn mentioned while he discussed the notion of traditionist exegesis (*tafsīr naqlī*). See az-Zarkashī, Badr ad-Dīn Muhammad ibn 'Abd Allāh, *Al-Burhān fī 'Ulūm al-Qur'ān* (*The Demonstration in the Qur'ānic Studies*), Volume II, Beirut, Dār al-Kutub 'Ilmīyyah, 2001/1422, pp. 173–181 & Ibn Khuldūn, 'Abd ar-Rahman ibn Muhammad, *Muqaddimah Ibn Khuldūn* (*Ibn Khuldūn's Preface to History*), Beirut, Dār al-Kutub al-'Arabī, 2001/1422, p. 408

[45] az-Zarkashī, Badr ad-Dīn Muhammad ibn 'Abd Alābh, *Al-Burhān fī 'Ulūm al-Qur'ān* (*The Demonstration in the Qur'ānic Studies*), Volume II, Beirut, Dār al-Kutub 'Ilmīyyah, 2001/1422, p. 174

[46] Ibid., p. 175

[47] According to Betti, in order to reconstruct the meaning of a text adequately only the interest of an interpreter in understanding is not enough rather he essentially needs 'an intellectual open-mindedness that enables the interpreter to adopt the most suitable position for his investigation and understanding.' Adopting this position the interpreter has to go through the process of 'self-effacement' to 'honestly overcome' his own 'prejudices' and attitudes that may stand in the way of unbiased understanding of the text. This is Betti's hard-line objectivist position that is just opposite to that of Gadamer's subjectivist stance which leads him to the notion of 'prejudiced interpretation' of a text as we have discussed above. See Bleicher, Josef, *Contemporary Hermeneutics: Hermeneutics as Method, Philosophy and Critique*, London, Routledge & Kegan Paul, 1980, p. 85

[48] Ibn Khuldūn, 'Abd ar-Rahman ibn Muhammad, *Muqaddimah Ibn Khuldūn* (*Ibn Khuldūn's Preface to History*), Beirut, Dār al-Kutub al-'Arabī, 2001/1422, p. 407

[49] Ibid., pp. 406–407 & *The Muqaddimah: An Introduction to History*, Volume II, trans. Franz Rosenthal, London, Routledge & Kegan Paul, 1967, pp. 443–444

[50] *Qul mā yakūnu lī an ubaddilahu min tilq'ā'ī nafsī in attabi'u illā mā yūhā ilayya* (Say: "I have no right of my own to change it, I follow naught but what is revealed unto me.") *Yūnus* 10:15

SECTION IV

MARIA-CHIARA TELONI

TIME AND THE FORMATION OF THE HUMAN PERSON: A COMPARISON OF EDITH STEIN'S AND MARTIN HEIDEGGER'S THOUGHTS

1. INTRODUCTION*

The issue of education is tightly connected to the anthropological one. And this is for two main reasons: first, a science of education that may be really considered as such must recognize the nature of the object of the research, that is the human being, the means, and also the purposes of the education process. Then, the essential link between anthropology, philosophy of education and pedagogical practice depends on the humans' spiritual nature, as he is not a complete being, but an evolving one, who develops, is subject to a process of *formation (Bildung)*. Moreover, the anthropological research seems to be the main theme carried out by the phenomenological school, even though the emphases and results change between the different authors, among whom are Martin Heidegger and Edith Stein, whose arguments about it will be focused in our discussion.

The link between the two authors can be found in the *Appendix* to *Endliches und ewiges Sein (Finite and Eternal Being)*,[1] where Stein collects and comments the outcomes of the comparison with Heidegger's existentialist philosophy particularly expressed in *Being and Time (Sein und Zeit)*,[2] that she happened to read "soon after its publication, getting very impressed, however without managing to discuss about that topic" (EES 35).

2. THE *APPENDIX* TO *ENDLICHES UND EWIGES SEIN*

The *Appendix*, entitled *Martin Heideggers Existentialphilosophie (Martin Heidegger's Existential Philosophy)*,[3] that Stein refers to dates back to 1936, when the Authoress is still in the Carmel of Cologne. It is developed in two parts. In the first one Stein makes a summary of the contents of *Being and Time* – offering a clear and precise outline of the book, proposed in a fluent way and, above all, without any polemical tone (a clear proof of the

225

A-T. Tymieniecka (ed.),
Timing and Temporality in Islamic Philosophy and Phenomenology of Life, 225–266.
© 2007 *Springer.*

great intellectual honesty that inspires and connotes the Authoress's whole speculative activity. On the other hand, the second part of the essay contains Stein's critical analysis of Heidegger's theory. We will focus mainly on the latter.

In this study we are going to try and point out especially the anthropological deficiency that Stein ascribes to Heidegger's existentialistic approach, and the solutions she proposes, instead, to fill in this gap; at the same time, we will not neglect the developments of her confrontation with Heidegger between the lines of *Endliches und ewiges Sein* itself, and the significant contribution offered by other works by Stein from the anthropological, and therefore pedagogical, point of view.

3. FROM A PHILOSOPHY OF THE "ESSENCE" TO A PHILOSOPHY OF THE "EXISTENCE"

First of all, Stein believes – as stated in the essay *Meaning of Phenomenology in the Vision of the World*,[4] where she compares Husserl with Scheler and Heidegger – that Heidegger's main merit consists in indicating the dimension of *being-in-the-world*, against any naively realistic position, that accepts this without problematizing it, or rather idealistic, that absolutizes the subject. The Authoress, indeed, highlights:

As of Heidegger, he glanced at what he called *the being in the world* of the self. This could sound trivial, but nobody in the past did grasp the core meaning of this fact so keenly. The naïve realisms takes things as they look in front of man's eyes and sets them in an absolute way, without even suspecting what is influenced by the relation between man and his world in what is in front of him: he forgets himself as a factor in the constitution of his world. The idealist was so charmed by finding out the role of the subject in the constitution of the world, that he has absolutized it, losing sight of the dependence where he is. It was a hard task to show the *Being-There as being in the world*, where we are ourselves, and make it an object of search (DBP 105–106).

Indeed, even if Husserl admits in his famous *Cartesian Meditations*,[5] dating back to 1931, "to oppose every dogmatism, while he is still receptive in front of a new metaphysics",[6] the teacher's phenomenology remains, however, a philosophy of the essence, unlike Heidegger's, that will develop exactly as a philosophy of the existence, as Stein points out clearly:

The philosophizing self, that is the starting point to disclose the sense of the being, is for Husserl the "pure self", for Heidegger the concrete human person. Maybe this shift towards a philosophy of the existence is right a reaction to the bracketing of the existence and of all that is concrete-personal.[7]

Actually, Husserl, focusing on the category of the essence, studied from the subject's consciousness, reaches his idealistic shift, so opposed and criticized both by his pupils and by his opponents, especially by the Thomists, leading to a relativization of the existence of the world.

Therefore Stein affirms:

With regard to that [that is to a "turning towards realism"], I feel that Heidegger was more consistent: indeed he attained a philosophy of existence, while the Husserlian-Schelerian bracketing of the being there prevents us from accessing the last decisive question (LP 111).

She thinks, therefore, that the master's analyses, although innovative and useful, especially from a methodological point of view, as for rigor and open-mindedness, need, however, an integration in a more totally metaphysical sense. And this is exactly what Stein intends to realize – even aware of how ambitious the project is and of her scanty, recent knowledge on the matter – with *Finite and Eternal Being*, which has exactly the aim of reintroducing the eternal metaphysical question, but just in new terms, making use of the suggestions and directions coming from the philosophy of the past, especially the Thomist one, but also using the instrument worked out by the new-born phenomenology.

To that end Stein finds interesting the possible contribution offered by the philosophical speculations by Martin Heidegger, Husserl's former pupil, as it appear, especially in *Being and Time*.

4. ANTHROPOLOGICAL DEFICIENCY OF HIDEGGER'S METAPHYSICS

First of all Stein thinks that Heidegger did not succeed in specifying and outlining the essential features of the structure of this being that man is.

Indeed, on one hand he rejects the traditional definition of man's essence, which is dogmatically established according to him, as "composed by two substances, a spiritual one and a bodily one" (MHE 178), as this would clearly clash with the statement that man's essence ad existence coincide; on the other, however, he spends very few words for the *body* and does not give any clear meaning to the word *soul*.

Moreover, by setting aside both notions of body and soul, Heidegger also eliminates the *what (Was)* from the being as "something that is", and leaves only the *something (Etwas),* that he makes equivalent of *who* or *Self.*

His philosophical anthropology, therefore, looks insufficient to Stein and limited to one single aspect of the human being. In fact, as Angela Ales Bello well notices:

Whereas for E. Stein the human being exists with his own complex essential structure, for Heidegger the essence entirely levels out to existence. Thus when it comes to describing this essence, Heidegger gets entangled in some problems.[8]

For this reason, Heidegger never refers to either categories of *I* or of *Person* – that Stein cherishes very much, though, and she places the latter among those new categories that the beginning of Christianity (and the Judaeo-Christian culture in general) offered to the philosophical research notice; whereas she chooses the former as the main object of her reflections, like all the other phenomenologists, preliminarily refusing to examine the possible meaning of both words, and thus barring any chance to achieve a better and realer explanation of the sense of being. However, we can maintain that what Heidegger wants to reproduce with the Self is probably the man's *being a person.*

On this point, Heidegger's diverges from Husserl's, as well, as Ales Bello points out:

The analysis of the pure Self, according to Husserl, makes it possible to highlight the structures of the subject itself; on the contrary, Heidegger is interested in his life, his existence, his place in the world. So he isolates in his work *Sein und Zeit (Being and Time)* the theme of *Dasein*, the *Being-There*, that does no correspond exactly to that conception of human being, as traditionally meant from a philosophical and historical point of view or proposed, more recently, by human sciences, but is considered only for that aspect that throws it into existence and temporality.[9]

It is exactly here, namely in the fact that he does not consider the complexity of the human being as a body and a spirit, that the basic defect of Heidegger's definition resides, that affects all his following arguments, and that Stein repeatedly refers to as the root of all his mistakes.

Consequently, Heidegger's analysis of the so-called *emotional state* also results incomplete, since, as Stein states:

I reckon that the emotional state is very important to try to understand what belongs to the psychical being and how both aspects are connected; however, on the other hand, it cannot be explained according to his full meaning if it is not shown in its development as a psychical and physical being (MHE 180).

And this is even clearer in the *anguish* that reveals in the affective state. According to Heidegger, it is based *primarily* on the *having been,* and belongs to the past, as a *be-thrown,* compared to which the Being-There is set before its *repeatability (Wiederholbarkeit).* According to Stein, instead, the anguish connotes the emotional state on the base of which the human being recognizes his own condition of *dependence.* On this subject Annalisa Margarino states:

This emotional state, that for Stein arises from the sense of transitoriness, flimsiness and fleetingness of one's own being, places the Self in front of nothing: the manifestation of *nothing*, at the same time, according to Stein, means for the Self recognizing its link with the *Eternal being*. The Self is a being that, before any retrospective reflection, feels *anguish* in front of its own flimsiness, and by experiencing this mood, it finds and retrieves its relation with the Eternal being. [10]

We are confirmed this interpretation by Stein's words:

The inconsistency and faintness of one's own being becomes clear to the Self when he takes possession of it by its thought and tries to reach its foundation. He draws it, before any retrospective reflection and every analyses of one's own life, through the anguish, that goes with the unredeemed man along his life under different guises (as the fear of this or that), but in the last resort as an anguish in front of one's own being, and "brings him before the nothingness". [11]

In conclusion, according to Stein, even though Heidegger's considerations have the merit of carrying out authentic explanations about the human being, especially where the identification of the basic constitution is divided into the different ways of *daily being* and *authentic being*, however they stop surprisingly before some "references that stand out even imperiously through what had been already highlighted" (MHE 180).

5. FROM "THROWN-NESS" *(GEWORFENHEIT)* TO "CREATURELINESS" *(GESCHÖPFLICHKEIT)*

This is what happens, for example, in the category of *thrown-ness* (belonging to the Being-There of human being), or *decay* of the individual, accepted by Stein in principle, as seen in her arguments mentioned above. This category, indeed, perfectly shows Stein's personal belief, that is "man is in the Being-There ignoring how he came there, that he is not from itself or by itself and that he cannot expect by his own being any explanation about his own origin" (DAP 94). However, because the question of origin cannot be settled starting from the world, according to Stein, it "needs an established being, who is a being of this human being, without any foundation in itself, that must be founded, *somebody* that lays the *thrown*" (MHE 181), then. In her personal ontological consideration, specifically in *Finite and Eternal Being*, Stein identifies this somebody right in the *Eternal being*. Indeed, Stein states:

It is unconceivable to receive the being apart from the eternal being, because nothing outside it really possesses any being. Every finite being is something placed and kept inside the being and, therefore, it is unable to give itself or keep the being by itself (EES 92).

And more:

Therefore, in my being I meet another being, that is not mine, but rather the stand and foundation
of my being, which has no stand or foundation in itself (EES 97).

Another of Heidegger's mistakes, according to Stein, which makes his philo-
sophic framework incomplete, is omitting entirely the question about the
beginning and the end of the Being-There. About this issue, Ales Bello
summarizes:

Heidegger uses words as "decay" of the individual or "thrown-ness" of the Being-There in
an absolute way, without wondering what positive situation should be considered to apply the
concepts of decay and fall, or wondering where those who are thrown come from. It looks like
he isolated one moment, one stretch of the way that cannot be ignored in whole its extension at
least for the need to know the beginning and the end.[12]

Actually, Heidegger answers this question someway, as he places and delimits
the Being between two nothings, one before life, and one towards death. Even
in this case Stein cannot avoid pointing out that the answer is unsatisfactory,
because on one side Heidegger does not analyse thoroughly the theme of
death, that he himself emphasises continuously as the essential dimension
which mostly affects the Being, that emerges, therefore, as a *being-for-death*;
on the other hand he does not consider at all the question about the lot of the
soul, which is impossible, however, as he has already excluded this category
from the scope of the Being-There, thus negating any validity of this concept
in the metaphysical field.

Moreover – Ales Bello continues – Stein remarks that, if on one hand it
is true that everyone should experiment his own death personally, it is also
true that before this event, that constitutes the possibility that denies all the
other possibilities, we acquire a certain knowledge of death starting from the
others' death. Seeing the others die, someway, we become aware that we are
going to die.

From these considerations we deduce the deep value given by Stein to
intersubjectivity as a source of knowledge, and also about this she must
take some distance from Heidegger again. Probably, this also derives from
their different considerations of associated life. Indeed, although Heidegger
seems to enhance the *being-with (Mit-sein)*, right in the daily being there, so
that human life appears "above all and mostly" (MHE 181) *living-with-the-
others*, therefore what he says about the *Self of the chat* denotes "some scorn
towards the others".[13] On the background of the objections made by Stein,
in this respect, to Heidegger, we find two of her important essays where she
focused on the analysis of associated life, *The Philosophical Foundation of*

Psychology and the Sciences of the Spirit[14] and *A Research on the State,*[15] where it is clear that the Authoress states that the associated life should not always be considered only anonymous and negative, so that the individual in order to find himself is obliged to escape it. On the contrary, the community is necessary as a place of perpetuation of traditional values, which should not always be scorned. It is rather a question of being able to judge the validity of what is given by the associated life: if it proves negative the individual must escape, but it cannot be stated that it is always the case.

Stein continues and declares that, if on one hand everyone is aware that he will die, on the other, however, in healthy natural life there is a very strong certainty of existing. Indeed, as Margarino maintains, even if the *finite* being still implies the *non-being* – and, therefore, also according to Stein, "continuously exposed to the *nothing*, in an incessant *insecurity*"[16]-, and even if the *anguish* "is a primary emotional state, as it comes before any reflection and analysis about one's own life, unlike it is presented and defined in Heidegger's thought", the latter, however, "is not a basic prevailing feeling in human life",[17] but, as Stein continues:

It becomes so in some cases that we define morbid, while in normal conditions we behave very confidently, as if our being belonged to us in a stable possession (DAP 95).

According to Stein, therefore, human life wavers between *certainty*, resulting from a superficial idea of our own existence, "that, because of the "lasting" time, shows us deceptively a "stable lasting being", and that prevents us, through the "care" for life, from perceiving its vacuity" (DAP 95), and *uncertainty*. However, it is right this uncertainty that Edith Stein does not identify with the emotional state of anguish, that "brings the soul far from itself",[18] which allows the *finite being* to recognize, together with its own finitude and the possibility to face the *nothing*, the Eternal everlasting being, from which every created being comes. Indeed, Stein declares:

In general and in an absolute sense we can talk about the certainty of the being as a simple outcome of this illusion or self-illusion. The retrospective disarticulation of our being, made through the thought, shows how little foundation of this certainty is in itself and how it is actually exposed to nothing. Does it show us, then, that the certainty of the being is objectively unfounded, then "irrational", and that the behaviour of a rational life is a "freedom for death ..." passionate, self-confident and "anguished"? Not at all. Before the undeniable reality that my being is transitory, delayed, so to say, from one moment to the other and always exposed to the possibility of nothing, the other reality stands, as much undeniable, that this transitoriness is me and from one moment to the other I am kept in being and in this transient being I catch something lasting (EES 96).

Thus, the human being, according to Stein, perceives himself as transitory and temporal, but at the same time kept in the being. Indeed, Stein goes on:

I know I am kept and for this reason I feel calm and safe: it is not the certainty of a man who stands on a steady ground by his own power, but the sweet, blessed certainty, objectively considered, not less rational. Or should we consider "rational" the child living in the incessant fear that his mother may let him fall (EES 96)?

This is probably the Self-image of biblical ascent[19] that summarizes more than anything else Stein's religious phenomenology, which consists, according to Beate Beckmann's words, in the "experience of being kept by God",[20] and in identifying God as stand of one's own life:

In my being, therefore, I meet another being, which is not mine, but rather the stand and foundation of my being, which has no stand or foundation in itself (EES 97):

According to Stein, essentially, the *thrown-ness* is revealed as *creatureliness*.

This is the conclusion Stein comes to, who in *Finite and Eternal Being*, quoting just Heidegger, about the problem of *Geworfenheit*, states:

As life is the being of the Self, this could mean that life received the being by the Self itself. But this obviously does not correspond to the unique properties recognized in this being, that is the being what belongs to it (its contents) and keep it inside; and above all it agrees with what the Self is and with how it experiences its own being. It perceives itself as something living, of being at the present; and at the same time as coming from a past, and cast in living a future already: it and its being are unavoidably there; it has been thrown into being. However, this kind of existence is the extreme opposite to self-control and self-understanding of a being that is from itself. The being of the Self is something that lives from one moment to the other. It cannot stop, because it runs unstoppably. Thus, it never succeeds in possessing itself really. And this is why we must define the being of the Self, this living present continuously changing. It is placed in the Being-There and kept there moment by moment. This way we can talk about a beginning, an end and also a break of its being (EES 90–91).

Hanna-Barbara Gerl comments Stein's reflections as follows:

Thus, even though it exists in an eminent sense, the Self appears, nevertheless transient, as it is not able to keep alive what it needs to exist: "Its life needs contents and without contents it is empty, void". The aware Self, therefore, depends on a "afterlife depth", that gives it or denies both an exterior and an interior world. The philosophical consequence that can be drawn is that the human being, deeply searched, does not exists by himself, does not control himself, or is not intelligible to himself. However it longs for it, he never possesses himself, it is always a received being.[21]

About the *being for death (dying,* or *anticipation of death)* it is possible to find a new meaning of anguish, different from the anguish as an emotional situation, that discloses to man his own *being for death*: it is the *decision* that he takes upon himself:

In the decision the anguish has reached understanding. The anguish as such does not understand itself. Heidegger means it at the same time as anguish *before* its own being and anguish *for* its own being [...]. This *before* which one feels anxious is the *impossibility-of-being* that the anguish itself attests: it is the experience of our being nothing. That *for* which one feels anxious and, simultaneously, on which the being of man depends, is being like a *fullness that one wishes to keep and does not want to let go – this topic is not discussed in whole Heidegger's analysis of Being-There* (MHE 191).

Heidegger, according to Stein, does not realize that one could not feel anxious *before* the impossibility-of-being and *for* its own being, if the human being were not part of a "fullness, of which something always escapes him and from which something is received: life and death at the same time" (MHE 191). This may depend on his general overestimation of the future and underestimation of the present, that leads him to neglect in every experience the essential event of *realization*. Indeed, Stein notices that in general the rule is valid that knowing the limit implies knowing how to overcome it; Heidegger, on the contrary, wants to remain in the finiteness, and he is not able to explain how finiteness itself can be reached, and does not admit that it can be so only compared to what is finite.

6. TEMPORALITY (*ZEITLICHKEIT*) OF THE BEING-THERE (*DASEIN*)

Thus, the theme of the thrown-ness is linked to the *temporality of Being-There*.

With this regard, Stein accuses Heidegger to assume a meaning of being, that is precisely the conviction of the temporality of being, before starting his analysis, even if she agrees with Heidegger when he considers the finished being a temporal being:

The being in this sense [that is in the passage from *ideal* or *possible* to the *present-real*] is a "becoming" and remains as such forever, it never becomes a "being (at rest)". This being needs time (EES 77).

However, while Heidegger thinks that temporality is the essential dimension of the Being-There, without devoting any place for eternity in his analysis, Stein considers temporality, connoting the finite, *creatural* being of the Being-There, what distinguishes it from the eternal immutable Being of God, where being and essence really coincide, stating that, vice versa, the authentic being, of which we are able in temporality, does not identify with the achievement of authenticity. As even Nietzsche declares, indeed, every pleasure (to be meant not in a restrictive sense, but rather as every thing that can satisfy us) requires eternity. We read in *Finite and Eternal Being*:

My being is a continuous motion, a flow, a transitory being in the strictest sense, in utter opposition with the eternal being, immutable-present [...]. The becoming cannot be from the being, that is from the being in a proper, true sense, from the being in the very sense of the word. It cannot be the authentic real being, because, accordingly to its meaning, it is a passage towards the being. As such, however, it can only be determined by the being. If we wanted to negate even the possibility of a being which is different from the becoming, we should also negate the possibility of the becoming itself and we would come to nothing (EES 82).

Heidegger's doctrine of temporality, therefore, must be reversed, that is the temporal ecstasies do not allow to understand the finite without infinity. However, Stein thinks that it is possible to find in it, beyond the author's intentions, a chance for eternity, that she perceived in the *moment*: indeed, it is right the moment that lets us understand the finiteness of anything non-temporal. The human being, in short, experiences *caducity,* right because it tends to fullness, the fullness of joy, of happiness, of love.

At this point, Ales Bello says, Stein puts forward an observation with a great sensibility, referring to Heidegger's psychological attitude, wondering why he thematizes anguish, care, that is painful situations, and never joy, happiness, that is positive moods. Even his looking at the future reveals this attitude. The *future*, indeed, is only *being for death*. She agrees that the future is the most important dimension, but this should be interpreted as the *future of hope*, the inclination towards fullness and stability. Thus, Heidegger's underlying pessimism seems to emerge, with its nihilist implications.

In another of her essays, already mentioned – *The Meaning of Phenomenology as a Vision of the World* – indeed, Stein catches the nihilist cues of Heidegger's position with a great sharpness and foresight, expressing her perplexity as to Heidegger's position, which is deeply influencing the contemporary cultural world. In her essay Stein affirms:

Currently I think it premature to indicate for Heidegger his image of the world. The central position of the Being, the emphasis given to the Care as basically belonging to it, to death and to nothingness, as well as some extreme formulations, show an image of the world without God, or better clearly nihilist (DBP 104).

And more:

About how Heidegger has formally worked to represent the vision of the world of our times, currently I barely dare give a judgment. Actually he is being charming young students for some years, as well as mature men. It is unquestionable that this should affect the attitude towards the vision of the world of the time. Actually I cannot determine what is the nature of this influence. It can lead to a closer analysis of life because he placed at the center of his interest the matters which are crucial to life. But I assume that the way that he followed, until now, insisting on the caducity of the Being, on the darkness where it comes from and to which it goes, and on the Care, will foster a pessimistic, if not nihilist, interpretation and will bury the orientation towards the absolute being, crucial to the survival or the end of our Catholic faith (DBP 106–107).

Stein summarizes, moreover, the relation that Heidegger establishes in the Being-There between the past, the present and the future as follows:

"The sense of Being-There is nothing hazily different from or outside the Being-There, but the Being-There self-understanding". The self-understanding is understanding one's own possibility of being, and this can be because the Being-There in its being *meets itself*. At the same time, it is *what it has been* and is *present at something*: future, having been (past) and present are the *out of itself* or the *ecstasies* of its *temporality*. The *future is primary*. Therefore Being-There, future, temporality are given as *finite*. It must still be shown what infinity means compared to this original time (MHE 168–169).

About the self-understanding of the finite being that in Heidegger assumes the form of Being-There, Margarino points out how, according to Stein, it is proper of all the *finite beings* to send to a *infinite Being*, but it is only proper of the human being to understand himself and be in this relation in every moment of its continuous transformation. The becoming of the human being makes possible for the Self to understand the idea of the *eternal Being*. Actually, the Authoress declares between the lines of *The Structure of the Human Being*, that we already quoted:

The Self can achieve the idea of the eternal Being not only thanks to the becoming and passing and failing its contents of experience, but also thanks to the peculiarity of his being that extends from one moment to the other: the Self draws back horrified before the nothing and does not want only a continuation without an end of its being, but the full possession of the being, a being that may take in all its contents in an immutable present, instead of seeing what has just start to live disperse again. Thus it achieves the idea of fullness, eliminating from its own being what it knows as deficiency (DAP 92–93).

Consequently, the relation of the human being with the *eternal Being*, that is *God*, is essential not only as a foundation of its own being, which is insubstantial in itself, but also for its understanding. Indeed, Stein specifies:

A peculiar characteristic of everything finite is the Impossibility to understand itself, referring to a *primum* that must be finite, better, the Infinity, because infinity cannot be but one. We define this first finite being God, as its features correspond to our idea of God. This way we must consider as ontological evidence that the human being, like all finite things, sends to God and it would be incomprehensible without this relation with the divine being, that is, it would be incomprehensible both that it is (its existence) and that it is what it is (DAP 215).

On the contrary, if on one hand Heidegger, maintaining the perspective of the *metaphysica generalis*, states that in order to understand the being it is necessary to understand the sense of being, on the other he links the understanding of the being to the finiteness of the human being, thus trying to use as a justification what should have been justified.

From these consideration, according to Stein, another problem emerges, concerning Heidegger's position in front of the being's transcendence, meant as God, and in front of the creation. The Authoress, indeed, stating from the analysis of some basic ideas, such as transcendence and nothing, catches the distance with a metaphysical formulation similar to Christian philosophy, that Heidegger seems to despise quite a lot, even if its relation with all the previous speculation, starting form the Greek, and above all Aristotle, through Scholasticism, should be analyses thoroughly.

Indeed, Heidegger states that the attempts, although important, made by Plato and Aristotle would not have succeeded in giving a sufficient explanation to the sense of being, since the ancient ontology considered *a certain way of being – the being simply present –* as the being as such. Afterwards, the being has always being assumed as the more general and obvious concept, with no need of an appropriate definition. For the rest the ancient ontology was followed and, precisely, not only during the Middle Ages, but also in the attempts entailing more consequences of the modern age: Cartesian and Kantian.

So, even though he puts "in the first place the being in its full total right" (MHE 201) – even if in a single place, that is in the Self – whole of Heidegger's search is supported by a certain preconceived idea of being, as "from the beginning every thing so as to prove the temporality of being" (MHE 202). This is why, according to Heidegger, no *essence* can exist separate from the existence that is realized in the Being-There, nor any *sense* different from the understanding that is contained by understanding itself, nor least of all, any *eternal truths* independent from human knowledge: they are only the remains of the "Christian theology not completely expelled by the philosophical issues yet" (MHE 203).

Stein writes in a long note replying to Heidegger's criticism that Christian dogmatics has not considered the problem of nothing, reinterpreting, in the light of Revelation, the phrase of the traditional metaphysics *"ex nihilo nihil fit"* in the sense *"ex nihilo fit ens creatum"*:

Now, how should the phrase "ex nihilo fit ens creatum" be interpreted? Only as follow: the Creator, in the creative act, is not influenced by any other being, because no being is given in absolute which is not the Creator or the creature [...]. This does not mean, however, that it [Christian dogmatics] is not interested in the being and in the nothing. It speaks about the being when it speaks about God; and speaks about the nothing in several contexts; for example when it speaks about creation and it means as creature a being whose being intends a non-being. since we "are so finite ... that we are not able by our own decision or will to take ourselves out of nothing originally", the manifestation of our being's nothing means, at the same time, the opening of this being of ours, finite and affected by the nothing, to the Infinite being, pure, eternal (DAP 94–95).

Thus, from a certain point of view, we should hold as true what Heidegger states, that being and nothing are together, but not because the Finite is between the chiefly authentic being and the nothing, but rather because the disclosure of the nothing to our being is an opening to the Infinite, pure, eternal, to a dimension that, in our opinion, could be defined as *eschatological*.

7. THE "CARE" AS ESSENTIAL DIMENSION OF THE BEING THERE

The temporal dimension of Being-There is connected to the theme of Care. "The *calculation of time*", indeed, as Stein affirms, "is inevitably based on the essential constitution of Being-There as Care", that is as *anticipating-itself*, as developed in the *chat of One*, for which time, interpreted to *take Care* (in the manifold meanings of *performing, realizing, get something, being afraid*), that characterizes the *being in the world*, is always "time of . . .". It belongs to the world worldliness and is called, therefore, *worldly time*.

Indeed, man in his concrete and daily life is first of all a *being in the world,* which is nothing but *taking care* of the things that he needs. And this taking care, according to Heidegger, has the features of *transcendence* (in a clearly *existential* sense) and of *project,* as the Being-There, that is man, *transcending* the actual reality as it appears at first sight, it *projects* it, taking it to him, that is subordinating it to his aims and needs, and translating it, in the final analysis, in a totality of *usable* tools.

As the relation between man and things develops as a taking care, so the relation between man and the others consists in *having care* of the others. This having care, however, as Heidegger points out, has two different meanings. It can be meant both as taking away from the others their cares, and in this sense, the man would not take care so much of the others but rather of the things to get them, realizing an *unauthentic* form of coexistence, that is a "pure being together"; and as helping the others to be free to take on their own cares, and in this case it will be the *authentic* form, that is to say the real *coexistence*.

Therefore, with respect to the ideas stated so far, the Care expresses the essential condition of a being, the man, who, thrown into the world, projects forward his *possibilities*. This *projecting-forward* of life, however, cannot but fall backwards on what it is already *actually*, thus revealing the *circular*, and therefore concluded and finished structure, of the Care. The being in the world of the man, therefore, necessarily falls into the *daily anonymous existence,* which is unauthentic as such, and according to Heidegger it is a great part of human life, including even the moral laws and the theories that search for its foundation.

Moreover, man, even finding himself as the foundation of himself, as a choice among the various *possibilities*, however, as he is planned-thrown, Heidegger rightly notices, cannot be the foundation of his own *foundation*. Thus, for Heidegger, the basic *nonentity (Nichtigkeit)* of which human existence consists would come out, both because man can never master his most proper being, and, on the other hand, because planning himself on some possibilities is possible only through the exclusion of other possibilities, or on the fact of *not* planning himself in other possibilities. The Being-There, then, is *doubly* crossed by the nothingness.

At this point it is right to wonder, I think, what is the sense of the Care, as it is described by Heidegger, where sense means what makes something possible and understandable. On the other hand, this was the aim of Heidegger's whole treatment: that is achieving a real understanding of the true sense of being. Heidegger answers that this sense would reside right in the very *temporality* of the Being-There. Or better, time would represent the horizon of every understanding and of every interpretation of the being. The very structures of the Being-There, indeed, in Heidegger's existential analysis refer to as many temporal dimensions, so that the *plan* projects the Being-There towards the *future*, the *being-thrown* nails the Being-There to the *past*, the *dejection* (see the following paragraph) roots the man in the *unauthentic present* of taking care of things, in opposition to the authentic present of the *moment*, that is the *anticipating decision of death*.

Likewise the *historicity* appears like the assumption of the past heredity, that is the intentional, conscious *resumption* (*"repetition"*) of the transmitted possibilities. A resumption that coincides with destiny, that is with the original historicization of the Being-There, that is nothing but the act by which the man transmits himself in an inherited possibility and, therefore, chosen. Indeed, as the existence, even planning itself as a radical nonentity of the world and of itself, is still a coexistence with the other men and among the things of the world, Heidegger states, the authentic existence gives the man the possibility to remain *faithful* to the destiny of the community or of the people he belongs to.

However, in my opinion, the answer given by Heidegger to the question about the sense of being is rather reductive and unsatisfactory. Indeed, should the fact of taking care and of having care, on the background of a Being-There founded on nothing, or better, nothing in itself, not be rather (more consequently) a *waste of time,* a *wasted time*? And then, how the *projection forward* and the essential phenomenon or *realization* can be conciliated with the *being-for-death* and the circular structure of the Care?

The anthropological outcome is rather a real *insignificance*, or better a sense of time and of human existence that reveals morally as a "dangerous" *indifference*.

Stein gives an outstanding answer to the problem issued by Heidegger's existentialism, making reference to the *Eternal Logos,* as the ultimate sense-giver, as discussed in the following paragraphs.

8. "DEJECTION" (*VERFALLEN*) AND THE ORIGINAL SIN

Dejection enters this subject, as it is, Stein declares:

a deviation from one's own free possibilities of being, towards the being-in-the-world and towards the One itself. In the possibilities there is always already an "anticipating-itself", and this belongs to the thrown being; its self-anticipation (*Vor-weg-sein*) is called *Care* and is the foundation of every worry and every solicitude, of every wish and every will, of every inclination and impulse (MHE 161).

Moreover, dejection is described as a way of being, in which the Being-There is not with himself or with the thing or with the others, but only implies all this.

"This *non-being*", Heidegger states, "must be meant as the way of being nearest to the Being-There, in which it is mostly maintained. The state of dejection in the Being-There should not be meant as a fall from a purer and higher original state" (MHE 186). After this statement, however, Heidegger adds that:

dejection occurs when *those that give tone* in the chat of One, are not the required experts at all and express loudly and irresponsibly their groundless opinions; and on the other hand, the mass submits irresponsibly to those incompetents' judgment and is influenced even in those cases that would require an autonomous responsible behaviour, closing their eyes and trying to deceive themselves (MHE 186).

Thus, dejection should not be meant as community life as such or being guided, but rather as the uncritical participation at the expense of authentic life, to which one is called, without paying any attention to the *call of conscience*.

This leads Stein to wonder what is the sense, then, of speaking about a dejection without any reference to a *fall*, which is exactly like putting a *being-thrown* without a *throwing*. If, indeed, Heidegger characterizes the average daily human being as declined, that is dejected, it must also admit that this is impossible only in contrast with an authentic being, that we must be aware of clearly, and that is *consistent with the original being.*

Every dejection, however, presupposes a temporal fall, not necessarily in the Individual's existence, but as an historical event that affects him. Moreover, Stein continues:

The peculiar nature of the fall, as we know it from the Revelation, cannot be deduced by that. But we must say that the Church teaching concerning the original sin is the solution to the enigma emerging from Heidegger's description of the dejected Being-There (MHE 187).

It is important to notice, as Margarino does, that within Stein's speculation the idea of original sin and of its consequences helps to understand the opposition between the actuated essence and the pure shape. Actually, Stein writes, taking up some Old Testament words:

Because of the curse cast against creation, elements are not only corrupted, but also one against the other, so as in nature the becoming is realized continuously hindering the essence development, and can carry out destruction. And if man must "earn bread with the sweat of his brow", this does not depend on the earth that gives him trouble and thorns and only after a hard work produces good fruits, but by the resistance of all the matters that he touches working. So the original sin and the state of punishment give us the key to understand the opposition between actuated essence and pure shape (EES 276).

The state of *fall*, that from the philosophical point of view, should be meant "only as a possible alteration of nature" (EES 275), and from the theological one as "subversion of the original order" (EES 275), is considered by Stein as the hinderer of the essence development:

It is possible to admit that in the original order everything happens in nature should help things to achieve the full realization of their essence and, thus, to reproduce the divine model in its integrity; moreover, the forces in them be proportional to the perfect shape of every single thing and of all the universe, and that they attend to this aim and do not act without sense and destroying as "brute forces". Even man's action should attend to emphasize more and more the resemblance with God (EES 276).

The ontologic distance between the essences and the original one – for which finite things are "always a mirror of the divine perfection, but a broken mirror"(EES 276), since there is a "difference between what they should really be and what they actually are, and also between what they should become and what they actually become" (EES 276) –, is ascribed, consequently, to the *original fall:*

In the world as it was originally created the matter should serve to effect the shapes; it should have been formed only and accordingly to the essential shape. Only owing to the "fall", losing its original unity, it can prevent from achieving a perfect structure (EES 276).

Stein connects the fall to the theme of man's *responsibility* with regard to the creation. An issue which is not at all minor with reference to the education of the Individual, or better, as Edith Stein says, of the person.

The category of responsibility is present in Heidegger too, differently described, however. In Heidegger's existential philosophy, indeed, "the Individual, in front of his more personal authentic being, which is a single responsible being, escapes in the community, and shifts his responsibility on the community, more narrow or wider" (MHE 184). So, in Heidegger's opinion, we can talk about *responsibility*, only when the single individual awakes from his *authentic* life. Instead, we speak about *irresponsibility*, as previously remarked, when *dejection* occurs. However, the two positions considered seem to be closer that expected, because, according to Stein:

Man, as a created being, is exposed to the finiteness and weakness of creation, but since he is endowed with rational knowledge, he is called to make himself responsible for the creation, or better, the sin in man actually consists in forgetting his own responsibility for the creation and in not considering the Creator's intents.[22]

So the original sin, according to Stein, did not consist in a "simple formal disobedience to God",[23] but in contradicting the original primordial hierarchical order.

On this subject it is useful to consider what Edith Stein writes about the relation between the sciences of nature and creation:

Gradually understanding in a rational way the effect connections in nature, and building with this a base to determine in advance the possible future events and intervene regulating them, is the original task of the sciences of nature. The domination of nature based on knowledge allows man to preserve the creatures in the ontological sense recorded in them. Modern technique, to the extent that it considers as its task subjecting nature to man and putting it at the service of its natural wishes, without worrying about the Creator's thought and in clashing contrast with it, represents a radical fall from the service that was originally imposed to it. Man is responsible of everything that, in nature, is not as it should be; moving away nature from the Creator's project is due to him. Let us remind again that, according to his structure, man is able to bear such a responsibility (DSP 86–87).

Man, on the other hand, as Stein adds, who is *helpless* by himself, is responsible of creation, since he is the first to be saved and freed:

Man is called to be the redeemer of all creatures. He can be so to the extent that he himself is saved (DSP 85).

And, if it is true that doing this he is part of nature, and therefore he can understand its language and its troubled sigh, on the other hand:

he can help not as part of nature, but as a son of God elevated over nature. Freely elevated, he is able to recognize the anguish as anguish, that in the animal remains only in the darkness. And to the extent that he is filled with the divine love, man is able to embrace lovingly the animal soul full of anguish. And it finds peace in pacified man's support (DSP 85).

9. THE IMAGE OF TRINITY IN MAN: BODY, SOUL AND SPIRIT

Stein's reflection continues in *Finite and Eternal Being* through the description of man's structure, made of body and soul, that is in the wake of that traditional conception rejected by Heidegger, instead, with intrinsic consequences on all the rest.

Indeed, Stein declares that, if it is true that man, integrated in creation, is not the only one to participate to the being of God, since all creation is an *imago Dei*,[24] and if it is true that he is neither the most perfect being, since his essence is not simple like that of the pure spirits created, however man's personal being is still the most accessible to our reason, and a special synthesis of matter and spirit is fulfilled in him, where all creation is summarized. Human nature, moreover, represents the top of creation owing to its peculiar participation to God's personal being. The triple internal structure of human beings, indeed, as Stein declares, seems to reproduce the Image of Trinity so good, that it results to be the more sublime imprint left by the dynamism of Trinitarian love in the creation, the most perfect *analogia Trinitatis*, according to a phrase by Theodor Haecker. The three basic forms of the real being (body, soul and spirit) in their unity are in close connection with Trinity, since they correspond to the *proprium* of the three divine Persons:

To the Father, the first Creator from whom everything originates, who is only by Himself, the being of the soul should correspond; to the Son as the essential shape "born", the bodily being should correspond; the free disinterested flow should merit the name of *spirit*, but in a peculiar sense (EES 384).

After that, Stein analyses more closely the three basic elements that form the human being's personal structure and their relevant functions.

10. THE BODY AS "ANIMATE BEING" (*LEIB*)

The most evident element is certainly the body, that is not the simply bodily "being" (*Körper*), however, as we mean it, a purely physical reality, but rather the body belonging to a living being (*Leib*). It "is 'my' living body, it is mine like anything else is; because I dwell in it as in my "innate" abode and I feel what happens in it and on it, and feeling I perceive it" (EES 389).

The actuality of the body, however, is given to us through different types of perception: the external perception shows us the living body as an object, but it does not reveal it in all its fullness. As Stein writes, indeed:

In this perception I am subject to strange limitations like no other body; in front of my body I am not completely free to move, I cannot watch it from all sides because I cannot "get rid of it" (EES 389).

However, there is also an "internal perception" – a typical Husserl's expression – of my body, that discloses it as bearer of sensations and subject of motion. The peculiar motion of the living body is not purely mechanic, almost as if the body were a simple tool, but is due to the *animate being* of the body, that is the fact it has a soul:

What differentiated the human body by a pure and simple body is that it is animate. Where there is a human body there is also a soul. And vice versa: where there is a soul, there is also a human body (EES 390).

11. THE SOUL (*SEELE*) AS "PRINCIPLE OF INTERIOR FORMATION"

Stein, then, analyses the second basic element that makes the human being, that is the soul (*Seele*). She continues by "subsequent layers". The soul is defined, first of all as "essential for every living creature" (EES 390), even though in different degrees, according to whether we are dealing with plants, animals or men. The soul, moreover, is the principle that gives form to the matter and, therefore, to the human body. It is able to give a structure to its own life, by transforming the matters of which it is made. Better, as it cannot be parted by the body, it is the very source of life:

Its "*being is life*, and life consists in giving *structure to the matter* in the three degrees: *transformation* of the constituent matters, *self-formation* and *generation*" (EES 391).

The human soul is seen, from this viewpoint, "creative", and for this reason connected to its divine Archetype that, "as divine life, creates itself eternally and gushes from its own source" (EES 384). It is, however, a "hidden source", as H. Conrad-Martius states in *Realontologie*, out of which the being and the visible of every living creature gushes. The soul has the property of being the "*centre of the being* of the living creature and the whole is made moving from the centre of the being" (EES 303). The soul gives shape to the body that, in turn, becomes its expressive means and bearer. Among all the living beings, the human soul, Stein states, on the wake of the reflections offered by the real ontology by Conrad-Martius, is in a privileged position. While in the plants, indeed, the life of the soul is mainly pushed outside, and in the animal as a passive purely sensible activity, in man, on the contrary, the soul represents "an 'interior world' complete in itself", "the place where the being has sprung up towards the Interior" (EES 391). It possesses an autonomous life, a being in itself. The human soul, far from being a simple middle course, a desert land between the body and the soul, is the place of self-determination, namely of free actions, where the Self places itself, decides the content of its experiences and the orientation of its actions:

the Self is an awake open spiritual eye looking the inside and the outside: it can receive what is close to it and can understand it and as a free person it can answer one way or the other. Man *can* do this and *since* he can, he is a spiritual person, a *support* of his life in the sense he "has it in his hands" (EES 392).

Even in the human soul, however, a sensible component remains, concerning the passivity of impulses, that makes man a being with limited, or, better, "conditioned" freedom (EES 393). Spirituality and sensitivity in the human being result to be two irreducible components, but inseparable at the same time that find their meeting point in the soul specified by the Authoress as follows:

[The soul] as *sensible soul* lives in the body, in all its limbs and parts, is fecundated by it, acts giving it shape and preserving it; in this *spiritual soul* it elevates over itself, looks at the world outside its Self [...] ; as *soul*, in the proper sense, however, it lives in itself, in it the person Self dwells. Here is gathered everything enters from the sensible and form the spiritual world, and here the internal disputation takes place, starting from which a side is taken up, drawing what will become more properly personal, the essential component of its own Self, what (metaphorically) "transforms into flesh and blood" (EES 394–395).

Stein lingers on this last meaning of soul, associating it to the image of "interior castle" of Saint Teresa of Avila, through which the former does not want to emphasise the idea of God "inhabitation" in the innermost part of the soul (the central room) – that we will find described in detail inside *The Science of the Cross* –, but rather present the *Seele* as a building, namely a being with its own depth and an essence to fulfil. The soul, indeed, far from being a simple empty container, "with its peculiar properties gives the body, and every personal spiritual activity, its characteristic imprint" (EES 395). This happens "unconsciously and unintentionally", but is perceived by the Self at conscious life level. The Self represents the "access" to the depths of the *Seele,* through the experiences that operate at a hidden depth, on one side showing what happens in the soul and then, increasing self-knowledge; on the other, fulfilling the essence of the *Seele*. The Self, therefore, shows us a soul structured on a "layered order". In the conception of the soul as "dark depth" the mystery at the base of the person is once more revealed, that is never totally knowable.

Moreover, the soul presents itself as a "spiritual creature", not only as non-extended, but also because it gives shape to man starting "from inside", or "the innermost part" of itself:

The "inside and the innermost part" are nothing but "the most spiritual", what is farthest by matter, which moves the soul in its depths (EES 399).

What Stein writes about the process of formation in *The Structure of the Human Person*, following the Aristotelian concept of *entelechia*, is quite interesting:

The body with its given form, closed in itself and articulated to comply to specific rules, is perceived by us as a reality held together interiorly. Its exterior shape is formed from inside. It brings something in itself that makes it, each time, what it is, and this happens in a progressive formative process; indeed, we have already seen that the body goes through changes in the shape. This taking shape from inside is a peculiar way of being, the way of being of the living. What enables the formation from inside is indicated by Thomas of Aquinas as interior shape. He also calls it soul in accord with Aristotle who thinks that it is only the vital principle, a vegetative soul. Aristotle uses the word entelechy, as well. Thus we understand that the formation process has an *aim (τελος)* tending to a specific shape. This aim is the developed articulated structure operating from inside, in order to keep itself in this completed shape – precisely, it operates so as every limb performs a specific duty within the whole, that is an organ for which the whole is an organism – but that goes beyond itself, produces other shapes of the same type (DSP 76–77).

In order to better explain the concept of *telos,* connected with the organic development of the individual, the Authoress refers to the concepts of *species* and *individuality*:

The *τέλος*, to which the development of the individual tends, is, like in a plant, the most accomplished sign of the species and its preservation in time by reproduction. It seems that an individuality which has a meaning as such does not exist. Of course the individuals are imperfect specimens and the less accomplished of the species and distinguish from one another (DSP 87).

In Stein's religious anthropology, moreover, individuality is also the foundation of a teleological order:

The individuals are inserted in a wider vital formative process. Where there are male and female individuals, they have in this process, their specific functions that interlace. Thus we should consider the species an original shape that dominates its whole real scope, in which the "division" in a male and a female shape and the birth of shapes of new peculiar members is based on their union. It is the standing formative principle determining in their structure all the individual formations of a scope. To the extent that in the "varieties" we can recognize a necessary structure, this can be understood starting from the original shape. What in it appears "casual" cannot come from the species (DSP 112–113).

12. THE ETERNAL *LOGOS* AS THE ULTIMATE SENSE-GIVER

The idea of *telos* in Stein's considerations is tightly connected to that of *Logos*, as the ultimate sense-giver, that Stein widely discusses also in *Finite and Eternal Being* and that, in my opinion, deserves to be deeply analyzed here, as it is well connected to our treatment, because it is actually Stein's answer to the question about the sense of the being in general and, then, to man's.

In the third and fourth chapters of *Finite and Eternal Being,* indeed, Stein refers to what she calls the "Aristotelian way" (EES 305) that, starting from things, as they are given in the experiences and in their finiteness, – instead of in the being of the Self, as it is peculiar, on the contrary, of the "Augustinian way" – tends to trace in them those essential contents, not reducible to the subjective conscience, pre-existent in the being unlike it, and explicative of a sense. The Authoress's intent is, therefore, achieving an essential ontology, from the onto-phenomenological argument of self-conscience, that finds in the *Eternal Logos* right its ultimate sense-giver. From the catch of the being to the question of the being of things, pre-existent to the subject that, in turn, leads to notice their essential consistence.

Stein starts making a distinction between *finite* and *infinite*: finite is "what does not belong its own being, and needs the time to reach the being", that is to become what it is; infinite is the eternal being. At this point Stein remarks that, if on one hand, the finiteness is connected to temporality, on the other, it does not perfectly coincide with it.

Then, Stein draws attention on the difference between *essence* and *essentiality*. First of all, essences can be *individual* or *universal*. Stein identifies this difference in that the universal essence can be found in every individual essence, without being subject to any change, as well as in that it is "communicable and can become actual in a variety of individual things [...] it is *not independent*, as in order to be realized it needs the individual being and its subjects, [...] however it is a unique thing [...]. It is that very thing that is realized [...] in all the individual essences that pertain to it" (EES 120). On the contrary, the individual essence cannot be communicated, moreover it is subject to change and it is "actual and possible only in an object, its own. It can have its equal, but cannot recur more than once" (EES 120). Moreover, Stein, like Hering, who defines the essence as a part of the object depending on the existence of the object itself, affirms:

Every essence is, according to its essence, essence of something, that is essence of this something and of no other something [...] specificity makes the object [...] it is what determines the *quid* of the object (EES 108).

This reveals that the essence not only differs from the *concept* defined "a structure independent from the object, referring to the object, that intends it. The precondition for its formation is the essence apprehension; and it draws it from this" (EES 111), but also differs in essentiality, both because it is independent from the object, and because, while for the essentialities the only being is the essential being, for the essences the actual-real being is also possible in the objects so much that it determines their *quid.*

The essential being, moreover, unlike the actual-real being, is *out of time*, is "immutably what it was. More precisely: the difference between present, past and future is abolished here" (EES 131).

In relation with the Self becoming being, indeed, we find in the *units of experience* (*Erlebnisse-Einheiten*) some contents that are not subject to the *time flowing*. Among them Stein takes as an example the experience of "joy":

There are many *Erlebnisse* of joy: they differ in the Self that experiences them, in their object, in their time determination and their duration and in many more things. *The essentiality "joy" is only one*: it is not mine or yours, it is not now or later, it has no short or long duration; it has no being in space and time, but the essentiality "joy" *is realized* always where and when one feels joyful (EES 101).

This essentiality of which Stein talks referring to the "joy", however, should be distinguished from the Platonic ideas, as it is not completely split from the sphere of the objects, but it can be found in the experience and, particularly, in that special experience made by the being of the Self. Moreover, we owe to the essentiality the sense and the intelligibility of everything. Indeed, in *Finite and Eternal Being* Stein also states:

The life of the Self would be an inextricable chaos where nothing could be distinguished, if in it some "essentialities" were not fulfilled (EES 103).

And more:

The essentiality represents the ultimate meaning [...] the proper intelligible. So it must be certainly them, in the end, to give sense to the words. Actually, the ultimate foundation of every intelligibility is also what makes possible the understanding of language and each other's understanding through it. *What the nouns properly express and in the end they are the essentialities* (EES 117).

The essential being, moreover, as it is not subject to the becoming and as it is out of time, will also be "quietness in itself", rest, opposed to the becoming of what exists and, for this, it is called *wesen,* that is "lasting".

However the essentialities, for Stein, remain in themselves an "unfathomable mystery" for the man.[25] They belong to an intermediate ontologic level between the eternal being and the real beings, therefore expressing the *eternal logos* or the divine archetypes of the created world, through their essential being (*wesenhaftes Sein*).

Now it is necessary to explain what kind of relationship exists between the essential being and "the actual-real being of things and the eternal being of the first Being" (EES 133).

The basic distinction between the *essential being* and the *actual-real being* is given here by the essential *quid* that, as Stein affirms, is not "universal or individual" in itself. "In the field of the essential being it has no limits [...] it can be mediated, communicated and allows the identification and what divides it from the individual being, this gives the possibility to ascribe to it the characteristic of universality" (EES 140). There follows that we can ascribe to the essential *quid* a being of the species of actual-real things. Moreover, it must be pointed out that the essentialities become elements through which the *quiddities* are built, that in turn enter the *quid* of things, and through the *quiddities* and the essences, the essentialities have relationships with the actual-real being.

It must be highlighted that it is said "to have a relationship" and not "to enter". About this, Stein, affirms, that "What is essential does not enter the existence" (EES 131). How could the link between the world of the essential being, timeless in itself, and the existing real world be justified? To answer this question, Stein has recourse to the Augustinian interpretation of Platonism, also followed by Thomas Aquinas who, in *De Potentia,* states the following:

The quiddity is said to *be created,* since before it has the being it is not but in the Creator's mind, where it is not a creature, but a creating essence (EES 132 our italics).

The *quiddity* and the essences become current-real in things, that is to say they become part of the compound of the thing as a steady core, through creation (following the model of the essences contained in God's mind), and the *quid* becomes actual in them, because it is their *flowing core.*

The knowledge of the essence, therefore, is like catching an eternal meaning. This can also happen only indirectly.

The eternal Being thus proves to master not only the being but also the sense. And the being of essentialities and of quiddities, far from representing an autonomous being next to the eternal being, appears, in turn, as "the eternal being itself, that moulds in itself the eternal forms – not in a temporal happening – forms according to which it creates the world in time and with time" (EES 145–146).

This way Stein explains the reality and effectiveness of the essential being, and also brings the philosophical questions before the "Eternal Wisdom": the *Logos*, the ultimate sense-giver. Stein, indeed, turns to theology for help, and takes the first verse of *John's Prologue* where it is written "In the beginning was the Word", and, as Margarino well notices, interprets it through Goethe's

Faust who says "in the beginning was the sense, the meaning" (EES 146). Stein affirms that by the word "sense" John meant the divine Person, namely the more actual-real something existing, that should be meant as a divine Being, as it is contained by the divine knowledge and, therefore, by the Revelation itself, and then called the Word. In other words:

in the first Being the Logos (the sense or the divine essence) was included – in the Father was the Son – the sense of the original actuality-reality (EES 147).

The being and the essence, therefore, are the same thing both for the Father and for the Son.

On the other hand, even St. Thomas did not think that by the mere philosophical speeches it was possible to achieve a "filling vision" of what one wishes to discover. Stein affirms:

We cannot catch an essence that is only being. We draw it again just because our spirit, beyond every finite, tends – and is led by the finite itself to tend – towards something that includes in itself every finite, without drying up in it. No finite can fill it up [...] it cannot even catch what could fill it up. It escapes its vision (EES 149).

Then, is it possible to separate the Persons and their distinguished being-person from the divine essence, if in the Eternal Being being and essence are inseparable?

The solution to this question, according to Stein, lays in considering the being in three Persons as essential, and "then without any doubt the separability of essence and being, of essential being and actual-real being in the *Logos* also turns into a matter that establishes an identity" (EES 151). The *Logos*, moreover, besides considering the divine essence in all its fullness, also embraces in its totality the sense of the creation. Indeed, Stein notices:

the sense of things, of which we should rather say that it is "not become", that it "has not made itself", *has* its seat in the divine *Logos*. What, since eternity, has its own consistency, as a member in the divine plan of creation [or *ars divina*, as Thomas calls it], is "participated" to the things as their sense and actuated, fulfilled in them (EES 154).

The passage to the Absolute is, then, in full harmony with Paul's words that he says about the Word:

He is before all things, and in him all things hold together.[26]

A deeper analyses, then, shows between all the beings and in the life of all mankind, the existence of a "significative relation", of a connection, actually, that in the *Logos* finds its totality of sense.[27] It can be found also in everyone's life, that "in front of the all-seeing eyes of God is a perfectly intelligible context" (EES 153) that we can understand only in part. For Stein, moreover, the fact that things "consist" in the *Logos* shows that the creating archetypes of all the realities created, having a being both essential and real, that is active, dwell in Him:

Thus we get a double meaning of the finite being in the eternity: every sense is embraced in the divine mind, every being has in the divine Being its archetypical-causative foundation (EES 155).

Therefore, we could say that the *Logos*, "the divine essence contained in the divine mind that reflects the divine essence" (EES 159), is at the same time God and creation.

To complete the argument hereto, it is interesting to quote Stein's words at the beginning of *The Structure of the Human Person*, where her idea of the human person is more clearly and systematically explained, with regard of the meaning of the Greek word "λόγος":

It means on one hand an objective order of what exists, where the action is also included, on the other a living comprehension by the human being of this order, that makes him able to operate in his praxis in accordance with it ("in accordance with sense") (DSP 37).

And still at the beginning of the same work, she writes:

All the human actions are led by a *logos* (DSP 37).

The *Logos*, then, – as Margarino writes, commenting upon what Stein maintains – "since it is the objective order of what exists, is the cosmos itself, the reality where the human being lives".[28]

And, Margarino continues, since the *Logos* is indicated by Stein also as the *living comprehension* – that is as the ability and the care to catch the sense, namely the order of what exists – the latter is also the main spiritual activity that calls man.

The philosophical thought, however, cannot catch autonomously both meanings (*order* and *sense*) which are part of the first Being, since the man has not intuition that lets him to. The paradox of the man, indeed, as Stein notices, is right this continuous tension between finite and infinite, and the continuous search of God, that also shows itself differently for the believer and the non-believer. The former, indeed, "hurls himself above the abyss, the non believer stops on its borders" (cf. EES 150). The theological reflection, therefore, opens the way to the achievement of some solutions, overcoming the limits of philosophy, even if it is still true that, through the philosophical analysis around the being we can disclose the sense of the truths of religion.

Moreover, Stein calls the concept of *logos* even in her close, hard comparison, in the fourth chapter of her book, with traditional metaphysics, especially about the concepts *ousia*, form and matter.

Here Stein, taking inspiration from the comparison with the Aristotelian speculation, repeats both the indicative and the constituting role of the being essentiality, both the common origin of pure form *(eidos)* and individual form *(morfé)*, in the horizon of the divine being that is the *Logos*, or the essential reason to justify the specular harmony of two worlds that would be totally separate otherwise. The creative and conservative act of God, indeed, not only gives a movement to the real, attracting it to Himself as a final cause, but also keeps the law actuated in the evolution of becoming, determining its going towards perfection. It is a *present* God, or better a God that makes *present* all things in Himself:

> If things appear to us as copies of the pure forms and the latter as models, with the essential forms working at their actuation, we cannot think of a casual concordance of two worlds that are totally separate. Both send to the same original reality, that makes their relation intelligible. Included in the unity of the divine Logos, the pure forms are the prototype of the things in the spirit of God, that gives existence to things by the form of the aim ascribed to them. Thus we can talk of a being of things in God, and Saint Thomas says that this being in God is even truer of the one they have in themselves. The causality of the eternal prototypes identifies with the efficiency of God that creates, preserves and orders (EES 266–267).

And:

> If Aristotle deduces the existence of a first mover from the present movement in the world, and attributes to that a merely spiritual being, this causality should be considered a final causality, for which all that is becoming is directed towards a higher aim. Thanks to the original forms, we can imagine now the divine Being not only as a mover of the world, but also as having a special link to every creature. Between the original and the essential form, there must be a particular relation, very solid and tight. This is why I think that the Platonic and Aristotelian doctrines of forms are not satisfactory, right because one only sticks to the original form and the other to the essential form (EES 267).

Indeed, she thinks that the eidetic intuition of ideas in the *Logos* cannot be compared to the *beatific vision* in eternity. The reality remain just a dull reflection of the true life, since it has on itself the signs of corruption. The degeneration of the actuated essence compared to the pure form would be the outcome of a fall[29] – identified by theology in the original sin and in the following state of the man's punishment, that Stein, as already seen, connects to the state of *dejection* or *throwness* proposed by Heidegger in *Sein und Zeit* – of the matter structured in the space outside the essential unity.

13. THE SPIRIT (*GEIST*) AS A CONSTITUTIVE COMPONENT OF WHAT EXISTS

As she goes on analysing the three basic components of the human being, Stein affirms that the spirit (*Geist*), being the third element, should not be meant only as the innermost part of the soul, or as the immaterial scope, but also as the constitutive component of everything material that exists. Actually, there is no matter totally devoid of spirit: even the dead matter is a figure of sense, created by the *Logos*. Stein writes:

> Everything that is *material is made by the spirit*. This does not mean only that all the material world is created by the divine Spirit, but that every material product is filled with *spirit*. Everything brings in itself its own shape [...] and for this shape it is made the support of a sense (EES 399).

If on one hand, indeed, the person-being of man shows an incommunicable individuality, on the other it supports a rational nature, *rationalis naturae individua substantia*,[30] strictly connected to spirituality, a "*spirit* and *reason* look inseparable implying each other" (EES 383). Actually, Stein affirms, referring to spirit:

> The spiritual has been defined unextended and immaterial; it has an "interiority" which is totally unextended, remaining "in itself", as it originates from itself. This going out of itself is essential for it; it is the total "lost of itself"; not in the sense that it has not an in itself, but in the sense that it give completely its self without losing it (EES 383).

Also the reason, as ability of "understanding one's own laws" and of "adapting the behaviour to these laws" (EES 385), shows a dynamics similar to that of the spirit, in the correlation between the permanence of intellect in itself and the exit of the behaviour from itself.

This does not mean only, in short, that everything is created by the spirit, but that the spirit also fills every person with itself, allowing them to act overcoming the natural mechanisms; that is to elevate themselves above nature and its laws and offering it, this way, the possibility to open itself to God's requests. Thus, the spirit makes man available to the intervention of the divine Grace, that does not destroy man's nature, but elevates it and transforms it, making it adequate to meet God and the change that results from this meeting.

With this theological investigation in the internal structure of the human being, even the empathic experience receives a somewhat Trinitarian justification, so that the three moments of the empathic process that could characterize intersubjectively the person's *selfness* in its constitutional opening to the otherness are connected to the Trinitarian dynamism of self-possession and spiritual free self-donation of the three divine Persons, obtaining a theological valence.

14. HUMAN FORMATION AND THE DIFFERENT DEGREES OF SELF-KNOWLEDGE

After explaining that the soul is the shape of the body, the Authoress analyses closer the *human formation*, outlining three stages: one *unintentional*, in the first period of life, consisting in physical growth; one *out of habit* (boosted also by imitation) in the little child; finally, one *intentional and personal* formation, also defined "formation or self-formation", which starts when the life of the spirit awakes and the Self becomes completely aware of itself, able to self-determine and self-educate. It applies especially to the souls, as it consists in the ability of addressing one's own *Leib* towards a specific aim that one is aware of.

Stein, then, distinguishes the different "degrees" of self-knowledge. They divide essentially in two modalities: that of *original knowledge* consisting in the "awareness that goes with the life of the Self" (EES 445); and that of *internal perception,* consisting, instead, on addressing to one's own self as if it were an external object. The latter is a reflex knowledge that sees the soul as "a whole" (almost as if it were an "inanimate being"). However, the internal perception never achieves the essence of the soul, as, Stein explains:

It is not the *reflex* establishment, but the original experience that reveals something of the essence of the soul, that is not only manifested in this experience, but *lives* and is revealed in it. And the authentic essential structure is possible only as a vital original process (EES 447).

To clear up the difference between the two kinds of self-knowledge the Authoress uses the example of the *moral self-knowledge.* The constitutive moment of the original self-knowledge is the experience that man makes of himself as a subject of his own behaviour. However, it is not really possible, according to Stein, to watch oneself from inside:

It almost seems that the Self perceiving itself as watched and moulded as something external [...] has left the castle to observe it from outside. This is not possible, of course; indeed the self-observation is the *life of the Self* itself, and the Self has no life unless it is the life of the soul; if it were not in relation with it, it would be nothing. Even if spiritually it places itself as an observer of itself, it remains prisoner in itself. But we can say that [...] it has abandoned the original direction of life, and that it does not possess the full vital force, undivided and intact. However, if we find a point where it is not interiorly and indivisibly "itself", it cannot understand itself completely, either (EES 448).

The human soul, moreover, not only forms a body, but it also *bears* in itself a shape: its peculiar essence from which the life of every single individual springs. Within this essence we can perceive a *sense* which is the aim of the soul by essential determination; and a *strength,* or power of being, that allows it to become what it must become, and breaks up in several strengths, corresponding to the three directions of the Self aware life, that the soul forms: the receipt of impressions, their working-through and the response to them.

These considerations bring Stein to stress those possible accesses that lead the Self to an original awareness at heart of its *Seele*.

The first gateway is found by Stein in *memory,* defined "the first species of interior preservation acceptance" of the sense contents (EES 451). It proves the depth of the soul, since the permanence of a memory depends on the "degree" of its original penetration, and showing the opening of the subject to a specific sense content, lets us understand how deep the Self lives its contents and, then, in which "room" of its interiority it dwells. Only if the Self is placed in the heart of its soul, it is revealed something of its being:

In the innermost part, the essence of the soul has opened towards the inside. If the Self lives here – on the foundation of its being, where it really feels at home and where it should stay – it feels something of the sense of its being and its strength altogether, before it is divided in single strengths. And if it lives from here, it lives a *full* life and reaches the culmination of its own being (EES 452).

Besides:

Those who live deeply absorbed see also the "small things" in wider wholes, they can only estimate their weigh [...] correctly, and can consequently regulate their own behaviour. Only in them is the soul going to the most complete formation and to the perfection of their being. In those who retire only occasionally in the depths of their soul, to get back to the surface again, the depth remains shapeless and cannot even developed its strength of formation towards the external layers (EES 454).

The Self, however, can also choose not to live starting from the heart of its soul. In this case every content that enters its *Seele* proves to be for the person a "call" for freedom, to take up side to himself:

The person is not "constrained" by what it goes through; it [...] must "take position" freely as of its position – whether to reach it or accept it – it must use its reason, it must clear up its situation, it must intelligently find how to behave and apply freely its strength in the direction required (EES 453–454).

After memory, Stein identifies with the voice of one's *conscience* (*Gewissen*) the element that allows the Self to remain in the heart of its *Seele*. It acts as (occasional) link between the life of the Self, the deed and the innermost part of the *Seele*. It is the same interior life of the soul, however, attracts to itself anyone who has experienced it a little. In it one experiences "a new life spring up, higher and more powerful: the supernatural, divine life" (EES

457), where the flower is God's inhabitation in human soul, bearer of that deep peace the Carmelite spirituality tends to, through what John of the Cross called "ascent to Mount Carmel".

The last gateway to the innermost life of the soul proposed by Stein is the experience of *ability* and *obligation*. About this Stein quotes the famous Kantian categorical imperative: "you can, because you must". According to the Authoress, however, the obligation can never force the person beyond its strength (*ultra posse nemo obligatur*). If it does, this means that "it can rely on a source of energy out of his nature", that is the Spirit of God:

The spirit of God is sense and strength. It gives the soul a new life, it makes it able to do what it could not, by nature, and simultaneously it points out the direction of its actions. After all every need full of *sense* appearing in the soul with a binding strength is a *word of God* [...]. And those who accept such a word of God promptly receive at the same time the strength to correspond to this word (EES 459).

Human freedom that accepts to be supported by the divine Grace, then, *can* everything, and the soul inhabited by God is able of finding in itself the very image of Trinity:

The soul filled with divine Life is the image of the Trinity of God in a new higher sense, more than any other creatures are, or better more than it is according to its natural structure (EES 460).

15. THE DEVELOPMENTS OF STEIN'S ANTHROPOLOGICAL REFLECTION IN THE *SCIENCE OF THE CROSS*

Let us analyse now what is usually considered the most original part of *The Science of the Cross* (*Kreuzeswissenschaft*).[31] The reflections mentioned therein by Stein are not just digressions from the central theme of the book; they are rather the fruit of what the Authoress, after a whole life spent for truth, thinks she has understood about the *laws* ruling the existence and the spiritual life, connecting the mystical life shown by St. John with the results of the phenomenological research carried out by her about the individual's *structure* and, then, about the human soul. Indeed, Stein writes:

The soul, as spirit, is part of the kingdom of spirit and spirits [...] it is not only the vital shape of the body [...]. It feels really at home only in its innermost part, in its essence and in its extreme end (KW 173).

Thus, she takes up again the theme of the *innermost part of the soul*, as she had left it in *Finite and Eternal Being*, devoting it a whole paragraph in *The Science of the Cross*, entitled, indeed, *The Soul, Spirit in the Kingdom of*

Spirits, a important transition section between the first and the second part of her work.

16. THE "INNERMOST PART OF THE SOUL": SELF-KNOWLEDGE AND RECIPROCAL KNOWLEDGE OF THE HUMAN SOULS

Here Stein divides the soul into two parts: one more "external", aimed at meeting and communicating with the exterior world, through the natural activity of its faculties; another, "internal", made of its innermost part. Now, as the Authoress states, since the being is certainly the innermost part that a being, like the soul, possesses, and since God is the foundation of this being, and is in constant relation with it, the created spirit, attaining the being, also attains God who gives it to the spirit every moment. Thus, the spirit, which lives collected in itself is, at the same time, in relation with God. Namely, penetrating into its own innermost part equals for the soul to elevating to God, finding itself out of itself.

John of the Cross, to explain this dynamics of interior life, uses a spatial image deduced from the field of science and nature of his own times, that of the gravitational attraction force. Actually, as every object is attracted to the centre of the earth, so that it falls more and more headlong, so it is for the soul, that finds no peace until it has not reached its deeper centre, where God dwells, who moves the soul towards himself through love. Love, as a force of attraction of the soul towards God, however, has different degrees, so that the more the soul comes closer to its deeper centre, the more it is attracted by it:

the more it elevates to God, the more it descends sinking in itself: the union has place in the innermost part of the soul, in its extreme end (KW 175).

The relation between God and the human soul, however, remains asymmetrical: so, on one hand, the Creator, preserver and founder of the being, penetrates everything with his own knowledge and, then, also the innermost part of the *Seele*, where He himself lives, peering its more secret thoughts; on the other, however, not only the human soul can attain the full knowledge of God on this earth, but it cannot embrace its interiority completely, either, unless allowed by divine concession.

The innermost part of the *Seele*, on the other hand, is all the more precluded to the other spirits created, be they pure spirits (angels or demons), or other human souls. Indeed, Stein states:

The innermost part of the soul is barred, there is no human eye so strong to probe it (KW 176).

At this point of the discussion a theme follows, cherished by Stein, since her dissertation, the relation and reciprocal knowledge between human souls. With this regard, Stein declares how the knowledge of the other's soul passes through perceptible exterior displays, from which we try to deduce the interior behaviour. Even succeeding, through this way, in identifying the existence of an interior emanating source, be it intentional or unintentional, conscious or unconscious, however it can never come to a precise idea of the other's innermost vitality, unless, even in this case, a divine enlightenment intervenes. Indeed, Stein states:

> What comes from the innermost depths will also make something emerge from the innermost depths. It will not be cleanly outlined, nothing comprehensible in a certain and determining way, until we remain in the natural path and we are not guided by the extraordinary divine enlightenment; it rather remains something mysterious (KW 176).

Instead, as for the relation of the human soul with the pure spirits created, that is bodiless, the latter can communicate with the former, either through cognitive ways, that can be considered "normal", namely appearing sensibly, or through "spiritual" ways (interior words, etc.). The innermost part of the soul remains for them, too, "naturally" unapproachable, unless God wants to display it.[32]

17. THE "PRIMORDIAL" LIFE OF THE SOUL AND THE "THOUGHTS OF THE HEART"

In the following paragraph, entitled *The Innermost Part of the Soul and the Thoughts of the Heart*, Stein describes what she defines "original life of the soul", characterized, indeed, by the so-called "thought of the heart". Actually, in the text we read:

> The *thoughts of the heart*: here is the original life of the soul in is essential lines. This basic structure is in the deepest psyche and goes before the articulation of the soul in its different powers and activities. The soul lives in it, as it is in itself, beyond all the reactions that the creatures provoke in it. Even though this innermost refuge is the dwelling of God and the place where the union between the soul and God is fulfilled, before this union occurs the proper personal life ferments in it, even when this union will never be achieved. Every soul has then its own innermost part, the essence of which is already a form of life. This primordial life, however, in unknown not only to the other spirits, but also to the soul itself (KW 178 o.i.).

C. Bettinelli[33] emphasises how this paragraph, logically speaking, should have come before the mystical analysis of the "night" of the soul. This proceeding, however, in a deeper analysis, results completely connected to Stein's typically phenomenological structure, which investigates the innermost essence of things only after a thorough description of its exterior phenomena.

Moreover, Stein here proposes a theme already mentioned in *Finite and Eternal Being*, where (still in the same chapter devoted to the image of Trinity in the creation) she spoke about original self-knowledge as a "perceiving with the heart" (EES 513), meaning with "heart" precisely the innermost part of the soul. Actually, we read in *Finite and Eternal Being*:

The heart is the real centre of life, the organ of the body the activity of which is connected to the life of the body. But usually the heart is meant as the innermost part of the soul, obviously because it shares more strongly what happens in the innermost part of the soul, because the link between the soul and the body is felt there most than anywhere else (EES 452).

In *The Science of the Cross*, however, the description of this "primordial" life of the soul results to be much richer and more detailed, exactly because the "thoughts of the heart" have been inserted.

These thoughts, as Stein specifies, should not be confused with those produced by intellect, since they "have no precise outline, are not articulated and expressible" (KW 178), as they are "shapeless", and as they consequently remain unknown to the soul, more often that not. Indeed, we read in the text:

The thoughts of the heart are not at all thoughts in the usual sense, nothing outlined strictly, before they become such products. They must only emerge from the bottom of the heart. Then they reach the first threshold, where they become perceivable. This perception is a very original way of conscience, more than a knowledge suitable for the intellect. It can also be found before the separation of powers and activity. It lacks the clearness of pure knowledge suitable for the intellect. What comes up is perceived as an indication of value offering the decision to accept or not accept what comes up (KW 178-179).

At this degree of awareness, the division of the powers of the soul (in intellect, memory and will) starts and therefore, their "interior perception", namely the proper intellectual knowledge.[34] Indeed, Stein declares:

The *life of the soul* in no longer only the primordial life in the depths, but also something comprehensible in the *interior perception*, a totally different way from the first perception of what comes up from the depths. How, in turn, this ascent from the depths is different from the emergence of an already formed figure, present in the memory and now alive again (KW 179).

Anyway:

Not everything that starts ascending thus becoming perceivable is really comprehended. A seizable part emerges, transforming into interior word, expressed word, desire [...] "still before the subject realizes it". Now, only those who live all absorbed in their Innermost part, preserve an accurate vigilance on these *first motions* (KW 179).

Thus, only those who live absorbed in themselves attains the knowledge of the thought and of their own heart. However, Stein must recognize that very few people live in such an absorption. She had already made a similar remark in *Finite and Eternal Being*, where we find:

The personal Self feels at home in the innermost part of the soul. If it lives here it has all the strength of the soul and can use it freely. It is also closer than ever to the sense of every event and open to the needs that occur, and prepared in the best way to measure its meaning and its purport. However, there are few people who live so "absorbed". Mostly, the Self lives on the surface, occasionally shaken by "great events" and attracted to the depths, it tries to answer this with a suitable behaviour, but after a period that can be more or less short, it goes back to the surface (EES 454).

Most people, therefore, live absorbed in the exterior world, and ignore that it is possible to attain what in the world is of value, without leaving their own interiority.

Stein, now, thinks she should explain better the structure of the soul, as indicated by the image of the "interior castle" by Teresa of Avila, that the Authoress, on the other hand, had already used in *Finite and Eternal Being*, where we read:

The soul as "interior castle", as our Saint Mother Teresa called it, is not punctiform like the *pure Self*, but is already a space, a castle with several residences, where the Self can move freely, sometimes going towards outside, sometimes retiring more and more inside (EES 395).

In the castle of the soul, therefore, Stein explains, the Self wanders "like inside its own spatial circle" (KW 181). Indeed, as said in *The Science of the Cross*:

The possibility to move on itself pivots on the structure of the soul which has the *configuration of the Self*. The Self is for the soul the characteristic through which it possesses itself and everything that moves in it like inside its *spatial circle* (KW 181).

18. THE "INNERMOST PART OF THE SOUL" AND THE PROBLEM OF HUMAN FREEDOM

The analysis of the relation between the Self and the innermost part of the soul is also important for Stein to clear up the problem of human freedom. Actually, as the Authoress continues:

The deepest point – of the soul – is simultaneously the seat of its freedom: the place where it can embrace integrally its own being and decide about it (KW 181).

Thus, only if he starts from the depths of his soul, according to Stein, can man really confront with the exterior world and understand his own place in it. This does not eliminate the possibility of taking a decision even from a point of his own soul far from its centre. In this case, however, these cannot be really true decisions since the man who does not live absorbed in his innermost part, and then, "does not hold firm in his hands the reins of all his self, is not up to determine himself in a really free way: on the contrary, he will also let something influence him" (KW 181).

However, as Stein admits, living in one's own innermost part does not mean to understand oneself completely. The innermost part of man, indeed, remains a secret of God, "that only He can reveal to the extent that He prefers" (KW 181). He protects the soul, that He has chosen as His dwelling, placing in it some spirits created, the angels, anyway without violating the "right of self-determination" of the *Seele*. This right, indeed, which the Authoress defines as "inalienable", is the great mystery of personal freedom, before which God Himself stops. Actually, even if He knows the thought of human heart and longs for leading the soul to the beatifying unity, He never forces it to subdue it to Him; instead, He waits until it consents to it by free love.

Now Stein tries to check if what she has said about the relation between freedom and its deepest interiority agrees with the doctrine of the holy father Giovanni. This agreement, Stein declares, is carried out perfectly in the mystical marriage as a reciprocal entrustment of God and the soul, as the highest degree of personal life. Indeed, the soul, which has now attained the highest degree of perfection,

has nothing more to do, it can only remain receptive [...]. Then, it is exactly in this remaining—in-receptivity that the participation to its freedom is expressed. Moreover, freedom intervenes in a much more crucial place: here, therefore, God operates everything, because the soul entrusts to Him completely. And this entrustment is the highest act of its freedom (KW 184).

However, now it is necessary to wonder, according to the Authoress, which freedom most people that never reach the mystical marriage enjoy. More precisely:

Can they also retreat in the innermost part and send their decisions from there, or are only able to take more or less superficial decisions? (KW 184).

Stein tries to answer this question analysing some human types. First she states that the Self usually takes its decisions "from that certain seat where it preferably dwells" (KW 184), which is, precisely, different in every human type. The "sensual man", the hedonist (*Genussmensch*), indeed, always in search of new pleasures, takes his decisions from a very far place from the innermost part of the soul. The "man searching for truth" (*Warheitsmensch*), instead, entrusting himself to his intellectual researches:

if he actually aims at the truth, *as such*, (not simply at collecting single particular notions), he may be closer to God – who is truth itself – and consequently to his own innermost centre, of what you do not think (KW 184).

Finally, there is the "man aware of his self" (*Ichmensch*), that is, the man who, placing himself as a centre of gravity of his own world, blocks by himself the road leading to the his innermost part. On the other hand, as Stein remarks, "something like this contains in itself every man, until he has stood the test of the dark *Night* to the end" (KW 185).

Anyway, is there a possibility for these people to move the seat of their self? What is the freedom that their decision enjoy? And finally, can they reach the innermost part of their soul? The answer to these three questions is, according to Stein, positive, but the ways vary from one type to the other.

For the sensual man the passage from a lower to a higher pleasure does not imply in itself any variation of place inside the soul, but the self is left to rest always in a place rather external from the innermost part. Anyway, starting from the consideration that "no human kind is exclusively connected to a specific category of values" (KW 185), it can also happen that one day he meets something belonging to a totally different kind of values (for example it can be urged to renounce a certain kind of pleasure to help another person). In this case the sensual man's will be asked to take a decision about it, not easy at all. It is true, theoretically, that there may also be some souls so absorbed in sensual life that they cannot perceive any interior call, any longer. However, as Stein states, they are only "borderline cases", where not only the single free decision is compromised, but also freedom itself has been sacrificed since long.

Anyway, there may also be a case where the man who has heard the call, rejects it, because he has not understood its whole purport. This rejection would originate a *superficial decision*, since the self would decide "taking care not to return to the deepest seat" of his soul, thus abdicating also the possibility of taking a consistent, rational, free position as to the facts.

Finally, there is also the possibility of an *objective refusal*, resulting from a previous weighing of the several pros and cons. This type of refusal assumes, according to Stein, like an adhesion, that the sensual man abandons his hedonist attitude and that, consequently, he adopts an ethical behaviour, that is a "a mentality ready to recognize and do what is morally right" (KW 186). Actually, as Stein explains:

No man is up to embrace with his eyes all the pros and cons that occur in a decision (KW 186).

Despite this, it is possible to make some choices suitable to a specific situation, "starting from the most remote depths of the soul" (KW 186). This is what the believer does, after all, who, because he is aware of his own cognitive narrowness, chooses to make everything God's omni-embracing look shows him to be right in his innermost part.

The hedonist man, instead, so used to taking decisions based only in the most external layers of his soul, will certainly have to undergo a transformation to reach his innermost part. About this Stein remarks:

Maybe a similar deed is not even possible by a natural way, but rather it will be solely by means of an extraordinary resurrection (KW 186).

According to the Authoress, therefore, "only a behaviour based in religiousness is really ethical" (KW 186). Indeed, if the man is ready to admit that only God knows all the pros and cons of every choice, it follows that "man must certainly strain to know what is right in the eyes of God" (KW 186) and, then, to do it. If so, he would solve, theoretically at least, the problem of his self-determination for good. Indeed, it will be enough for him to remain joined to God in his innermost part (not so stock, on the other hand), and let his Spirit lead his choices, to have "always and everywhere the certainty to act uprightly" (KW 187), that is ethically, in the sense mentioned above, and completely free.

True freedom, therefore, according to Stein, consists in entrusting oneself completely to God: "this entrustment is the highest act of freedom" (KW 184). Stein tells this relation with God through the image of divine filiation, which she celebrates like an inexpressible gift and that she tries to live as a necessary commitment:

Being sons of God means walking hand in hand with God, doing the Father's will, not one's own, putting in the hands of God all the worries and hopes, worrying no longer about oneself and one's own future. The freedom and the joy of God's sons rest on this [...]. Living in the firm trust in the Lord is possible only when this includes the availability to accept everything from the hand of the Lord. *Fiat voluntas tua!* In its full dimension it must be the rule of a Christian life. It must regulate the day from morning till night, and the unravelling of the year, all life long. Then it becomes the only worry of a Christian (KW 21).

This is what the Authoress calls *realism of the saints*:

an original interior receptivity of the soul regenerated by the Holy Spirit; everything approaches the soul, the latter welcomes it in the suitable way and in the corresponding depth; and finds a living strength in it, dynamic and ready to be moulded, that lets what it has welcomed imprint and lead it sweetly and joyfully, without any absurd restrain and without any impeding hardening. When the strength of a holy soul welcomes the truth in the faith in this world, then it attains the *Science of the saints*. The mystery of the Cross becomes its *interior form*, then attains the *Science of the Cross* (KW 7).

All that has been said so far, however, does not eliminate the possibility of a natural search towards the right and the good. In order to better understand what Stein means, her analysis of the second type can be useful:

The one who "*hic et nunc*" looks for true good following the upright reason, deciding according to what he thinks he has sensed, finds himself already on the way leading to God and consequently to himself, even if he does not know (KW 187).

Even if he has not placed his Self in the depths of his the innermost part, anyway he has decided in himself, placing himself, by principle, in search for the good, "with the intent to fulfil it always and everywhere" (KW 187). Despite that, this man has not identified yet his upright reason with God's will and, therefore, the road he is walking is not completely sure yet, nor is he able to decide for himself completely with the absolute freedom of things. According to Stein, this is what happens, on the other hand, to many believers, too, who, even if they have chosen to do God's will, however, they have not attained the mystical union with Him, yet, the only way that, according to the two Carmelite reformers, allows to dwell permanently in one's own innermost part. In our opinion, we cannot avoid recognizing in these words a clear autobiographical reference to Authoress's own life, who knows well these interior dynamics, since she has experienced them in her soul.

CONCLUSIONS

I think that what we have tried to present in these pages shows very clearly the importance held by the soul in Stein's philosophical speculation – and, particularly its connection with the transcendent dimension of reality, which makes it God's dwelling in man and the principle of interior formation pre-eminently – in the knowledge of the human being as a person and, then, for an adequate philosophical anthropology that may act as a solid foundation, from which we could start to re-think education in perspective of life, as well as life.

The other basic consequence to be drawn from Stein's words is the dimension of *eternity* – connected to the conception of man as made of body and soul – and, then, what we have called the *eschatological opening*, which allows to give formation and education of the human individual a different direction from the nihilism that Heidegger's existentialism seems to propose and that results in being *for death*, rather than *for life*. The future described by Stein and that stands before the eyes of the believing Christian, is, on the contrary, a future full of hope, life, eternity, happiness, for which it is worth to spend his own strength, his own *time*. A future supported not only by human abilities, by that Being-There that man is, as Heidegger would say, but that is especially the outcome of the cooperation between man and the One who is in the time, and at the same time, – to use a pun – out of it, since He is the same yesterday, today, always. The One who offers himself as a sure guide of human actions, through the assistance of His Holy Spirit, and that makes them ethical salvific actions. The only One who can be called Father with full rights and pedagogue of every single man and of mankind.

This is what Edith Stein, wanted to communicate to us not only with her writings, but mainly with her life, according to that beautiful image of divine filiation, that is fulfilled in proceeding hand in hand with God, doing the Father's will, not one's own, no more worrying about oneself and one's own *future*, but placing in Him every worry and hope. This, as Edith Stein would state, is the true freedom of God's sons.

Università degli Studi di Macerata

NOTES

* All English translations from Italian editions herinafter are by myself.

1 E. STEIN, *Endliches und ewiges Sein. Versuch eines Aufstiegs zum Sinn des Seins*, in *Edith Steins Werke*, Band II, Herder, Louvain-Freiburg i. Br. 1959. It. tr. edited by L. Vigone, *Essere finito e essere eterno. Per un'elevazione al senso dell'essere*, revision and presentation by A. Ales Bello, Città Nuova, III edizione, Roma 1999. Hereinafter EES with the number of pages in the Italian translation.

2 M. HEIDEGGER, *Sein und Zeit*, Niemayer, Halle a.d.S., 1927. It. tr. *Essere e tempo*, edited by P. Chiodi, Longanesi, Milano 1970.

3 E. STEIN, *Martin Heideggers Existentialphilosophie* (1936), in *Welt und Person. Beiträge zum christlichen Wahrheitsstreben*, in *Edith Steins Werke*, Band VI, Herder, Louvain-Freiburg i. Br. 1962. It. tr. edited by A. M. Pezzella, *Filosofia esistenziale di Martin Heidegger*, in E. STEIN, *La ricerca della verità. Dalla fenomenologia alla filosofia cristiana*, edited by A. Ales Bello, Città Nuova Editrice, Roma 1993, pp. 153–226. Hereinafter MHE with the number of pages in the Italian translation.

4 E. STEIN, *Die weltanschauliche Bedeutung der Phänomenologie* (1932?), in *Welt und Person. Beiträge zum christlichen Wahrheitsstreben*, *Edith Steins Werke*, band VI, Herder, Louvain-Freiburg i. Br. 1962. It. tr. *Significato della fenomenologia come visione del mondo*, edited by A. M. Pezzella, in E. STEIN, *La ricerca della verità*, quot., pp. 91–107. Hereinafter DBP with the number of pages in the Italian translation.

5 E. HUSSERL, *Cartesianische Meditationem und Pariser Vorträge*, in *Husserliana*, vol. I, a cura di S. Strasser, 1963; It. tr. *Meditazioni cartesiane*, edited by F. Costa, Bompiani, Milano 1960.

6 A. ALES BELLO, *Introduzione*, in STEIN, *La ricerca della verità*, quot., p. 35.

7 E. STEIN, *La Phénoménologie*, Journée d'études de la Société Thomiste, Jusivy, 12 sept. 1932, Edition du Cerf, Paris 1932; It. tr. *La fenomenologia*, editeb by P. Conforti; *La ricerca della verità*, quot., p. 112. Hereinafter LP with the number of pages in the Italian translation.

[8] ALES BELLO, *Introduzione,* in STEIN, *La ricerca della verità,* quot , p. 45.

[9] Ibidem, p. 29.

[10] A. MARGARINO, *In statu viae. La fenomenologia religiosa in Edith Stein,* Edizioni OCD, Roma Morena 2002, pp. 104–105.

[11] E. STEIN, *Der Aufbau der menschlichen Person,* in *Edith Steins Werke,* Band XVI, Herder, Freiburg i. Br.-Basel-Wien 1994. It. tr. edited by M. D'Ambra, *La struttura della persona umana,* Città Nuova Editrice, Roma 2000, p. 94. Hereinafter DAP with the number of pages in the Italian translation.

[12] ALES BELLO, *Introduzione,* in STEIN, *La ricerca della verità,* quot., p. 46.

[13] Ibidem.

[14] E. STEIN, *Beiträge zur philosophischen Begründung der Psychologie und der Geisteswissenschaften: 1) Psychische Kausalität; 2) Individuum und Gemeinschaft,* in "Jahrbuch für Philosophie und phänomenologische Forschung", Band V, Halle 1922. Published with the essay *Eine Unterschung über den Staat,* by the publisher M. Niemeyer, Tübingen 1970. It. tr. *Psicologia e scienze dello spirito. Contributi per una fondazione filosofica,* edited by A. M. Pezzella, presentation by A. Ales Bello, Città Nuova Editrice, Roma 1996.

[15] E. STEIN, *Eine Unterschung über den Staat,* in "Jahrbuch für Philosophie und phänomenologische Forschung", Band VII, Halle 1925. It. tr. *Una ricerca sullo Stato,* edited by A. Ales Bello, Città Nuova Editrice, Roma 1993.

[16] MARGARINO, *In statu viae,* quot., p. 106.

[17] Ibidem.

[18] E. STEIN, *Die ontische Struktur der Person und ihre erkenntnistheoretische Problematik* (1932?), in *Welt und Person. Beiträge zum christlichen Wahrheitsstreben,* in *Edith Steins Werke,* band VI, Herder, Louvain-Freiburg i. Br. 1962. It. tr. edited by M. D'Ambra, *La struttura ontica della persona e la problematica della sua conoscenza,* in E. STEIN, *Natura persona mistica,* p. 70. Hereinafter DSP with the number of pages in the Italian translation.

[19] "If I was not humbly minded, but exalted my soul: As a child that is weaned is towards his mother, so reward in my soul." (*Sal 130*) , or: "My soul hath stuck close to thee: thy right hand hath received me." (*Sal 62*).

[20] B. BECKMANN, *Fenomenologia dell'esperienza religiosa secondo Adolf Reinach ed Edith Stein,* in *Edith Stein, Testimone di oggi, profeta per domani,* Atti del Simposio Internazionale, Roma-Teresianum, 7–9 ottobre 1998, edited by J. Sleiman-L. Borriello, Libreria Editrice Vaticana, Città del Vaticano 1999, p. 327.

[21] H.-B. GERL, *Edith Stein,* Morcelliana, Brescia 1998, p. 170.

[22] MARGARINO, *In statu viae,* quot., p. 84–85.

[23] E. STEIN, *Die Frau, ihre Aufgabe nach Natur und Gnade,* in *Edith Steins Werke,* Band V, Nauwelaerts, Louvain-Freiburg i. Br. 1959. It. tr. *La donna: il suo compito secondo la natura e la grazia,* edited by O. Nobile, preface by A. Ales Bello, Città Nuova Editrice, Roma 1998, p. 73.

[24] Stein states: "Saint Thomas distinguishes between *vestigium (Spur)* and *imago (Abbild)*: [...] he finds in all creation a vestige of the Trinity; an image only in the creatures endowed with reason, who have intelligence and will (*Summa Theol.,* I, q. 45, a. 7). Nevertheless we find a certain image even in those creatures that for Saint Thomas reveal only a vestige of the Trinity and therefore we talk only about images" (n. 1, EES 379).

[25] Cf. n. 8, in EES 104.

[26] *Col 1, 17.*

[27] The text states: "The link connecting "all" in the Logos must be imagined as a unity of a significative totality (*Sinn-Ganze*)" (EES 152).

[28] MARGARINO, *In statu viae*, quot., p. 67.

[29] Cf. n. 240, EES 271.

[30] Phrase by Boetius, taken later by Thomas Aquinas in his *Summa Theologiae*.

[31] E. STEIN, *Kreuzeswissenschaft. Studie über Joannes a Cruce*, in *Edith Steins Werke*, Band I, Ed. Nauwelaerts, Louain 1950. It. tr. edited by C. Dobner, *Scientia Crucis*, Edizioni OCD, Roma-Morena 2002. Hereinafter KW with the number of pages in the Italian translation.

[32] The Authoress distinguishes between what is called "spiritual" and what is defined, instead, "purely spiritual". Referring the former to what, even if not falling under the external senses, is influenced by it, however; the second, instead, refers only to what happens in the innermost part of the soul, that is "the life of the soul lived in derivation from God and plunged in God" (KW 178).

[33] E. STEIN, *Vie della conoscenza di Dio e altri scritti*, edited by C. Bettinelli, Edizioni Messaggero, Padova 1983, n. 4, p. 59.

[34] About this, it may be useful to remind the difference already made by the "original knowledge of oneself" and the "internal perception" in *Finite and Eternal Being* (cf. EES 445–447).

EDITH STEIN'S WORKS

Abbreviations:

EES   Endliches und ewiges Sein. Versuch eines Aufstiegs zum Sinn des Seins

MHE   Martin Heideggers Existentialphilosophie

DAP   Der Aufbau der menschlichen Person

DBP   Die weltanschauliche Bedeutung der Phänomenologie

LP   La Phénoménologie

DSP   Die ontische Struktur der Person und ihre erkenntnistheoretische Problematik

KW   Kreuzeswissenschaft. Studie über Joannes a Cruce

A.L. SAMIAN

VIRTUES IN AL-BIRUNI'S PHILOSOPHY
OF SCIENCE

1. INTRODUCTION

Abu Rayhan Muhammad ibn Ahmad al-Biruni[1] was born on Thursday, 3rd of Dhu al-Hijjah, 362 A. H. (4th September 973 A.D.) at "Madinah Khwarizm".[2] His exact birth place is still a matter of dispute. It is suggested that he was born in the outskirts (birun) of Kath[3], at al-Jurjaniyah[4], Khwarizm[5] or at a place called Biruni[6], as implied by his nickname al-Biruni. Al-Biruni was a devout Muslim yet there is no conclusive evidence of him adhering to any particular madhhab throughout his life.[7] His native language was the Khwarizmian dialect. He knew Persian but preferred Arabic, because to him the latter is more suitable for academic pursuit. Most of his numerous books and compendia were written in Arabic.[8] He received some of his early education under the tutelage of the astro-mathematician Abu Nasr Mansur b. Ali b. Iraq al-Jilani (d. ca. 427 H)[9] and ᶜAbd. Al-Samad b. [1]Abdal Samad from Khwarizm.[10] This is in addition to his formal elementary religious education at the madrasah.[11]

His *Kitab fi tahqiq ma li'l-Hind....*, was finally published in 421/1030 A.D. The Ghaznavid Sultan Mahmud invaded and conquered the city in 407/1017. Al-Biruni's other book, *Kitab al-Tafhim li-awa'il sinaᶜat al-tanjim* which was dedicated to Rayhanah, daughter of al-Hassan, was written in Ghaznah, 1029 A.D. Al-Biruni's *magnum opus*, *al-Qanun al-Masᶜudi fi al-Hay'ah Wa'l-Tanjim*, an astronomical encyclopedia comprising eleven treatises divided into 143 chapters was completed at a later date, in 427/1035 A.D., and was dedicated to the son of Mahmud, Masᶜud. Apart from emphasizing the importance of astronomy, he gives accurate latitudes and longitudes and also geodetic measurements.[12] His *Kitab al-Jamahir fi Maᶜrifat al-Jawahir* was completed less than a decade later (about 435/1043) and was dedicated to the Ghaznavid Prince Sultan Shihab al-Din Abu'l Fath Mawdud b. Masud, Sultan Mahmud's grandson.[13] His *Kitab al-Saydanah* was written towards the very end of his life.[14]

A-T. Tymieniecka (ed.),
Timing and Temporality in Islamic Philosophy and Phenomenology of Life, 267–283.
© 2007 *Springer*.

Al-Biruni lived during a period of intense scientific activity. Among his contemporaries were al-Haytham (975-1039 A.D.) and Abu ᶜAli al-Husayn bin ᶜAbd Allah ibn Sina (370/980 A.D.–428/1027 A.D). Others include Abu Nasr Mansur ibn ᶜAli ibn Iraq who was one of al-Biruni's patrons; Abu al-Hassan ᶜAli ibn Said ᶜAbd ar-Rahman ibn Ahmad ibn Yunus who was an astronomer of distinction (d. 1009 A.D) and last but not least, Abu Sahl ᶜIsa ibn Yahya al-Masihi al-Jurjani (d. 1000 A.D.) who was a close associate of al-Biruni and wrote twelve books under his name.[15]

Al-Biruni was a philosopher-scientist, but in him "science prevailed over philosophy"[16] and he appeared not to have identified himself with any school of philosophy. It was reported that he started doing astronomical observation as early as 18 years old.[17] In addition to his *Kitab al-Tafhim* and his *Kitab fi ifrad al-Maqal fi amr al-Zilal*, we can also find notable remarks which reflect his conception of nature in his other works. As an example, the introduction to his *Kitab Al-Jamahir Fi Maᶜrifah Al-Jawahir* consists of fifteen *tarwihah* which gives his view on the attitude of man towards nature. It is more than a book on pearls and precious stones.

In order to understand his overall view on ethics and morals, and the underlying concepts related to them such as truth, realities, The Good, and man himself, we have to examine his philosophy of science, particularly his philosophy of mathematics since he considers himself more so of a mathematician. Says al-Biruni, ".... I belong to a branch of mathematics (*riyadhi*), and since my coming into this world. I have been holding it strongly and have been known by it and may intention never exceeded it ..."[18] Therefore it is his philosophy of mathematics that by and large determines his philosophy of science.

2. SCIENTIFIC PROBLEMS AS RELIGIOUS PROBLEMS

First and foremost, al-Biruni never uses the word "science" in the sense that the word is understood today; that knowledge which is "exact", objective, veritable, deductive and systematic. The closest term that he ever used is the Arabic word "ᶜilm", which also means knowledge. Al-ᶜilm in the language of the Quran and *sunnah* (traditions of the Prophet) implies knowledge which makes man conscious of God, of His attributes, of the eternals, of the next world and of the return to Him and Him alone.[19]

Science, to al-Biruni, is a problem solving activity. As trivial as it may sound, we will argue in this section that such is the position of this industrious and dynamic scholar to science. Scientists seek solutions to scientific problems. Solving scientific problems, which to al-Biruni is analogous to "untying knots,"[20] are the main activities of scientists. But what is a scientific problem to al-Biruni? A scientific problem to him is a problem *circumscribed* by the Holy Quran and Sunnah which is enjoined by God. It is a problem that arises and needs to be solved in order for a Muslim to improve his "taqwa". It is also a problem posed by an Islamic society, arising out of their efforts to practice Islam as correct, and accurate, as possible, in order to please God. A scientifc problem, to al-Biruni is not just any problem under the sun.[21] The orientation of the problem[22] determiness its "scientificity".

A scientific, to al-Biruni, does not solve a scientific problem simply for the sake of solving problem. He does not solve a problem because the problem ought to be solved since it is technologically possible to do so.[23] His motive of solving problems is *dominated* by this consciousness of seeking God's pleasure, "that which yields Him satisfaction".[24]

The interesting thing is that the evaluation of the problems tackled is not given post hoc or ad hoc. It is not the case that al-Biruni solved scientific problems before thinking of its necessity, its worthiness for the ummah, viz., its *legitimacy* from the Quranic and *Sunnah* point of view. Concerning geography and astronomy, he states: "... For whoever determines the longitude and latitude of this country with precision will thereby enabled him to find out ... the end of evening twilight and of dawn, times which are needed ... for fasting".[25] Realising the comprehensiveness of Islam as a complete way of life, he adds; "... the usefulness here exceeds specific religious matters and extends to worldly affairs ... is also beneficial in finding the correct direction towards one's destination".[26] Clearly, to al-Biruni, there is a "sacred" orientation in scientific problems. Scientists *qua* scientists should solve problem in a manner which bring them closer to God, that can "yield His satisfaction (*rida*)".[27]

In yet another one of his book, *The Exhaustive Treatise on Shadows*, we can see very clearly the orientation of scientific problems expounded by al-Biruni. In studying shadows, not only did he analyse shadows of this world but also shadows in the Hereafter! He investigates in detail their differences, similarities and nature of existence. He differentiates between shadows in Heaven from shadows in Hell. Concerning the latter, he states:

However, as for the people worthy of punishment, the shadow they know (in hell) is characterised as smoke (*yahmum*) because the utility of shadow is relief from distress of heat and the a hot wind (*simum*), and if it were other than cool and not present it would increase the painful torment, like the distress present at the strata of the sky which (takes) the breadth (or souls) away and which (chokes).[28]

Thus al-Biruni shows that there is a "revealed perspective" on scientific problems which the scientist should take into account. The scientist should always be mindful of the connection that the problems have to this world and to the Hereafter.

Moreover, from the perspective of the Quran and *Sunnah*, nature and history (the days of God (*ayyam Allah*)), can enlighten man in knowing more about himself and his Creator. Says the Holy Prophet: "He who knoweth his self knowest his Lord". The Holy Quran views the alternation of night and day, the lengthening of shadows, the variation in human colour and language, the vicissitudes of nations, as signs of God that warrant examination in our quest of knowing Him,[29] so that we will not be "blind to the realities of the life to come".[30] The science of astronomy to al-Biruni, for an example, has its origin from Prophet Idris[31] (the Biblical Enoch). These are example of scientific problems enjoined solving in the Holy Quran and *Sunnah* that from al-Biruni's point of view, merit investigation.

There is an element if transcendence in seeking scientific solution to the end that problem solving is an act of contemplation. Al-Biruni, more often that not, is always conscious of God while solving problems. He strives to be among those who ". . . remember Allah, standing, sitting and reclining and consider the creation of the heavens and the earth, (and say): O Lord; Thou created not this in vain".[32] Examples are abundant in his writings there he invokes God's help. In *India*, be beseeches God so that He will "help him to a proper insight into the nature of that which is false and idle, that he may sift it so as to distinguish the chaff from the wheat". Elsewhere he writes:

And I pray for God's favour and spacious bounty to make me fit for adopting the right course and help me in perceiving and realising the Truth (*al-Haqq*) and facilititate its pursuit and enlighten its course (*sabil*) and remove all impediments in achieving noble objects.[33]

General speaking, within the schema of contemplation, al-Biruni solves problems mathematically. He solves problems "from the eyes of a mathematician" because al-Biruni considers himself as a mathematician, more than anything else.

3. NATURE OF MATHEMATICAL KNOWLEDGE

Al-Biruni's believes in the mathematical structure of the universe and the presence of numbers and geometrical figures in created things. According to him these concepts serve as the foundation of mathematical knowledge, consequently mathematical knowledge is knowledge derived from our understanding of numbers, geometry and the view that the universe has a mathematical structure.

According to al-Biruni, our understanding of numbers and geometry in turn depends upon our virtuous ability to reason and memorize arguments. The interesting thing about this ability is that it cannot be achieved from manual labour. To use a phrase from education psychology, it is not a learned behaviour. Al-Biruni believes that this ability is a gift grom God. He writes:

> Memorizations of arguments and reasoning is an even more useful implement for the attainment of knowledge and all the proofs concerning the facts evolved will stay in memory very long and easy to draw upon at will but this is *a gift from God*. It cannot be attained by means of toil or sedulousness. *God gives it to some and denies it to others.*[34]

Because one's expertise in mathematics depends heavily on this ability, his above statement points to the notion that mathematical knowledge is likewise a gift from God. Mathematical knowledge originates from Him.

That in al-Biruni's philosophy of mathematics mathematical knowledge and its basic entities such as numbers and geometrical figures issues forth from God can also be established from a different angle. The soul of the mathematician does not have the actual mathematical entities; other wise the soul would be conscious of them and consciousness in this case, implies "automatic" mathematical intellection. It the mathematical entities are not in the soul, they must be located elsewhere. In order for them to exist elsewhere, they must exist by themselves or existing in an independent substance from which they originate, a substance which has the propensity to impose mathematical entities on sensible things and on the soul so that mathematization is possible. And to al-Biruni, only God exists independently and the rest are nothing but His creations because "it is not possible to have an endless chain of succession . . ."[35] Consequently it follows that mathematical entities issues forth from God, The Good. It is no other than The Substance, the Most Virtuous, which al-Biruni rightly and humbly admits, "All good comes from Him".[36]

In his philosophy of mathematics, al-Biruni maintains that mathematical knowledge is governed by religion. He believes that both the theoretical and practical aspects of mathematics are guided by religion. Let us consider the theoretical aspects first. By "theoretical aspects" we meant those values that are connected with formulation of mathematical theories such as "simplicity" as opposed to "complexity". For example in his astronomical discussion concerning the formation of eclipse, al-Biruni maintains that "the sentences of the Quran on these and other subjects necessary for man to know are not

such as to require unnecessary complexity (i.e. myths and the like)". He is
referring to the Hindus who he believes had to create myth corresponding to
the doctrine of the Purana in order to explain the astronomical phenomena.[37]

From the practical point of view, al-Biruni believes that mathematics in
governed by religion because mathematics is extremely useful in solving
problems sanctioned by it. Mathematics enhance prayer, almsgiving, distribution of wealth and so forth, the many virtuous exoteric acts in Islam. In
this sense, mathematics is a subset of Islam. There is an organic relationship
between mathematics and that of Islam. In response to those who disagree
with this point of view, he writes:

> ...that prayer is the buttress of religion and that its perfection is restricted to (its observance)
> at its (proper) time and facing in the proper direction for it, and that both matter are connected
> with astronomy and a due amount of geometry; and almsgiving follows them, and [inheritances]
> there being no escape from them, just as there is no escape from buying and selling as a means
> of subsistance, in the Muslim Law and (since) all of them require arithmetic either in the lowest
> degree, in imitation of the method(s) of the computers, or else at its highest level, it being the
> deep investigation or geometry... for he is obliged to apply two (arithmetic and geometry) in
> almsgiving for the manufacture of weights and measures, and in charity the making of standard
> units[38]

As reflected in the above statement, al-Biruni views mathematical knowledge
as that knowledge which is extremely useful because it solves problems.

According to al-Biruni, there is another aspect in the nature of mathematical
knowledge which some branches of knowledge may not have. As al-Biruni
has shown, mathematical knowledge has tremendous applications. This is true
because it is very difficult to think of anything that cannot be mathematized.
Yet mathematical knowledge is not easily grasped by everyone. Al-Biruni
maintains that most people have difficulty with it. Thus:

> The other two parties are of the common people, whose hearts are disgusted by the mentions of
> shadows, or altitude, or sines, and who get goose-pimples at the mere sight of computation or
> scientific instruments.[39]

Therefore it is the nature of mathematical knowledge that only few people are
attracted to it. There is a reason for this. Al-Biruni believes that mathematical
knowledge involves a great deal of abstraction and not every people have
this virtuous mental capability. Mathematical knowledge is not that kind of
knowledge one acquires simply by "seeing and believing". In order to illustrate
the processes of abstraction involved, let us consider the case of a point.
The point is certainly a very basic mathematical entity. Yet to understand
the concept of a point is not that easy. "Seeing" a point is not like seeing
an amoeba or a stag. A dot from the ink of a pen is not a point, however

small it is. It is only one of its many physical representations. Points can only be grasped through our intellect. The same form of reasoning applies to al-Biruni's concept of lines and surfaces. Says al-Biruni:

> If a line is finite, its extremities are points. Points have one dimension less than lines, viz., length; they have neither length, breadth, nor thickness, and are indivisible. The point of a sharp needle may be taken as an illustration from the sensible world, but surface, line, point, although they accur on solids which bear them, apart from them cannot be apprehended *except by the intellect.*[40]

Although al-Biruni concedes to the importance of the intellect in acquiring mathematical knowledge, he does not submit to the philosophical position that mathematical knowledge is localized. Mathematical knowledge is not personal, so to speak. Mathematicians have their own academic communities and al-Biruni believes that this social aspect also contributes in the development of mathematical knowledge and values.

The social aspect is what we coin as the "external factor". It also determines the nature of mathematical knowledge. In more specific terms, al-Biruni believes that there are basic agreements between mathematicians on some mathematical concepts and the progress of mathematical knowledge is based on these concepts. Let us take the case of numbers. Al-Biruni defines numbers operationally and collectively. When we claim we know what numbers are, it is not the case that we can enumerate all of the natural numbers, just as we known what we mean when we say "al-Biruni is a man" although we do not know all men individually. In defining numbers operationally, he writes:

> Since the unit of measure is not a natural unit, but a *conventional* one assumed by general consent, it admits both practical and imaginary division. Its subdivisions or fractions are different in different periods in one and the same country. Their names, too, are different according to place and times; changes which are reproduced, either by the organic development of languages or by accident.[41]

Although al-Biruni's definition has a tinge of conventionalism,[42] he was far from being a conventionalist in his conception of the nature of mathematical knowledge in the sense this term is understood today. Admittedly mathematical conventionalism deserves substantial credit for the manner it has helped in clarifying the rapport between theory and experiment. It underscores the importance of the role played by the mathematician's activity which is executed in accordance with collective agreements, *mores* so to speak, in conducting and interpreting scientific experiments. Conventionalists believe that laws of nature and our values are our own free creations; our arbitrary decisions and conventions.[43] The laws of nature are simple but nature is not. For the conventionalist, mathematical description is not a picture of nature but a simply a logical construction. It is not the properties of this world which define this construction; on the contrary, it is this construction that defines the properties of the world. A measuring rod is "accurate" and a clock is "precise" only if the measurements of these instruments satisfy the axioms of mechanics which physicists of mathematicians have agreed to embrace. In short, applications of mathematics come about by fiat and mathematical truths as well as ethics and morals, could be merely social agreements. We can see that in the conventionalist's conception on the nature of mathematical knowledge, there is hardly any room for God. Yet God, who is the Most Virtuous, is fundamental in al-Biruni's concept of mathematical knowledge since according to him it is religion that licenses mathematical knowledge. Therefore al-Biruni's concept of the nature of mathematical knowledge, for that matter values and morals, is certainly not that of a conventionalist.

Moreover al-Biruni believes that there is an aspect in the nature of mathematical knowledge where conventionalism is out of place. It has to do with the noble concept of truth and virtues related to it. Al-Biruni maintains that truths transcend the rule established by convention. For example in elaborating the astrologers view of the order of planetary spheres, he states:

> ... it was known that the people of this craft are (sic) *agreed among themselves* that the nearest sphere to us is the sphere of the moon and the farthest of the spheres of the planets from us is the sphere of Saturn. And if they said, it was regarding the transit of the moon, that it is above Saturn, it was denying their saying that one planet, the extreme distance from the earth of which is sixty four times its (earth's) radius, passes over another, the nearest distance of which from the earth is fourteen thousand eight hundred and eighty one times its radius. But it is an expression without leading to this meaning, which is well-known among them by agreeing on it by *convention, although the order of the planets is not necessarily thus.*[44]

However al-Biruni believes that there are parts of mathematics wherein community decisions or *mores* are needed. In more specific terms mathematicians agree on what assumptions are considered fundamental to a branch of mathematics. These assumptions are known as axioms or first principles. Al-Biruni states:

> Arithmetic and geometry are impossible to understand unless on proceeds systematically from first principles, unlike other sciences in which he may acquainted with something of their middle (parts) or their ends without knowledge of their beginning.[45]

In our opinion, what he meant by the phrase "unless one proceeds systematically from first principles" is best understood from the perspective of the virtuous act of acquiring mathematical knowledge. From al-Biruni's point of view, mathematical knowledge is knowledge about the structure of the universe. It is not so much about story and events. The underlying assumptions of mathematics are truths (such as two point determine a line or things equal to the same things are equal to one another) and mathematical knowledge is constructed upon these truths. Thus without first knowing what these truths or first principles are, how can the student "proceed" from them?

So far we have not established the claim that al-Biruni's "first principles" are self evident truths. We have only mentioned that they are truths. We can examine the claim that they are self-evident truth by analysing one of his statements on geometry. Al-Biruni believes that one can arrive at truth concerning the universe by way of mathematics. He states:

By it [geometry] the science of numbers is transferred from the particular to the universal, and astronomy removed from conjecture and opinion to a basis of truth.[46]

In other words, if one "proceeds systematically from first principles," one can arrive at truth. But ontologically speaking truth cannot follow from falsehood.[47] In this sense, a true theory has to be a consequence of a true axiom. It is instructive to quote Aquinas who states:

Plato said that unity must come before multitude; and Aristotle said that "whatever is greatest in being and greatest in truth, is the cause of every being and of every truth," just as "whatever is the greatest in heat is the cause of all heat".[48]

In similar vein, al-Biruni's "first principles" are self-evident truths because it is "the greater truth" that is the cause of the "great truth". This way of reasoning in his view applies to all truth, including those of ethics and morals.

Although it is the nature mathematical knowledge to produce true theorems, al-Biruni believes that it is also the nature of mathematical knowledge that whatever theorems it produces are not necessarily guaranteed truths. That they are not necessarily true laws is because they are *ceterus paribus* generalizations; generalizations that hold only under particular, usually ideal conditions. *Ceterus paribus* is translated as "other things being right".[49] Al-Biruni believes that the truth or falsity of a theory is connected to the conditions attached to it. There are instances where theories could turn out to be false, especially when the conditions are not "right". Alluding to the significance of *ceterus paribus* in mathematical knowledge, he writes:

Whichever of the two theories may be correct, whether the Anwa are to be traced back to the days of the year or to the rising and setting of the Lunar Stations, in any case there is no room for a third theory. To each of these theories, whichever you may hold to be correct, *certain conditions attach*, on which the correctness of the Anwa depends.[50]

Since mathematical laws have conditions attached to them, al-Biruni is very much aware of the uncertainty aspect of mathematical knowledge, the virtues of doubt that is. Let us take for instance, the law of the excluded middle. Al-Biruni used it extensively in his mathematical reasoning. For example in his correspondence with Ibn Sina concerning infinite divisions, he gives the following argument:

According to your view, it becomes necessary that the side of a square be equal to its diagonal; if you deny it you have opposed your own principles. Or you will say that between the part there is a separation; in this case I ask if the separation is *greater or smaller* than the indivisible parts.[51]

Yet al-Biruni did not elevate the law of the excluded middle, or for that matter any mathematical law, to the level of an absolute truth on a par with revelation. He is conscious of the realm of possibilities even in mathematics; that with the ever creating God, literally anything is possible. Between A and not A, there can exist things which are not only plausible, but also true. There can be two contradictory worlds existing simultaneously.

A group of sages have been of the opinion that it is possible for another world to exist which differs from this world in nature. Aristotle has considered their views detestable, but his hatred is untimely and out of place. For we find information about natures and element of things when we observe them with our eyes like a man born blind who can find about sight only when he hears about nature from other people. And if there were no faculty of hearing he would not know that in the world there is such a sense as sight, the fifth sense, by means of which colours and heights and shapes become visible and observable. To sum up, what harm can there be if there is a world which as we say differs in the directions of motion and is separated from this world by an isthmus so that each is hidden from the other?[52]

To recapitulate, al-Biruni believes that the whole corpus of knowledge issues forth from God. Mathematical knowledge is invaluable because it is of great utility to religion. And not everyone can master mathematics. This is in part due to the variations in their intellectual virtues.

4. VIRTUES OF SAFE-GUARDING THE SOUL

Since the pursuit of mathematical knowledge is a virtuous act , it is crucial to safeguard the soul. Al-Biruni believes that the joy of the spirit in the virtuous act of discovering the true nature of things is better than the pleasures of the flesh since the former is more lasting.[53] Therefore in order for the soul to "have proper insight into the nature of that which is false and idle"[54] in the course of mathematical abstraction and for the soul to experience the pleasure of being immersed in Divine Presence while mathematizing, al-Biruni emphasizes cleanliness of the heart and purity of intention of the mathematician, that cleanliness is part of faith (*al-nazafah min al-iman*).[55]

Since the mathematician does vacillate between the two levels of awareness and forgetfulness of the Good, al-Biruni gives some advice for the mathematician so that the latter can always be in the blessed state.[56]

Al-Biruni maintains that as a seeker of a sacred knowledge, the mathematician should live according to a set of virtues revealed by God through His Prophets (peace be upon them). According to him, the mathematician should be actively involved in solving problems for the society because man cannot live by himself.[57] His research priorities should not be decided with the objective of hoarding wealth because those who are blinded by wealth will suffer in the hereafter and he quotes verses from the Holy Quran to buttress his view.[58] We believe that al-Biruni humbly rejects Sultan Masud's gift of an elephant load of silver upon the completion of Al-Qanun al-Masudi[59] because he wants to safeguard the purity of his intentions in studying God's creation.

In addition to the above, al-Biruni recommends that the mathematician strives earnestly "for the suppression of evil and for welfare of truth".[60] Quoting ᶜAli b. al-Jaham's statement, al-Biruni maintains that the mathematician should not feel shame if he loses his prosperity but "the real disgrace is if he loses courtesy, generosity and etiquette".[61] The mathematician should not labour for his personal fame. Instead, the mathematician should put the pleasure of God above everything else in his quest of mathematical knowledge. He should let the pleasure of God, who is the Most Virtuous, to be the ultimate arbiter between his choice of actions.[62]

The code of conduct described by al-Biruni rests on the mathematician's constant remembrance of God. Al-Biruni realizes this most important axis, the continuous consciousness of God as the most important aspect that binds and characterizes the mathematician's quest of mathematical knowledge. For instance, commenting on Abu Bakr bin Zakaria' Al-Razi book entitled The Secrets of Secrets, he quotes the verse from the Holy Quran: "Any one who does not seek God for light on his path has no light in him (stays in darkness)".[63] The mathematician should be mindful of God constantly. His private and public life should be in accordance to the famous saying of the Holy Prophet : "that you should worship God as though you saw Him..." (an taᶜbuda Allaha ka 'annaka tarahu...). In other words, the mathematician should always be in a state of gratitude to his Lord and al-Biruni cites at least four Quranic verses to support his view.[64]

In light of al-Biruni's view on virtuous conduct for the mathematician or scientists, we should never interpret that his problem solving activity equals to the utilitarian normative ethical doctrine. Utilitarians maintain that if a mathematician is faced with a number of mathematical problems related to the society, he should prefer solving the problem that can promote the greatest happiness of the greatest number irrespective of guidance from the scripture. Choices are judged by their consequences and the amount of pleasure derived from those consequences. Clearly al-Biruni's code of ethics cannot be called utilitarian because choices are never analysed entirely through actions and consequences. Rather, motives and underlying *intentions* are crucial in his problem solving approach. As we have shown earlier, al-Biruni believes that problems are religiously defined. From the external aspect, problems are solved for the betterment of the society but to al-Biruni, the welfare of the society is never the endpoint. The endpoint, the ultimate cause, the foremost reason problems are solved by the mathematician is so that both he *and* the virtuous society will enjoy continuous Divine Blessing from the Most Virtuous in this transitory world and the hereafter.

CONCLUSION

Al-Biruni believes that mathematics is a primary link that connects nature, science and religion. Guided by his belief that everything is rooted in the The Good who is the Most Virtuous, the Divine, mathematicians' contemplation of nature are facilitated by mathematics through which they can know and internalize the various levels of reality and the qualitative aspect of God in the world of quantities.

He looks at mathematics as a very powerful tool of studying nature. However to say that he was an instrumentalist as the word is understood today would not do justice to his philosophy of mathematics. Instrumentalists believe that in the case of mathematics, the latter is nothing more than a tool in our noble quest of knowledge where as al-Biruni believes that mathematics has an important role in man's understanding of the relationship between nature, science, religion and in order for him to become a virtuous man. Nature can be scientifically analyzed through mathematics and religion plays a critical role in some of the processes. In more specific terms, mathematics as practiced by al-Biruni are circumscribed by religion wherein the mathematician is immersed above all, from observing God's handiwork in deciphering nature with the consequence of knowing more about his mode of existence and as a matter of fact, about Existence Itself.

Central to al-Biruni's philosophy of mathematics is his conception of The Good. He views the sensibles and mathematical objects as related to God in a manner corresponding to their mode of existence. The Good is the center for all there is. In point of fact, it is his notion of God, the Most Virtuous, which dominates his conception of mathematics and a virtuous seeker of knowledge. According to him , by doing mathematics one should in the end knows more about God. The total worthiness of mathematics corresponds to the extent that mathematics can bring the mathematician closer to God, the Most Virtuous, to the degrees that it can improve his piety (*taqwa*).

Since he realizes the significance of the rational soul, it is not surprising that al-Biruni's ethics sought to purify the rational soul of the mathematician. He believes that since it is the Most Virtuous, the Most knowledgeable, that imparts mathematical meanings to the soul and since God is the Most Pure, consequently having a "pure soul" will facilitate the process.

Al-Biruni believes in the existence of levels of reality. There is a hierarchy of reality, so to speak. In the case of al-Biruni, material objects and the infinite divisions of its constituents, the nature of light as represented in his *Treatise on Shadows*, the belief in the existence of Angles, the frequent mentions of God's Divine Qualities and the stated humility of not-knowing the Divine Essence correspond respectively to the levels of reality consisting of the material, subtle and angelic world circumscribed by the world of Divine Qualities and Divine Essence.

As a consequence of his belief in the existence of various planes of reality, we can chart a one to one mapping between the faculties involved in the virtuous process of deciphering nature mathematically and the levels of reality. The external senses map into the world of brute facts which is the terrestrial world. The mind and other internal senses are mapped into the so-called intermediate world or the subtle world. Finally the soul who attains the mathematical meanings and ultimately the spirit, each corresponds to the celestial world and the world of infinity, which is none other than the world which includes Divine Qualities and the Divine Essence.

More importantly, in accord with these metamathematical tenets espoused by al-Biruni is the belief that man is a microcosm. He is a reflection of the macrocosm. It is the incognizance that man is the microcosm, that the heaven and the earth are ontologically related and that The Good is the Lord of both; become the principle cause of the secularization of mathematical experience. The mathematical experience of the mathematicians are no longer part of that illuminative experience with Divine Unity and Aspects of Existence. Instead, the mathematical experience they undergo are only fruits of their descent to the dry and morbid world of sophisticated quantification.

As a corollary to the one-to-one relationship between man (the microcosm) and the cosmos (the macrocosm) manifested in al-Biruni's philosophy of science, we can explain the reason mathematics functions as a bridge connecting the world of sensibles to the world of intelligibles; simply because by the virtuous act of mathematization, we facilitate our comprehension of the abstract world. We brought ourselves yet closer to the world of the infinite and ultimately to the Most Virtuous.

National University of Malaysia

NOTES

[1] "The spellings Al-Biruni and Al-Beruni are both legitimate". See Percival Spear, ed. *The Oxford History of India*, (Oxford: Clarendon Press, 1961) p. 209, footnote 1. Also the forms Alberuni and Albiruni, without the hyphen that is, are equally acceptable from the usage there and elsewhere. In this paper, I adopt the form al-Biruni because it is more conventional.

[2] See *Tahdid Nihayah Al-Amakin*, (Ankara, 1962), p. 5. Hereafter cited as *Tahdid*.

[3] See S.H. Barani, "Al-Biruni and his Magnum Opus Al-Qanun 'al-Mas^c udi" in *Al-Qanun Al-Mas^c udi*, (Hyderabad: Deccan, 1956), p. v.

[4] S.J.H. Kramers, "Al-Biruni's Determination of Geographical Longitude by Measuring the Distances", Commemorative Volume, p. 189. Krenkow, for example, maintains that the birth place was the outskirts rather than in al-Jurjaniyah. See his "Beruni and the MS. Sultan Fatih No. 3386", *Commemorative Volume*, p. 196.

[5] See Ghadanfar's *Risalah al-Mushshatah li-Risalah al-Fihrist* which is reproduced in E.C. Sachau's introduction to al-Biruni's *Al-Athar Al-Baqiya*, (Leipzig, 1923), p. xvi. See also A.S. Nadwi, "Alberuni", Commemorative Volume, p. 255 and H.M. Elliot, *The History of India as Told by its Own Historians*, (London, 1869), Vol. II, p. 1.

[6] For example, see S.H. Barani, *op. cit.*, p. 34; *Al-Athar al-Baqiyah*, p. LIII; and Ibn Abi Usaibi'ah, *'Uyun al-Anba fi Tabaqat al-atibbs'*, (Beirut, 1957), pp. 29–30.

[7] See, for example,. E.S. Kennedy, "Al-Biruni, Abu Rayhan Muhammad ibn Ahmad " in G.C. Gillispie, ed. Dictionary of Scientific *Biography*, Vol. II, p. 156; that he was a Sunni in S.H. Barani, "Ibn Sina and Al-Beruni" *Avicenna Commemoration Volume*, Iran Society, (Calcutta, 1956), p. 7; that he was attracted to Shi'i in his early years but adopted a Sunni tendency towards the end in S.H. Nasr. *An Introduction to Islamic Cosmological Doctrine, op. cit.*, p. 114 and that he was a Zaidite but later became a *'tafdili'* Sunni in H. Said & A. Zahid. *Al-Biruni: His Times, Life and Works*, (Hamdard, 1981), p. 198.

[8] See Hakim Mohammed Said (ed.), *Al-Biruni's Book on Pharmacy and Materia Medica*, v. 1, pp. 5–16, v. 2, pp. 17–57.

[9] For an insight into one of Abu Nasr's works, see Claus Jensen, "Abu Nasr Mansur's Approach to Spherical Astronomy as Developed in His Treatise 'The Table of Minutes' ", *Centaurus*, (16) (1971) pp. 1–19.

[10] See, for example, G. Sarton, *Introduction to the History of Science*, Vol. 1, Robert Kreger (ed.), (New York, 1975), pp. 693–709.

[11] Education and instruction in *'awa'il'* sciences such as astronomy, geography and geometry were usually given by individual scholars. See Aydin Sayili, *The Observatory in Islam*, (Ankara, 1960) pp. 416–417. Until the end of the Umayyad Caliphate, subjects taught as part of a normal curriculum include Quranology, Tradition, Arabic language, poetry and mathematics. For a further discussion on education during this period, see M. Abdul Mu'id Khan, "The Muslim Theories of Education During The Middle Ages", *The Islamic Quarterly*, (3/3)(1956), pp. 420–428.

[12]   See for example E.S. Kennedy et al., "The Hindu Calendar as described in al-Biruni's Mas'udic Canon" *Journal of Near Eastern Studies*, 4:1965, pp. 274–284.

[13]   See M. Nazim, *Sultan Mahmud Ghaznawi*, (Cambrige, 1931), and F.C. Auluck, (Ed.), *Al-Biruni*, (New Delhi, 1971), pp. 1–16.

[14]   See Hakim M. Said (Ed.), *Al-Beruni's Book on Pharmacy and Materia Medica*, (Karachi, 1973) and the *Introduction* in Vol. II.

[15]   See H. Said, A. Zahid, *"Al-Biruni" His Times, Life and Works*, *op. cit.*, pp. 98–114.

[16]   See S.H. Nasr, *Three Muslim Sages*, (New York, 1976), p. 10. Cf. S. H. Barani, "Ibn Sina and Al-Beruni; A Study in Similarities and Contrasts" in *Avicenna Commemoration Volume*, op. cit., p. 6.

[17]   See S. H. Barani, "Ibn Sina and al-Beruni: A Study in Similarities and Contrasts", *ibid.*, p. 3.

[18]   See al-Biruni's preface to *al-Qanun al-Masudi*.

[19]   See S.H. Nasr. *Living Sufism*, *op. cit.*, p. 42.

[20]   See al-Biruni, *The Exhaustive Treatise on Shadows*, *op. cit.*, p. 2.

[21]   It is important to note here that the claim is not that all problems are scientific problems although all problems in a sense, are religious problems. For instance, it is already established that some problems of astrology, for example, are not considered as scientific problems by al-Biruni although these problems are religious problems. Rather the claim is that problems which al-Biruni considered as scientific are also problems sanctioned by religion.

[22]   By orientation of a problems, we mean the origin of the problem, method (s) used to solve it and its worthiness.

[23]   Critics of modern science such as Erich Fromm and Orwell argue that one of the major maxims of modern science is that "something ought to be done because it is technologically possible to do so. If it is possible to build nuclear weapons, they must be built even if they might destroy us all . . . One the principle is accepted that something ought to be done because it is technically possible to do so, all other values are dethroned, and technological development becomes the foundation of ethics." See E.D. Klemke, R. Hollinger, A.D. Kline (eds.) *Readings in the Philosophy of Science*, (New York, 1980), p. 298.

[24]   See *India*, Vol. II, p. 246. See also *The Exhaustive Treatise On Shadows*, *op. cit.*, p. 2.

[25]   See *Tahdid*, pp. 323–324. See also A. Sayili, *The Observatory in Islam*, (Ankara, 1960) pp. 22–23.

[26]   See *Tahdid*, pp. 323–324.

[27]   See al-Biruni's supplication in *India*, Vol. II., p. 246. See also S.H. Nasr, *An Introduction . . .*, *op. cit.*, p. 174.

[28]   See *The Exhaustive Treatise On Shadows*, *op. cit.*, pp. 20–21. Al-Biruni also quotes the *Quran* (7:41).

[29]   *al-Quran*, 25:46, 10:6, 3:131.

[30]   *ibid.*, 17:72.

[31]   See al-Biruni, *The Exhaustive Treatise on Shadows*, *op. cit.*, Vol. I, p. 230.

[32]   al-Quran, 3:191. See also al-Biruni's introduction in *Tahdid*.

[33]   See *Tahdid*, *op. cit.*, p. 45.

[34]   See al-Biruni, *Kitab al-Saydanah fi'al-tibb*, transl. By H. Said, (Karchi, 1973), p. 2 cf. To the Quranic verse (2:269):

"He (Allah) giveth wisdom (*hikmah*) unto whom He will, and he unto whom wisdom is given, he truly hath received abundant good".

[35]   See the translation of S.H. Nasr in his *An Introduction . . .*, pp. 116–117 which is based on the next written by al-Biruni in his *Kitab Tahdid Nihayat al-Amakin*. See also al-Biruni's

Chronology, p. 116 and his *Kitab al-Jamahir* ..., "Chapter on Pearls ...," trans. and reproduced by F. Krenkow, *Islamic Culture*, (15; 421)(1941).

36 See *India*, Vol. II, p. 246.

37 See *al-Biruni Commemorative Volume*, p. 326.

38 See al-Biruni, *The Exhaustive Treatise On Shadow*, p. 8. It is interesting to note that wih the exception of music (*'ilm al-musiqa*), al-Biruni's enumeration of the mathematical enterprise closely resembles that of al-Farabi. See O. Bakar, *Classification of Sciences...*, *op. cit.*, pp. 194–195.

39 See al-Biruni, *On Transits*, *op. cit.*, p. 75.

40 See *Elements of Astrology*, p. 3.

41 See *India*, Vol. I, pp. 160–161.

42 For other passages of his wherein convention is mentioned, see *The Exhaustive Treatise On Shadows*, pp. 40–41 and *Elements of Astrology*, p. 2.

43 The argument that natural laws are nothing more than shared definitions and therefore tautologies will ultimately support the belief that man, by himself, can know; thus solving the problem of induction.

44 See al-Biruni, *On Transits*, (transl. By M. Saffouri & A. Ifram), (Beirut, 1959), p. 14.

45 See al-Biruni. *The Exhaustive Treatise On Shadows*, p. 6.

46 *Ibid.*, p. 1.

47 Surely in terms of pure logic, everything follows from falsehood.

48 See under "Treatise On the Creation" in Aguinas, S.T. *The Summa Theologica* (transl. By Fathers of the English Dominican Province), (The University of Chicago, 1952), p. 238.

49 See Cartwright, N. *How the Laws of Physics Lie*, (Oxford University Press, 1983) p. 45.

50 See *Chronology*, p. 232.

51 See S.H. Nasr. *An Introduction...*, p. 171. See also F.A. Shamsi. "Ibn Sina's Argument Against Atomicity of Space/Time", *Islamic Studies*, 23(1984), pp. 83–103.

52 See the translation of S.H. Nasr in his *An Introduction...*, *op. cit.*, p. 168.

53 See S.K. Hamarneh's discussion on al-Biruni's concept of *futuwwah* in his "Evaluation of Al-Biruni's Book on Precious Stones and Minerals (Al-Jamahir Fi Maᶜrifat Al-Jawahir", *Hamdard Islamicus*, (21) (2) (1988), p. 12.

54 See *India*, Vol. II, p. 246.

55 See al-Biruni, *Kitab al-Jamahir...*, pp. 12–22. Also *al-Quran*, s:22, 27, 126. Cf. S.H.H. Nadvi, "Al-Biruni and His Kitab al-Jamahir fi maᶜrifat al-Jawahir: Ethical Reflections and Moral Philosophy", in *Al-Biruni CommemorativeVolume*, p. 534.

56 A contemporary of al-Biruni who once served in the same Court with him, Ibn Sina, likewise emphasizes the importance of preparing the soul in order for the heart to see the truth for "the Spirit bloweth where it listeth." See also Osman Bakar, "The Question of Methodology in Islamic Science", in *Tawhid And Science*, *op. cit.*, p. 27.

57 See *Kitab al-Jamahir...*, pp. 6–8.

58 See *ibid.*, pp. 8–10.

59 See H. Said & A. Zahid, *Al-Biruni: His Life, Times and Works*, *op. cit.*, p. 95.

60 See *Kitab al-Jamahir...*, pp. 10–12.

61 See *ibid.*

62 See *ibid.*, pp. 24–26.

63 See for example, S.K. Hamarneh, "Notes on Al-Biruni's views of Al-Razi's works", *Al-Biruni Commemorative Volume*, p. 475.

64 See *Kitab al-Jamahir*, pp. 4–6.

BIBLIOGRAPHY

al-Biruni, *al-Athar al-baqiya min al-qurun al-khaliya*. English trans. By Edward Sachau, The Chronology of Ancient Nations. London:MinervaGMBH, 1879

_____*al-Qanun al-Masudi* (Canon Masudicua). Hyderabad: Osmania Oriental Publications Bureau, 1954–1956.

_____*Kitab al-Jamahir fi marifat al-jawahir*. Ed. By F. Krenkow. Hyderabad-Dn: Osmania Oriental Publications Bureau, 1936

_____*Kitab al-Saydanah fi'l –tibb*. Ed. and trans. By hakim Mohammed Said et al. Pakistan: Hamdard Academy, 1973

_____*Kitab al-tafhim li-awa'il sina'at al-tanjim*. Tehran: Jalal huma'l, 1940. English trans. By R. Ramsay Wright, The Book of Instruction in the Art of Astrology. London: Luzac, 1934

_____*Kitab fi ifrad al-maqal fi amr al-zilal*. Hyderabad-Dn: Osmania Oriental Publications Bureau, 1948. Ed. and trans. As The Exhaustive Treatise on Shadows. E.S. Kennedy. Syria: University of Aleppo. 1976.

_____*Kitab fi tahqiq ma li'l Hind*. English trans. By Edward Sachau, Alberuni's India. London: Trubner, 1888.

_____*Tahid nihayat al-amakin li-tashih*. English trans. By Jamil Ali, The Determination of the Coordinates of Cities, al-Beruni's Tahdid al-Amakin. Beirut: American University of Beirut, 1967.

KATHLEEN HANEY

THE ONTOPOIETIC TIMING OF LIFE VERSUS THE KAIRIC UNFOLDING OF THE TRANS-NATURAL DESTINY (A-T. TYMIENIECKA)

1. ANNA-TERESA TYMIENIECKA'S TIME

Life times itself! Life develops itself in temporal sequence albeit not necessarily linear sequence. Living involves forward and seemingly backward movements, illness, loss, destruction, as well as advances in various spheres. Time then is not what clocks and calendars record; time provides the possibility for measuring movements of all sorts, though the measures, as human history shows, are themselves somewhat arbitrary cultural constructions. The logos of, the rational thrust of, finite life intrinsically includes the stages of beginning, middle and ending. Various life forms reveal virtualities in a progression that leads to the human condition, which expresses the fullness of timing in the consciousness of itself as questioning. Its questioning reveals a *telos* that finds its fulfillment in making the stories and fables of historical consciousness. The human condition works out its life as it times its becoming. Tymieniecka's theory of time moves beyond Paul Ricoeur's notion that time is a proto-constitution. Rather, because life times itself, constitution of worlds and others is an opportunity for the creativity that fulfills the promise of the human condition.

Anna-Teresa Tymieniecka's philosophy suggests her precursor, Edmund Husserl, insofar as it too upends the pre-phenomenological conception of time. Time, as calendars and clocks measure it in homogenous units of years, months, days, hours, minutes, second and even nano-seconds, is not itself lived time, according to Husserl's analysis, though measurement of time must be grounded in the time of experience. The time of subjective experience is not homogenous or even very predictable. Experience of time, which seems always to be enclosed within the time of common measurement (yesterday, waiting in dread for the dentist, time seemed to stand still) is more basic than its measurement. Thirty-five minutes felt as if it were two hours. That same evening, the delightful concert rushed by in no time, "sweet sounds

285

A-T. Tymieniecka (ed.),
Timing and Temporality in Islamic Philosophy and Phenomenology of Life, 285–294.
© 2007 *Springer.*

do not cease." We often refer to these two senses of time as subjective or dramatic time and objective or mechanical time. Yet, there was time before clocks or clock-makers, the time which provides a foundation for that which is measurable. For Husserl, "objective" time is founded on the time of the *Lebenswelt.* After all, infants and children grow and change before they recognize what day it is or that the end of night signals a "new day," while the end of nap continues the "same day." Likewise, generations lived and died without a formal measure for time, without naming the day or the year, while they creatively struggled to invent hourglasses, sundials and lunar and solar calendars so that they could share a time, external to them all. Tymieniecka's theory of time is neither that of a perspective of objectivity or subjectivity, though both poles of temporality comprise it. Her analysis of time suits to measure the life that the generations expend, in the growth and decay of each individualizing life as it becomes and ends. Living intrinsically requires processes of timing insofar as the logos of life acts in an individualizing life to gather together a past into its own dispersion for a future. Life, then, contains a temporal structure that human life embraces through enacting it.

The purpose of this examination of Tymieniecka's theory is to awaken insight into her understanding of time within her philosophy of life. In order to achieve an intuitive grasp of her thinking, I shall begin with a description of the privileged, empirical sense of time as it unfolds in Husserl's critique before moving on to the temporality of consciousness and thus to the ways in which life times itself, particularly within the human condition. "Timing" aptly expresses Tymieniecka's understanding of the nature of time as it functions in the processes of living. More basically than in Husserl's thought, Tymieniecka's includes a recognition of the timing that life enacts in finitude, a dimension not to be found in earlier phenomenologies. First, let us open up the problematic of time and the impossibility of responding to the questions of time, as we can conceive of them within the pre-phenomenological attitude.

The modern natural sciences take for granted that time predates its record so that pre-historical time is a commonplace notion, but we do well to wonder what it may refer to. Doesn't time imply history? A sense of time before history reifies time into a kind of spatial thing or at least a space-time matrix, which it is possible for time-machines to travel backwards and forward in. We know the image—the mad scientist and his buddies load into the ship to go back to the 17th century or pre-history etc. Time, then, as a spatial thing, seems somehow independent of living and changing entities whose progress marks time's realization. Classical phenomenology, distressed at taking ordinary presuppositions for granted, provides a means for withholding the contemporary understanding of time (that which can be served up in discrete units) in order to inquire into the subject's experience of the time thus structured. Here we return to experiences of dramatic versus mechanical time. Mechanical time can be the subject's experience only if it is stuffed into experiential time. Without my watch or the dentist's clock, I could not propose that objective time felt differently than the subjective time of my dread. So, experiential time must be more basic than any other experiences of time recorded within it.

Time, for Husserl, as for Kant before him, is the necessary condition for the possibility of perception. He means this, however, not only in the depreciated Kantian sense that the space/time matrix is the *a priori* condition for the possibility of any experiences, but also in the sense that perception in the now involves dimensions of past and future, as well. Perceptual experience of a melody or of a sentence or of everyday objects requires temporality. Such experiences can be grasped as units of intentionality since they protend meanings in a future that validates the relation that these meanings have to prior anticipations that have sunk down into the past without, however, being annihilated. The structure of internal time consciousness, in Husserl's telling, is essential to all perception of objects or subjects since it brings fulfillment and growth to sedimented meanings that consciousness uses to grasp further perceptions. The future may include their modifications and developments insofar as protentions are fulfilled or annulled Time and its necessary function in intentional consciousness make it basic, according to Husserl.

1.1. Time in Tymieniecka's Theory: An Overview

Not so, for Tymieniecka, though I doubt that she would argue that the above account is irrelevant to a full analysis of the workings of transcendental consciousness. Tymieniecka does argue, however, that life is more funda- mental than consciousness of it. After all, for Tymieniecka, it is life that times itself. Internal time consciousness in its incessant flow, is essential for conscious reflection, as Husserl holds, but time consciousness requires life. Without life in its intrinsic intelligibility, its logos, the time of the human condition can have no measure. There may be change, but there cannot be time since there would be no vital experience of change as unfolding in the course of life. The cold and lifeless planets may revolve, but without conscious appreciation of the movement, there is no apprehension of movement or its meaning. This seems to be the end of the story, for Husserl. Yet, for Tymieniecka, the organic alterations in their irreversibility are basic since they exhibit life timing itself from within and manifesting its changes in the world. Not to doubt, change can be stimulated by "external" events, but the meaning that flows into the world from the changes must be filtered through their effects on the "internal" equipoise of the organism and its impetus to continue. Then must we say that trees experience time? Or that the mountains are affected by it? Is this the pathetic fallacy run riot? How about victims of comas? They do not express any appreciation of the passage of time; nevertheless, they age, though interestingly, more slowly than we who encounter the travails of the 21st century world more directly.

Tymieniecka's account of time upsets the analysis that classical phenomenology provides. The life that times itself does so in different registers, depending upon life forms, but carries within itself an intrinsic entelechy that directs it to its *telos*. Yet, the life that times itself includes the expression of the alteration in the world in a fashion that may be shared by other consciousnesses and self-consciousnesses. Regardless of its own registration of events, bios projects itself as temporal as it lives its organic life. "It measures itself, and thus its temporal spread, by its natural constructive advance in the cyclic cosmic order." Tymieniecka writes, "each occurrence in the course of bios' unfolding is significant in various inward/outward radiating directions (*inwardly*: the opening of a flower is a phase preparatory to fruition; *outwardly*: it is the opening of a source of nectar that nourishes bees, wasps, hummingbirds, etc.)"[1]

This temporal structure does not exhaust the meaning of time for the human condition or its description for temporal consciousness. Lived time is not only peculiar to the distortions that one may experience while awaiting the dentist. Dramatic time or "kairos" time involves more than the order of life that is objectively measurable by counting devices or by mere survival. Human life engages not only the chronos of continuous existence; but also human life includes becoming oneself, through difficulties, disappointments, serendipities and strivings. "Life-constructive fulfillments marking ontopoietic progress, and their occurrence within the play of favorable and contrary conditions, are the moments of kairos."[2] Such moments are possible for human life that registers its accomplishments, its strivings and its stories as well as its physiological survival. Human life surely incorporates the logos of life as it struggles to meet the needs of body, but the human condition crowns the logos of life insofar as it provides for transnatural destiny. Human creativity takes and makes its streaming temporal experiences and measures them not only by clocks, but also by goals that are implicit in life lived in the human condition.

The logos of life, the lawfulness of the nature of life lived in the human condition, thrusts the creative imagination of self- conscious life forward onto a path that is already marked out, but invisible until traced through the living of it. This process, though uniquely enacted by each traveler, enacts life's self-individuation, a motive that forces onward the achievements that make the maker. Surely, these processes are temporal and in time, but they cannot account for themselves in the simple fashion that biological life begins, strives and ends. Setting goals and achieving ends is latent in the virtualities of the human condition as the means whereby biological life is transformed into meaning by the creative imagination and its acts. Paradoxically, the interrogative quest to know what life is about motivates the products that concretize possible meanings in accomplishment. And, as Aristotle pointed out, the poesis, the making, makes the maker. So engaged, the maker makes his life, uses his time and recognizes his history. But, what then is time? We thus join with St. Augustine in his plaintive plea.

1.2. Timing in Tymieniecka's Philosophy of Life

At this point, at the limits of what we wonder about when we wonder what time is, we turn to the details of Tymieniecka's account of time. First, we present her depiction of time and secondly its answers to the conundra associated with the typical, hasty, thoughtless evaluation of the phenomenon. Tymieniecka writes, "Life times itself!" Life becomes through the activities whereby it makes itself this and that in reaction to others, to natural disasters and political catastrophes and in its creative activities whereby it extends itself by producing what is not yet and thereby producing its own being in becoming, as human creator. To return to our opening example, the felt time of waiting in the dentist's office can be enfolded within Chronos, but if the visit to the dentist amounted to some kind of production or denouement then Kairos time, or the dramatic time of accomplishment, comes into play, as well. If this is the case however, though chronos or its measures may be an intersubjective agreement of sorts, neither the constitution of time nor the passage of time is identical with the possibilities for its measurement.

All natural life is finite, thus temporal. As individualizing life processes through its stages, it manifests and expresses itself differently. It makes its being in its acts of becoming. Tymieniecka's term, "ontopoiesis," etymologically refers to making being. The forms of life express their own potential for being, but all life "times its advance at each and every one of its steps." The logos of life, manifests itself in "organic, vital, sharing-in-life, gregarious, creative, societal, etc."[3] Only human life participates in all of these stages, manifesting specifically human reality. Human life gathers up or includes sub-human life forms since it necessarily bases itself on its animal life, which concerns itself with eating, sleeping, moving, exploring, reproducing, cooperating, competing, participating, aging and dying. Through such acts, normal animal life times itself through growth and maturation to its end.

Human life is necessarily more complex, since self-consciousness characterizes it. Though higher animals experience heightened sensitivities, consciousness, as self-consciousness, requires the human propensity for the language that can name experience in order to be able to reflect on it and to question its meaning in the context of the meaning of life. Regardless of how base a human life may be, it always reaches beyond the survival of organic and even animal life. Human language ensures that human individualizing life can creatively uncover its full potential through its capacity to synthesis and summarize the past to which it is heir and the future that it can bequeath through fables that present a truth.

None of us alive would suspect that the course of life is linear. We experience life's ebbs and flows, its constructions and destructions, its forward and its retrograde movements. We try to make sense of life. We attempt to discern its meanings. These attempts are developments of the logos of life itself, in its manifestation in the human condition. Even to figure that there is no meaning to life beyond survival is to grapple with the question of the meaning of life, a struggle indigenous to the human condition as well as exclusive to it. According to Tymieniecka, the creativity that characterizes the human mind lifts it above the requirements of living unto the domain of questioning, of seeking after a variety of perspectives on the logos of life and recognizing universally valid responses. Such interrogation and the answers that it yields cannot be simply absorbed into life's flow. They change the direction of the flowing insofar as the course can be determined. The impetus and equipoise of the logos' rhythm must find touchstones so that the forces can achieve a balance and can develop implicit virtualities. Tymieniecka thus provides an account of rising above the lifeworld to measure its timing through space/time coordinates that provide a grid for the construction of the time that we pre- philosophically come to take as time itself. In this way, her analysis provides an explicit motivation for the foundation of homogeneous time on the basis of intersubjective lived time and perhaps the impulse behind water clocks and digital watches, as well. Humans base their practical lives on this founded time, though we usually forget its second order status. Yet, as Tymieniecka points out, such grids (calendars, clocks, measures of distances in light years and so forth) fail to venture beyond their instrumentality into meaningfulness. What am I to do with the years to come? An answer to such a question rests on what I take the purpose of human life, especially my own human life in the fabric of human history, to be.

Though incessant activity that fills the slots on the grid may all too often occupy us, the question of purpose lurks in the background, waiting to lead us back to the history of the logos that others have discovered throughout its evolving course. Specifically human questioning refers us to all of our inherited knowledge as well as to our own creative responses. We move beyond the merely vital into the realm of purpose and freedom. In this way, humans ever more deeply enter into perspectives that can provide vantage points for timing. Soon, we find that we have moved beyond our intellects into what Tymieniecka refers to as the subliminal realm of "our profound yearnings, tendencies, and wishes." We move beyond the merely intelligible that cannot fully satisfy our need to know. To know and to know how to proceed to become ourselves we reach into memory, which Tymieniecka considers as "the crucial modality of the creative timing of the conscious life." The ceaseless flow of human ontopoesis moves out of the processes of acting and knowing and these slip into an irreversible "past,". The living present retains experiences so that they can be of service in recalling kairic "knots of attainment or accomplishment" within an understanding that supplements their present by bringing their (hidden) genesis and (recollected) stages to the foreground again.

Next, the logos of questioning, awakened by the creative imagination turns to making stories or fables about meanings, which result in another plateau for "plotting reality." This phrase of Tymieniecka's suggests both the will and the cognition functioning as indispensable elements in understanding. His-story emerges from reflection on what has been accomplished and what has been known to point us to a prospect which enables us to see into the meaning of the human condition. Questions initiated pragmatically reach forward into various perspectives, "psychological, cultural, rational," which lead into individual "fears, longings, dreams" that enlighten us about the "universal Human Condition."[4]

The universal Human Condition includes more than individual, parochial perspectives. As we advance along the way of the logos of life, we come to recognize that all of life determines its boundaries. Our questions reach out for answers in the evolution of life, in the various cultural constructions of values and techniques and in the traditions of humankind. Consciousness can push beyond vital significance to significance for humanity in the fabrications which have shaped history. Communication of facts and fables passes on bestowed meanings of the worth of the most profound human experiences and realities in their depths. The present amplifies the narrated past as it resonates in its own time. Thus, the tapestry of the past is further embroidered so that hidden images emerge, which reflect the perennial questions that continue to vex the human condition. Thus, the interrogative logos leads us beyond a singular destiny into the history shared (more or less fully) by those who partake of the human condition.

The search for truth and the love of wisdom lead to moving beyond the communication of past events into their re-configuration in present creative imagination. Since flowing life can provide no direction or obvious purpose, we turn for answers to eternal questions in the human condition itself. Present events, feelings, creation and destruction take their places within the shared legacy of the human mode of being so that our new stories reprise the old in the inevitable newness of reenactments. The fruit of these processes is renewed understanding of the past as well as a tempered view of the present in the wisdom that season our fables with the salt that preserves them and spices them. Our gropings for wisdom have been transformed so that, without losing their personal character, they have become suitable flavor for common humanity, despite the tastes peculiar to each culture and epoch.

1.3. Concluding Thoughts

Human history, though set in systems of biological and chronological time, cannot be merely a record of survival. History, as we learned from St. Augustine, ties together the time of life in the nexus of the logos of life. History is the story that a community of others tells itself about what life means until its members move forward beyond the accomplishments that ready them for the love that fulfills them.

The human soul makes use of the time it has lived to forge a fuller understanding of itself as it turns towards others. The soul propels itself unto the temporal horizon since its bios demands its development. The logos of life projects the soul beyond the temporal now to a not yet that it owns itself, but in conjunction with others. The logos of bios has a sequence from its beginnings, but the logos of life includes more and other than biological life. The life of meaning, the life of giving, the life of creating intensifies perhaps even as chronological time ticks off moments towards death, yet the feeling of life grows as it opens to include cherishing and nurturing lives that are not immediately its own.

In the human condition of creation and discovery through accomplishments of productive syntheses or the misses of enlightening disappointments and unavoidable suffering, the logos of life interrogates these phenomena in order to understand and to make sense. In its memories, in its stories, in elucidating itself and its situation, the logos of life advances the sacral logos of transnatural destiny. In time, the creature swims away from biological destiny into its self-realization in a transcendental destiny, which unites earth and sky. The facile illusion of time that the world disposes dispels the ineluctable facticity of life by enabling the logos of life to manifest itself in the growth of meaning and of spirit. The events of history slip away into the historical reckoning of spirit as it accumulates the fruits of its acts into its self-making, which undergo revisions as it fulfills itself in its unfolding of Logos. Husserl's account of the constitution of the inner time consciousness becomes thus a detail in the larger process of self-realization of the core of the person, as it extends outward beyond the confines of biological life alone. Husserl and Tymieniecka both recognize that life is not limited to bios alone, but necessarily strives to complete itself in meanings that extend beyond the temporal into an eternity.

John Paul II makes Tymieniecka's point:

" . . . it is a question here of an interior dimension, which eludes the external criteria of historicity, but which, however, can be considered historical. It is precisely at the basis of all the facts which constitute the history of man—. . .—and thus reveal the depth and very root of his historicity."[5]

The logos of life effects a timing of the individualizing life that locates it within the system of life, as a member of the community of life in its own particular circumstances and virtualities. Without knowing its path or goal, the logos of life leads consciousness to seek for the wisdom that allows each individualizing life to recognize and to realize its nature. The steps along the way in this process are not the minutes and the hours, but the milestones of the journey whereby life makes of its becoming a being, not via a total actualization impossible for finitude, but through its acquisition of understanding of a historical place for itself with the timing of its life. The faculties in play in the human condition include the intellect, the memory, the imagination, the creativity and the freedom of the person who comes to understand its part in the whole, which is as a center that enacts its own vision of the common human condition. Seeking to communicate its version, living out the human condition as an individualizing life, the logos of life drives individualizing life to make the time of its life, through the generations and the stories that engendered it through the fables it leaves as its contribution to the legacy of the human condition.

NOTES

[1] Anna-Teresa Tymieniecka (ed.) *Analecta Husserliana*, Vol. L. 3–22. (The Netherlands: Kluwer Academic Publishers, 1997), p. 9.
[2] *Analecta Husserliana*, Vol. L. 3–22, p. 11.

[3] Anna-Teresa Tymieniecka, *Logos and Life, Book 4: Impetus and Equipoise in the Life-Strategies of Reason, Analecta Husserliana*, Vol. LXX (Dordrecht: Kluwer Academic Publishers, 2000). pp. 660–663.

[4] Anna-Teresa Tymieniecka (ed.) *Analecta Husserliana*, Vol. L. 3–22.

[5] John Paul II, *Theology of the Body*, p. 124.

JAD HATEM

PURE LOVE IN MULLA SADRA

1. THE NEED OF A CRITERIUM

There is no theory of love that doesn't conceive of levels (that are sometimes stages) and of the distribution of grades. When Mullâ Sadrâ determines the signs through which one can recognize the love of God, he does not enumerate all of the possible and imaginable forms it can take. Indeed, he considers that the signs not only include the effects, but also the conditions of validity that must be met by the feeling toward the absolute, not necessarily the absolute of its strength, but that of its quality. That is why among the proofs of the sincerity of the lover's cause "... *shart li-Sidq al-da'wat*", one must count secret-keeping (*kitmân*), martyrdom and the pain of killing for God.[1] As is death in the service of God supposed to lead to Paradise, the Shirâz philosopher conceives of a ladder at the bottom of which the Righteous (*Abrâr*) take pleasure with the houris and the ephebe, and at the top of which the Near Ones, full of disdain for sensual pleasures,[2] associate their beatitude to the divine Presence.[3] The consideration of Hell intervenes in a negative fashion when it comes to evaluating the fear of God: it is the sign of love provided that it is not awaken by the fear of chastisement, it expresses the reverential fear of the Majesty.[4]

Through this criteriology research, Mulla Sadra welcomes a multiple inheritance in which he performs cuts. We hear the persistent echo of Râbi'a Al-Adawiyya, which he received from an attribution to the Imâm Alî of the sentence that says that one should worship God for Himself et not by fear of Hell or desire for Paradise.

According to Rabi'a, the contemplation of the beauty of God is worth more than a paradise. Hence her answer to the question about what her nostalgia of Paradise is like. She answers: "The Resident comes before the Residence" (*Al-jâr qabl al-dâr*),[5] which becomes in Mullâ Sadrâ: "What the Near want from the Residence is its Lord".[6] Remains the fact that where God is, Paradise is.

The system I suggest to follow in order to identify and comment the apparitions of the theme of pure love in Mulla Sadra is a system which organizes, without neglecting its inner tensions, the station of love. The latter

A-T. Tymieniecka (ed.),
Timing and Temporality in Islamic Philosophy and Phenomenology of Life, 295–309.
© 2007 *Springer*.

might not be the supreme one, on the ladder on which it is but a grade, since love implies separation.[7] As a means, love is secondary in regard to the purpose. But for it to be itself a purpose is a hypothesis which is supported by the use of the hyperbolic pure love here and there.

Simple pure love:
1. Exclusive love.
2. Indifference toward Hell and Paradise.
3. The love of the sole glory of God.
4. The interceding for sinners.
   Pure Hyperbolic love:
1. Identification to the loved one.
2. Love of the enemy.
3. Love in spite of damnation.
4. Substitution to the sinners.
5. Self-sacrifice.

Although Mulla Sadra does not obviously support pure hyperbolic love, he has conceived its theoretical possibility in a lapidary sentence that I'm using out of context: "Absolute perfection is realized [or is verified] as soon as the thing is perfect and more than perfect (*fawq al-tamâm*)".[8] Remains the point of knowing whether an excess, be it an excess in love, is a "more than perfection", if it is superfluous, or incongruous.

The outbidding is often called for by the lover's excessive scruple. The extra purity seems to be the sole way to eradicate the last bit of self-love. This will be criticized by the Hanbalites as being excessive, for love perfects itself in not conciliating Law and Nature. It matters to note nevertheless that, though positioned in the pure love scale, exclusive love proceeds from the essence of love as such. As for its deep truth, (although not necessarily in its practice), every love is already excess in the election.

2. MERCY FOR THE DAMNED

When Râbi'a tries to sift love through indifference toward salvation, the movement of her thought doesn't even meet Bistâmî's, since the latter intends to save the damned. This is confirmed by one of the Saint's prayers: "My God, all that is destined to me of this world's possessions, give it to your enemies, and all that is in store for me in Paradise, distribute it among your friends; for you alone are what I seek".[9] It's the same old story, but the context of its revival is original. Râbi'a is giving up the pleasures of Paradise (hence perceived as being physical), since she can get something better. She has no problem giving up all possessions in this world. Fine. But why should they be offered to God's enemies? For the ascetic she is, these are factors of perdition (halâk). It's as if she's applying to her theory this sentence attributed to the Prophet Mohammad: "This world is the believer's prison, and the unbeliever's paradise".[10] Therefore, she is far from thinking of saving the sinners (or infidels): she is getting rid and putting upon them the weight that prevents her soul from rising. This allows me to say that she does not subscribe to any of the hyperbolic forms of love that I enumerated. Nothing that she says defies our understanding.

On this point, Mullâ Sadrâ's position seems more interesting to me, for it is submitted to an internal tension. He tells the story of a man who's full of shame because he thought he loved God deservedly, suitably, which brings him to offer the results of his good deeds to the damned, in order to reduce their sufferings.[11] Although there is no substitution to speak of, nor some decision to empty the Pit from its occupants, this man's communial gesture is part of the goodness one should show to any man. This is confirmed by the shirâzian Master's injunction: "He who loves (ahabba) God must love all things, for all things are his products and his effects. The passionate love ('ishq) of the Cause does not cease to love what depends of the latter, and constitutes Its traces. The love of traces as traces is love of their author". It follows that man is asked to feel compassion for all creatures (khalq).[12] Fine! But then at the same time, the philosopher does not feel he's contradicting himself when he adds that one of the signs of the love one bears for God envelops the necessity of being merciful toward His worshippers and full of hate for His enemies, namely the infidels, the unfair, the decadent and the mean.[13] How can one hate those one should pity? Even if Mullâ Sadrâ doesn't suggest one should follow the example of the man who offered the product of his good deeds to the damned, he does acknowledge him as having a greater love for creatures, and thus for the Creator; the difference should be marked between hatred of evil and those who become its voluntary or involuntary accomplices. Even a soufî like Abù al-'Abbâs ibn Mutâ professed a hatred in God (bughd fî Allâh), meaning a detestation of those the Coran designated to this effect. Fudayl ibn 'Iyâd goes even so far as to imagine that, on Judgment Day, God blames one of his followers for not making an enemy of one of His enemies.[14] This failure in spiritual chivalry might reveal a weakening in God's service and is a call for an inversion of love (which is more than a tearing renunciation) if God's enemy is my friend. It can also originate from a mercy that doesn't dare to be more merciful than the Merciful Himself (like we say of some that they're more kingly than the king). Or they might be more eager to intercede in favor of men than the Prophet Mohammad, who's accused by Shiblî, (the latter is thus blamed by Ibn al-Jawzî of doing so), of interceding for his sole community, whereas he would like to empty Hell of all its occupants.[15]

The true thought of Mullâ Sadrâ is revealed to the light of a displacement in the transcendantal and of the logic of *a fortiori*. He remarks on the fact that some, himself included, are merciful to all God's worshippers, though sinners. Nevertheless, he says that those merciful people are creatures who are submitted to passions. God, on another hand, declared that He Himself was the most merciful of merciful. It follows then that he could not condemn the guilty to eternal punishment, especially since God is not injured by transgressions, nor is he privileged by obedience, and men are in all things determined by Him.[16] It is debatable as to know if in this remarkable page Mullâ Sadrâ's good dispositions concern all kinds of enemies, for only those sinners who are God's worshippers as well are mentioned, in conformity with stories of Mohammad's intercessions for his Community, where are freed from infernal slavery men of little merit, or those whose only deed in existence was to acknowledge that there's no other god then God.[17] This excludes the idolatrous and the atheists, which is confirmed by his interpretation of a sentence attributed to Jesus that rules on the difference between both divine Names *Rahmân* (which applies to this world) and *Rahîm,* (which applies to the next world). Mullâ Sadrâ explains: the first Name is even exerted in favor of the unbelievers and the mean, whereas the second is exerted only in favor of the believers.[18] Let us notice though that Mullâ Sadrâ considers afterwards, following in that Ibn 'Arabî and Qaysarî, that everyone worships God.[19] He even goes as far as to profess, basing himself on the theory of universal eros, that there is no being that doesn't pray.[20] Mercy is exerted on pagans in a subtle way, for, as long as they've worshipped God Himself in the form of idols, they please God who transmutes their torture into pleasure.[21] Unless he contradicts most verses of the *Koran,*[22] Mullâ Sadrâ does not pull them out of the Gehenna. He's content enough to modify their nature, so that these men created for Hell enjoy their stay there as much as they would in their homeland, and would only suffer from being excluded from it![23]

Another possible attenuation of the matter: the philosopher considers that men who think this way have been modeled by God after the attribute of mercy ("*mimman jabalahun Allâh 'alâ al-rahmat*"), which makes us suppose that others are not that worried about the sinners' salvation. Some could even pass for anti-merciful.[24] A statistic enquiry could support this restriction. But it would suffice that the merciful quality holds true for some: this transcendantal ability that supports it would then be held as universal. The theology of creation confirms this, as it holds Man as such as originating from mercy rather than from prepotency. The theology of eschaton supports this as well, since it teaches, through Ibn-'Arabî's voice[25], that God's Mercy precedes His Anger[26], or wins over it[27]. The first is substantial to God, while the second remains accidental, even though both still envelop all beings.[28] Pure love that is love of the Essence and which doesn't exclude any attribute, changes colors as soon as it is modified into love of the enemy, to the point that pure love prefers henceforth to consider that certain Names of God prevail upon others (their servitors), although they're in fact all identical.[29] In reality, the attribute of Mercy is identified with Existence, which *is* Mercy enveloping all quiddities, amongst which that of Anger.[30] The antecedent is not chronological, it belongs to ontology. As the Andalusian Master puts it: "Any existent (*mawjûd*) is subjected to mercy (*marhûm*)".[31] By divine grace, he is borne to existence in his distinctive qualities. Isn't he saved by the power of an identical grace? But doesn't the prime act of salvation consist, for him, of passing from the state of being subjected to mercy to that of being merciful, as wishes Ibn 'Arabî? But then, more so in the sense of the love of the enemy than that of the approval of the beloved's being.

If one is restrained to the trenscendantal dimension (in criticist meaning of the word), while putting aside the theologal (and Mullâ Sadrâ doesn't), the *a fortiori* argument (God must even more so show mercy to the damned, which doesn't necessarily mean forgiveness) implies the passage to the hyperbolic which is disposed to suspend or to reinterpret the torments, and implies a summon to Him, Who is more than Man, of not being less capable of mercy than the latter (on the transcendantal level), for some do show pity (empirical level). Of course, the theologal doesn't identify itself with this emphasis that makes of Man the model of God. This is why he cuts short: "And God is the most merciful of merciful (*arham al-râhimîn*) as He Himself said it of Himself".[32] Nevertheless, Mullâ Sadrâ attacks elsewhere those who believe that God, being God, won't exert any punishment. The reason for doing so is not only to prevent the risk of anomism (absence of laws). The reason is that torment emanates from the nature of the guilty itself![33] All things return to God,[34] and are included those that were created from attributes of Vengeance and Power. Punishment is only another name for divine Indulgence.[35] The inscription at the entrance of Dante's hell becomes the Sadrian's hell as well.

3. THE DAMNED LOVE

Love of the enemy, however crucial, especially for reason itself, remains accessible to Man when the enemy is Man. What is there to say or to do if the enemy is God? Can one love whoever throws you in tribulation? Wouldn't be then to love against all reason, and not only the healthiest one?

This is nevertheless, says Mullâ Sadrâ, the perfect occasion to identify the authentic lovers from the hypocrites, for love and trial are twins.[36] However, by separation and rebuff I don't mean the pains or dryness that God inflicts or gratifies with his lovers as purifications. These are included, but also surpassed by the insurmountable ordeal of the hopeless abandonment to which corresponds the conviction that the obstacles in the way of the union are not of a transitory nature, and that an impassable barrier is erected by the Beloved. Majnoun is safe from hope through his mad imaginary appropriation. Damnation offers a superior degree in maximalism.

It convenes here to put away any use of the metaphor, as one can suspect it in Isfarâyânî who says a magnificent verse:

"If Hell offers us union (wasl) with you, Then we are ashamed of all the inhabitants of Paradise".[37]

Indeed, if the sentence is taken literally, the idea falls on a logical contradiction, for how can union occur with He Who addresses the individual such a definitive word of reprobation? If the contradiction can be diminished and become a paradox, it would be in benefit of a return to the theme of purification. And if the idea is grounded on the Majnounian experience of union in spite of the absence, we are sent to the modality of a union in the immanence of the lover, offering to the pure hyperbolic love its affective base, in the sense of its condition of possibility as love, in the clarity of the heart. Then we'd say: there is no union but in separation, and no beatitude but in Hell. To remain in joy, Majnoun must repudiate Laylâ, for he can only be the beloved in intimacy.

The typical represent of the second figure of the pure hyperbolic love can only be a real damned. I mean Iblîs, as Hallâj has conceived his spirit and drama. It seems risky to classify the Iblîsian attestation of absolute monotheism in pure love, since it's tinted with insubordination. In reality, Iblîs only rebels against the Creator of Man who should be honored. Ghazâli denounces as being an incongruity[38] the fact that pure love could be asserted in rebellion, if it is true, as teaches it Muhâsibî, that obedience is the sign of love (and not only its result).

However, rebellion is truly in the manner of an emphasis of jealousy. For as irrational as it can be, it is still full of meaning, though it spoils the good relationship to the Beloved, Who deserves adoration and respect. I'm neglecting the other suspicion that comes to mind, that of imputing hypocrisy. Ghazâlî is more subtle in that he accuses Iblîs of deceiving himself in believing that he loves God.[39] Hallâj, that exceptional man who could be satisfied with the sole idea of pure love, doesn't follow up with either hypothesis, for he has spotted a rejected love that remains firm in a seemingly absurd faithfulness, only because it was able to become as clear as crystal in the heart of the rock.

To the Faithful of pure love that are encountered by Sarî al-Saqatî during an ecstasy, and whom God dissociates from all his worshippers who worship Him for some other reason than Himself, the Beloved says: "Between me and you exist a torment out of my torments, that none could bear". _ "O our Prince! O our Lord, You must inflict it". – "Could you bear what I have described to you?" – Aren't you He Who projects the torment on us? – Indeed!-This is enough to satisfy us".[40] Refinement has reached here its extreme, which implies no sadism nor masochism, for God doesn't enjoy inflicting pain, nor do the faithful of pure love enjoy suffering from it. But if God wants it, whatever the reasons, madness, perversion, justice for unknown motives, game, then, let it be! Mullâ Sadrâ remembers this, in his own way, when he specifies that torment inflicted to the Gnostic who's thrown in Hell for ethical mistakes is at once painful and sweet (*'adhb*), for the promiscuity with the Executioner is offered. His torment allows him hence to contemplate God (*al-haqq*), which is for him extreme beatitude.[41] For the Gnostic, Hell is a Paradise of which the modality of being is the divine Majesty.

But to think still of pure love as immolation (which leads the central thesis of pure love to its most radical consequence), that is due to the imponderable fact that a tiny part of self-love is preserved in the continuous practice of hyperbolic pure love if to love the Lovable rejoices the soul (without having to make the category of pleasure intervene, nor even the consideration that the reign of the beloved depends on the lover's bondage, whose gain is hence guaranteed).[42] And, in a more radical manner, if the simple fact of loving rejoices the soul, if love is union. The idea is powerfully undertaken in the sentence Hallâj reserves to Iblîs: "*al-hubb wâjid*", which involves a pun: love allows to find, and it leads to ecstasy.[43] Hallâj is not saying anything different when he proclaims, on his own account, that "the sun of the hearts never sets".[44] But if the *wajd* is the indissociable attribute of love, isn't there a risk of having a speck of interest penetrate the superlative of the very pure?

Hence the following declaration by a lover, transmitted by Mullâ Sadrâ: "Love is the way, and the sight of the beloved is Paradise, and separation is the fire, *God's fire, fanned, which rises to the hearts*".[45] The text doesn't intend to banally say that the infernal condition is of separation. He considers rather that remoteness throws the lover in an extreme pain. Although the Koranic quotation context (104:7) – that I put in italics – is Hell that is promised to the calumniators, our sentence sees in the fire that spreads in the heart the influx of an affliction of love. To make the idea more concrete, I'd say that the Hell of the love passionate (already distinguished from the other by Mullâ Sadrâ in the same page), could be what the common people call Paradise, this garden of delights – hadn't God offered Himself to be seen. And from this same verse Ja'far ibn Muhammad opposes two fires, one that rises in the lover's heart, and one that burns the unfaithful.[46] This theory of two fires should not be confused with another that Mullâ Sadrâ got to know from Ibn 'Arabî, and that distinguishes in the Place of torment a fire that lacerates the flesh of the decadent, from an imaginary fire that is printed in the heart of the hypocrites and the pagans, although the Persian philosopher happens to superpose them sometimes.[47]

4. THE DESIRE TO DIE

We owe Mullâ Sadrâ the introduction in philosophical thought the theme of the desire to die as a criteria of love's sincerity. I privilege first the notion of sincerity (which is only a sub-category in the classification of pure love), since it is a departure point to the Shirâzian Master's thought who comments this fragment of the verse: "... wish for death if you are sincere" (Koran 62:6).[48] The accent is put on the conjunction. The question is to know if one truly loves God. Death on another hand is one of the causes of the junction (*waslat*). The wish for passing away toward God is hence a sign (*'alâmat*) of the friendship (*walâyat*) we bear for Him, in other words, of the true love (*al-mahabbat al-haqîqiyyat*). Holding on to life would be equivalent to being attached to earthly possessions, or to people. Mullâ Sadrâ holds that "love of any thing that is not God is a ramification of self-love". A powerful sentence that, if it skips love of the enemy, (unless we still see in the enemy humanity, and, thus, oneself), allows to integrate the *jihâd* (a term that, it seems to me, should be taken here in its martial sense), to which self-love is an obstacle. This integral purification that is accomplished by the walk in love bears, for Mullâ Sadrâ, a tensional value that determines the stages of elevation. A verse by Hallâj summarizes all his intention:

"Kill me, my friends, in my killing is my life!".[49]

Mullâ Sadrâ doesn't reveal the name of the author, as it is often the case when he quotes verses. It is not because of a prejudice against this victim of the orthodoxy that he shuts his name, (since he doesn't mind otherwise attacking orthodoxy in the pages here analyzed) and he does mention it elsewhere, in good terms.

If the verse summarizes well the philosopher's intention, it doesn't mean that the intention of the great martyr corresponds to his. For Mullâ Sadrâ, death offers, through liberation from the physical world, an access to a way of superior realization, at the end of which the junction could be hoped for. For Hallâj on the other hand, it's crucial love itself that accomplishes, here and now, through the dislocation of flesh, what the love through identification has succeeded in spirit and in truth. But truth itself demands of man the verification. Crucial love doesn't differ hence from love through identification when it comes to essence, but only when it comes to form. In other words: *I am whom I love* or *I am the Truth* have risen to the unsurpassable point. It is only up to the Cross to authenticate the extinction. In the tension between Being and love, insofar as Being designates the conatus and its narcissist variations, and insofar as love implies the heterocentrism of whom brings nothing to himself, the overcoming of one by the other is dealt with in the intimacy of the decision. But how will the lover know (and *a fortiori* the others) that the accomplishment has occurred? Madness and utterance inaugurate the visibility that is demanded by every authentication. And both passages, be it from the possible to the real, and from the essence to the phenomenon lead to quartering. Elevation toward the Golgotha is a process of manifestation. The hypothesis which is noted by Jîlâni[50] and according to which Hallâj dared to utter his *I am God* for the sole reason of provoking his own death is not a pertinent one, though it has the merit of linking both events.

5. UNION OF THE INTELLECT AND THE INTELLIGIBLE

Mullâ Sadrâ mentions the sentence of loving expulsion (*ilayki 'annî*) in the context of his interpretation of burning desire (*'ishq*) understood as an exaggerated will for the union (*ittihâd*). "Majnoun al-'Amirî was sometimes so immersed in burning desire that, upon his beloved's arrival and call: "O Majnoun! I am Laylâ", he did not look at her and he told her: "By my passion for you, I'm better off without you (*lî 'ankî ghinâ*)".[51] Although he doesn't quote the identification sentence (*anâ Laylâ*), the Shîrâz philosopher implies it. I carefully distinguished them. It is nevertheless obvious that one could be linked to the other for one could think that it is only where the lover is the beloved that he has no more need of his physical presence, and a fortiori of sharing beds with her. In opposition, as soon as he discovers himself to be a lover through his love, and not (or not any more) through the physical person, the beloved's image itself can progressively fade away in the proclamation of identity. Mullâ Sadrâ will precisely interpret the latter as a union to the image of the beloved. A proof that both sentences are combined: he quotes, and rightly so, verses by a poet he does not name, Hallâj, following closely the *I am Laylâ*: *I am whom I love and whom I love is myself.*[52] Mullâ Sadrâ, who doesn't ignore that this poem is by Hallâj,[53] interprets it elsewhere as an effect of deification (which is investment with divine qualities,[54] in conformity with the definition given by Junayd of *mahâbbat*).[55] For the moment, it all goes as if, like Sarrâj, he only saw in it a profane poem.

Mullâ Sadrâ objects to any union between individuals conceived as a corporal mix. To be consequent with himself, he links the *'ishq* to the psychic, not to the physical. Operation of the spirit, the union that is brought by burning desire is explained as a junction of the rational soul (*'âqilat*) with the form (*sûrat*) of the Intellect in action, and the union of the feeler with the form of the felt,[56] without which there's no possible intrasubstantial movement. Nothing indicates that he understands the Majnounian sentence, or even Hallâj's poem, in a divine sense. He could have done so, since he supports, according to a tradition he's surely inherited from Tûsî explaining Ibn Cinnâ, that there are two kinds of human love, the true and the metaphorical. But we have no right to operate the translation, not only because he does not himself do so, but mainly because it would weaken his intention instead of strengthening it. It is important that a man is able to say *I am whom I love* and still make sense even if but a woman is concerned. By saying so, he has intellected the form of the beloved (it is not, hence, the essence of the other that becomes his) and he has received the influx of the Intellect agent itself, from the world of the Imperative.[57] Science dematerializes its object as soon as it identifies in it an intellective existence. Upon being intellected, Laylâ becomes, from a physical thing, a spiritual reality, and is perceived in the Intellect agent. It is hence useless to allegorize the sentence. There's no profane meaning next to or underneath a sacred meaning. Each intellective operation achieves union, for intellect is the things it intellects. It becomes the intellected forms, which means that it changes itself. It can increase its intellections, until it unites with the Intellect agent itself. If it is right to mention a transport, it is not from profane to sacred, but from singular to general. The loving passion brings the daily matter to language, it allows to have an intuition of the fact that the soul becomes what it intellects.

What prevented Ibn Sînâ from admitting the thesis is that he couldn't see how substance could modify itself. With his theory of intrasubstantial movement, Mullâ Sadrâ made possible the fact that an evolution implies the access to superior (or inferior) modalities of the being, more so, hence, than faculties that are increased or diminished. Knowledge doesn't add up to existence, it *is* existence as such, in a way that one intellection doesn't abolish the one that precedes it (which usually occurs in the case of accidents of the substance). Being is growth, with the exception of the divine being. There is indeed here a determined theory of deification that authorizes us to say that the mystic is God, meaning that he has freed himself through divine grace from the slavery of the corporal soul and of human attributes.[58]

"I have embarked on the sea and the ship is broken": this sentence by Hallâj isn't tragic at all for Mullâ Sadrâ, since it expresses a turn in the personal evolution.[59] What perishes in man is only what is not God, in a way that man becomes eternal through God's eternity.[60] And as the lover's substance becomes complex from all it intellects, Laylâ doesn't end up being identified to a singular form,[61] but to the greatest number of intelligible things, if not to all.[62] The latter are constitutive of the Intellect agent, which is origin and end of the beings, but that, aside from its own existence, possesses an existence *in* and *for* the soul as being its perfection.[63]

Although our author professes unity of the knower and the known in regard to sensation as well,[64] the junction of the intellect and the intelligible is of a superior dignity, and the passage from one to the other, which is precisely the Majnounian moment, is here to confirm that the soul becomes receptive for the imaginative form, while the latter becomes matter for the intelligible form.[65] This is because the soul is potentially intellect, since the substance modifies itself at the rhythm of its ascension.[66] Gradually, it passes from a vegetative state (that of a fetus), to the imaginative, to the practical intellect, to the intellect in act (case of the Gnostics and the Faithful), to the Spirit of holiness (reserved to God's friends).[67] It doesn't gain attributes, it perfects its substance. To each truth correspond intensities in existence. It suffices hence to perfect existence in order to achieve the essence.

The truth of the Majnounian attestation holds, according to Mullâ Sadrâ, to the acknowledgement that the desired essential form is not this exterior accidental form.[68] Far from being released by the process of abstraction, the perceived form emanates from the soul itself,[69] to the point that Majnoun substitutes to the notion of the exterior form expressing the beloved's being, the idea according to which this form, which couldn't occur to him, (or mix with his spirit), must correspond with what is his, that is the beloved's form as he configures her.

A Sadrian treatment of the Majnounian configuration could be continued against the backdrop of the spiritual theologal union to God[70] and of the doctrine of the oneness of existence, which allows to identify in Laylâ an intensive expression of the being, as in Majnoun himself actually. That's how God has two faces, at once beloved by all creatures and all creatures' lover ('âshiq), since they are his effects.[71] Among the traits the Gnostic describes, some derive from the Majnounian constellation (like wilderness, taken in a simply ethical sense, and madness), without the need, henceforth, to name Laylâ's lover.[72]

In this light, Hallâj's poem allows Mullâ Sadrâ to subscribe to a known register. He illustrates extinction as identification: the butterfly burnt by the candle has become fire. Mystical translation: the soul illuminated by God's light, coupled with the world of lordship, is covered with God's attributes, to the point that seeing it is seeing God.[73] It is to say that the mystic is exhausted only as much as he is transsubstantiating through the Lordly Spirit.[74] Isn't it right then to involve our philosopher in a rehabilitation of the *shath,* if we only take notice of the word's etymology, which is *movement*?[75] What is, indeed, the intrasubstantial movement if not a transgression of the limits by identification to that which one is not? The veiled is uncovered in proportion to the power of change. More exactly, the unveiling is change itself. The becoming intellect in act of the soul has to necessarily go through the conversion of the human self that's cuddled on itself so that it entirely turns itself toward the Real (*al-haqq*). And Mullâ Sadrâ quotes Hallâj's verse (with Qaysarî's variations):

> Between me and You, there is an "it's me" that fights me. Remove hence
> By Your subtle [work] my "it's me" from the interval" (D, P. 90).

As this same verse serves him to illustrate extinction, it is possible for us to superpose the mystical *fanâ'* to the philosophical becoming intellect in act. Among all definitions of mystical love, Junayd's (where are co-implied the acts of casting off one's own qualities and to endorse the Beloved's) seems to fit best his thought, if one admits that the theory of intrasubstantial movement does circumscribe its core. Against those who see in the state of union an illusion due to sole promiscuity, Mullâ Sadrâ thinks about a real junction that is neither fusion nor inhabitation in the Christian sense.[76]

The Sadrian interpretation of *Anâ al-Haqq* renounces to simply fall into line with *Anâ Laylâ,* for the sentence is taken in its strong meaning of identification to the divine essence (and not only to the Intellect agent). The philosopher subscribes rather to a well defined context, that of the miscomprehension by Hallâj of the event of which he is a subject. He's kind enough to qualify his error as *Kufr al-qalb,* in other words, a heresy due to love.[77] He actually imagines that Hallâj repented from his error, by renouncing at the literal content of his paradoxes.[78] Christians haven't recovered from this error as they misunderstood the "christic soul".[79]

Of course, the polished[80] heart reflects "God's light and the beauty of oneness", but it should not lead us to think that God's image (*Sûrat*) remains (*hallat*) in (*fî*) the mirror of human self. It only manifested itself to it (*lahâ*).[81]

CONCLUSION

The Unification of God in the rule of exclusive love.

Mullâ Sadrâ characterizes pure love as absolute adoration, freed from self-preoccupation that is imprisonment in oneself, for he situates the idea in a theological context and not only a psychological one. Indeed, the tenants of pure love worship God because He deserves to be worshipped, and not because of such or such attribute, like Mercy, Benevolence or Vengeance (through which Paradise or Hell are assigned). No preference should be granted to an attribute over the other. Indeed, the worshipper of Mercy isn't that of Vengeance. Pure love transcends hence these preferences and adores the divine Essence only. It envelops hence love of all the attributes, to the point that to love truly leads to love *equally* the humiliations and pains inflicted by the Beloved, for "all the Beloved does is loved". The philosopher quotes then the verse 81 of the *Great Tâ'iyya* with an interesting variation:

"If the lovers are charmed by some of your beauties, everything in you charms me".[82]

Ibn al-Fârid had written *nussâk* (anchorites), not *'ushshâq*. Must we see in the philosopher's choice a generalisation?

Saint-Joseph University, Beirut

NOTES

[1]   Mulla Sadra, *Kasr Asnâm Al-Jâhiliyyat*, Tehran, 1962, pp. 71, 65.
[2]   Based on the *Coran* 52:16—24.
[3]   *Kasr Asnâm Al-Jâhiliyyat*, p. 69.
[4]   *Ibid.*, pp. 69—70.
[5]   Muhammad Bahâ' al dîn al-'Amilî, *Al-Kashkûl*, Cairo, 1228h, p. 134.
[6]   Mulla Sadra, *Kasr Asnam Al-Jahiliyyat*, p. 69. One should note that our author distinguishes two kinds of paradise, a sensible one, and an intellectual one (*Tafsîr al-Qur'ân al-karîm*, Beirut, Dâr al-Ta'âruf, 1998–1999, VII, p. 24).
[7]   See on the subject Ibn al-'Arif, *Mahâsin al-majâlis*, Paris, Geuthner, 1933, p. 97.
[8]   *Tafsîr al-Qur'ân al-karîm*, VII, p. 346.
[9]   Quoted by Jîlânî in his *Sirr al-asrâr*, Ms BO 1618, p. 37v: "My share in this world, give it to the infidels, and my share of reward, reserve it to the believers, for all I want from this world is the sole mention of You, and as sole reward I want the sight of you ".
[10]   Bayhâqi, *Anthology of renunciation*, Lagrasse, Verdier, 1995, p. 99 ; cf. pp. 126–127.
[11]   *Kasr Asnâm al-Jâhilyyat*, p. 72.
[12]   *Ibid.*, p. 67. It is legitimate to wonder if the Sadrian theory of resurrection of all creatures does not secretely proceed from this universal compassion.
[13]   *Kasr asnâm al-Jâhiliyyat*, p. 67.

[14] Both quotations in Jâmî, *Nafahât al-uns*, Cairo, n.d., pp. 61–62. Cf. Muslim, *Al-Sahih*, Beirut, n.d.,VIII, pp. 40—41.

[15] *Talbîs Iblîs*, **Beirut, Dâr al-Nadwat, 1994,** p. 347.

[16] *Tafsîr al-Qur'ân al-karîm*, II, p. 237.

[17] *Tafsîr*, IV, pp. 351—353.

[18] *Tafsîr Sûrat al-Tawhîd*, in *Majmû'at rasâ'il falsafî Sadr al-Muta'allihîn*, Teheran, 1420h, p. 415.

[19] Glosses on Sohravardi, *Le Livre de la Sagesse Orientale*, tr. H. Corbin, Lagrasse, Verdier, 1986, p. 531. He explains how in *Al-Shawâhid al-Rubûbiyyat*, Mashhad, 1966, p. 144 (cf. p. 316).

[20] *Tafsîr*, VII, p. 389.

[21]   *Tafsîr*, II, p. 242. Same ambivalence (soft pain) for the gnostics who were guilty of reprehensible acts (*Al-Hikmat al-muta'âliyat fî al-asfâr al-'aqliyyat al-arba'at*, Qom, 1378h, 1958–1959, IX, pp. 360–361).

[22] With the exception of 11 :107 that makes God free of cancelling the terrible verdict.

[23] *Tafsîr*, II, p. 237.

[24] See *Tafsîr*, II, p. 309.

[25] See The Verb of Zachariyya in the *Fusûs*, a chapter that is indicated by our author.

[26] Cf. *Tafsîr*, II, p. 237 ; VII, p. 89.

[27] Cf. *Tafsîr*, IV, p. 350.

[28] *Tafsîr*, I, p. 203. Cf. *Koran* 7 :156.

[29] *Sharh Usûl al-Kâfî*, III, *Kitâb al-tawhîd*, Teheran, 1370h, p. 248.

[30] *Ibid.*, p. 249.

[31] *Fusûs al-hikam*, Cairo, 1946, p. 178.

[32] *Tafsîr*, II, p. 237. Cf. *Koran* 12:64, 92 ; 21 :83.

[33] *Tafsîr*, VIII, p. 236.

[34] *Asfâr*, IX, pp. 278–279, 347.

[35] Cf. *Asfâr*, IX, p. 353.

[36] *Tafsîr*, IV, p. 96.

[37] *Le Révélateur des mystères*, tr. H. Landolt, Lagrasse, Verdier, 1986, p. 143.

[38] *Ihyâ'*, IV, p. 331.

[39]   *Ihyâ'*, IV, p. 318.

[40] Quoted by Rûzbehân, *L'ennuagement du cœur*, p. 232.

[41] *Asfâr*, IX, pp. 360–361.

[42] Cf. the gloss 31 on the *Kitâb-e 'Abhar al-'âchiqîn* (p. 157), from an anonymous commentator.

[43] Hallâj, *Dîwân*, edited, translated and annotated by Louis Massignon, Paris, Geuthner, 1955, p. 50.

[44] *Ibid.*, p. 45.

[45] *Tafsîr*, V, p. 394.

[46] In Sulamî, *Haqâ'iq al-tafsîr*, **Beirut, Dâr al-Kutub al-'ilmiyyat, 2001,** II, p. 240.

[47] Cf. *Tafsîr*, III, pp. 186–187.

[48]   *Tafsîr*, VII, pp. 180–186.

[49] *Tafsîr*, VII, p. 186. Hallâj, *Dîwân*, edited, translated and annotated by Louis Massignon, Paris, Geuthner, 1955, p. 33.

[50] *Dîwân*, Cairo, Akhbâr al-yawm, 1990, p. 273.

[51] *Asfâr*, p. 178.

[52] *Ibid.*, p. 178.

[53] Cf. *Mafâtîh al-ghayb*, Beirut, Al-Irshâd, 1999, p. 321.

[54] *Mafâtîh al-ghayb*, p. 557.

[55] " Substitution of the lover's qualities with the Beloved's " (Al-Risâlat al-qushayriyyat, p, 321).

[56] Asfâr, VII, p. 177.

[57] The intellect agent corresponds to the holy Spirit (or of holyness) in the terms of the Revelation (Asfâr, VII, p. 23).

[58] Tafsîr, V, pp. 398–399.

[59] Mafâtîh al-ghayb, p. 628. See, Ibid., p. 637. The Asfâr (IX, p. 238) which resume the body-ship metaphor declare that death is good since it is natural.

[60] Cf. Tafsîr, VI, p. 11.

[61] Mullâ Sadrâ knows from Ibn 'Arabî that are focused on Laylâ rays of love that are in fact addressed to God (Glosses on Sohravardi, Le Livre de la Sagesse orientale, p. 531).

[62] " The human soul is capable of knowing all the realities of the universe and to unite with them intellectually " (Mullâ Sadrâ, Risâlat ittihâd al-âqil wa-l-ma'qûl, in Majmû'at rasâ'il falsafî Sadr al-muta'allihîn, Teheran, 1420h, p. 98). In fact, the active intelligence in us is all the beings (Asfâr, III, p. 326).

[63] Asfâr, IX, p. 140 (See also Al-Shawâhid al-Rubûbiyyat, Mashhad, 1966, p. 245). The difference between both states is a matter of point of view.

[64] Asfâr, III, p. 316.

[65] Asfâr, III, p. 331.

[66] Asfâr, III, p. 366.

[67] Asfâr, IX, p. 97; Kitâb al Mashâ'ir, Paris-Teheran, 1964, p. 62.

[68] Asfâr, VII, p. 177.

[69] Asfâr, VIII, pp. 179–180.

[70] Cf. Al-Mabda' wa-l-ma'âd, Beirut, Dâr al-Hâdî, 2000, p. 342.

[71] Cf. Mafâtîh al-ghayb, p. 347.

[72] Cf. Asfâr, VII, p. 189.

[73] Tafsîr, IV, p. 204.

[74] Tafsîr, VII, p. 205.

[75] Cf. Sarrâj, Luma', p. 453.

[76] Sohravardi, Le livre de la Sagesse orientale, p. 636.

[77] Mafâtîh al-ghayb, p. 251.

[78] Ibid., p. 542.

[79] Ibid., p. 542.

[80] "Tasfiyat al-mir'ât", which is the necessary step, though negative (Mafâtîh al-ghayb, p. 548 ; Tafsîr, VII, p. 97). But the veiling can be due to superior causes (Ibid., pp. 580–581).

[81] He could also write in her (fîhâ) without modifying the meaning. (Cf. Tafsîr, VI, p. 266).

[82] Mullâ Sadrâ, Iqâz al-nâ'imîn, Téhéran, 1361h, pp. 67–68.

SECTION V

ROBERT J. DOBIE

١ ذأ١

THE PHENOMENOLOGY OF *WUJUD* IN THE
THOUGHT OF IBN AL-'ARABI

The concept of *wujud* or "existence" stands at the center of Ibn 'Arabi's thought with his most immediate successors attempting to capture the essence of his thought with the formula, *wahdat al-wujud*, or "the unity of existence."[1] But like most translations from Arabic, the word "existence" only gives us a flat and abstract idea of what Ibn 'Arabi means by *wujud*. *Wujud* means "existence" or "being" only derivatively and in its passive sense: originally and actively it means, "to find," "to hit upon," "meet with," "get" or "obtain," "to invent" or "to find (good or bad)." In other variations of pattern upon the basic root, which makes the meaning of every Arabic word so rich and polyvalent, *wajada* can mean, "to produce, originate, create or bring about," or it can mean, "to be passionately in love with" or "to grieve for," or, yet again, "to turn up," "appear," "be there." I submit that if we look at all of these different but related meanings of the root *wajada* we have before us in the thought of Ibn 'Arabi and in the Arabic language itself a phenomenological understanding the "matter" or *Sache* of Being and time. "To be" is "to be found" or "to turn up," "to be there" or, in other words, "to appear" or "to presence" out of the flow of temporality. As such truth is the self-disclosure of Being out of the flow of created temporality that evokes or should evoke a human response of appropriation or, as Heidegger puts it, of *er-eignis* – of "en-owning." For, by doing so, the human subject finds his or her true ground in the divine Essence, in which lies his or her "secret of destiny" (*qadr*).

I

To explore the phenomenological nature of Ibn 'Arabi's thought, I shall look at the thought of the later Heidegger and, in particular, the relatively late lecture, *On Time and Being*. This is because I find Heidegger's thinking, of those in the phenomenological tradition, closest in content and spirit to Ibn 'Arabi's. In his lecture, Heidegger attempts to think yet again the relationship between Being and time some thirty-five years after *Being and Time*. For

313

A-T. Tymieniecka (ed.),
Timing and Temporality in Islamic Philosophy and Phenomenology of Life, 313–322.
© 2007 *Springer.*

him, the great puzzle that he did not adequately address in his great work is the idiom, when we talk about what is there in the world, that "there is" Being or time or, as the idiom is in German, "it gives (*es gibt*)" Being or time. Being or time "is," and yet Being or time is no-thing; it is not an entity like other entities. As Heidegger puts it:

> Being is not a thing, thus nothing temporal, and yet it is determined by time as presence. Time is not a thing, thus nothing which is, and yet it remains constant in its passing away without being something temporal like the beings in time. Being and time determine each other reciprocally, but in such a manner that neither can the former – Being – be addressed as something temporal nor can the latter – time – be addressed as a being.[2]

Time determines Being as a "presencing" or "making present" to the "being-there" or *da-sein* of human existing; Being determines time insofar as without the coming-to-presence of being, there would be no time. Thus, for Heidegger, what we need to think is not "Being" or "time" insofar as they are things or entities, but we need to think their presencing: the "there is" or "It gives" of time and Being.

Heidegger argues that the German form of the idiom, "there is," – "It gives" or *es gibt* – is the most pregnant with possibilities for understanding the relationship of time and Being. We must think not the being that is given nor even the "being" or "entity" that is presumed to give being but the giving of Being itself: "To think Being explicitly requires us to relinquish Being as the ground of beings in favor of the giving which prevails concealed in unconcealment, that is, in favor of the It gives."[3] But it is Heidegger's contention that the Western philosophical tradition has forgotten and ignored the "it gives" in favor of that which is given: "At the beginning of Being's unconcealment, Being, *einai, eon* is thought, but not the 'It gives', 'there is'. Instead, Parmenides says *ein gar einai*, 'For Being is'."[4] According to Heidegger, then, the temporality of Being has been forgotten; the primal giving or presencing of being has been obscured in favor of what is given in the "present" as such. It follows that the primal nature of truth as *aletheia* or "unconcealment" or "bringing-to- presence" has been forgotten.

Heidegger argues that this is the historical destiny of a particular "epochal sending" of Being that has its origins in the Greeks. If to think the "It gives" of Being is the more primordial thinking of Being, then the primordial meaning of Being is always conditioned by temporality: a sending and simultaneous withdrawal of the "It gives": "The history of Being means the destiny of Being in whose sendings both the sending and the It which sends forth hold back with their self- manifestation. To hold back is, in Greek, *epoche*. Hence we speak of the epochs of the destiny of Being."[5] Since this original sending of Being that is the root of every "epoch" of Being's understanding is gradually forgotten and obscured, it is the task of thought to think back into the original sending of our epoch so as to be open to a new sending of Being.

But this opening given in thought is also essential to the sending of Being. Heidegger argues. "There is no time without man."[6] "There is" no Being without the "being-there" of human *Dasein*. This is not to say that time or Being is a "creation" of human beings; quite to the contrary, human beings are constituted as such by time and Being. But nevertheless, there can be no giving of Being or time without the space that human *Dasein* opens up: "Presence means: the constant abiding that approaches man, reaches him, is extended to him."[7] Thus, while Being and time are nothing human, "there is Being" and "there is time" only insofar as there is human *Dasein*. As such, the understanding of Being is through and through historical and thought is an opening of space for a new sending and understanding of Being: "The giving in 'It gives Being' proved to be a sending and a destiny of presence in its epochal transmutations."[8]

Thus, Heidegger asserts that if we are to think this giving of Being in its primordial sense, we must think it in the sense of *Ereignis*, which can mean "event," "appropriation" or "en-owning." Here, in the German word, we have entwined a temporal sense – that of "event" – and an existential sense – that of the "appropriation" or "making one's own" of Being. These two senses are connected for Heidegger, because to make Being "one's own" is to think back to the original "event" or "It gives" of Being:

In the sending of the destiny of Being, in the extending of time, there becomes manifest a dedication, a delivering over into what is their own, namely of Being as presence and of time as the realm of the open. What determines both, time and Being, in their own, that is, in their belonging together, we shall call: *Ereignis*, the event of Appropriation. *Ereignis* will be translated as Appropriation or event of Appropriation. One should bear in mind, however, that "event" is not simply an occurrence, but that which makes any occurrence possible. What this word names can be thought now only in the light of what becomes manifest in our looking ahead toward Being and toward time as destiny and as extending, to which time and Being belong.[9]

Being thought primordially is not a thing or a being, but it is an "event" in which the "It gives" of Being is appropriated in time; which is to say, it is appropriated in human *Dasein*. Indeed, it is this appropriation that constitutes the "It gives" as such and human *Dasein* as such: as Heidegger says, it is not the human being that appropriates, but it is "Appropriation that appropriates" or *Das Ereignis ereignet*. And with this expression, Heidegger asserts the essential temporality of Being and its understanding.

II

As was mentioned at the beginning of this paper, the Arabic root *wajada* from which comes the word, *wujud*, "being" or "existence," has precisely many of the phenomenological connotations that Heidegger sees in the originary understanding of Being. And Ibn 'Arabi is particularly adept at bringing out many of these. Perhaps most pertinently, Ibn 'Arabi sees *wujud* or existence as constituted by the play of Manifestation and Nonmanifestation: on the one hand all things manifest Being by virtue of the fact that they are "found" in the world by us; but by the same token, Being itself remains hidden in all of these manifestations, because Being as such does not manifest itself in any particular manifestation. This is because all manifest things are limited, possible beings, whose essence does not imply their existence; their "what-ness" does not include their existence or being found. Only in God is what-ness the same as existence. Thus, insofar as creatures are "found" in the world, they manifest God *qua* existent; but they conceal God *qua* being each a particular "what." Thus, as Ibn 'Arabi says, "God is identical with the existence of the things, but He is not identical with the things."[10] God both reveals and conceals Himself in things at the same time or, to put it in a way that is closer to the Arabic, God is both found and not found in creatures. This dialectic is demanded by the very nature of *wujud* itself as that which reveals itself as something found but conceals itself behind the variety of forms in which it manifests itself.

As limitations upon existence, finite created forms have no positive existence; these forms are not existent in themselves. For Ibn 'Arabi creatures really have no being or existence of their own; they are utterly "poor" with respect to God, Who is rich in Himself. All the existence that is found in a creature does not come from the creature nor is it possessed by the creature in any way; its existence comes in and through God alone. Or, to put it in another way, the creature is just the "locus or manifestation" or the "there" of Being:

> God says to the thing, "Be!" He does not address or command any but that which hears, yet it has no existence ... It receives coming to be. But our view of its reception of coming to be is only the fact that it becomes a locus of manifestation for the Real. This is the meaning of His words, "[Be!] And it is." This does not mean that the thing "acquires existence" (*istifadat al-wujud*). It only acquires the property of being a locus of manifestation ... Hence He is identical to all things in manifestation, but He is not identical to them in their essences. On the contrary, He is He, and the things are the things.[11]

The creature "is" only insofar as the creature's form is the "place" of the manifestation of the divine Being. But it is no more.

The Being of creatures, therefore, is not a quality of the creatures themselves. Creatures cannot exist in and of themselves for even one moment. They must, then, be created anew every moment. What at first glance looks like a static and stable world is really, according to Ibn 'Arabi, a world in a constant state of flux: at every moment, every creature is being created, which is to say, receiving existence, anew. Two passages from the Qur'an that Ibn 'Arabi likes to quote in relation to this insight are, "No indeed, but they are in confusion as to a new creation (*khalq jadid*)" (50:15) and "Each day He is upon some task (*sha'n*)" (55:29). Thus, as Ibn 'Arabi explains:

> God has decreed for each thing a term in a given affair which it reaches. Then the thing passes to another state in which it also runs to a stated term. And God creates perpetually at each instant (*ma' a'lanfas*). So among the things, some remain for the length of the moment of their existence and reach their term in the second moment of the time of their existence. This is the smallest duration (*madda*) in the cosmos. God does this so that the entities will be poor and needy toward God at each instant. For if they were to remain [in existence] for two moments or more, they would be qualified by independence (*ghina*) from God in that duration.[12]

Neither the being nor the time of any creature is in or out of itself but from God, the Real in Itself. When we say "there is" a being or "there is" a time, what we mean is that there is the constant giving of being every instant and that this giving is identical with the divine activity. It is of the nature of the creature to receive its being at every instant of its duration and it is of the nature of God to give being every instant. Thus, neither being nor time are entities or accidents of entities, but rather the entities are the loci of their manifestation.

The giving of Being is constant and unstinting. The differentiation of beings that we perceive in creation is due not to the character of Being Itself, but due to the preparedness of the various possible creatures to receive that Being. In themselves, creatures are nothing but mere possibilities within the divine existence. Nevertheless, once they are actualized by the divine existence, they inflect that existence only to the degree that their essence or what-ness is able to receive and reflect it. Thus, Ibn 'Arabi compares God's Being to the Sun that spreads its rays over all existent things and does not stint anything its light and warmth. Nevertheless, each thing receives that light and warmth differently, such that it blackens the face of the washerman, while it whitens the clothing that he is washing. In the same way, God gives Being to all things in every instant and for their appointed time, but the degree to which they reflect that Being and for how long depends on their preparedness to receive that Being so that some creatures receive Being more fully than others.

The preparedness of creatures to receive the unstinting flow of divine Being takes on particular importance for the human creature, insofar as the human being's preparedness is not determined by his or her essence but by his or her openness to the gift of divine Being. This is because the human essence is a microcosm that contains virtually and potentially within itself all other essences. In the first two chapters of his *Bezels of Wisdom*, for example, Ibn 'Arabi compares the human being to a mirror that reflects unified within himself the entire cosmos and, hence, the divine Essence. The human being, alone among creatures, has no fixed essence but is open to existence as such. In this way, the human being is superior even to the angels:

> The angels do not enjoy the comprehensiveness of Adam and comprehend only those Divine Names peculiar to them, by which they glorify and sanctify the Reality, nor are they aware that God has Names of which they know nothing and by which they cannot glorify Him, nor are they able to sanctify Him with the [complete] sanctification of Adam.[13]

And, Ibn 'Arabi continues, "Adam enshrines divine Names the angels have no part in ..."[14] As al- Qaysari remarks, Adam receives all degrees of being without himself being a degree. This is why Adam represents (or *is*) the Universal Spirit.[15] Only Adam (not the angels) worships God with all His names.[16] In this sense, then, the human being in his essence mirrors the totality and absoluteness of the divine essence.[17] As such, the human being, alone again among creatures, is capable of receiving God's self-disclosure of Himself as such or of covering it over completely in forgetfulness and evil acts. The human being, therefore, truly exists only to the degree that he or she reflects the divine Essence. And this happens only to the degree that the mirror of his or her intellect is polished smooth by a detachment from all created things and an abiding in existence as such, God. Only then can God "find Himself" in the heart of the gnostic; for it is not the gnostic who ultimately knows God but rather it is God who knows Himself in and through the gnostic. For "none knows God but God."[18]

This faculty by which, according to Ibn 'Arabi, the human being becomes open to the gift of divine Being is through the heart (*qalb*) which corresponds roughly to the medieval scholastics' *intellectus*.[19] The "heart" is not, of course, the bodily organ of that name but a higher faculty of the intellect that is distinct from discursive reason or *'aql*. Reason is the discriminative faculty: it divides things into categories and knows by separating off one quality or essence from another. But the heart is that faculty that looks past division and classifications: its root, *qalaba*, means to "turn over," "rotate," etc.; it is thus that faculty that conforms the soul to the constant turnings-over and rotations of beings in their ever-new manifestations of God. It is that faculty that appropriates the ever-new givings of Being in creatures, looking past the entities to the giving of Being itself and to the giving of the time of beings itself. As William Chittick puts it: "... reason knows through delimitation and binding, while the heart knows through letting go of all restrictions."[20] As such, the heart knows the eternity of the divine Being not through abstraction – the process whereby it separates out the "standing now" from the past and future – but through a complete appropriation through letting go of the ever repeating self-disclosures of God. In this way, the heart becomes united with God by constantly shedding His finite manifestations and by encompassing Him, for as the hadith *qudsi* says, "My heavens and My earth embrace Me not, but the heart of My believing servant does embrace Me." This is why, as Ibn 'Arabi asserts at the beginning of his *Bezels of Wisdom*, that the self-disclosure of God could not take place without the human heart; for it is in the perfected human heart, or *al-insan al-kamil*, that God is reflected back upon Himself and therefore brings both Himself and humanity to full self-consciousness.

But because of the power of reason, the human being is trapped in dualism. He cannot but think of himself and all other creatures as other than God, as separate from God. He cannot help but think of God as a "thing" or "entity" over and against creation. And, to a certain degree, this is necessary, for otherwise, as Ibn 'Arabi notes, the creature would be annihilated and there would be no gift of existence and no self-disclosure of God:

> One of the mysteries of knowledge of God lies in the interrelationship between the God and the divine thrall, or the Lord and the vassal. If God did not undertake to preserve the thrall and the vassal constantly, they would immediately be annihilated, since nothing would preserve them and keep them in subsistence. Were He to become veiled from the cosmos in the Unseen, the cosmos would become naught. Hence the name "Manifest" exercises its properties forever in existence, while the name "Nonmanifest" exercises its properties in knowledge and gnosis. Through the name Manifest He makes the cosmos subsist, and through the name Nonmanifest we come to know Him.[21]

In order for the human being to think existence in the play of its manifestation and nonmanifestation, there must be a separation – a space or "locus of manifestation" – between Being in Itself, God, and the human being. In other words, God cannot be known as such, i.e., God apart from all reference to anything other than God, without first being known as Lord, viz., as first being among beings. To think of God as Lord of creation is, therefore, a necessary presupposition for the authentic thinking of *wujud* in both its manifestation and nonmanifestation; but at the same time, to think of God as "Lord" – as a being distinct from creation – must also be overcome because such thinking limits the Reality or *al-Haqq* to a distinct and limited mode of being. What is necessary is a sort of thinking, that Ibn 'Arabi calls *gnosis* or *ma'arifa*, that is able to think the manifest and non-manifest together, to think the concealment in the unconcealment and the giving of existence in the given of the existent. If creatures are to exist, God must become manifest and "found" (*mawjud*) in them as their *wujud*. But at the same time, God cannot become manifest or "found" in any particular thing; God is also the Unseen or Nonmanifest that is essential to manifestation. Through the nonmanifest in the manifest, the human intellect is moved beyond appearances to their true being in God. As such, we come to know God as God only through what is nonmanifest in manifestation.

But, most of all, we have the play of manifestation and nonmanifestation, of unconcealment and concealment, in the very act of knowing by the human subject: God is found in the human subject insofar as the human being is a microcosm, a mirror of the divine Essence Itself. But, at the same time, insofar as the human subject sees him or herself as an "I" separate from the divine Essence, God is not found but concealed behind the "I." Only to the degree that the gnostic is able to strip away the created "I" and see him or herself only as a manifestation or "theophany"[22] of God will the gnostic come to know his own "secret of destiny" or *qadr*, which is nothing but the gnostic's own archetype in the divine Essence. For by finding his own "secret of destiny" does the gnostic see himself as God sees him and only then does he exist in such a way that his existence is his own for it is now seen *sub speciei aeternitatis*. The gnostic him or herself becomes a locus of divine manifestation, but, unlike other creatures, in a whole and complete way. Thus, the "destiny" of the gnostic is not so much a fixed "pattern" as it is a fixed and providential "event" in the history of the divine self-manifestation.

III

We have seen in what ways Ibn 'Arabi's understanding of Being and time is thoroughly phenomenological: in order to understand Being or the Real, we cannot enclose It in a science that confines It in categories. Rather, in order to understand Being, the human intellect must let Being show itself in the loci of its manifestations and, most importantly, in that locus of manifestation which is him or herself. It must let beings come to presence in time. Thus, if the intellect is to know – which is tantamount to saying, to unite with – Being or the Real, it must be open to the appropriation of Being. And this appropriation can only come through the heart: reason abstracts from the giving of being and thus separates the knower from what is known while the heart, in conforming itself to the play of divine manifestations, actually comes to move "behind" the manifestation so as to embrace God's concealment in his unconcealment and, hence, to embrace God Himself. The heart enters into

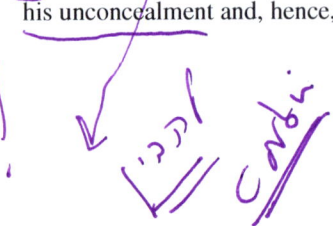

the divine Being as such and appropriates it for one's own. Thus we have, I submit, a real convergence between Ibn 'Arabi and a phenomenological understanding of being like one that we find in Heidegger.

But they converge without really meeting. I do not think it is too much of an oversimplification to say that Heidegger's thought is an inversion of Plato: whereas for Plato time is an image of eternity, for Heidegger, eternity is an image of time or, to be more exact, the erection of eternity as an ideal is an inauthentic attempt to "freeze" time and thus lift the human subject out of the flow of life and its essential temporality. Ibn 'Arabi, by contrast, is essentially a Platonist: authentic existence is in God whose essence is also His existence. We exist authentically only to the degree that we are not prisoners of our time but, through the heart, embrace God's eternity which is not an abstract "now" that is "frozen" in a particular form, concept or manifestation but the fullness of time that realizes itself in a constant and dynamic flow of manifestations. For there cannot be existence without the fullness of existence nor can there be any self-disclosure of Being in general without a hermeneutical key to that self-disclosure – the Holy Qur'an. For, according to Ibn 'Arabi. God's self-disclosure in creatures cannot be understood as such without His direct and particular self-disclosure in Scripture. And here we have a gap that cannot be reconciled.

Robert J. Dobie La Salle University

NOTES

[1] As Claude Addas makes clear, this term is not Ibn 'Arabi's but that of one his closest and most important followers, al-Qunawi. See: Claude Addas, *The Quest for the Red Sulphur: The Life of Ibn 'Arabi* trans. Peter Kingsley (Cambridge: The Islamic Texts Society, 1993), 232. That the term was not Ibn 'Arabi's does not mean, of course, that al-Qunawi was necessarily unfaithful to the deepest meaning of his master's teaching.

[2] Heidegger, Martin. *On Time and Being* translated by Joan Stambaugh. (Chicago: University of Chicago Press, 1972), 3.

[3] *On Time and Being*, 6.

[4] *On Time and Being*, 8.

[5] *On Time and Being*, 9.

[6] *On Time and Being*, 16.

[7] *On Time and Being*, 12.

[8] *On Time and Being*, 17.

[9] *On Time and Being*, 19.

[10] This citation as well as all others in this essay are from Ibn 'Arabi's "Meccan Revelations" (*Al-Futuhat al-makkiyya*) as translated in: William C., Chittick, *The Sufi Path of Knowledge: Ibn Arabi's Metaphysics of Imagination* (Albany, NY: State University of New York Press, 1989), 89.

11   *The Sufi Path*, 90.

12   *The Sufi Path*, 98.

13   *The Bezels of Wisdom* trans. Ralph Austin (Mahwah, NJ: Paulist Press, 1980), 52.

14   *Bezels*, 52.

15   Daud Al-Qaysari, *Sharh Fusus al-hikam* 2 vols. (Dar al-'Itisam: Qom, no date), I 156. For al-Qaysari, what the angels do represent are the ruling spirits of the world in the same way that the faculties of the rational soul are ruling spirits of the body. Thus we have here a correspondence between macrocosm and microcosm. Nevertheless, the human being represents the unifying "soul" of the world and, as such, is higher than the angels. See: Al-Qaysari, I 167.

16   Al-Qaysari, I 183.

17   " . . . the human self, in its primordial universal condition, is a point of vision which possesses 'no essential characteristic other than totality and absoluteness'. Its very nature is to mirror the totality and absoluteness of the Unity of Being. This *is* the human potential. If this potential is to be realized by the individual it requires an approach to reality which involves the whole of oneself, so that the polishing of the mirror of the heart can take place and the heart can become devoid of 'wrong beliefs' about the nature of the Real." Peter Coates, *Ibn 'Arabi and Modern Thought* (Oxford : Anqa Publishing, 2002), 167.

18   *The Sufi Path*, 153.

19   One usually sees the Arabic term *'aql* translated as "the intellect," but I think that this is misleading. As we explain in the text, *'aql* more properly corresponds to what the scholastics called *ratio* or "reason," the calculative and discriminative faculty of the human soul. By contrast, *intellectus* refers to the unitative intuition or insight into the first principles of all things. Or, to put it another way, whereas *ratio* is analytical, breaking things down into their constituent parts, *intellectus* is synthetic, grasping all the parts in their unity.

20   *The Sufi Path*, 159.

21   *The Sufi Path*, 89.

22   "The authentic mystic wisdom (*ma'rifa*) is that of the soul which knows *itself* as a theophany, an individual form in which are epiphanized the divine Attributes which it would be unable to know if it did not discover and apprehend them in itself." Henvi Corbin, *Alone with the Alone: Creative Imagination in the Sufism of Ibn 'Arabi* (Princeton, NJ: Princeton University Press, 1969), 132–33.

MICHEL DION

"IBN KHALDÛN'S CONCEPT OF HISTORY AND THE QUR'ANIC NOTIONS OF ECONOMIC JUSTICE AND TEMPORALITY"

Before Ibn Khaldûn (1332–1406) began to write the Muqadimmah,[1] he worked on Averroes' works (1126–1198). During that period of his intellectual life, he was forging his "philosophical mind". From 1377 to 1400, Khaldûn wrote his "History of the World". The Muqadimmah was then considered as the Introduction of the "History" he had in mind. What Khaldûn has done is to discuss his general theories on historical development within the Introduction (Muqadimmah) of his "History of the World". Because he was politically involved throughout his life, he was sensitive to the way means were required to reach given ends. Indeed, he believed, like Machiavelli[2](1469–1527) after him, that all means to reach an end are justified insofar as they are required to reach that end. In the Muqadimmah, Khaldûn tried to present the basic principles of historical development and the way true historians should authentically reconstruct the past events.

In this paper, we will analyze Khaldûn's concept of history and thus the way historical development can be explained. We will also see to what extent the Qur'anic concept of economic justice is revealing deep concerns for temporality as such. Insofar as historical development is the result of the flow of time, and thus of earthly temporality, we can analyze how we relate such temporality to given human behaviours. We choose here to express the basic link between (earthly) temporality/(divine) eternity, on one hand, and economic justice on the other hand.

1. IBN KHALDÛN'S WAY TO ANALYZE SOCIAL ORGANIZATION AND SOCIAL LIFE

According to Khaldûn, civilizations appear when human beings, impregnated by God's power, cooperate with each other and jointly create forms of social organization. Indeed, civilizations cannot grow without such cooperative acts.

323

A-T. Tymieniecka (ed.),
Timing and Temporality in Islamic Philosophy and Phenomenology of Life, 323–340.
© 2007 Springer.

The more people cooperate one with each other, the more their civilization is growing. Cooperation is indeed a way to avoid extremes. As said Khaldûn, in the case of human qualities, the extremes are reprehensible, while the middle road is praiseworthy (p. 385). Khaldûn's concept of history presupposes that the human world ultimately depends on man. Indeed, for him, there is no social group without the involvement of its individual members. History is impregnated by human activities, whose common orientation is the self-preservation.

Khaldûn is quite concerned with the deep feeling of belongingness to a given social group and/or family. He said that such a feeling is basically natural, and is experienced when our relatives, friends or neighbours are unjustly treated, or harmed or killed. This is the natural meaning of the group feeling, according to Khaldûn. This group feeling is considered as exerting a very positive influence on social cohesion itself (p. 374–376, 379–383). The objective of group feeling is ultimately self-defence (p. 374). Every group feeling exercises its own authority and superiority over the people and families that adhere to it (p. 381). The group feeling is sometimes so low or weak that it makes impossible for that group to impose its own authority. Indeed, such a group is then subjected to another group (whose group feeling is stronger) (p. 382).

In this paper, I will present Ibn Khaldûn's concept of history. Insofar as historical development of social groups and institutions arises within temporal (worldly) existence, we will analyze how temporality in the worldly life is conveyed in the Qur'anic concept of economic justice.

2. KHALDÛN'S CONCEPT OF HISTORY

Khaldûn's concept of history cannot be isolated from the idea of a divine destiny and divine nature. According to Khaldûn, there is a "book of destiny" in which God has fixed the final term (death's day) of everybody (p. 4). The final term of every thing is decided by God (Surat XXXI.21).God is seen as the Living One who will never die (p. 4), the Creator of the Universe we should all worship (p. 33). God creates whatever He wants (Surat III.42). God has the knowledge of everything, the full knowledge (p. 65) (Surat XII.76). God is the Knowing One (Surat XV.86; XXXVI.81). God could increase our knowledge (Surat XX.113). God is our refuge from human desire for power and from misfortune (p. 33). God gives guidance and help (p. 65). He gives success and support (p. 68, 85). God guides with His Light whomever he wants guide (Surat XXIV.35). At the begging of Creation, there was nothing but Allah (Sahih Bukhari, vol. 4, book 54, no 414). The division of a year in twelve months (out of which there are four sacred months) is reflecting the original division of time when Allah created the Heavens and the Earths (Sahih Bukhari, volume 4, book, 54, no 419). The Prophet Muhammad is presented as a pre-existing being: he existed before the arising of time and space, not corporeally but rather spiritually (p. 4).

2.1. The Nature of History

According to Khaldûn, history is information about political events, dynasties and events of the past. Such information is "elegantly presented and spiced with proverbs". The inner meaning of history involved two basic dimensions or viewpoints: (1) speculation and the attempt to get at the truth (philosophical viewpoint) (2) a subtle explanation of the causes and origins of things and social, economic and political phenomena, a deep knowledge of how and why given events are arising : history makes possible to better know the conditions explaining the arising of given events or organizations (the "early conditions"), and the principles through which such events or organisations are led (the "subsequent history") (p. 10, 13). Social organization actually reveals the cooperative nature of human beings. There is a natural (human) trend towards co-operation (p. 79, 84). Human being cannot live without social organization and cooperation concerning the way to get their necessities of life (p. 380). Laws are nothing but means to preserve civilization (p. 80). History is information about social organizations and thus deals with conditions affecting civilizations such as "group feeling" and the various ways by which some social groups became superiors over others (p. 71). Khaldûn said that historians must deeply know the differences among nations and periods with regard to ways of life, customs, and basic social institutions. History refers to events that are specific to some social groups or historical periods (p. 63). Historians must know the origins and conditions through which given groups are born and their basic influence on social and historical development. They must reflect the historical facts such social groups were confronted to and the history of such leaders' groups (p. 56). It is the only way to deeply understand the origin of every historical event. History makes us more aware of the conditions in which given nations reflected their "national character" in the past. History thus implies to get in touch with various sources of historical information and thus to have a deeper and varied knowledge (p. 15).

History is rooted in philosophy, since it implies the (speculative) knowledge of the nature of things. It is not only a field that makes us possible to better know the evolution of societies and the events given societies faced or are facing. It is also a branch of philosophy. In searching for truth, history is a philosophical venture. It implies that we will never deny the authority of truth and that the way speculation is be developed will avoid any kind of falsehood (p. 6–7, 16). History is then also a speculative science that will make possible for historians to reach the truth itself and to avoid the basic errors of historical research (p. 15). The truth often lies behind the historical information (p. 46). To actually reach the truth, historians must have a clear knowledge of the principles of action that follow from customs. They must deeply know the political facts and the nature of the civilization they are working on. They must deepen their knowledge of the conditions that have determined the arising of given social organizations. Historians must also compare their materials inherited from past authors with contemporary materials (p. 15–16). They must consider the similarities or differences (and their causes) between the present and the past conditions (p. 56). Any comparison is not safe from error. Historians often apply their knowledge of the present to the historical information and measure the historical information by what they can observe in their own present situation. This is a basic error historians must absolutely avoid (p. 58). Untruth afflicts historical information, said Khaldûn. According to Khaldûn, this is due to the partisanship (and prejudices) for opinions and schools. Historian should be impartial in receiving historical information. Only in that way can they assess the truth or untruth of such historical information. The lack of impartiality will guarantee that falsehoods will be socially accepted and transmitted (p. 71).

Khaldûn said that there is another factor for the appearance of untruth in historical research: the reliance upon transmitters (p. 71–72). Moreover, in some cases, transmitters (of historical data) are not really aware of the purpose of a given historical event. The transmitter can attribute to the information a significance that is overestimated or underestimated, thus resulting in falsehood. Very often, the assumption that a given event or phenomenon is true is not rightly founded; it is often due to the reliance upon transmitters. It is also possible to ignore how conditions (for the arising of a given event or phenomenon) actually conform to the reality itself. The transmitter can neglect to consider some conditions or overestimate some other conditions. Indeed, Khaldûn said that personality criticism makes possible to assess the probity and exactness of the transmitters (p. 76). On the other hand, people usually approach high-ranking persons with praise, so that they will spread their fame. We pay too great attention to this worldly life so that the status and wealth persons have can be decisive for the way we will interpret their role in given historical events or phenomena. But Khaldûn insisted that there will be untruth in historical information because of the ignorance of the nature of the conditions arising in civilizations. Knowing the nature of events and the circumstances for their appearance will make possible to distinguish truth from untruth in investigating and criticizing the historical information (p. 72–73).

According to Khaldûn, the past deeply resembles the future (p. 17). If the future would resemble the past, it would mean that the past is the reference pattern, so that any future event can be "compared" to past events or phenomena. It would mean that every future event is a somewhat repetition of the past. The repetition of the past would then become the basic principle of historical research. But Khaldûn explicitly said the opposite. If the past resembles the future, then the future is the reference pattern, so that any past event cannot be understood without being compared to future events or phenomena. It means that the past cannot be grasped without the light of future. Future is the best way to grasp the essence of the past. The final result of such a strange assertion is that the past is unknowable in itself. The basic principle of historical research is then the overwhelming power of future.

2.2. Errors Committed by Historians

Khaldûn described in details four (4) main errors historians should never commit if they want to safeguard the objectivity/reliability of their field of research:

1. *1st error: blind trust in tradition*: critical insight is always required in order to reveal the hidden truth (p. 7). Civilization actually conveys various elements to which historical information could be related. We must always safeguard our critical insight towards imaginary or genuine aspects of given historical events. Historians must criticize the way historical information were found and/or expressed in various kinds of official documents. Khaldûn said there is a very common desire for sensationalism, so that people tend to overestimate (or underestimate) some figures or data, in order to improve their own situation or to reinforce their self-esteem (p. 19–20, 371). The exercise of self-criticism is also very important for historians, said Khaldûn. It implies to analyze our own errors and intentions, to check to what extent we report historical events with fairness and to continuously search for more precise historical information. If historians fail to do that and then are quite attracted by sensationalism, they could lead others away from God's path (Surat 31.6). Khaldûn is also very concerned with the way historical information has been transmitted. Given historical information could be suspect if the way it has been transmitted is not sound (p. 25). God is the guide to the truth, to reliable historical information. (Surat XXXIII.4) (p. 21, 25, 55). Khaldûn is concerned to get rid of storytellers' fictions (silly stories or fictitious fables)(p. 23, 27–28,

38–39). Khaldûn qualified such people as "envious talebearers" (p. 38). He said that those stories should be analyzed as to their plausibility, that is, its compatibility with sound sources. If they are implausible, they should be rejected (p. 28). According to Khaldûn, factual proofs and circumstantial evidence are required to test the plausibility of given tales and stories (p. 41). There is a difference between what is known and what is guess. Khaldûn admitted that all guesses are equally probable. Moreover, there is a difference between what is absolutely certain and what is considered as possibly true (p. 52). Common sense should be used to distinguish between the possible and the impossible. A possibility is inherent in the matter that belongs to a given thing: for instance, the size, the strength and other characteristics of a given thing makes some conclusions possible and other impossible about the data we got from the evolution of that thing. Everything that is possible should be accepted and everything that is considered as impossible should be rejected (p. 371–372). According to Khaldûn, to establish the truth of given historical information, we should consider its conformity; with general conditions. Is it possible that given facts have happened? So, external evidence is required to go beyond the personality criticism (criticism of the way transmitters interpret the data). In order to distinguish truth from untruth conveyed in historical information, we should distinguish: (1) the conditions that are closely linked to the essence of civilization, (2) the conditions that are accidental to civilisation; (3) the conditions that cannot be related to civilization (p. 77).

2. *2nd error: disregarding the changes in conditions and in the customs of nations and social groups that happened throughout their historical evolution*: historians must never consider some historical forms without deepening their substance. They must rather analyze what make them genuine and what is conditioning them from an external viewpoint. Historical information can never be presented without deeply know the origins of the events themselves. In that sense, historians cannot only repeat what earlier historians have said. Historians must take into account the (cultural) changes in the way given historical materials are considered, particularly changes in social customs. Historians must take for granted that such changes are methodologically important. Such changes constitute the basis for every critical insight historians must be able of (p. 8–9). According to Khaldûn, conditions in which nations and social groups are evolving actually change with historical periods (p. 56). The whole world and it constituencies (the nations and social groups, the social institutions, families and individuals; rural and urban areas) do not persist in the same form throughout human history (p. 57). Changes in social

institutions and cultural (societal) customs are due to the decisions of the ruler, the customs emphasized by the ruler (p. 58). Khaldûn said that when political leaders refer to the customs of their predecessors and neglect the customs of their own nation or social group they belong to, they can create a discrepancy between the customs of the new ruling class and the customs of the old social group or nation (p. 58). The final result is a distinct set of customs and social institutions (p. 58). When there is a general change of conditions within a given society, a new world is then born (p. 65).

3. *3rd error: making a too brief presentation of history*: historians should never be satisfied by some fragmentary historical information. They should rather deepen their knowledge of the various elements of the events, peoples, leaders and nations that constitute the core of a given historical period (p. 10). Only the knowledge of the nature of civilization makes possible to have a critical investigation of such civilizations. A deep knowledge of the nature of a given civilization is the only way to investigate historical information critically and thus to distinguish truth and untruth conveyed in such information (p. 76).

4. *4th error: taking into consideration some silly or fictitious (implausible) information*: Khaldûn said that the storytellers who invented idle, silly or fictitious tales were generally characterized by a deep search for forbidden pleasures and the desire to smear others' reputation. It is a way for them to justify their own blind search for pleasure in mirroring the fact that people in the past behave in the same manner (p. 27–41, 47, 75).

3. TEMPORALITY AND THE WORLDLY LIFE: THE QU'RANIC CONCEPT OF ECONOMIC JUSTICE

In the Islamic society, the production of necessities of life has the priority over that of luxuries. Necessities of life must then be in sufficient quantity before there could be any real demand for luxuries (luxuries being those goods that are beyond the average standards of consumption in a given society).[3] The Islamic Economic system tries to safeguard the common good in the long-run, rather than in a short-term perspective.[4] So, temporality of worldly life is thus focusing on long-term scale. Common good is seen as closely linked to a long flow of human time.

The Islamic economic system presupposes that every economic activity is a way to worship God as the Ultimate owner of the Universe (Surat VI.165; VII.157) and the opportunity to help the poor and the needy (Surat CVII.3–7). Social and economic justice implies that we give to others what is actually due to them (Surat IV.37). According to Siddiqi (1988), Islamic economy is promoting a pattern of quest for wealth that actually must fulfill spiritual needs and moral ends.[5] According to Haneef (1995), Naqvi does not assume that there is an "Islamic man". Naqvi rather asserted that human being only has egoistic motives, so that State intervention is required to avoid social injustice. However, Naqvi does not mention the possibility for the Islamic state to take unjust decisions, because Islamic economy is ruled over by ethical concerns, including the best ways to get rid of poverty (zakah, sadaqah, riba). So, Naqvi adopted the framework of philosophical egoism when he considered human nature, while keeping an idealistic political view of the Islamic state. Taleghani (1982) adopted a similar concept of State as the Guardian of public welfare and social justice, so that the Islamic State must be involved in all economic sectors. To Taleghani, equity means an equitable distribution of wealth.[6]

As said Naqvi et al. (1984): 14–15), an Islamic economy is dominated by ethical concerns, mainly the best ways to favour the poor and the needy.[7] According to Haneef (1995), it reflects an emphasis on social justice that Naqvi interprets as implying egalitarianism. On the other hand, the Qu'ran acknowledges that economic differences follow from various talents God has given to human beings (Surat VI.165; XVI.71; XVII.30; XLII.12). As said Haneef, Islamic economy limits the size of private property to what is socially required (for the common good) and broadens ownership to the whole society (Siddiqi, 1986: 156).[8] Siddiqi believed that the Qu'ran and the Sunnah of the Prophet have provided principles to be applied in the economic life, but that they way such principles will be applied can vary, depending on cultures and circumstances. It is a way to recognize that temporality actually influences the way se understand basic sacred texts. However, there are specific behaviours following from the implementation of Islamic principles. Indeed, it makes Islamic economy quite unique as such.[9] So, Siddiqi is acknowledging the principle of cultural relativism, but only in a very specific meaning. It does not imply that truth will be defined differently in various countries, but rather that there will be different cultural patterns to actualize Qu'ranic principles of economic justice. As said Kahf (1989: 75–76), Islamic economy actually promotes moral values such as social justice and personal honesty, cooperation and equality.[10] Briefly, while Siddiqi and Kahf are open to a lower degree of State intervention (like it was the case in Adam Smith's works), Naqi and Taleghani supported the view of a higher level of State intervention in all sectors.

We will discuss here the concept of economic justice as it is conveyed in the Qu'ran. The concept involves three basic issues as it is discussed in the

Qu'ran : (1) material goods (earthly life) and spiritual needs (the hereafter life); (2) the duty to give alms to the poor ; (3) honesty in business transactions.

3.1. Material Goods and Spiritual Needs

3.1.1. Temporary Pleasures and Permanent Life: Earthly pleasures seem beautiful in our human perspective. However, there are only temporary, perishable pleasures (Surat X.71; XLIII.34; LV.26) within a perishable world (Surat III.12). There is a dualistic way to look at temporality and life itself: either there are temporary ("going-to-an-end") pleasures (worldly life, as temporality towards-death), or there are heavenly pleasures (eternal life, or temporality "without-any-end"). The earthly life should never make us blind (Surat VI.69, 130; VII.49; XLV.34; LVII.13, 20). If we only wish to get the pleasures of the earthly life, we will not be rewarded in the hereafter life (Surat XI.18–19). Human temporality is thus always linked to temporality in the hereafter life (eternity). The hereafter life is permanent, while the earthly life is perishable (Surat LXXXVI.16–17). Earthly pleasures are nothing in comparison wit those of the hereafter life (Surat IX.38; X.59; XVI.110, 119; LXII.11). They constitute delusive and temporary goods (Surat III.182; VII.23). We should then be detached from earthly goods and rather prefer the rewards of the hereafter life (Surat IX.38). Too often, we deepen our desires to own earthly goods, while God promises His rewards in the hereafter life (Surat VIII.68). Rewards in the hereafter life are reflecting that worldly life is full of suffering and thus that temporality "is" suffering, while eternity is spiritual liberation. We should rather remind that spiritual health is better than material prosperity (Surat LXII.9). Material goods actually stimulates temptations, but God's rewards are infinitely more precious (Surat VII.82; VIII.2; LXIV.15). God has given to us such goods in order to check the scope and depth of our faith (Surat XX.131).

3.1.2. Detachment from Earthly Goods The earthly life is seen as usufruct; the hereafter life is considered as the real, permanent life (Surat XL.42; XLII.34). Earthly life is nothing but a game and a frivolity (Surat VI.32, 69; XIII.126; XXIX.64; XLVII.38; LVII.19). The worth of the hereafter life is greater than that of the earthly life (Surat XCIII.4). In other words, eternity is considered as superior over world temporality. We love too much the earthly (perishable) life in comparison with the hereafter life (Surat LXXV.20–21; LXXVI.27). Through such an attitude, our hereafter life will be spent in hell (Surat II.80; LXXIX.38–39; CII.1–6). We should be detached from material, perishable goods since they give us a minor pleasure in comparison with the joyfulness of the (eternal) hereafter life (Surat IX.38; XVI.99). Again, temporal pleasures seem inferior to heavenly pleasures, so that eternity is substantially and qualitatively richer than worldly temporality. God's mercy is much more precious than earthly goods (Surat III.151; XXVIII.60; XLIII.31). We should cherish God rather than earthly goods or trading activities (Surat IX.24), since luxuries are useless for the hereafter life (Surat VII.46; XXVI.205, 207; XLV.9; LXIX.28–29; XCII.11). The usefulness of worldly goods is thus connected to eternal life as a reference framework. Worldly temporality is a means to get in touch with worldly goods. But we should be wholly attached to God only our basic desires and pleasures should focus on eternal life.

Wealth can make us neglecting God (Surat XCVI.6–7). God's grace is more precious than any earthly good or prosperity (Surat X.59). Any treasure already exists in God's essence, since it has been given by Him to the Universe (Surat XV.21). Trade and contracts should never make us neglecting God: that is, not remembering God, not observing prayer, not giving alms to the poor and the needy (Surat XXIV.37; XXIX.44). Luxuries or treasures cannot help wealthy people to be closer to God (Surat XXXIV.36). Wealthy people are rich because their prosperity reflects the Divine Will. Everybody receives what God wants to give him or her. Everybody will receive a part that will be in accordance with his or her works (Surat IV.36). Indeed, social inequalities are seen as a consequence of the Divine Will. God's aim is to test our faith, particularly when we own much more goods than others (Surat VI.165). God's Providence is a basic principle of the Islamic faith (Surat VI.15; XV.20).

3.1.3. The Infinite Quest for Wealthy and the Existence of Social Evils: We should never hoard in accumulating goods, properties and money for our personal interest. We should rather keep the wealth we need and give the superfluous through charity or good words (Surat II.217). The infinite (blindly) quest for wealth is perceived as the source of all social evils (Surat C.8). We must never make a "god" from our passions (Surat XLV.22; XLVII.15, 18; LIV.3). When we love material goods above all other beings, we consider such goods as if they were gods (Surat LXXXIX.21). We should never pursuit happiness through the ownership of earthly goods (Surat XXVII.36). Loving earthly goods rather than God is committing idolatry (Surat XXIX.24). Passions must be followed with discernment (Surat XXX.28). God does not like people who are arrogant because of their wealth (Surat XXXI.17). Focusing on the fulfillment of our passions is going far away from the "way of God" (Surat XXXVIII.17; LXIII.9). Being attached to earthly pleasures makes our remembering of God disappears, since we are then considering our passions as our gods (Surat XXV.45; XXVIII.63).

We should rather use our material goods "for the cause of God" (Surat XLVII.40). Spending our goods in order to purify our heart will be rewarded by God (Surat XCII.18–21). Everything we have spent "in the way of God" will be reimbursed so that we will lose nothing (Surat VIII.62). Those who accumulate goods and become wealthy without spending money or using their goods "in the way of God" (serving community and helping the poor) will be punished by God (Surat IX.34). Moreover, we should never use our goods and properties to wrongly influence others (Surat VIII.36). Punishments and rewards are imposed to human beings by God's Will. But they are here projected in both the earthly life and the hereafter life. God's intervention to reinforce human behaviour is thus actualized in two temporal dimensions: worldly temporality and the divine eternity.

It is clearly asserted that human beings naturally tend towards greed or cupidity, although it is detrimental to their interest (Surat IV.127; XLVII.40). Greed or cupidity destroys us (Surat C.8). It makes us neglecting others (Surat XCII.8). Those who accumulate material goods "for the future" believe that their treasures will contribute to give them the eternal life (Surat CIV.1–3). There seems to be a dualistic way to look at future when accumulating material goods is at stake: either a perishable (worldly) future (it is useless to do that), or a permanent (eternal) future (that is, a temporality that goes beyond worldly life limitations, a temporality that is characterized by a continuous flow of time; such a renewed temporality excludes any possibility to be eroded by the flow of time). Eternity is the reality that expresses such a renewal of temporality when we reach the hereafter life.

Although avarice is a natural trend (Surat XVII.102), we should adopt neither an attitude of cupidity, nor an attitude of material indifference. Somewhere between those extremes, there is a right attitude towards earthly goods (Surat XXV.67). God does not like cupidity (LXX.18). He does not like greedy people (LXX.18) who try to convince others to imitate them (Surat LVII.24). Felicity is the reward for having struggled against cupidity (Surat LIX.9). Our desires should be focused on heavenly treasures rather than earthly goods (Surat LIII.30). Earthly life is nothing but the desire to accumulate goods and become wealthier, thus stimulating the feeling of envy towards others (Surat LVII.19). We still keep the benefits we received from God as long as our heart remains pure (Surat VIII.55). God can make us wealthier than we presently are (Surat IX.28; LXXI.11). But nobody who distorts the Word of God will become wealthy (Surat XVI.118). During the pilgrimage, it is allowed to ask God to increase our wealth, through honest trade and to improve the collective well-being (Surat II.194). Because are righteous believers, we have received many benefits in this life (Surat VIII.71). But our rewards will be much greater in the hereafter life (Surat XVI.32, 43; XVII.19; XVIII.44). Those who rightly act are rewarded by God (Surat VII.160). Indeed, right actions increase the benefits (rewards) we receive from God (Surat X.27) in the worldly life and the hereafter life as well.

3.2. The Duty to Give Alms to the Poor

The Qu'ran includes a long list of verses dealing with alms (Surat II.40; IV.79, 160; V.15, 60; VIII.3; XXII.36, 42, 78; XXIII.4; XXIV.55; XXVII.3; XXXIII.31, 33; LI.19; LVII.17; LXXIII.20; LXXIV.45; LXXVI.8; XC.14, 16; XCIII.4, 10). The duty of give alms implies to treat with kindness the poor and the needy (Surat II.77).

3.2.1. Spending "in the way of God": The fact that we will give alms to the poor and the needy will be rewarded by God, since it is "spending in the way of God", that is, gifts given in order to please God and to strengthen our soul (Surat II.104, 263, 267, 274, 277). However, our gifts should never be followed by reminders of our generosity (or an attitude of ostentation) or with injury; otherwise, God will not reward us for our actions (Surat II.264, 266; IV.42). Kind and honest words are better than charity followed by injury (Surat II.265). Those who give alms to the poor are virtuous and just people (Surat II.272). Alms can be given secretly or publicly (Surat XIII.22; XIV.36; XVI.78; XXXV.26). But we should never regret to give alms (Surat IX.54). We should never make the following deal with God: "If I receive benefits from God, I will give alms". When God will accomplish His promises, we would then go far away from truth (Surat IX.76–77).

3.2.2. The Motives for Giving Alms God has given better gifts and talents to some persons, so that it is natural (and suitable to the Divine Will) that a given level of social and economic inequality follows from such a distribution of gifts and talents (Surat XVI.73). Believers must not aim at a social and economic egalitarianism since it would mean that God's decision to distribute gifts and talents in the way He did would have been wrong (Surat XVI.74). Allah's Providence has made possible for us to own some goods so that we are able to give alms to the poor (Surat II.255). That's why we should never refuse to provide the necessities of life to the poor and the needy. We should never encourage others not to give alms to the poor (Surat CVII.2–7). Wealthy people (as well as influential persons) should always help financially, or in other ways, their parents as well as the poor and the needy (Surat XXIV.22). But giving alms to the poor is an act that only God makes possible for humans to do (Surat II.277). It is a way for believers to practice mutual aid (Surat VIII.74) and an opportunity to remind that everything we have comes from God (Surat IV.80–81; XVI.55). The Surat II.211 said that we should help our parents, kindred, orphans, the poor and the needy, the wayfarers as well. Helping people implies that we could give advice to people, or simply pronounce kind words, or help others to fulfill their duties and satisfy their desires. It does not necessarily consist in property or money. Our right actions will be known by God (so that God will reward us). Our intent (when we are helping others) must never be unethical (such as vain glory, false indulgence, or encouraging idleness). The nature of the action must never be unethical. Alms must always be given in order to please God (Surat IV.114), that is, to receive God's rewards (Surat XII.88; XXX.38; XXXIV.38). In that sense, giving alms is in our interest (Surat LXIV.16). Sacrificing part of our goods gives us an advantage for our hereafter life (Surat LXI.11). But we should never give alms in order to become wealthier (Surat LXXIV.6). Giving alms is thus connected to our "way of life" in the hereafter life. It is a way to ensure that eternal life will be in accordance with what we have done in our temporal (earthly) existence.

3.2.3. The Nature of Alms   Giving useless things or pronouncing useless words or giving dangerous objects (for instance, a dangerous car) is not charity at all. In Islam, charity is practiced in order to show the unselfishness of the believer. We should always give to others what is due to them (Surat IV.37; XXX.37). That's why those who ask for alms must be in want, due to honourable causes rather than unethical causes (such as fraud, unpaid services : Surat II.274). However, alms are due to poor who have abandoned their country and to those zealous believers who have been required to leave their home and have lost their gods and properties because of their zealous attitude (Surat LIX.8). Alms must be distributed to the poor and the needy, to those who give them hospitality, to the recent coveted, to wayfarers, or for the cause of God (Surat IX.60).

We should give the best things we have earned (goods that have been acquired through honest, honourable, legitimate and ethical means: it thus excludes ill-gotten gains through fraud and robbery). We should never distribute part of our goods that are bad or disgusting (Surat II.269). Alms should be composed of those goods we cherish the most profoundly. They should be given at every moment of our life, without regard to our level of wealth (Surat III.128). We should not take the excuse of a misfortune in order to justify our inability to give alms (Surat IX.99). However, we can give alms proportionally to our wealth (Surat LXV.7). And we should always remind that alms come from goods that have been given by God, the Owner of the Universe (Surat IV.43; XXVIII.54; XXXII.16; XXXVI.47; LVII.7; LXII.7; LXIII.10). Alms are means to get closer to God and to participate in His mercy (Surat VII.154; IX.100). Giving alms is a way to get in touch with God's Will and then to get an advantageous position before the nature of our eternal life (Heaven or hell) will be decided by God. Giving alms is a temporal action undertaken in order to gain a somewhat "fragmentary guarantee of eternity". Giving alms publicly is good, except if it is done with motives of ostentation (Surat II.275). Generally speaking, it is better to secretly help the poor and the needy. Such a conduct is more morally right so that it removes from us some of our sins (Surat II.273).

3.3. Honesty in Business Transactions

3.3.1. Prohibited Business Practices: We must never conclude unjust or fraudulent transactions (Surat II.279; VI.153; XI.85-86; XXVI.181, 183; LV.7–8), because believers would then sin against God (Surat VIII.27). Even business transactions made in the name of God will not be taken into account by God if the person proves to be treacherous (Sahih Bukhari, vol. 3, book 34, no 430). Sinners would be punished in their hereafter life (Surat LXXXIII.1–6). Muslims must lead their business with honesty, truthfulness and a sense of justice (Surat III.129; VI.153; VII.82; XI.86; LV.7–8), since justice has great worth and beauty (Surat XVII.37), and because for God, everything is equal (Surat XIII.11). Those who rightly act will be rewarded by God (Surat VII.160). God does not make wealthy people who wrongly act (Surat VI.21; X.18; XII.23; XXVIII.37). We should never use our goods for vanity, frivolity or useless motives, or in order to corrupt others (particularly, people holding authority), although the action is undertaken to get a legal advantage (Surat II.184).

There are many kinds of business transactions. Islam is particularly concerned with two types of transactions: (1) transactions involving a future payment or future conditions: goods are bought now, and the payment is promised at a fixed (future) time and place. In such a case, a written document is recommended (but not obligatory), in order to prevent doubt. The scribe must act with probity, as if such transactions would be made in the presence of God. If we cannot find a scribe, we could give something on trust. The trustee must safeguard the interest of the person on behalf of whom he holds the trust and must give back the property or money when he is required to do so (Surat II.283); (2) transactions in which payment and delivery are made on the spot: in that case, having witnesses to such transactions is enough (Surat II.282). In one or the other type of business transactions, we should always fulfill the obligations following from a contract we have signed since in doing so, we are virtuous and just people (Surat II.172).

However, if our debtor is in difficulty, we should give him more time, until it is easier for him to reimburse the money (Surat II.280). In that context, giving more time to our debtors is a way to be generous. As an analogy, we could say that Allah has given to us a lot of time to "change our heart". In the same way, we must provide our debtors enough time to reimburse their money. Generosity in the human and the divine realms is always an issue of "time that is done" (a delay).

There are four basic business practices that are prohibited by the Qu'ran: (1) pollution: we should never pollute God's Creation (Surat XI.86); (2) gambling: it is a means to get profit without having worked for it (Surat II.216; V.91–92); (3) stealing: it is generally prohibited (Surat V.42). It is acceptable only in a situation of misery, when the person (robber) has a good intent and acts with good faith. The sin will then be forgiven by God (Surat V.5); (4) usury: it is the undue profit made (excluding any legitimate trade, that is allowed by God) out of loans and of necessities of life. Usury is prohibited (Surat III.125, 130; IV.159), since it is a means to accumulate goods and properties and a way to become attached to earthly pleasures (Surat XXX.38). So, God is looking at human actions (and sins) as if human soul would be a "container of sins and merits". Sins are related to past actions. God's rewards and punishments are projected in divine temporality. They are actualized in the present human life and/or in the hereafter life. Those who, after receiving the guidance from God, desist from practicing usury will be forgiven for their past sins, while others will be condemned to the hell (Surat II. 276, 278). To be forgiven also means that we will safeguard our capital in doing so (Surat II.279). God has allowed trade, not usury (Surat II.275).

3.3.2. God's Rewards and Punishments   Every believer must never fear to be subjected to fraud or to be "unjustly" treated (Surat LXXII.13). Muslims must strictly observe justice and honesty (even in transactions with non-Muslims: Surat III.68–69) and remind that God is closer to rich and poor than anybody else (Surat IV.134). Muslims should even never say dishonest words (Surat XXIII.3). They should never lie (Surat XXII.31). Business success will not be achieved, if we try to create some kind of dispute (Surat VIII.48). God loves the equitable (Surat XLIX.9). He has ordered equity (Surat VII.28; LVII.25). Those who kill people teaching equity will be severely punished by God (Surat III.20).

CONCLUSION

Now, *is it possible to find out convergences or divergences between Khaldûn's concept of history and the Qu'ranic concept of economic justice?* We would like to make the following three remarks:

Firstly, both *Khaldûn's concept of history and the Qu'ranic concept of economic justice imply a theological view of earthly life*: a specific (critical) way to look at earthly pleasures. In the Qu'ranic concept, earthly pleasures are considered as an illusion and a sub-product of the perishable/temporary (earthly) life, while God's rewards for the hereafter life are seen as the (permanent) reality, directly linked to God's promises and God's mercy. God is and will always be the Creator and thus Owner of the Universe. God will increase our benefits (rewards) in this life and in the hereafter life. Such a theological view of earthly pleasures is quite important, since it influences that way Islamic faith is looking at social justice;

Secondly, *Khaldûn's concept of history and the Qu'ranic concept shares a deep concern for common good*. The Qu'ranic concept of economic justice implies that we use (and share) goods "in the way of God", that is, in serving community, and helping the poor (giving alms to the poor: the amount of alms should be proportionate to the level of wealth we own). Both objectives are linked to an improvement of collective well-being and the attitude of unselfishness. However, in Islam, the poor and the needy must not be poor because of their unethical practices (such as fraud). The goods we actually share must have been acquired through ethical means and ends (excluding fraud and robbery). If there are social inequalities, they are due to the Divine Will (various talents are given by God). So, we should not aim at an "absolute" (economic and social) egalitarianism, since it would contradict God's decision to distribute talents in the way He did. Our material prosperity reflects the Divine Will, God's Providence. In Islam, natural inequalities are due to the Divine Will; however, we should struggle to improve collective well-being and help the poor and the needy. That's the reason why God has given us our material prosperity. In God's view, natural inequalities cannot imply any necessity for poverty. Poverty is a human product, not a divine one. Due to God's Providence, poverty is indeed a scandal.

Thirdly, *both Khaldûn's concept of history and the Qu'ranic concept of economic justice constitute grounds for human (social) justice.* In Islam, God is seen as essentially Just: everything is equal for Him. That's why we must reach a high level of justice. While Islam is defining human justice as closely linked to God's justice. Both Khaldûn's concept of history and the Qu'ranic concept of economic justice are theocratic;

Finally, the Islamic economic system is dominated by ethics.[11] It is based on the following main principles: (1) the interdependence between a good (moral) behaviour in (earthly) temporal life and a good life after death (eternity), or between the way we use material goods and the way we fulfill our spiritual needs. Our success in the hereafter life (eternity) is based on our actions during our (earthly) temporal life; (2) brotherhood/sisterhood : the interest rate is perceived as destroying the moral principle of brotherhood; (3) a social and economic justice: it implies a circulation of wealth and a moderate consumption of material goods. However, it does not exclude the fulfillment of material needs in the (earthly) temporal life.

University of Sherbrooke (Quebec), Canada

NOTES

[1] Ibn Khaldûn (1967) The Muqaddimah. An Introduction to History, Coll. "Bollingen Series XLIII", Princeton: Princeton University Press, vol. 1.

[2] N. Machiavelli (2003) The Prince, London/New York: Penguin Books.

[3] M.U. Chapra (1992) Islam and the Economic Challenge, Herndon: International Institute of Islamic Thought.

[4] T. Kuran (1986) 'The Economic System in Contemporary Islamic Thought: An Assessment', International Journal of Middle East Studies, 18: 135–164.

[5] Mohammad Nejatullah Siddiqi (1988) 'From Contemporary Economics to Islamic Economics', in Abdullah Omar Naseef (ed.), Today's Problems, Tomorrow's Solutions, London: Mansell Publishing Ltd.

[6] Ayatullah Sayyid Mahmud Taleghani (1982) Society and Economics in Islam, Berkeley: Mizan Press, p. 23-72.

[7] Syed Nawab Haider Naqvi, Rafik Ahmed H. U. Beg and Mian M. Nazeer (1984) Principles of Islamic Economic Reform, Pakistan Institute of Development Economics.

[8] Mohammad Aslam Haneef (1995) Contemporary Islamic Economic Thought. A Selected Comparative Analysis, Kuala Lumpur: Ikraq, p. 52–65; Mohammad Nejatullah Siddiqi (1986) 'The Guarantee of a Minimum Level of Living in an Islamic State', in Munawar Iqbal (Ed.), Distributive Justice and Need Fulfillment in an Islamic Economy, Leicester: The Islamic Foundation.

[9] Muhammad Nejatullah Siddiqi (1983) Issues in Islamic Banking. Selected Papers, Leicester: The Islamic Foundation.

[10]   Monzer Kahf (1989) 'Islamic Economic System – A Review', in A.Ghazali and S. Omar (Eds.), Readings in the Concept and Methodology of Islamic Economics, Petaling Jaya: Pelanduk Publications.

[11]   M. Saeed, Z.U. Ahmed and S-M Mukhtar (2001) 'International Marketing Ethics from an Islamic Perspective: A Value-Maximization Approach', *Journal of Business Ethics*, 32: 127–142; Gillian Rice (1999), 'Islamic Ethics and the Implications for Business', *Journal of Business Ethics*, 18.4 : 345–358; Abdel H. Bashir (1998) 'Ethical Norms and Enhancement Mechanism in Profit-Sharing Arrangements', *The Mid-Atlantic Journal of Business*, 34.3: 255–271.

AMERICAN PHILOSOPHICAL ASSOCIATION, EASTERN DIVISION

DECEMBER 27-30, 2005
NEW YORK HILTON

World Institute for Advanced Phenomenological Research and Learning

Fifth Symposium in:
Islamic Philosophy and Phenomenology of Life in Dialogue

Topic: The Temporal and Temporality in Islamic Philosophy and Occidental Phenomenology

Session I:
Chair: William Chittick (State University of New York, Stony Brook)

Speakers:William Chittick (State University of New York, Stony Brook)
"The Temporal Unfolding of the Soul"
Robert Dobie (La Salle University)
"Existence and Temporality in the Thought of Ibn Al-'Arabi"
Anna-Teresa Tymieniecka (World Institute for Advanced
Phenomenological Research and Learning)
"Chronos and Kairos, Ontopoietic Timing of Life and the Kairic
Unfolding of the Sacral Spirit"

Session II: Roundtable
Topic: The Temporal and Temporality in Islamic Philosophy and Occidental Phenomenology
Chair: Anna-Teresa Tymieniecka (World Institute for Advanced
Phenomenological Research and Learning)

A-T. Tymieniecka (ed.),
Timing and Temporality in Islamic Philosophy and Phenomenology of Life, 341–342.
© 2007 *Springer.*

Speakers: Nader El-Bizri (University of Cambridge, Great Britain)
             "Perspectives on Time from the History of Philosophy
             and Phenomenology"

             Mehdi Aminrazavi (Mary Washington College)
             "Mir Damad on Time and Temporality"

             Michael F. Andrews (Seattle University)
             Topic to be announced

             Kathleen Haney (University of Houston-Downtown)
             "The Ontopoietic Timing of Life Versus the Kairic Unfolding
             of the Trans-natural Destiny
             (A-T. Tymieniecka)"

NAME INDEX

ISLAMIC PHILOSOPHY AND OCCIDENTAL PHENOMENOLOGY IN DIALOGUE

Printed in Great Britain
by Amazon